The Elections in Israel 1999

SUNY series in Israeli Studies

Russell Stone, editor

THE ELECTIONS IN ISRAEL 1999

Edited by
Asher Arian and Michal Shamir

in conjunction with
The Israel Democracy Institute

State University of New York Press

Published by
State University of New York Press, Albany

Printed in the United States of America

For information, address State University of New York Press,
90 State Street, Suite 700, Albany, NY 12207

Production by Judith Block
Marketing by Patrick Durocher

Library of Congress Cataloging-in-Publication Data

The elections in Israel, 1999 / edited by Asher Arian and Michal Shamir in
conjunction with the Israel Democracy Institute.
     p. cm.—(SUNY series in Israeli studies)
    Includes index.
    ISBN 0-7914-5315-4 (alk. paper)—ISBN 0-7914-5316-2 (pbk.: alk. paper)
    1. Elections—Israel. 2. Israel. Keneset—Elections, 1999. 3. Israel—
Politics and government—1993– I. Arian, Alan. II. Shamir, Michal, 1951–
III. Makhon ha-Yisre'eli le-demokratyah. IV. Series.

  JQ1830.A95 E44 2002
  324.95694'054—dc21

                                          2002017625

10 9 8 7 6 5 4 3 2 1

Contents

Introduction

MICHAL SHAMIR AND ASHER ARIAN

The 1999 elections, held on May 17, 1999, featured two parallel races. One was for the office of the prime minister, and the second was for the Knesset (Israeli Parliament). This was the second time that the rules for the simultaneous direct election of the prime minister and the selection of the Knesset based on a fixed-list proportional representation formula applied. The change in the electoral system was legislated before the 1992 elections, but was activated for the first time in 1996. The prime minister was elected under a winner-take-all system, with a second-round runoff between the two candidates with the most votes two weeks later if no candidate received a majority in the first round. The Knesset was elected as in the past, using a strict proportional representation list system with very few procedural or technical obstacles facing a group that chose to compete. The threshold for Knesset representation was 1.5 percent, in effect since 1992. In 1999 there were five candidates for prime minister a week before the election, and almost three dozen parties were running. But just before the deadline, three of the candidates for prime minister and two of the competing lists withdrew.

The government of Prime Minister Benjamin Netanyahu, elected in 1996, had been plagued with instability from the outset. The style of his rule, his inability to cooperate with other leaders of his Likud Party, such as Benny Begin and Dan Meridor, and the fragile majority he commanded in the Knesset, combined to weaken him. In addition to these, he lost support from parties of the right because of his begrudging acquiescence to pursue the path of peace outlined by the Oslo accords initiated by the slain Yitzhak Rabin. Netanyahu signed the Wye River Accord with Palestinian Authority Chairperson Yasser Arafat in October 1998 to the dismay of many in his right-wing coalition.

1

The opposition in the Knesset made a motion in December 1998 for early elections, originally scheduled for the end of 2000. According to the provisions of the law regulating the direct election of the prime minister, had Netanyahu been voted out of office by the Knesset, new elections for the prime minister and the Knesset would take place within sixty days. After initially opposing the move, Netanyahu finally decided to embrace the inevitable and to control the length of time available for the campaign. Netanyahu agreed to legislate early elections and the date finally agreed to was May 17, 1999, thus giving the parties and candidates six months to prepare for the showdown, rather than the two months that would have been the preference of those who drafted the legislation.

Many shifts of affiliation occurred during the campaign period. One member of the Knesset, Eliezer Zandberg, actually changed his parliamentary affiliation five times, beginning with membership in the extreme right-wing Tzomet and ending up on the anticlericalist dovish Shinui list. The Center Party emerged, formed by leaders from various parties (see the chapter by Nathan Yanai, in this volume), and the Labor Party coalesced with two smaller parties to form One Israel (see the chapter by Gideon Doron, in this volume).

The front-runners for the prime minister post were Netanyahu, and Labor Party leader Ehud Barak. Netanyahu's campaign used the slogan, A Strong Leader for the Future of Israel, signaling that only he could properly defend Jerusalem, and a variation on the Peace and Security slogan that brought him to power three years earlier. Netanyahu, engaged in political infighting, found himself unable to heat up the torpid campaign during the long election period. Ideological differences were muted as both candidates appealed to the center, most notably narrowed because the right-wing Netanyahu government had approved the Wye River Accord and had actually handed over some West Bank land to the Palestinian Authority.

Most Israelis accepted the land-for-peace formula although differences remained regarding how much land would have to be given up. There was also a growing realization that a Palestinian state was inevitable. Ironclad ideological credos of the past were downplayed as the party dealigned because of the international political developments and the changes introduced to the electoral system (see the chapter by Asher Arian and Michal Shamir, in this volume). Rather than dwell on the difficult issues of concessions in the West Bank, the future of Jerusalem, or how much of the Golan Heights should be returned to Syria, the campaign focused on one issue: Netanyahu's performance as prime minister. In a TV debate months before the election and just after resigning as Netanyahu's defense minister to run at the head of the Center Party, Yitzhak Mordechai blasted Netanyahu with unforgettable phrases accusing him of engaging in "compulsive lies," "dangerous adventurism," and "unethical leadership."

As Election Day approached and as support for Barak grew, Netanyahu became more desperate. The prime minister had the Likud replay commercials that featured scenes of suicide bombing attacks in Israeli streets, blaming the Labor opposition for being soft on terror. His appeal to such controversial arguments indicated to many just how embattled he felt.

Close to the election, the polls showed that Barak was likely to win a majority even in a field that featured many candidates. Hence three of them, all opposed to Netanyahu, decided to withdraw their candidacies a short time before the final deadline as provided by the law. The three candidates were Benny Begin, formerly of the Likud and a candidate of the nationalist right; Azmi Bishara, an Arab member of the Knesset; and former defense minister Mordechai, head of the newly formed Center Party.

Table I.1 presents the results of the elections in both the prime minister and the Knesset races. The prime ministerial race came down to Netanyahu against Barak. Barak won by a landslide (56% to 44%) but the parties of the candidates, Likud and Labor, won fewer seats in the Knesset than they had in decades, and only middle-size and small parties were elected to the Knesset. Table I.2 brings the vote results for the prime ministerial candidates, and for Likud and Labor in selected communities in 1999 compared to 1996.

The dual system of elections led to a very fragmented Knesset, and with it, a high probability of an unstable government. The prime minister is the focus of power and policy and since he was directly elected this concentration of power was increased. But since the prime minister cannot rule without a majority in the Knesset, he becomes hostage to coalition negotiations, and these are very costly in terms of the prime minister's time and the public's money. The dual ballot system fostered middle- and small-size parties, and those parties had greater bargaining power in the absence of large-size parties.

The reform that provided the voters with two ballots instead of one changed their voting calculus, and altered the nature of the campaign, the party system, and the relations between the legislative and executive branches. The electoral reform and its repercussions are featured in all of the chapters in this volume. The major aspect of the electoral reform, the direct election of the prime minister, receives considerable consideration but there were developments in other areas, such as in the selection methods of candidates (see Gideon Rahat, chapter 12, in this volume).

The voters intuitively understood the potential of the reform and acted accordingly. Large parties were abandoned since voters assessed that policy

Table I.1   Results of the 1999 Elections

Prime Minister	% of Valid Votes	Votes	
Ehud Barak	1,791,020	56.1	
Benjamin Netanyahu	1,402,474	43.9	
Knesset	**Valid Votes**	**% of Valid Vote**	**Knesset Seat**
One Israel[a]	670,484	20.3	26
Likud[b]	468,103	14.1	19
Shas	430,676	13.0	17
Meretz	253,525	7.7	10
Israel b'Aliya	171,705	5.2	6
Shinui	167,748	5.1	6
Center	165,622	5.0	6
National Religious	140,307	4.2	5
United Torah Jewry	125,741	3.8	5
United Arab List	114,810	3.5	5
National Union	100,181	3.0	4
Hadash	87,022	2.6	3
Israel Beiteinu	86,153	2.6	4
Balad	66,103	2.0	2
One Nation	64,143	1.9	2
Pnina Rosenblum	44,953	1.4	0
Pensioners	37,525	1.1	0
Green Leaf	34,029	1.0	0
Third Way	26,290	0.8	0
Greens	13,292	0.4	0
Hope	7,366	0.2	0
Casino	6,540	0.2	0
Heart of Immigrants	6,311	0.2	0
Negev	4,324	0.1	0
Tzomet	4,128	0.1	0
Natural Law	2,924	c	0
Romanian	2,797	c	0
Raam	2,151	c	0
New Arab	2,042	c	0
Male Rights	1,257	c	0
Heritage	1,164	c	0
TOTAL	3,309,416	99.6%	120

Minimum needed for representation (1.5%)—49,642 votes.
Quota per Knesset seat—25,936 votes.

SOURCE: *Central Bureau of Statistics.* There were 4,285,428 eligible voters; 3,373,748 (78.7% of eligible voters) participated in the elections. In the prime minister vote, 3,372,952 participated (78.7%) and 3,309,416 (77.2% of eligible votes) participated in the Knesset vote. For the prime minister, 179,458 (5.3% of votes cast) were invalid because they were blank ballots, or they were cast for candidates no longer running (9,826 votes). For the Knesset, 64,332 (2.2%) were disqualified, and 197,093 (6%) were for parties below the minimum required.
[a]Labor with Gesher and Meimad in 1999; Labor in 1996.
[b]With Gesher and Tzomet in 1996.
[c]Less than 0.1% of the vote.

Table I.2 Voting Support (in %) for Prime Minister,
Likud and Labor in Selected Communities, 1999 and 1996
May 17, 1999 (May 29, 1996)

	Netanyahu	Barak (Peres)	Likud[a]	Labor[b]
National Total	43.9 (50.5)	56.1 (49.5)	14.1 (24.9)	20.3 (26.6)
Jewish settlements	48.3 (55.6)	51.5 (44.3)	15.4 (27.4)	21.6 (27.7)
Non-Jewish settlements	5.3 (5.2)	94.3 (94.7)	1.3 (2.2)	7.7 (16.7)
Druze settlements	20.6 (21.3)	79.3 (78.6)	7.9 (11.7)	21.7 (40.5)
Bedouin settlements	8.6 (6.8)	91.3 (93.1)	0.7 (1.5)	4.0 (14.9)
Bnei Brak	88.7 (88.9)	11.2 (11.0)	6.5 (11.1)	4.4 (6.6)
Jerusalem	64.5 (69.9)	35.4 (30.0)	15.2 (25.6)	14.1 (16.3)
Nazareth	1.1 (1.3)	98.8 (98.6)	0.2 (0.3)	3.4 (8.5)
Nazareth Heights	46.0 (51.2)	53.9 (48.7)	19.3 (28.4)	12.9 (28.4)
Tel Aviv	35.6 (44.8)	64.2 (55.1)	15.4 (26.6)	27.4 (33.9)
Golan Heights	41.4 (49.7)	58.5 (50.2)	9.2 (16.3)	23.3 (31.2)
Jews beyond Green Line	78.0 (83.7)	21.9 (16.2)	19.5 (32.1)	8.3 (10.1)
Kibbutzim	6.8 (10.0)	93.1 (89.9)	1.8 (3.1)	50.5 (54.8)
Moshavim	44.2 (51.8)	55.7 (48.1)	16.3 (26.7)	30.8 (34.8)

SOURCE: *Election results of the Central Elections Committee, as reported in Haaretz and Maariv, May 19 and May 23, 1999; and in the Hayom supplement of Maariv, June 2, 1996, 8–17.*
[a]Likud-Gesher-Tzomet in 1996.
[b]One Israel in 1999, with Gesher and Meimad.

would be set by the election of the prime minister and not by the vote for the Knesset, and accordingly the vote for parliament became the arena for sectarian contestation. Fifteen parties won seats in the 1999 elections compared with 11 in 1996. The effective number of electoral parties rose from 6.2 to 10.3; the effective number of parliamentary parties rose from 5.6 to 8.7; electoral volatility rose from 17.3 to 24.8. These were the highest in the history of elections in Israel and one of the highest in Western democracies (Hazan and Diskin 2000, 632).

Four chapters in this volume analyze voting behavior, from four different perspectives. Our chapter (chapter 1) analyzes the 1999 election from a comparative and long-term perspective in terms of the party system and voting behavior. We discuss the different phases of the Israeli party system, its current dealignment characteristics, the increase in issue voting, the growing importance of candidates in voters' calculus, and the vitality of the bloc alignment. We consider changes in electoral behavior, and in particular the increased importance of issue voting, candidates, and performance evaluations. As the parties and voters' party identification weaken, the prime ministerial candidates replace the parties in the eyes of the voters, and the blocs of left and right gain in importance.

The next two chapters focus on strategic and split-ticket voting. Up to two days before the election, there were five prime ministerial candidates. Paul Abramson and John H. Aldrich (chapter 2) discuss strategic voting considerations in the prime ministerial race before three of the candidates withdrew, based on survey data we collected in the month before the election as part of the Israeli National Election Study.

There was a good deal of split-ticket voting as a result of the system, whereby a voter selects the candidate for prime minister representing the Likud or Labor, but selects a different party for the Knesset vote. Due to the two-ballot system, split-ticket voting became easy and popular. Dana Arieli-Horowitz (chapter 3) assesses this phenomenon based on aggregate data in the 1996 and 1999 elections, the two elections held under the hybrid system of simultaneous elections to the Knesset and for the prime minister.

The chapter by Michael Shalev and Sigal Kis (chapter 4) attempts to resurrect the role of class in electoral behavior. Indeed most voting research in Israel—including our own—has noted the relative absence of class politics and class voting. Using our 1999 survey data, in addition to ecological analysis of aggregate data, and multilevel analysis, they demonstrate class effects. However, they conclude their study by suggesting that in Israel "the most obvious correlates of these class-voting linkages are non-economic: disputed issues of collective identity, the role of religion in personal and national life, and management of the peace process and future borders." This indicates less of a disagreement with our work than a difference of emphasis. Collective identity, nationalism, religiosity, and ethnicity are exactly the factors we emphasize in our analyses. Class effects are mediated and depend upon the social and historical experiences of individuals and groups, and do not by themselves and directly define electoral behavior. The sophisticated and multifaceted analysis by Shalev and Kis is to be commended, and we join their plea for more ecological studies, and in particular for multilevel analyses and better data.

The list of special group parties that did better in 1999 than ever was wildly variegated: it included the Haredi, ultra-Orthodox, non-Zionist Shas; the passionate anti-Haredi secular Shinui; two parties appealing to immigrants from the former Soviet Union; and Arab parties. The usual large parties, Labor and Likud, became much smaller. Yoav Peled's chapter (chapter 5) analyzes the continuing electoral success of Shas; As'ad Ghanem and Sarah Ozacky-Lazar (chapter 6) focus on the Arab parties and voters. Zvi Gitelman and Ken Goldstein (chapter 7) discuss the "Russian" revolution in Israeli politics. Daphna Canetti, Howard L. Frant, and Ami Pedhazur (chapter 8) analyze these developments in terms of party system polarization.

This array of parties is especially interesting because it suggests the importance of domestic issues in determining the outcome. This appears to be the case for the Knesset vote, but not for the vote for prime minister. There was much evidence of rising unemployment, decline in the rate of growth of the gross domestic product (GDP), and misspending of public money, but the economic policy differences between the two main parties were not all that wide. Personalities seemed to matter, since many voters seemed attentive to the character of the contenders. The fact that Netanyahu had lost the support of many of the Likud leadership such as Begin, Mordechai, David Levy, and Meridor, worked against the prime minister.

Some observers, especially in the foreign media, interpreted the election of Barak as prime minister as a fundamental sea change in Israeli priorities and belief patterns. This analysis was encouraged by the fact that the voting resulted in the largest margin ever achieved in Israeli elections. Consider: No party had ever won an absolute majority of the votes; the Netanyahu-Peres contest of 1996 was decided by less than 1% of the vote; accordingly, the 1999 spread (Barak 56% and Netanyahu 44%) seemed like a landslide. But this view was incorrect. Old patterns funneled into a new system of voting produced the 1999 results. As always in elections, and probably more than before, the candidates played a fundamental role in determining the results. A more appropriate way to think of the 1999 Israeli elections is that a weak candidate (Barak) bested a wounded prime minister abandoned by most of his political allies (Netanyahu).

Based on the landslide, political scientists might be tempted to view 1999 as a realigning election. But that would also be incorrect at worst, premature at best. As we show in our contribution, the election results do not signify significant readjustments in the size or in the social and ideological makeup of the opposing camps. Barak's plans for peace with the Arab world may or may not be realized, but the election was not focused on those plans.

Both candidates made great strides toward the center of the Israeli political spectrum in forming their platforms and while their styles and temperaments differed, on fundamental positions they seemed not that far from one another. The contributions by Gideon Doron (chapter 9) and by Jonathan Mendilow (chapter 10) discuss these and other aspects of the election campaigns of the two candidates and their parties. Their analyses are complemented by Nathan Yanai's (chapter 11) investigation of the emergence and failure of the Center Party. Gabriel Weimann and Gadi Wolfsfeld (chapter 13) examine the struggle over the electoral agenda between the media and the prime ministerial candidates, comparing the elections of 1996 with those of 1999.

The Israeli political system has changed, and it has changed in complex ways. Just as a range of factors affects the decision of the individual voter, myriad forces drive the transformation of a society and its political system. There are not many settings more appropriate to study these matters than Israel in the 1990s. The rules of the game have been altered; new groups of voters have emerged; international and economic shifts present new challenges. Our collection explores all those in the context of the 1999 elections.

Reference

Hazan, Reuven Y., and Abraham Diskin. 2000. "The 1999 Knesset and Prime Ministerial Elections in Israel. *Electoral Studies* 19: 628–37.

Part I

Voting Behavior

Candidates, Parties, and Blocs

ASHER ARIAN AND MICHAL SHAMIR

Realignment and Dealignment

Political scientists who study elections resort to two major concepts useful in sorting out elections and interpreting electoral dynamics: partisan realignment and dealignment (Dalton, Flanagan, and Beck 1984). A realignment is electoral change that persists. It is characterized by "more or less profound readjustments . . . in the relations of power within the community, and in . . . new and durable election groupings. . . ." (Key 1955, 4). A partisan realignment involves significant shifts in the ideological and social group bases and in the strength of party coalitions. The realignment concept is anchored in a social cleavage model of politics, whereas the dealignment concept is rooted in a functional model, which evaluates party systems in terms of their relevance to social and political needs. Dealignment is defined in terms of weakening parties and party bonds, and as a result—increasing volatility and unpredictability of elections. Volatility also characterizes realignments, but only as a temporary state of affairs, after which new party alignments crystallize, and there is no change in the role of the party as an institution in politics.

This conceptual frame efficiently organizes the dynamics of the Israeli party system and the four turnover elections of 1977, 1992, 1996, and 1999. The first turnover of 1977 was the climax of a partisan realignment (Arian 1975, 1980; Goldberg 1992; Shamir 1986). Despite the fact that the 1977 results were extremely dramatic, it is more instructive to discuss realignment in terms of a realigning electoral era, rather than a single critical election, especially in a dominant party system. The 1977 turnover certainly signaled a realignment of the party system, of the electorate, of the elites, and of public policy. Ethnic and religious group allegiances crystallized, and demography combined with the territorial issue cleavage to redefine the political system.

The 1992 election was clearly different (Arian and Shamir 1993). Even though the policy shift following this election was as significant and perhaps even more abrupt and dramatic than the change following the ascent of the Likud in 1977, in terms of electoral alignment, 1992 was not 1977. The electoral shift in 1992 was less complex and numerically smaller than the one in 1977, and was grounded more in issue positions than in social groupings. It did not result in a notable and enduring restructuring of the power distribution and of the political cleavage structure. There was no realignment in 1992, nor were the two following elections of 1996 and 1999 elections of realignment. The elections of the 1990s do not involve significant and enduring shifts in the strength of the left, the right, or the religious party blocs (see table 1.1), nor are significant changes in the ideological and social group bases of party coalitions at the heart of these changes. Although religion became a more potent factor in the elections, the major characteristics of the elections in this decade are the increase in issue voting and in the role of performance evaluations of candidates (see table 1.2).

The 1992 election was the last one held under the old one-constituency proportional representation system. Even though it took place after the electoral reform legislation had been passed, and Yitzhak Rabin conducted his campaign as though these were personal elections, the reform took force only in 1996. Already in the 1992 elections there was evidence of greater individual and aggregate level volatility in the vote with an attendant increase of potential impact of leaders in the voting booth, and the sense of empowerment of the electorate "call[ing] upon Labor to perform for this term, with the implicit threat that they too could be replaced in future elections" (Arian and Shamir 1993, 341; Hermann 1995). Now that two more elections have taken place, it seems even more obvious that the 1992 election was the beginning of the dealigning era in Israeli electoral politics, soon to be exacerbated by the electoral reform.

For the first forty years of Israeli political history there was only one turnover election (1977); in the decade of the 1990s, each of the three elections was a turnover election. The 1990s were characterized by low predictability of outcomes, by unprecedented instability in party fortunes, and by the waning of party loyalties.

The two large parties, Labor and Likud, respectively, declined from 44 and 32 Knesset seats in 1992, to 34 and 32 seats in 1996, and to 26 and 19 seats in 1999. Labor and Likud together commanded almost 80 percent of the votes at the height of their combined grip on the system in 1981. From the midsixties through 1992 their combined strength was at least 71 seats in the 120-member Knesset. They dropped to 66 seats in 1996 and to 45 seats in 1999 (see table 1.1). The 1999 election left the Knesset without large parties, only with medium-sized and small parties.

Table 1.1 Knesset Election Results 1949–1999: Fragmentation, Competitiveness, Blocs

Election Year	1949	1951	1955	1959	1961	1965	1969	1973	1977	1981	1984	1988	1992	1996	1999
Fragmentation															
Number of lists	12	15	12	12	12	12	11	9	13	10	15	15	10	11	15
Largest party	46	45	40	47	42	45	56	51	43	48	44	40	44	34	26
Two largest parties combined	65	65	55	64	59	71	82	90	75	95	85	79	76	66	45
Competitiveness															
[Difference between two largest parties	27	25	25	30	25	19	30	12	11	1	3	1	12	2	7]
Turnover (+/−)	−	−	−	−	−	−	−	−	+	−	−	−	+	+	+
Blocs[a]															
Left	71	70	70	71	68	72	66	62	41	52	53	53	61	52	48
Center	5	4	5	6	−	5	8	4	16	4	7	2	−	4	12
Right	22	28	28	25	34	26	28	39	45	51	47	47	43	34	27
Religious	16	15	17	18	18	17	18	15	17	13	13	18	16	23	27
[Right + Religious	38	43	45	43	52	43	46	54	62	64	60	65	59	57	54]

[a]Left bloc includes One Israel, Labor, Alignment, Mapai, Ahdut Haavoda, Rafi, Mapam, Civil Rights Movement, Meretz, Communist, Haolam Haze, Shell, and Arab parties. Right includes Likud, Herut, Liberals, Free Center, Shlomzion, Tehiya, Tzomet, Moleder, Kach, and Ihud Leumi Parties. Religious bloc includes National Religious, Agudat Israel, Poalei Agudat Israel, Degel Hatora, Tami, and Shas Parties. Center includes Independent Liberals, Democratic Movement for Change, Shinui, State list, Telem, Yahad, Ometz, and Center parties. Not included in this analysis are Sephardi, Yemenite, Wizo, Flatto Sharon, and Israel Baaliya parties, and hence the total for some years does not add up to 120.

13

Considering the vote for prime minister and for the Knesset, split-ticket voting has become the rule. The floating vote for parties is steadily growing as large parties are drastically cut in size. In the late sixties and in the eighties the floating vote was around 25%. During the realigning era it was a third in 1973; 50% in 1977 and 40% in 1981. The elections in the 1990s exhibit similar levels of floating vote. In 1992, it was about a third, it increased to almost 40% in 1996, and exceeded 40% of the electorate in 1999.

Weakening parties, loosening party ties, and growing volatility all indicate trends of dealignment. The direct election of the prime minister provides much of the explanation for the partisan dealignment in Israel, but signs of it were already evident in the 1992 election (Korn 1998). Dealignment trends in other advanced Western democracies (Dalton 1996; Dalton, Flanagan, and Beck 1984; Kitschelt forthcoming) have been associated with changes in the mass media and its role in politics; in party organization and tactics; in the nature of social bonds; and in the education, political resources, and values of the electorate. All of these also apply to Israel.

Party System Phases

Israel has moved through three electoral phases in its political development, easily discerned in table 1.1. The dominant party period from 1948 and up to 1977 coincided with the period of nation building, during which the precursors of the Labor Party (Mapai, the Alignment, etc.) were by far the largest political party and formed all government coalitions.

A second, competitive party system phase began after the victory of the Likud in 1977, characterized by two large parties of similar size forming the nucleus of two party blocs. These two blocs, commonly labeled *left* and *right,* crystallized around the major cleavage dimension of security, peace, and the future of the territories. While the system indicated signs of competitiveness, in fact the Likud had a superior position during this fifteen-year period, because of the larger size of the right bloc. The parties of the right and the religious parties combined won the majority of Knesset seats and supported the Likud position regarding the Arab-Israeli conflict. This was true even in the period between 1984 and 1990, during which Likud and Labor joined in a National Unity government that featured a rotation of the prime minister position between the two antagonists. Throughout this period, the Likud dominated politics, even if it never achieved a dominant party status similar to Labor in the first decades of statehood.

The 1992 election broke this pattern with the left bloc winning a majority (61) of the seats for the first time since 1973. From that point on, power shifted between the two largest parties, the Likud and Labor, and between the right and left camps they led. The third phase began in 1996 and coincided with the introduction of the direct election of the prime minister, and with post-Oslo politics. Suddenly the Palestinian issue was being negotiated and territories were being returned. Up until the electoral reform, the winning coalition of parties determined who would rule. Since the direct election of the prime minister, the parties no longer determine who will be head of government, and the two parts of the Election Day ceremony became more and more separate from one another.

The combination of institutional reform and changing political realities reintroduced multidimensionality into the party system after some two decades in which the system was focused on the Israeli-Arab conflict issue dimension. The two large parties declined, and the small parties, in particular sectarian ones—Arab, Russian immigrants, Haredi, and anti-Haredi—flourished in the Knesset elections. The religious parties became willing coalition partners for any prime minister, just like most other sectarian and center parties. While irrelevant in the prime ministerial race, these parties gained in power in coalition politics since the growth of their share of the votes came at the expense of the large parties.

The change from one ballot to two ballots has confounded the measure of victory and defeat in elections. In the pre-Reform period (through 1992), the winner was the largest party in the Knesset elections. Until 1977, that party was always Labor; it always formed the government, and this dominant-party-system was highly stable. For the three elections in the 1980s Labor and Likud were very close to each other, and what determined the coalition government in this competitive decade was the bloc share. In the 1990s, since the legislation of the direct election of the prime minister, power shifted three times: from Yitzhak Shamir to Rabin in 1992, from Shimon Peres to Benjamin Netanyahu in 1996, and from Netanyahu to Ehud Barak in 1999. Under the new electoral system what determines the winner is the prime minister race, not the Knesset party shares. The fortunes of the political parties became detached from political victory and defeat.

Both Labor and Likud have suffered declining political fortunes in the last two decades. Labor's uninterrupted reign ended in 1977, after which Likud and Labor competed for power. Likud emerged as the largest party in 1977, grew more in 1981, and then began a downward trend. Labor peaked in 1969; its reemergence in 1992 was only relative to the poor showing of Likud that year. In the period of dominance the system was one-sided; the period of competition saw a heightening of the concentration of the vote for the two parties at first and then their weakening and the reemergence of smaller parties.

By 1999, One Israel (a list made up of Labor, Gesher and the moderate-Orthodox Meimad) won only 26 seats, with 670,484 votes (20.3%). Likud fell to 19 seats, reflecting the 468,103 voters (14.1%) that supported it. Netanyahu's 1999 total (1,402,474; 43.9%) was 100,000 votes less than he had won in 1996. Barak won 1,791,020 votes (56.1%), over 300,000 votes more than Peres won in 1996. Labor's size was now 37% of Barak's; Likud's was a third of Netanyahu's. In 1996, both parties still obtained over 50% of their leaders' votes in the prime ministerial race.

Throughout Israel's history the party system has been highly fragmented. The number of lists represented in the Knesset varied between 9 and 15 with no apparent trend. The 15 lists in the 1999 Knesset were no exception— three other elections also had that high a number of successful lists. However, unlike the others, the 1999 Knesset had no large party, only medium-size and small parties, and thus it was more fractionalized. Moreover, in 1992 the threshold for representation in the Knesset was raised from 1% to 1.5%. We can see in table 1.1 that this reform reduced the number of lists in the next two elections, but by 1999 the number of successful lists returned to the pre-Reform level. Thus it would seem that the two elements of the electoral reform from 1992 canceled each other out. Small parties competed and many of them achieved office. In 1999, two lists received 1.9% of the vote entitling them to 2 Knesset seats each; 3 other lists obtained between 1 and 1.5%, leaving them outside the Knesset.

Parties, Issues, and Candidates

It is clear that parties and voters interact in bringing about the dealignment of the party system. We focus here on the voters, and emphasize the increase in issue voting and the growing importance of candidates and their performance—trends in evidence throughout Western democracies (Dalton and Wattenberg 1993; Franklin, Mackie, and Valen 1992).

Table 1.2 presents data on the major factors in the vote for Barak versus Netanyahu in 1999[1] in comparison to voting patterns for Netanyahu versus Peres in 1996 and the vote for the right and left blocs in the years preceding the electoral reform. This bloc vote can be used meaningfully only for the elections since 1981, following the clear emergence of the bipolar structure of the party system. Table 1.2 covers then the period of 1981–1999, using the prime ministerial vote since the introduction of the direct election of the prime minister, in 1996 and 1999, and the right-left bloc vote for the Knesset (Israeli parliament) between 1981 and 1992.[2]

We conducted the analysis using logistic regression. For each year, we present three regression analyses, performed only on respondents who disclosed their voting intention. First we analyze voting behavior in reference to the major sociodemographic variables (Age, Gender, Density of Dwelling,

Education, Income, Religious Observance, and Ethnic Background). In the second stage we combine sociodemographics with indicators for the major issue dimensions in Israeli politics (the Territories Issue, the Socioeconomic Issue, and the State-Religion Issue). In the third stage we add performance evaluation variables (Performance: Economy and Performance: Security).[3]

To assess the relative importance of each group of variables in the three-step regression model, we consider the percent of correct predictions in each model. We find that the sociodemographic model achieved between 67% and 74% correct predictions, with no clear trend over the years. In 1981, the sociodemographic model correctly predicted 67% and in 1999—68%. Thus it seems that the predictive potential of the social characteristics of voters has not changed significantly over the two decades.[4] The contribution of the issues beyond the socioeconomic variables in the second-stage regression, however, increased over time. In 1981 issues added 3% to the sociodemographic model.[5] Starting in 1984, issues added between 8 and 16% correct predictions. The third-stage regressions indicate the growing importance of performance evaluations, especially since the direct election for prime minister.

Like most other advanced industrial democracies, in Israel issue voting has increased over time. Unlike these other systems, however, the predictive potential of sociodemographics (and of sociodemographic and attitudinal variables in combination) has not declined (Franklin, Mackie, and Valen 1992). The source of this pattern lies in the collective identity dilemmas raised by the issues on the agenda and their interrelationship with group characteristics (Shamir and Arian 1999). The rise of issue voting can be traced to the increased salience of the external collective identity dilemmas manifesting themselves in the policy issues relating to the peace process and the territories, and of the internal identity dilemmas around citizenship, nationhood, and religion.[6] These two dimensions are indicated in the regressions in table 1.2 by the willingness to return territories item and by the state-religion question about the role of government in seeing to it that public life be conducted according to Jewish religious law.

The territorial debate was clearly dominant throughout the period covered in table 1.2. Among the three issue domains, all measured on a similar range from 1 to 4, the issue of the territories is without doubt the most influential issue factor. Moreover, it grew in importance over time. The 1984 election seems to be the cutting point, the point in time in which the territory issue emerged as the overriding dimension ordering the party system and it has registered a major increase in its impact on the vote. That was the election that followed the war in Lebanon, and the first election in which Yitzhak Shamir replaced Menachem Begin as the head of the Likud. Since 1984, the impact of the territories issue on the vote remained very high. According to

Table 1.2 Logistic Regressions: Prime Ministerial Candidate/Right-Left Bloc, 1981–1999[a]

Variable	1981 (N = 1,249) b	(s.e.)	1984 (N = 1,259) b	(s.e.)	1988 (N = 873) b	(s.e.)	1992 (N = 1,192) b	(s.e.)	1996 (N = 1,168) b	(s.e.)	1999 (N = 1,075) b	(s.e.)
I. Sociodemographic												
Age	-.07*	(.03)	-.14***	(.04)	-.12**	(.04)	-.14***	(.03)	-.10**	(.03)	-.06*	(.03)
Gender	-.43**	(.17)	.11	(.18)	d	(.16)	.05	(.17)	-.60***	(.17)	-.27	(.16)
Density of Dwelling	.36**	(.13)	.29	(.17)	.43**	(.16)	.19	(.13)	.46**	(.15)	.36*	(.18)
Education	-.01	(.09)	-.10	(.10)	-.45***	(.15)	-.27**	(.10)	-.23*	(.10)	-.28*	(.12)
Income	.05	(.09)	.00	(.09)	-.01	(.09)	.05	(.07)	.14	(.08)	-.12	(.07)
Religious Observance	-.68***	(.10)	-.66***	(.12)	-.81***	(.13)	-1.01***	(.11)	-1.18***	(.13)	-.95***	(.11)
Ethnic Background	-.46**	(.18)	-1.68***	(.20)	-.39*	(.20)	-.82***	(.18)	-.57***	(.18)	-.52**	(.17)
	N = 723[b] 67%[c]		N = 676 74%		N = 596 71%		N = 821 72%		N = 771 73%		N = 795 68%	
II. Sociodemographic + Issues												
Age	-.05	(.04)	-.08	(.05)	-.09	(.06)	-.10*	(.04)	-.03	(.04)	-.05	(.04)
Gender	-.45*	(.18)	.25	(.24)	d	(.21)	.04	(.21)	-.52**	(.21)	-.27	(.21)
Density of Dwelling	.32*	(.14)	.24	(.22)	.41*	(.21)	.23	(.17)	.50**	(.18)	.14	(.20)
Education	.12	(.10)	.03	(.13)	-.46*	(.20)	-.39**	(.12)	-.02	(.12)	-.30*	(.15)
Income	.02	(.10)	-.07	(.12)	-.02	(.12)	-.06	(.09)	.08	(.09)	-.22*	(.10)
Religious Observance	-.52***	(.11)	-.60***	(.14)	-.67***	(.17)	-.75***	(.15)	-.87***	(.15)	-.31*	(.15)
Ethnic Background	-.59***	(.20)	-1.65***	(.26)	-.05	(.27)	-.80***	(.23)	-.56**	(.22)	-.56***	(.22)
Territories	.62***	(.10)	1.08***	(.11)	1.30***	(.12)	1.11***	(.09)	1.32***	(.11)	1.55***	(.13)
Socioeconomic	-.36***	(.10)	-.96***	(.18)	-.67***	(.13)	-.39***	(.12)	-.23*	(.12)	-.47***	(.13)

III. Sociodemographic + Issues + Performance Evaluation

State-religion	-.23** (.08)	[d]	-.13 (.13)	-.29** (.11)	-.38*** (.10)	-.51*** (.13)
	N=682	N=610	N=536	N=750	N=758	N=761
	70%	83%	86%	82%	81%	84%
	(+3%)[e]	(+9%)	(+15%)	(+10%)	(+8%)	(+16%)

Age	-.07 (.06)	-.04 (.06)	-.08 (.06)	-.06 (.05)	-.01 (.07)
Gender	.14 (.28)	[d]	.07 (.26)	-.36 (.25)	-.04 (.37)
Density of Dwelling	.39 (.25)	.61** (.25)	.18 (.21)	.41* (.20)	.11 (.35)
Education	-.05 (.15)	-.44 (.23)	-.36* (.15)	-.01 (.14)	.05 (.27)
Income	-.02 (.13)	-.09 (.14)	-.07 (.11)	.08 (.11)	-.22 (.17)
Religious Observance	-.57*** (.17)	-.47** (.19)	-.80*** (.19)	-.78*** (.18)	-.23 (.27)
Ethnic Background	-1.75*** (.31)	-.09 (.31)	-.88** (.29)	-.57* (.26)	.02 (.37)
Territories	1.00*** (.13)	1.23*** (.14)	.92*** (.11)	1.07*** (.13)	1.10*** (.20)
Socioeconomic	-.93*** (.20)	-.62*** (.15)	-.34* (.14)	-.20 (.14)	-.23 (.21)
State-Religion	[d]	-.06 (.14)	-.20 (.13)	-.24* (.12)	-.49* (.22)
Performance: economic [d]	1.17*** (.19)	.78*** (.19)	.67*** (.15)	.93*** (.17)	2.44*** (.30)
Performance: security [d]	.57** (.20)	1.07*** (.21)	1.51*** (.20)	1.28*** (.20)	1.52*** (.26)
	N=603	N=527	N=740	N=751	N=761
	87%	88%	88%	89%	95%
	(+4%)	(+2%)	(+6%)	(+8%)	(+11%)

[a] Dependent variable: Vote for prime ministerial candidate 1996–1999; for Right-Left bloc 1981–1992.
[b] Sample size. For details on the samples, the wording and the coding of the variables see Shamir and Arian, (1999, Appendixes A and B).
[c] Total percentage of correct predictions.
[d] Not available.
[e] Change in percentage of correct predictions.
*p < .05   **p < .01   ***p < .001.

19

the full equations, the largest-size parameter is observed in the 1988 election, but fluctuations since 1984 are not large.

According to the second-stage equations, which do not include performance evaluations, the territories issue effect reaches its highest point in 1999. The 1999 result is interesting in view of the fact that the differences between the Likud and Labor parties and between left and right on this issue have narrowed following the post-Oslo reality, Rabin's assassination, and Netanyahu's term in office. By 1999, after three years in which Netanyahu reluctantly pursued the Oslo accords, the process itself had become part of the consensus. The majority of Jewish voters preferred peace and a Jewish democratic state to greater Israel—Israel with its post-1967 war boundaries. Opposition to the Oslo process shrank, and the National Unity list, the right-wing alternative to the Likud and Netanyahu that placed greater Israel and outright opposition to the Oslo process at the forefront of its election campaign, won only 4 seats.

The debate that rages is still fierce, but it is no longer cast in metaphysical terms of divine promises and national destiny, but in pragmatic terms about borders, the nature of security arrangements, and the eventuality of a Palestinian state. In the 1999 survey only about 60% perceived large or very large differences between the two major parties on the territories issue, down from 80% in 1996, and from around two thirds between 1981 and 1992. Nevertheless, 1999 was similar to the other two elections of the 1990s and different from previous elections in that many more voters said that the territories would be an important consideration in their voting decision. In 1999 and 1996 about two thirds said that the issue of the territories would very greatly influence their vote, compared with half in 1992, and less than a third in previous elections. Summing the two positive categories of response, around 90% in 1999 and 1996 and about 80% in 1992 said that the territories issue "will influence my vote" or "will greatly influence my vote" compared with less than two thirds in previous elections.

The state-religion issue was the weakest issue predictor of the vote through 1992, but by 1996 and 1999 it placed second after the territories and before the socioeconomic schism. More important however is its increasing role over time in the explanation of the vote, with the highest coefficients in the 1999 equations.[7] Obviously this dimension has become more potent in structuring the vote and the party system. Before the 1999 elections, Shinui was represented by only one Knesset delegate, and seemed to be doomed to extinction. The party recruited an outspoken journalist to head its 1999 list, built its campaign solely on an anti-Haredi message, and leaped in size to 6 seats. The left-wing "Meretz" Party, which combined a dovish and secular agenda, grew from 9 to 10 Knesset members. On the other side, the religious parties increased their share of seats in the current Knesset to 27 from their previous record high of 23 seats in 1996, based mostly on the spectacular rise of the ultra-Orthodox Sephardi party Shas. Shas grew from 10 to 17 seats. The strife between religious and secular and between the Jewish and democratic Israel will clearly be on the agenda.

The third-stage regressions illuminate another change in Israeli voting behavior, and that is the increased role of performance evaluations. Voters' evaluations of the performance of the candidates are becoming more important considerations in their voting decision. In 1999 the impact of performance evaluations in security and foreign affairs and in the economic realm reached record highs in the explanation of the vote. The 1999 result may be partly due to the change in question wording[8] or to the candidates running in the race and in particular the Netanyahu factor, to which we will return. Whatever the explanation, there seems to be a trend here, with performance evaluations contributing 4 and 2% in 1984 and 1988, respectively, to the explanation of the vote beyond sociodemographics and issues. In 1992, performance evaluations added 6% beyond the other variables. Since the move to direct elections for prime minister in 1996 and 1999, this number jumped to 8% and 11%, respectively. The election campaigns are more and more candidate-oriented and less party-centered (Lehman-Wilzig 1995), and how well the candidates did or will do in office takes on increased importance in the voting booth, as in other democracies (Bean and Mughan 1989; Wattenberg 1991).

Another indication of the importance of candidates is provided by our 1999 postelection study, in the field immediately following the election. We presented our sample with a list of alternative explanations for the results of the election. The statement receiving the highest level of agreement was that "the elections were basically about Netanyahu's personality and his performance as prime minister." Seventy-two percent of respondents agreed with this assessment of the election. Many also agreed that "Barak's victory showed that the public wants to continue the peace talks and reach a compromise with the Palestinians" (67%) and that "Barak's victory showed that the public thinks that he will better keep the rule of law" (59%). But when asked to choose the primary theme of the elections, 41% chose Netanyahu's personality and performance. An additional 24% chose the social and economic situation, 17% picked security and foreign affairs issues, 10% said the rule of law, and 9% religious-secular relations. The primacy of the Netanyahu factor in the elections cut across political affiliations.

That the prime ministerial candidate seems to have replaced the party in the eyes of the voter is evident from a consideration of the love-hate thermometer scales for Labor and Likud and for the candidates, Netanyahu and Barak in 1999, Netanyahu and Peres in 1996, and Shamir and Rabin in 1992. Table 1.3 presents means, t-tests for the difference in the means, and correlations between party and candidate thermometer scores for these three elections. The thermometer scores for the candidates and for their respective parties are highly correlated (the lowest being the correlation for Labor and Rabin in 1992). But more interesting are the differences in means. Using the t-test for the difference in means, we see that the party-candidate differences for Likud and Labor and their respective candidates are statistically significant in 1992 and in 1996, but not in 1999. Only the Mordechai-Center difference in 1999 is statistically significant, although it too is small. With the 1992 election still conducted under the old electoral system and the 1996 election as the first in which the candidates ran directly for prime minister, the distinction between candidate and party was fresh enough for respondents to differentiate between the two. By 1999, the role of the Labor and Likud parties had receded and the importance of the prime ministerial candidates had become so central as to blur the difference between candidate and party almost completely.

Table 1.3   Thermometer Scores—Parties and Candidates

	Mean		Correlation	N	t-test
1992					
Labor	5.5	\			
Rabin	5.8	/	.69***	1,162	−6.335***
Likud	5.6	\			
Shamir	5.3	/	.83***	1,157	5.682***
1996					
Labor	5.8	\			
Peres	6.2	/	.82***	1,135	−7.741***
Likud	5.9	\			
Netanyahu	5.7	/	.85***	1,141	2.852**
1999					
Labor	6.3	\			
Barak	6.4	/	.86***	1,030	−1.210
Likud	5.6	\			
Netanyahu	5.7	/	.89***	1,025	−1.071
Center	6.0	\			
Mordechai	6.1	/	.81***	1,034	−2.169*

*$p \leq .05$ **$p \leq .01$ ***$p \leq .001$.

A Glimpse of the Future: Blocs not Parties

The division between left and right has characterized Israeli politics since independence. This distinction organizes the multiparty system combining politics and ideological stance. Politicians use the labels, as do political commentators and the general public. Over time, with the passing of the dominant party system and with the establishment of the two-bloc competitive system, the left and right terms became more meaningful, useful, and prevalent. The key electoral division in the multiparty system was no longer between the dominant party, Mapai/Labor, and all other parties, but between the left and right blocs or ideological families. These proved to be useful shorthand codes that organized the complex political world for the public. In intergenerational socialization, passing on the side in the left-right division was more important and relevant than a specific party identification (Ventura 1997). Left and right were defined in terms of the Israeli-Arab conflict dimension, the major cleavage dimension in the polity (Arian and Shamir 1983; Shamir 1986; Ventura and Shamir 1992).

Using respondents' self-identification in terms of these labels, it is clear from our surveys that the left and right demarcation has increased in relevance and coincides with shifts in power distribution in Israeli politics. The data[9] we have at hand relate to the years 1962 to 1999 and are displayed in table 1.4. The response categories changed somewhat over time with the changing structure of the system, but the general pattern is very clear.

The dominant party system, in which many more identified with the left than with the right, eroded gradually. By 1973 the two camps were about equal in size, and by 1977 with the turnabout in government, the right superseded the left. The right continued to grow until 1988, when it comprised about half the Jewish population, but from then on its strength decreased. The fortunes of the left presented a mirror image with the low points in 1977 and 1981, after which it increased in size. By 1999, the size of the two groups was almost equal. There was obvious interaction between election results and the left-right self-identification of the electorate.

Of even more interest in terms of our concerns here is the increase in the number of respondents defining themselves as right or left. As the two-bloc party system established itself in the 1980s, more and more respondents adopted the labels and identified themselves accordingly. By 1988, 75% did so, compared to 50% in 1981, and 39% in 1962. In the 1999 survey, 79% divided themselves almost equally into the two blocs. The depletion of the center and no-identification categories is the other half of the same process. Adding together those who defined themselves in the center and those who

Table 1.4　Left-Right Identification (in %), 1962–99

	1962	1969	1973	1977	1981	1984	1988	1992	1996	1999
Left/moderate left	31	25	22	18	17	23	26	30	36	39
Center	23	26	33	29	39	21	11	18	16	11
Right/moderate right	8	16	23	28	33	38	49	42	39	40
Religious	5	6	7	6	6	2	4	3	3	2
No interest in politics; no answer	33	27	15	19	6	15	10	7	6	9
[Center and no answer	56	53	48	48	45	36	21	25	22	20]

[a]The question was, "With which political tendency do you identify?" The first responses were suggested to the respondent, the "religious" and "no interest in politics; no answer" responses were not. In 1962, "Left" and "Right" were not used; "Marxist left" and "Herut" were offered in their place. From 1962 through 1977 the surveys were conducted by the Israel Institute of Applied Social Research; from 1981 through 1992 by the Dahaf Research Institute, in 1996 by Modi'in Ezrachi, and in 1999 by Machshov.

did not identify themselves along this continuum presents a convincing trend. From about half of the sample up to and including the 1981 elections, this group declined to about a third in 1984, and between a quarter and a fifth in the next four elections.[10] Two processes were at work: The electorate had become more and more identifiable using the left and right labels, and has also become more polarized with fewer center and nonidentified voters, more left and right identifiers, and growing parity in the size of the blocs.

Juxtaposing bloc representation in the Knesset with the public's right-left self-identification, indicates that the curves of identifiers and Knesset seats for the left and the right move quite closely together, albeit in different trajectories for the left and the right. When the trends of bloc vote and prime ministerial vote diverge (as in the case of the left between 1996 and 1999, when the bloc vote declines whereas the prime ministerial vote share increases) the (left) identification trajectory goes with the latter rather than with the former, reemphasizing the predominance of the prime minister race in electoral politics.

While there is general correspondence between the fortunes of the left and the right in the voting booth and in the self-identification survey data, this is not the case with respect to the center. The proportion of the electorate defining itself as center declined over the years, but there is no simultaneous trend in the voting for center parties.[11] Center position or identification does not necessarily translate into party choice, and voting for a center party does not rule out identifying with either the left or the right. What the center means, which parties qualify for it, and whether the center exists at all (Duverger 1964; Hazan 1996) are questions for which there are no straightforward answers. But the analysis offers striking evidence of the transitory nature of the political center in Israeli politics.

Many of the center parties served politicians and voters as vehicles for electoral mobility when they did not feel they could move to the other side. The Democratic Movement for Change (DMC) provides the most prominent example in the 1977 election; it allowed a vote against Labor without supporting Likud. The Center Party in 1999, and especially the role of Yitzhak Mordechai as candidate for prime minister, signaled a preference for a right of center persuasion without supporting Netanyahu.

In many ways, center parties perform the function of train platforms, something to get in on, not to stand on. Once in, the pulls of coalition bargaining quickly transform ideals into bargaining chips. Center parties are often formed to perpetuate the leader's hold on office. Some voters might be attracted to the leader, others to the usual call for "clean government" and a new kind of politics. But after the election, history has shown these parties almost always find themselves in the coalition, and gone by the next election.

This interpretation of the center position as inhospitable to long-term occupancy is supported by the survey results. Respondents were asked about the possibility of shifting from one bloc to another. Of the 15% of respondents who located themselves in the center of the political continuum, 73% said they would consider moving to either left or right. A very different picture obtained for respondents who identified themselves with the left or the right. Only 10 and 12% each of those groups, respectively, indicated that they could see themselves changing blocs. Of the small minority who indicated that they might shift, only a handful said that it would be easy for them to do so. Seventy percent of right-wingers and 78% of leftists did not think that it would be possible to feel at home in the other camp after such a shift. The left was more apprehensive than the right, but large majorities in both camps did not think that such a switch could be done with comfort. Identification with the bloc, with all it implies in terms of politics and ideology, is highly entrenched.

The party system has undergone dealignment, almost deconstruction, but another gird of the political system, the division into identificational blocs of left and right, is as sturdy as ever. The blocs are alive, well, and vigorous. It is no coincidence that we observe the growth in vitality in bloc alignment and the simultaneous weakening of political parties and party ties. Also in the new party system, structured by the direct election of the prime minister and multiple cleavages, there will be a need for the structuring power of the ideological families or political blocs of left and right.

Conclusion

The Israeli party system, its parties and its voters, have undergone tremendous change since independence in 1948. From a stable dominant party system through a competitive two-bloc system, it finds itself at the beginning of the new millennium in a most unstable state. It was always a highly fragmented system, but after the 1999 election there was no large party to structure its political life. In the past, the parties—large and small—were by far the most powerful actors in the system. While we do not yet see "the demise of parties" (Korn 1998) we definitely observe a decline in their power, and serious shrinking in the size of the large parties. Turnovers, unpredictability, volatility, and instability are the rule—in stark contrast to the dominant party era.

Electoral politics have become privatized and candidate-centered. The nomination process has been democratized, with primaries highlighting the process. Campaign financing in 1996 and in 1999 was essentially privatized, with claims made that the restrictions on party spending did not apply to candidates for prime minister. Sectarian single-constituency and single-issue party lists abounded. Issue and performance considerations, along with identification with the labels of *left* and *right,* gained in importance.

Many of these changes are similar to those occurring in other advanced industrial societies. Changes in political communication and in the value structure of postindustrial societies occurred in Israel as they did in other countries. With all the similarities, the direct election of the prime minister makes the Israeli case unique. The Arab-Israeli conflict structured electoral politics for many years; the unfolding of the Oslo process will be played out within that familiar form, but it is likely that the system will be transformed in the process.

If the parties are in disarray and the mobilizing potential of the establishment has disappeared, the lust for power has not been diminished. Ambitious candidates will make use of the direct election of the prime minister to foster their own chances. As of the 1996 elections, these candidates had no incentive to reinvent the party system since political goals could be achieved without investing the hard work that it takes to build a party. The separation between prime minister and party was acceptable to them. Their parties were simply one more group to bargain with once the election was won and the coalition had to be formed. This characterizes the entire spectrum. The new system has been used twice so far. Once, in 1996, the last of the founding father generation, Peres, competed with a young upstart from the right-wing of the Likud, Netanyahu. In its second use, in 1999, Netanyahu competed against Barak, a prince of the left with a brilliant military record. The younger candidates were from the party system but not of it, and they both ran campaigns that ignored their parties. This abandonment of the parties in favor of the candidates and the blocs with which they are loosely identified is a clear symptom of the privatization of the electoral system. The parties have been sorely weakened; alternative forms of democratic governance have yet to emerge. In the short-term, the prognosis is for turnover, volatility, and instability; long-term complications could be much more severe.

Competition in the future is likely to be based on the ideological families and political blocs of left and right. Political parties are likely to persist in the emerging system, mostly because the future will be played out under rules that were fashioned for political parties in a different era under different conditions. Parties will persist in name and form because the law provides that the candidate for prime minister must be the head of her party's Knesset list in the parliamentary elections. Parties are also the main building block of the coalition needed by the prime minister once the Knesset is formed. Also, the structure of campaign financing is focused on party competition. But these are throwback arrangements to an earlier system. The party in Israel is unlikely to be a mass organization with a defined and articulated program. The large party will be in hibernation mode until it is awakened for a few golden moments by people seeking to be candidate for prime minister immediately before elections.

Dealignment of the party system is easy to discern and to document. Outlining the potential realignment is harder. Certainly issues of social equality, the tensions between religious and secular Jews, and an appropriate role for Israeli Arabs in the Jewish and democratic state of Israel will fashion the parameters of this realignment. The emergence of significant groups of voters will have to be taken into consideration. The immigrants in the 1950s from the Middle East and North Africa impacted the electoral arena by largely switching from Labor to Likud in 1977, thus bringing about the demise of the dominant party system and the 1977 realignment. The immigrants in the 1990s from the former Soviet Union came to a different system, and seem to have had an immediate impact, but of a different sort. They vote in large numbers for sectarian parties, and they were important forces in the three turnovers in the 1990s, casting a protest vote against the incumbent in each election. They are thus fundamentally dealigning the Israeli party scene.

Israeli democracy has witnessed the imperfect dissolution of major institutions while the media-driven increased personalization of politics has fostered the dominance of a political center, peopled by potential prime ministers but not by political parties. Organizations of control have been eclipsed; individuals of previously dominant groups are still in control, but the trends toward personalization underscore the expression of a new Israeli liberalism. This liberalism champions individual rights and the courts, leaving weaker groups doomed to pursue their quest in the back-corridors of coalition bargaining. Dominant groups will generate candidates to appeal to the center of the electorate for the now personalized and less-encumbered office of prime minister; in the meantime, the tensions between sectarian and universalistic demands will likely grow if they remain unresolved.

Notes

1. The survey was conducted during April and May 1999 in face-to-face interviews among a representative sample of voters by the Machshov Research Institute. It was funded by the Sapir Center for Development of Tel Aviv University and the Israel Democracy Institute. The data analyzed in this chapter cover only the Jewish electorate.

2. All surveys, including the 1999 survey, were preelection surveys collected through face-to-face interviews in the respondent's home. They were representative samples of the adult Jewish population, not including kibbutzim and Jewish settlements in the territories under Israel's control since 1967. The surveys between 1981 and 1992 were carried out by the Dahaf Research Institute, the 1996 survey by Modi'in Ezrachi, and the 1999 survey by Machshov. The sample sizes were 1,825 in October 1969; 1,917 in May 1973; 1,372 in March 1977; 1,249 in March 1981; 1,259 in July 1984; 873 in October 1988; 1,192 in June 1992; 1,168 in May 1996; and 1,075 in May 1999. The 1981 and 1984 surveys were supervised by Asher Arian; those since 1988, in collaboration with Michal Shamir.

We conducted a similar analysis of the vote for the two major parties, Likud and Labor, throughout the period for which we have survey data, from 1969 through 1999. It is not presented here because the distinction between these two parties has become less meaningful as the contest generated by the direct election of the prime minister has won most attention. The overall pattern of results is similar to that for the bloc vote in table 1.2. For the 1969–1996 results, see Shamir and Arian (1999).

3. For the wording of the questions, see Shamir and Arian (1999), Appendix B.

4. The same stability in the percent correct predictions of the sociodemographic model also holds for the Likud-Labor vote throughout the 1969–1999 period (not presented here).

5. In the analysis of Likud-Labor vote (not presented here), issues added between 0 to 5 percent between 1969 and 1981.

6. The impact of the socioeconomic issue oscillates over time, with the highest levels observed in 1984 and 1988.

7. This issue dimension is closely related to religiosity, measured in our surveys by a question asking the degree to which an individual observes the strictures of rabbinic Jewish law (Halacha). This measure of religious observance is based on behavior but indicates at the same time one of the most meaningful definitions of an individ-

ual's social affiliation and identity in modern Israel. Among the sociodemographic variables, religiosity has become the most meaningful social distinction. It has increased in its impact on the vote up to 1996. In 1999 it weakened somewhat, while the role of the state-religion issue increased.

8. Up to and including 1996, the question asked for a comparison between the two major party (Likud and Labor) teams. In 1999 we asked the respondents to compare the prime ministerial candidates, and assess who will deal better with the country's problems in the two areas. Since up to the eve of the election three major candidates were in the race, our question referred to all of them. The answers were recoded as 3—Netanyahu; 1—Barak; and 2—other answers (other candidates, none of them, all of them).

9. The surveys between 1962 through 1977 were conducted by the Israel Institute of Applied Social Research and were based on a representative sample of the adult urban Jewish population. Later surveys were representative of the adult Jewish population, excluding kibbutzim and settlements in the territories. The following institutes carried out the surveys: Dahaf between 1981 and 1992; Modiin Ezrachi in 1996, and Machshov in 1999. Each survey, except for 1962, was a preelection survey.

10. A reflection of changes in the party system can be seen in the responses of those who identified themselves as religious using this measure. Through the 1981 elections about 6 percent were not willing to identify themselves in left-right terms and voluntarily offered self-identification with the religious camp. From 1984 on, this number shrank by about half, as the religious dimension became more and more associated with the hawkish, right-wing position on the Israeli-Arab conflict dimension, the major dimension of the left-right continuum. This dimension evidently overrode other calculations for many religious voters; with growing multidimensionality this pattern may well reappear.

11. Based on commonly accepted classifications and the self-definition of parties, Center parties include the following: the Independent Liberals through 1977, the State list in 1969, the Democratic Movement for Change (DMC) in 1977, Shinui in the 1980s and in 1999, Telem 1981, Yahad and Ometz in 1984, the Third Way in 1996, and the Center Party in 1999 (see in Arian 1998).

The Independent Liberals obtained 4–6 seats in most elections throughout the 1950s and 1960s; in 1977 the DMC won 15 seats; in 1981 4 Knesset seats went to two Center parties, in 1984 7, in 1988 2, and none in 1992. In 1996 the Third Way elected 4 Knesset members, and in 1999 the reinvigorated Shinui and the newly established Center Party won 6 seats each. Counting Israel B'aliya as a center party (rather than as a sectarian ethnic party representing immigrants from the former Soviet Union), the figures for 1996 and 1999 jump to 11 and 18 seats, respectively.

Most of the party lists defined as center since 1977 were candidate-centered ad hoc groupings that did not survive more than one election. Yadin's DMC, Dayan's Telem, Weizmann's Yahad, and Kahalani's Third Way are good examples. The 1999 Center Party featured Mordechai, Lipkin-Shahak, Meridor, and Milo.

References

Arian, Asher. 1975. "Were the 1973 Elections in Israel Critical?" In Asher Arian (ed.). *The Elections in Israel—1973*. Jerusalem: Jerusalem Academic Press, 287–305.

———. 1980. "The Israeli Electorate, 1977." In Asher Arian (ed.). *The Elections in Israel—1977*. Jerusalem: Jerusalem Academic Press, 253–276.

———. 1998. *The Second Republic: Politics in Israel*. Chatham: Chatham House.

Arian, Asher, and Michal Shamir. 1983. "The Primarily Political Functions of the Left-Right Continuum." *Comparative Politics* 15: 139–158.

———. 1993. "Two Reversals in Israeli Politics: Why 1992 Was Not 1977." *Electoral Studies* 12: 313–339.

Bean, Clive, and Anthony Mughan. 1989. "Leadership Effects in Parliamentary Elections in Australia and Britain." *American Political Science Review* 83: 1165–1179.

Dalton, Russell J. 1996. *Citizen Politics: Public Opinion and Political Parties in Advanced Western Democracies*. 2d ed. Chatham, NJ: Chatham House.

Dalton, Russell J., Scott Flanagan, and Paul Beck (eds.). 1984. *Electoral Change in Advanced Industrial Democracies*. Princeton: Princeton University Press.

Dalton, Russell J., and Martin P. Wattenberg. 1993. "The Not So Simple Act of Voting." In Ada W. Finifter (ed.). *Political Science: The State of the Discipline II*. Washington, DC: American Political Science Association, 193–218.

Duverger, Maurice. 1964. *Political Parties*. London: Methuen & Co.

Franklin, M., T. Mackie, and H. Valen. 1992. *Electoral Change: Responses to Evolving Social and Attitudinal Structures in Western Countries*. Cambridge: Cambridge University Press.

Goldberg, Giora. 1992. *The Parties in Israel—From Mass Parties to Electoral Parties*. Tel-Aviv: Ramot (Hebrew).

Hazan, Reuven Y. 1999. "The Electoral Consequences of Political Reform: In Search of the Center of the Israeli Party System." In Asher Arian and Michal Shamir (eds.). *The Elections in Israel 1996*. Albany: State University of New York Press.

———. 1996. "Does Center Equal Middle?: Towards a Conceptual Delineation, with Application to West European Party Systems." *Party Politics* 2 (April): 209–228.

Hermann, Tamar. 1995. "The Rise of Instrumental Voting: The Campaign for Political Reform." In Asher Arian and Michal Shamir (eds.). *The Elections in Israel—1992*. Albany: State University of New York Press, 275–298.

Key, V. O. 1955. "A Theory of Critical Elections." *Journal of Politics* 17: 3–18.

Kitschelt, Herbert. Forthcoming. "Linkages between Citizens and Politicians in Democratic Politics." *Comparative Political Studies*.

Korn, Dani (ed.). 1998. *The Demise of Parties in Israel*. Tel-Aviv: Hakibbutz Hameuchad Publ. (Hebrew).

Korn, Dani, and Boaz Shapira. 1997. *Coalition Politics in Israel*. Tel-Aviv: Zmora-Bitan Publ. (Hebrew).

Lehman-Wilzig, Sam. 1995. "The 1992 Media Campaign: Toward the Americanization of the Israeli Elections?" In Daniel Elazar and Shmuel Sandler (eds.). *Israel at the Polls—1992*, 251–280.

Neuberger, Benyamin. 1997. *Political Parties in Israel*. Tel-Aviv: Open University.

Shamir, Michal. 1986. "Realignment in the Israeli Party System." In Asher Arian and Michal Shamir (eds.). *The Elections in Israel—1984*. Tel-Aviv: Ramot, 267–296.

Shamir, Michal, and Asher Arian. 1999. "Collective Identity and Electoral Competition in Israel." *American Political Science Review* 93: 265–277.

Ventura, Raphael. 1997. "The Influence of the Close Family Circle on the Voting Patterns of the Individual in Israel." Ph.D. diss., Tel-Aviv University.

Ventura, Raphael, and Michal Shamir. 1992. "Left and Right in Israeli Politics." Medina Umimshal 35: 21–50 (Hebrew).

Wattenberg, Martin P. 1991. *The Rise of Candidate-Centered Politics*. Cambridge: Harvard University Press.

2

Were Voters Strategic?

PAUL R. ABRAMSON AND JOHN H. ALDRICH

Multicandidate contests always provide the opportunity for strategic voting, and the Israeli prime ministerial election began as a five-candidate contest. But of the five candidates approved by the Central Elections Committee, only three had any chance of winning: Benjamin Netanyahu, the incumbent prime minister who led Likud, Ehud Barak, the head of One Israel, and Yitzhak Mordechai, leader of the newly formed Center Party. For most voters strategic considerations would be reduced to a comparison of these three candidates.

Although Mordechai eventually withdrew from the contest, he had strong credentials. As a former minister of defense, he had considerable political experience. Being of Kurdish origin, and being born in Iraq, also gave him a special appeal to Jews from Asia or Africa, or whose parents were from Asia and Africa, the so-called Sephardim. Early in the campaign, pundits thought Mordechai had a reasonable chance of winning if he could come in first or second and face either Netanyahu or Barak in a head-to-head contest. But very few expected him to come in first or second. Mordechai faced the problem of many centrist candidates: he may have been the second choice of many voters, but the first choice of relatively few.[1]

The two remaining candidates were seen as having virtually no chance of winning. Benny Begin, running as the head of the National Union, claimed to be the true heir of Herut, the party that his father, Menachim Begin, had led. In practice, he drew relatively little support and that came primarily from voters who would otherwise have supported Netanyahu. The Christian Arab, Azmi Bishara, running as the head of Balad, acknowledged at the outset that he had no chance of being elected.

We are grateful to Asher Arian and Michal Shamir for providing the survey data we analyze in this chapter, and to Matthew L. Diamond, Renan Levine, and Thomas J. Scotto for their assistance with the data analysis, and to Renan Levine for his suggestions.

This chapter examines the strategic preferences among the Israeli electorate during the 1999 prime ministerial contest, focusing on comparative
evaluations of Barak, Netanyahu, and Mordechai. Israelis are often seen as
sophisticated consumers of political information and if voters anywhere are
likely to vote strategically they are likely to do so in Israel. So we cannot
claim that Israel provides a deviant case to demonstrate that voters act strategically (Eckstein 1975). All the same, often political scientists cannot demonstrate what they believe to be true. Fortunately, the surveys conducted under
the supervision of the editors of this volume, Asher Arian and Michal Shamir,
contain several questions that will allow us to demonstrate that Israeli voters
were guided by strategic considerations during the 1999 prime ministerial
contest.

What Is Strategic Voting?

William H. Riker defines strategic voting as "voting contrary to one's immediate tastes in order to obtain an advantage in the long run" (1986, 78).
Riker (1982) argues that strategic voting would be particularly prevalent in
plurality-vote win systems in which voters might decide to vote for their second or lower-placed choice so as to avoid wasting their vote on a candidate
who has little chance of winning. But the Israeli direct election for prime
minister is a runoff system in which there is a second election if no candidate
wins a majority on the first ballot. Under a runoff system many voters may
vote their true preference on the first ballot, expecting to have an opportunity
to vote for one of the two top candidates in a second ballot. Although the
Israeli system for choosing the prime minister calls for a runoff, in the two
elections in which the system has been used the voting has involved a head-
to-head contest between two candidates. In 1996, only two candidates competed since Netanyahu persuaded two potential candidates, David Levy and
Rafael Eitan, not to run. He did this by incorporating Levy's Gesher list and
Eitan's Tzomet list into the Likud list, giving them a large number of "sure
seats" to keep them out of the race. In 1999, however, the number of candidates was reduced from five to two only in the two days preceding the election. But the decision of the candidates to withdraw as Election Day approached was based upon polling information that strongly suggested that
they would do very poorly on the first round, and that Barak might win
a majority of the vote even if they did not withdraw. The election was on
Monday, May 17. On the Saturday before the election, Bishara withdrew from
the contest, and on the morning before the election Mordechai withdrew.
Begin waited until the late afternoon to withdraw his candidacy. As voters
expressed their preferences by choosing a ballot slip for one candidate, and

as the slips for Bishara, Mordechai, and Begin were withdrawn, it was now a certainty that either Barak or Netanyahu would win a majority of the valid vote cast. (Write-in votes are not allowed, although voters can cast a blank ballot.)

On Election Day, Israeli voters had the choice of only two candidates and therefore could not vote strategically for prime minister. This does not mean, however, that strategic considerations played no role in the decision of voters to move their support toward the two leading candidates during the course of the campaign nor does it mean that candidates failed to act strategically in light of voter expectations. Our goal in this chapter is to examine these possibilities.

Changing Support for the Candidates Over Time

To measure support for the three leading candidates we employed a feeling thermometer in which respondents were asked to rank candidates from 1 ("hate") to 10 ("love"). We examined the distribution of responses over the course of the six weeks preceding the election.[2] Affect for the candidates varied relatively little throughout the campaign, but our analyses suggest that support for Netanyahu rose somewhat two weeks before the election, while support for Barak rose during the week before the election. The assessment of their chances for winning, on the other hand, varied dramatically, and we present our results in figure 2.1. Only a small minority at any point in the campaign thought that Mordechai would win, and by the last week of the campaign only a handful thought he would win. But there was a huge shift in the perceptions about whether Netanyahu or Barak would win in the last two weeks of the campaign. Two weeks before the election more respondents thought Netanyahu would win than Barak. In the final week, a clear majority of the electorate thought that Barak would win. Of course, none of the candidates had access to these data, but public surveys, as well as private polls, showed Barak's support gaining and Mordechai's support falling.

Strategic Considerations among the Israeli Electorate

Are voters affected by their perceptions of who will win? Although voters were constrained to choose between Barak and Netanyahu on Election Day (or to abstain) we argue that strategic considerations played a role *before* Election Day. We will present evidence indicating that at least some of Mordechai's supporters may have already decided to abandon him and to cast votes for their preference between Barak and Netanyahu. This follows from

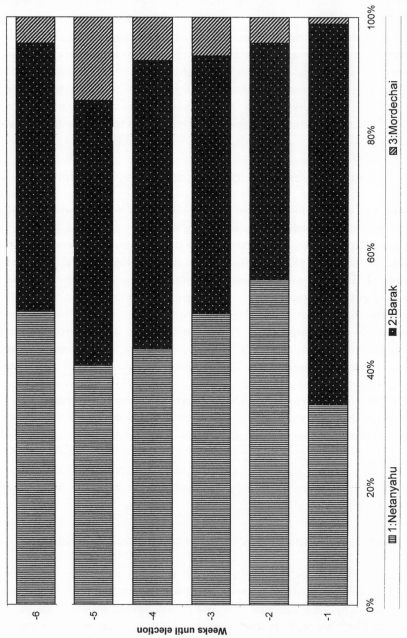

Figure. 2.1. Who Is Going to Win?

1:Netanyahu   2:Barak   3:Mordechai

the thesis that some voters will not want to "waste" their votes on candidates they believe have little chance of winning. Leading candidates often use the "wasted vote" argument, especially in political systems with two major parties, and minor-party candidates often try to refute it. That politicians use or refute the "wasted vote" argument does not mean that voters actually consider the chances that the candidate they favor will win. Yet there is empirical evidence that some voters are affected by strategic considerations.[3] Paul R. Abramson and his colleagues (1992) use data collected by the National Election Studies during the 1988 U.S. presidential primaries to suggest that at least some Americans were "sophisticated," assessing the viability of candidates in making their voting choices. Their analyses of the National Election Study data also suggest that there was strategic voting in the 1968, 1980, 1992, and 1996 presidential contests (Abramson et al., 1995; Abramson, Aldrich, and Rohde, 1999). On the other hand, there are scholars who argue that rational voters never vote strategically (Ferejohn and Fiorina 1974, 1975, 1993). They argue that voters follow a "mimimax-regret" strategy. In other words, they minimize their maximum regret, and for all such voters this regret would be greatest if their favorite candidate lost because they failed to support him or her at the polls.

Table 2.1 strongly suggests that at least some Israelis thought strategically. It shows the percentage who planned to vote for Barak among respondents who ranked him first among all the candidates. Likewise, it shows the percentage of respondents who planned to vote for Netanyahu among those who ranked him first, as well as the percentage who intended to vote for Mordechai. There are substantial differences among these three subgroups. Among voters who ranked Barak first, nine out of ten planned to vote for him, and four out of five who ranked Netanyahu first intended to vote for him. But among the voters who ranked Mordechai first, only three out of five planned to vote for him. The percentage who planned to vote for Mordechai is strikingly similar to the percentage of American voters in 1980 who voted for John B. Anderson among those who ranked him first in a three-way

Table 2.1   Percentage Who Intended to Vote for Barak, Netanyahu, and Mordechai among Respondents Who Ranked Them Highest on the Feeling Thermometers

	Percentage Who Planned to Vote for Candidate	Number Who Ranked Candidate First
Ranked Barak First	92	(343)
Ranked Netanhahu First	81	(321)
Ranked Mordechai First	59	(107)

comparison with Ronald Reagan and Jimmy Carter—57%. There are other parallels between Mordechai and Anderson, since both were centrists who started out with substantial support in the polls, but saw their support collapse as the election neared.

These data further support the thesis that Israeli voters may have been thinking strategically because the probability that a candidate's supporters would defect from him was strongly related to their perception of whether or not he would win. Of course, Barak and Netanyahu supporters were much more likely to think their candidate would win than Mordechai supporters were (82%, 88%, and 55%, respectively). Table 2.2 shows the percentage who planned to vote for Barak among respondents who ranked him first among all the candidates, controlling by whether or not they expected him to win. Among those who thought he would win, 94% planned to vote for him, whereas among those who thought he would not, only 79% did. Differences among Netanyahu supporters are far greater, although we should bear in mind that relatively few voters who ranked Netanyahu first thought he would lose. Among those who thought he would win, 88% planned to vote for him, while among those who thought he would lose only 24% did. Differences are greatest among Mordechai supporters. Among those who thought he would win, 95% said they would vote for him, whereas among those who did not think he would win only 21% planned to vote for him. Reading down the first column (which shows the results among those who thought that the candidate they ranked highest would win) shows very little difference among Barak, Netanyahu, and Mordechai supporters.

Table 2.2   Percentage Who Intended to Vote for Barak, Netanyahu, and Mordechai among Respondents Who Ranked Them Highest on the Feeling Thermometers, by Whether They Thought the Candidate They Ranked First Would Win

	Thought the Candidate They Ranked First Would Win		Thought the Candidate They Ranked First Would Not Win	
	Percentage Who Planned to Vote for Candidate	Number Who Ranked Candidate	Percentage Who Planned to Vote for Candidate First	Number Who Ranked Candidate First
Ranked Barak First	94	(282)	79	(61)
Ranked Netanyahu First	88	(284)	24	(37)
Ranked Mordechai First	95	(55)	21	(52)

Although these results suggest that strategic considerations among the Israeli electorate cost Mordechai support, they do not suggest that they caused him to lose. The bottom line is that relatively few Israelis ranked him first. These strategic considerations, however, could have affected the dynamics of the campaign. Strategic considerations among the electorate eroded Mordechai's support over the course of the campaign, eliminating his chances of making it to the runoff and reducing his chances of affecting the outcome. Ultimately, Mordechai withdrew from the contest even without promises of a cabinet position from Barak (Sontag 1999). Had Mordechai not withdrawn, Barak might have won a majority of the vote in a three-way contest, and Mordechai would have suffered a major embarrassment. On the other hand, had his candidacy resulted in Barak missing a majority by a narrow margin, Mordechai and the Center Party might have been blamed for forcing a needless and costly runoff. Of course, it is Riker's (1982) argument that politicians are more likely to follow strategic considerations than voters, and the Israeli campaign offers support for his contention.

Was Barak the Condorcet Winner?

It is widely recognized that different election rules can lead to different outcomes. But in the 1999 prime ministerial election it seems reasonable to conclude that the runoff rules did not greatly affect the outcome. We already know that Barak defeated Netanyahu by a substantial margin. Unless major events favoring Netanyahu had occurred in the two weeks between a first round and a runoff, Barak would have defeated Netanyahu in a second-round contest. The only question that remains is whether or not he would have defeated Mordechai in a runoff. If so, it seems safe to conclude that the runoff system did not lead to pernicious results.

One widely accepted criterion for "fairness" in elections is the "Condorcet criterion" (see Black 1958). The Marquis de Condorcet (1743–1794) argued that if there is an outcome that would be preferred by a majority over any other alternative, that outcome should be selected. A candidate who would defeat any of his or her opponents in a head-to-head contest meets this criterion. If there is a three-person contest in which candidate A would defeat candidate B in a head-to-head contest and would also defeat candidate C in a head-to-head contest, candidate A meets the Condorcet criterion. If candidate A wins the actual election, he or she is the Condorcet winner. But since in most elections (including the Israeli prime ministerial contest) voters can state a single preference for each office, a candidate can meet the Condorcet criterion but lose the actual election. We would view such a candidate as a concealed Condorcet winner. There also may be no outcome that meets the

Condorcet criterion. For example, candidate A might defeat candidate B in a head-to-head contest, candidate B might defeat candidate C, and candidate C might defeat candidate A.

In their analyses of the 1968, 1980, 1992, and 1996 U.S. presidential elections, Abramson and his colleagues (1995, 1999) used the National Election Studies to determine whether the third-party candidate might have been a concealed Condorcet winner. Of course, it seemed very unlikely that in 1968 an extremist candidate such as George C. Wallace could have defeated either Richard M. Nixon or Hubert H. Humphrey in head-to-head contests, and the data suggest he would have lost soundly to either of them. It seemed more logical that a centrist candidate, such as Anderson in 1980 or H. Ross Perot (especially in 1992, when he won 19% of the popular vote), might have been a concealed Condorcet winner. But Abramson and his colleagues' analyses provided no support for the thesis that any of these independent or third-party candidates would have defeated their major-party opponents. In fact, it seems very likely that Nixon in 1968, Reagan in 1980, and Clinton in both 1992 and 1996 were all Condorcet winners.

The Israeli survey data can be used to determine whether Barak was the Condorcet winner, and the evidence suggests that he probably was. We base this conclusion on using the ten-point "love-hate" scale to directly compare each of the three major candidates. Barak prevails over Netanyahu by 52% to 40%. Assuming that the relatively small percentage who tied these candidates split evenly, the overall result is precisely on target in predicting the election result. Barak also defeats Mordechai, but not decisively. Twenty-one percent of the respondents tie these two candidates, and we can assume that Barak will win only if he carries most of the respondents who rank them the same.[4] There is one major difference between the Israeli and American results. Whereas in the United States the third-party candidates would have lost to either of their major-party opponents, Mordechai defeats Netanyahu, and does so almost as decisively as Barak does. Fifty-one percent support Mordechai in a head-to-head contest against Netanyahu, while only 38% support Netanyahu. See table 2.3.

These cross-national differences may simply result from idiosyncratic differences among these elections. Netanyahu was very unpopular and may have been vulnerable to any reasonable centrist candidate. But we also suspect that the pull of party loyalties in the United States plays a major role in minimizing the vote for independent and third-party candidates. Party loyalties have weakened in the United States, but about three in ten voters are strong party identifiers who very rarely support the opposition or even an independent candidate (Abramson, Aldrich, and Rohde 1999; Abramson et al. 2000; Bartels 2000). Despite the widespread arguments that the U.S. party system

Table 2.3 Comparative Thermometer Ratings of Barak, Netanyahu, and Mordechai (Head-to-head Comparisons in Percentages)

Candidate Rated First					
Barak	52%	Barak	45%	Netanyahu	38%
Tie	8	Tie	21	Tie	11
Netanyahu	40	Mordechai	34	Mordechai	51
Total percent	100%	Total percent	100%	Total percent	100%
(Number)	(1,155)	(Number)	(1,162)	(Number)	(1,158)

is in disarray, presidential candidates attempt to use political parties to bolster their support and recognize that they are more likely to carry out their policy objectives if their parties win legislative support (Aldrich 1995). In Israel the party system has become increasingly fragmented, at least partly because of the direct election of the prime minister (Arian 1998). Before direct election, at least some Israelis may have voted strategically for the Knesset by voting for the party they wanted to lead the governing coalition, rather than voting for the party that they most preferred (Nixon et al., 1996). With the direct election of the prime minister, this function can be filled by choosing among the prime ministerial candidates. Having stated their preference in the prime ministerial ballot, voters are free to choose a small party for the Knesset.

Conclusion

From a comparative viewpoint, our main finding is that strategic considerations do occur even in runoff elections. This is an important conclusion since some scholars have argued that strategic considerations should not be important. Indeed, Maurice Duverger argued that there is little reason to expect strategic voting in runoff elections since "the variety of parties having much in common does not adversely affect the number of seats they gain since in this system they can always regroup for the second ballot" (1963, 240). For example, Abramson and his colleagues (1995) argue that the large number of candidates who gain a substantial share of the vote in the first round of French presidential elections results from high levels of sincere voting among French citizens who expect to have the opportunity to vote in a runoff election.

On the other hand, Gary W. Cox emphasizes the impact of runoff rules on the number of parties that decide to compete, focusing on what he calls "strategic entry." But he also argues that strategic voting will occur under runoff systems. He argues that "When voters are concerned only with the outcome of the current election and have rational expectations, strategic voting plays a role in dual-ballot elections similar to that it plays in single-ballot plurality elections: acting to limit the number of candidates" (1997, 123). Cox argues that the benchmark for the number of candidates is $M + 1$, where M is the number of first-round candidates who can legally quality for the second round. But Cox acknowledges that "in practice strategic voting in the first round of runoff elections is probably much rarer than the theoretical benchmark established by the model" (1997, 125).

Of course, the Israeli system of direct election has never actually given Israeli voters the chance to act strategically. Perhaps this results from holding the first round of the prime ministerial election simultaneously with the Knesset election. In 1996, side-payments to Levy and Eitan included safe seats on the Likud list. In 1999, Mordechai was not in a position to extract any side-payments, although he may have been in a better position had he withdrawn earlier. Even so, pressure from the Center List may have persuaded him to withdraw. In any event, we are not in a position to estimate the precise amount of strategic voting that would have occurred had Mordechai persisted with his campaign. Clearly, most Israelis would have voted sincerely, but, contrary to the arguments advanced by Duverger, some strategic voting would have occurred.

If the system of direct election is maintained there may be contests in which three or more candidates have a reasonable chance of advancing to a runoff. If such elections occur, they may create pressures for strategic bargaining among ideologically similar parties to assure that an acceptable candidate advances to the runoff (see Cox 1997). If voters are actually faced with a choice among three or more viable candidates, we would expect a larger proportion of the electorate to employ strategic considerations than the percentage who reasoned strategically in the 1999 election.

Notes

1. Brams (1978) has demonstrated how the center candidate can be "squeezed" from the left and right in a single, winner-take-all contest, even when the center candidate would defeat each opponent facing him or her one at a time.

2. We examined demographic differences among the electorate over these weeks. We did find that the percentage of Israeli-Arabs was somewhat higher in the fifth and fourth weeks before the election, which may partly account for the increase in "hate" for Netanyahu during these weeks.

3. For evidence for Britain, see Cain (1978) and for evidence for Canada, see Black (1978).

4. We examined head-to-head comparisons over the course of the campaign. Barak was the apparent Condorcet winner in every week except for the second week

before the election. In that week, consistent with the results in figure 1, Netanyahu narrowly edges out both Barak and Mordechai. Also, consistent with the results in the figure, Barak most clearly emerges as the winner during the final week.

References

Abramson, Paul R., John H. Aldrich, Phil Paolino, and David W. Rohde. 1992. "'Sophisticated' Voting in the 1988 Presidential Primaries." *American Political Science Review* 88 (March): 55–69.

———. 1995. "Independent and Third Party Candidates in American Politics: Wallace, Anderson, and Perot." *Political Science Quarterly* 110 (Fall): 545–574.

———. 2000. "Challenges to the American Two-Party System: Evidence from the 1968, 1980, 1992, and 1996 Presidential Elections." *Political Research Quarterly* 53 (September): 495–522.

Abramson, Paul R., John H. Aldrich, and David W. Rohde. 1999. *Change and Continuity in the 1996 and 1998 Elections.* Washington, DC: Congressional Quarterly Press.

Aldrich, John H. 1995. *Why Parties? The Origin and Transformation of Political Parties in America.* Chicago: University of Chicago Press.

Arian, Asher. 1998. *The Second Republic: Politics in Israel.* Chatham, NJ: Chatham House.

Bartels, Larry M. 2000. "Partisanship and Voting Behavior, 1952–1996." *American Journal of Political Science* 44 (January): 35–50.

Black, Duncan. 1958. *The Theory of Committees and Elections.* Cambridge: Cambridge University Press.

Black, Jerome H. 1978. "The Multicandidate Calculus of Voting: Application to Canadian Federal Elections." *American Journal of Political Science* 22 (August): 639–655.

Brams, Steven J. 1978. *The Presidential Election Game.* New Haven, CT: Yale University Press.

Cain, Bruce E. 1978. "Strategic Voting in Britain." *American Journal of Political Science* 22 (August): 609–638.

Cox, Gary W. 1997. *Making Votes Count: Strategic Coordination in the World's Electoral Systems.* New York: Cambridge University Press.

Duverger, Maurice. 1963. *Political Parties: Their Organization and Activity in the Modern State.* Translated by Barbara North and Robert North. New York: Wiley.

Eckstein, Harry. 1975. "Case Study and Theory in Political Science." In Fred I. Greenstein and Nelson W. Polsby (eds.). *Handbook of Political Science. Vol. 7, Strategies of Inquiry.* Reading, MA: Addison-Wesley.

Ferejohn, John A., and Morris P. Fiorina. 1974. "The Paradox of Not Voting: A Decision Theoretic Analysis." *American Political Science Review* 68 (June): 525–536.

————. 1975, "Closeness Counts Only in Horseshoes and Dancing." *American Poli-tial Science Review* 69 (September): 920–925.

————. 1993. "To P or Not to P? Still Asking After All These Years." Typescript. Harvard University.

Nixon, David, Dganit Olomoki, Norman Schofield, and Itai Sened. 1996. "Multi-party Probabilistic Voting: An Application to the Knesset." Political Econ-omy Working Paper 186, St. Louis, MS: Washington University.

Riker, William H. 1982. "The Two-Party System and Duverger's Law: An Essay on the History of Political Science." *American Political Science Review* 76 (December): 753–766.

————. 1986. *The Art of Political Manipulation.* New Haven, CT: Yale University Press.

Sontag, Deborah. 1999. "Peace. Period." *New York Times Magazine* (December 19): 58–63, 84, 86, 92.

3

Split-ticket Voting in the 1996 and 1999 Elections

DANA ARIELI-HOROWITZ

Split-ticket voting in Israel's general elections is a relatively new phenomenon that came about after the reform of the general elections system and after the 1996 transition to direct election of the prime minister. Before the general elections system reform, the ticket splitting discussed in Israel's research literature focused on one of two phenomena. The first referred to ticket splitting at the municipal and national levels in instances when individuals chose one party in the general elections and another at the municipal level. The second, after the 1975 municipal elections system reform, had to do with a voter's ability to split her vote between the candidate slated to head the local authority and the candidates for council seats. The transition to direct election of the prime minister created the potential for split-ticket voting at the national level in Israel, which is the focus of this chapter.

The theoretical literature worldwide on the subject of ticket splitting mainly addresses presidential regimes where voters split their ballots between the candidate for presidency and the candidate for legislative representative. A considerable portion of the research literature focuses on the United States, where the phenomenon of split-ticket voting has been investigated at length in recent years. The Israeli model is unique and exceptional in the sense that it combines both direct prime ministerial elections with an extreme form of proportional representation system. Beyond the tension between representative and direct democracy, as reflected in Israel's new election system, the phenomenon of ticket splitting in Israel has far-reaching implications for the relationship between the executive and legislative authorities, the authority of

The author expresses her gratitude to Tamar Edri, general director of the Central Election Committee at the Knesset; to Michal Shamir and Yossi Shain for reading an early draft; to Sigal Kis for her assistance with the database, and to Michael Shalev for granting access to his database, which matches the 1996 election results with the 1995 general census.

the prime minister, the Knesset's power, Israel's constellation of parties, and, indirectly, for the deepening cleavages in Israeli society.

Double-ballot voting—one for the premiership and the other for a legislative party—has naturally led to a significant increase in the level of split-ticket voting. In the case of Israel, however, the method by which the prime minister and the Knesset are elected allows a potential for many types of split-ticket voting—at least in theory. As opposed to the American scenario, which accommodates only limited ticket splitting, Israel's system allows for a much wider range of split-ticket voting. In this chapter, I will attempt to sketch the possible scenarios for ticket splitting in Israel as well as potential typologies for investigating the phenomenon of split-ticket voting.

To group the possible scenarios toward a systematic discussion of split-ticket voting, we propose differentiating straight voting, split-ticket voting within party blocs, and split-ticket voting that transcends the boundaries of political blocs.

We will investigate ticket-splitting trends in Israel with reference to the two most recent general election campaigns, in 1996 and 1999. A comparison of these two campaigns already points to a trend of steady increases in split-ticket voting in Israel. We will examine the split-ticket voting phenomenon in Israel by addressing a number of central issues. The first issue deals at length with the terminology and typology of the main concepts researchers employ in discussing split-ticket voting. This discussion will address the main reasons for split-ticket voting, as reflected in the current theoretical research on this subject worldwide.

The second issue concerns the split-ticket voting phenomenon in Israel's municipal elections in the wake of the 1975 local government reform. Within this framework, we will examine the approaches to split-ticket voting addressed in the research literature, summarized in Gad Barzilai's distinction between internal and external split-ticket voting (1993, 141–163). We will address the question whether Israeli citizens are consciously split-ticket voters, and whether they distinguish between the general elections—as a process involving existential values that require decisions based on a consolidated worldview and a sense of ideology—and the municipal elections, which deal with urban questions, and therefore do not necessarily encourage voting based on ideology or factional loyalty.

The third issue focuses on the rising trend toward ticket splitting in Israel on the national level, by examining the data relative to the last two election campaigns (for the Fourteenth and Fifteenth Knesset, respectively). Researchers who look into split-ticket voting agree that the phenomenon occurs whenever election methods encourage it (Arian and Shamir 1998, 15; Burden and Kimball 1998, 533, 538). The main question is whether the increase in split-ticket voting is the outcome of a procedural change, such as double-ballot voting, or whether—even had the election system reform not been adopted—we would still be witnessing a rising trend in split-ticket voting and increased fragmentation among Israel's parties (Kimmerling 1999, 42).[1]

Israel still lacks sufficient perspective to assess whether ticket splitting is the outcome of the system or the reflection of far-reaching trends such as a decline in the collective values of Israeli society, the adoption of patterns of direct democracy, and deepening social cleavages culminating in the assassination of Rabin. For the time being, it remains an open question whether Israelis are conscious split-ticket voters or not. Ascertaining the Israeli voter's sense of political influence, as well as the extent of accountability he exerts, will require qualitative research (Doron and Kook 1999, 102; Kaufman 1999, 124).[2]

A number of alternative reasons have been given for the split-ticket voting of Israelis. Thus, among other issues, we will attempt to examine whether there is a link between split-ticket voting in Israel and demographic distribution/geographic location, and whether ticket splitting is more prominent in some segments of Israeli society than in others. We will also address the question of the link between split-ticket voting and factional loyalty.

Split-ticket Voting: Definitions, Reasons, and Test Cases

"Split-ticket voting" is defined in the political science dictionaries as "electing candidates of two parties or more for different posts," as distinct from "straight voting" where the voter decides to choose representatives of the same party for different posts (Beasley 1999, 322; Plano 1989, 97).

Beyond the definition of ticket splitting are distinctions pertaining to split-ticket voters' motivation, as proposed by Morris P. Fiorina, for example, in arguing that "conscious intent" should be distinguished from "subconscious intent." The former applies to those who split their votes with the intent of dissipating the political power retained by the party in control of government policy making. According to this explanation, ticket splitting is the outcome of a rational decision by citizens desirous of enhancing mechanisms for balance and restraint (Fiorina 1992, 399).

The research literature also addresses levels of ticket splitting. In this context, the main argument is that one must distinguish between high rates of ticket splitting, which are liable to lead to a divided government, and relatively low rates that contribute toward maintaining a unified government (Burden and Kimball 1998, 534).

Split-ticket voting has been researched primarily in the United States, where in recent decades voters have shown a systematic tendency toward higher levels of ticket splitting. Since 1832 elections have resulted in a divided government 40% of the time (Fiorina 1992, 388) but, according to Barry C. Burden and David C. Kimball, 15 of the last 22 election campaigns have led to a divided government, which means that this issue must be investigated more systematically (Burden and Kimball 1998, 533).

Split-ticket voting has been rising steadily in the United States since the mid-1960s. At least one out of every four voters for a given party in the 1968 and 1972 elections, opted for a presidential candidate from another party (Niemi and Weisberg 1984, 498). An analysis of election campaigns in the United States revealed a higher tendency toward split-ticket voting in the South, primarily among Republican voters for the presidency who tend to elect Democratic candidates for Congress. Paul Frymer, Thomas P. Kim, and Terri L. Bimes point out that 32% of the Southern electorate overall voted for Republican presidential candidate Bush alongside Democratic candidates for the House of Representatives, versus an average of 19% nationwide (Frymer, Kim and Bimes, 1997, 197).

So far Israel has not experienced a divided government in which the prime minister heads an opposition parliament. Due to the profusion of parties, the probability of an oppositional Knesset—as it was termed during the debate on direct election of the prime minister—seems very low.

The research literature offers several explanations for ticket splitting based on voting behavior. Most researchers agree that this phenomenon reflects a decline in the electorate's capacity to identify with any given party. According to Barry C. Burden and David C. Kimball, split-ticket voting is more widespread during times of weakened party affinity (1988, 538). G. R. Niemi and H. F. Weisberg support this view with their claim that citizens no longer feel committed to a given party (1984, 501). The authors find support for this in the fact that young voters have a greater tendency toward ticket splitting than veteran ones—a phenomenon they interpret as a consequence of post-materialism that is characterized by, among other things, a decline in the capacity to identify with a given party (1984, 510).[3]

Notwithstanding the decline in citizens' capacity for party identification, some researchers find a variable that elucidates the ticket-splitting phenomenon in parties' ideological polarization. For example, Frymer, Kim, and Bimes claim that split-ticket voters react to ideological schisms within the parties, and that their behavior is systematic and genuine (1997, 196). Fiorina suggests that split-ticket voting actually stems from the blurring of ideological differences between parties, to which voters react by consciously splitting their votes (1992, 393). Burden and Kimball also support the claim that the blurring of ideological boundaries between parties is the leading cause of ticket splitting, but unlike Fiorina they maintain this is not a reflection of conscious intent, but rather an indication of comprehensive political change (1998, 533–538).

Beyond the ticket splitting that results from voting behavior, researchers claim that the trend is enhanced during times of pressure and strain. According to Fiorina, divided governments generally come about during periods of social hardship. He illustrates this by pointing out that it was no coincidence that the periods following the American Civil War and the Vietnam War, respectively, led to a rise in the ticket-splitting trend which, in turn, created divided governments (1992, 389, 392).

Further explanations for split-ticket voting stem from the election system or candidate behavior. In an era of mass communication when a candidate's charisma is brought to the fore, voter dissatisfaction with her party's "natural" candidate is liable to be expressed through ticket splitting. When a party candidate lacks a positive image or, alternatively, when the party of the voter's preferred candidate fails to yield a feasible candidate, the ticket-splitting trend intensifies (Frymer, Kim, and Bimes 1997, 196).

Beyond the question of candidate charisma, the literature deals with the link between voters and parties. Richard Born claims that when a party distances itself from the electorate, ticket splitting is likely to intensify (1994, 95). Similarly, the behavior of party elites is liable to lead to increased split-ticket voting. Frymer, Kim, and Bimes agree that there are three factors behind split-ticket voting, namely, ideological consistency, reaction to schisms and social fragmentation, and voters' perceptions of the candidates (1997, 197).

Split-ticket Voting at the Local Government Level: The Israeli Case

As of 1975, the reform in Israel's election system made it possible to track Israelis' voting behavior and tendency for ticket splitting, but only a handful of research studies singled out this issue. Arian and Weiss had already addressed the issue of split-ticket voting in 1968, when the election system itself still did not encourage ticket splitting at either the local or national level. Gad Barzilai defined this type of split as external, "a split between voting for a local authority (council or mayoralty) party candidate and voting in national elections." The other type is defined as internal ticket splitting, "a split between votes for candidates of various municipal parties," which only became an option after the reform (1993, 147).

Arian and Weiss use the term ticket splitting to describe a voter's support of different parties on the national level from those supported on the local level. They proposed a ticket-splitting index that they applied to 41 Jewish

municipalities comprising at least 10,000 individuals in the 1965 elections
(Arian and Weiss 1968, 78). They distinguished between an increase in
split-ticket voting, which occurred in 21 out of the 41 selected municipalities, and a low ticket-splitting index or lack of significant change.

Beyond discussing levels of ticket splitting, Arian and Weiss also considered the phenomenon on the basis of not only socioeconomic and demographic data, but also voters' evaluation and expectations of local versus national government. If it was reasonable to expect that the voter would "split
his loyalty so that security and fiscal policy needs would be met by the national government and education and transport needs by the local government" (Arian and Weiss 1968; 80), the fact is that few voters did so during
the late 1960s. It appears that the Israeli voter also remained faithful to the
party during the local authority elections.

Based on the local government election results during the two first election campaigns following the reform (1978 and 1983, respectively), Giora
Goldberg concludes that there are low levels of ticket splitting. An analysis
of the political blocs proposed by Goldberg (Labor, Likud, religious, local,
etc.) shows that in 1978, 34.9% of the national electorate voted for the
Labor Party for council versus 39.1% for council head (a 4.2% gap). Similarly, in 1983, 36.9% of the electorate voted for the Labor Party for council
versus 40.4% for council head (a 3.5% gap). There were similar gaps
between those who voted Likud for council in 1978 (26.3%) versus those
who voted Likud for council head—31.3% (a 5% gap). In 1983, 23.5%
of the electorate voted for the Likud for council versus 28.6% for council
head (a gap of 5.1%) (1987; 98). Hence, according to Goldberg, the accomplishments of the two large blocs are more prominent on a personal
level than on an election roster.

Goldberg's discussion reveals a steady increase over the years in split-
ticket voting during municipal elections with regard to the four main blocs:
"In 1955, the national weighted average was 6% in 1959, it increased to
7.6% and in 1965 it climbed to 9%; in 1969 it grew to 10.9% and in 1973,
it jumped to 15.8%" (1987, 105). Nonetheless, in the wake of the election
system reform, the ticket-splitting trend apparently came to a halt and stood
at a national weighted average of 11.7% in 1978 and at 14% in 1983. According to Goldberg, these data do not reflect a decrease in the scope of split-
ticket voting as compared to 1973. Rather, they reflect, more than anything,
the internalization process the voters have undergone in order to adapt to
new procedures. Goldberg concludes that it is safe to assume that "until the
procedure is fully integrated, the scope of ticket splitting will not be extensive" (1987, 103). Once the procedure is fully in place, however, one can expect a high level of ticket splitting, which is liable to create a situation in

which the elected council head does not have a majority on the council. The municipal election results in 1989, 1993, and 1998 corroborate Goldberg's conclusions (Diskin 1999).

Split-ticket voting, as reflected in the gaps between the rate of support for an elected candidate and the rate of support for the party promoting her, is steadily increasing—23.1% in the 1989 elections, 43.3% in the 1993 elections, and 54.4% in the 1998 elections. This led to the unprecedented situation in 1998, where Ehud Olmert was elected mayor of Jerusalem along with only 3 out of 31 city council members from the "Jerusalem United Behind Olmert" electoral list. Jerusalem's 1998 municipal election results bear witness to—as Avraham Diskin describes it—the "drastic decline in the power of the electoral lists identified with the major national parties, namely, the Labor Party and the Likud" (1999, 8).

Barzilai investigated the phenomenon of split-ticket voting in the 1993 Tel Aviv-Jaffa municipal elections. His research focuses on the impact of the constitutional change in municipal elections on split-ticket voting, while also looking at neighborhood voting distribution and Tel Aviv-Jaffa statistical zones. Barzilai does not agree with the conclusion that ticket splitting reflects a decline in party loyalty: In the 1993 elections, Roni Milo won 62,553 votes—47.15% of the electorate—and Avigdor Kahalani garnered the support of 56,383 voters or 42.5% of the overall electorate. In the confrontation between parties, the Labor Party won 29% of the vote (10 Council seats), the Likud 19.11% (6 seats), and Lev, 16.15% (5 seats). According to Barzilai, straight voting was more frequent and more noticeable than split-ticket voting, and ultimately it was the voter's capacity to identify with a party that best explained the extent of support for a mayoralty candidate (1993, 160). He emphasizes that "the possibility of a high profile candidate being the principal cause of ticket splitting has turned out to be incorrect; the statement that a rational, societal choice urges citizens to become split ticket voters also proved incorrect. Furthermore, the explanation that the local, territorial nature of Israel's government is the main instigator of ticket splitting has also been refuted." Barzilai distinguishes between short-term and long-term trends: "Thus, one can assume that in the short term split-ticket voting in the direct election of the prime minister among the Knesset electorate's two major parties will not be that pronounced. This is due to the impact of party identification on Israeli voting behavior." Nonetheless, in time the value of personal prominence and rhetoric will increase and lead to "a significant pattern of ticket splitting in the local and central governments" (1993, 160–161).

Amir Horkin, Yitzhak Katz, and Baruch Mevurach relate to the increase in ticket splitting at the municipal level. According to them, one explanation for the split stems from the shift in emphasis in municipal elections from ideology to local issues. "The Israeli voter distinguishes existential questions—such as the issue of evacuating the territories—from questions of well-being, such as garbage removal, and he splits his vote accordingly" (1998, 80).

Straight Voting and Split-ticket Voting Nationally: The 1996 and 1999 Elections

Observing the trend toward ticket splitting in Israel, which has been in effect in the general elections since 1996, is a very complex issue, for several reasons. The main ones are the extent of the broad cleavages in Israel society and its relationship to coincident cross-cleavages. Add to this the multiparty system and the high level of politicization of the Israeli citizen, and one can find countless prospects for ticket splitting. Therefore, to examine the levels of ticket splitting in Israeli society, a comparison was made between the results of the Fourteenth and the Fifteenth Knesset elections by focusing, on the one hand, on demographic distributions between kibbutzim, large cities (see table 3.5) and, on the other hand, on sociopolitical distributions between development towns, settlements, and cities with a high concentration of immigrants from the former Soviet Union (see tables 3.2, 3.3 and 3.4, respectively).

From a methodological viewpoint, for each category we attempted to select a variety of municipalities reflecting the spectrum of ideologies in Israeli society. For example, kibbutzim founded by the Shomer Hatzair, the United Kibbutzim Movement, Hapoel Hamizrachi, and even later kibbutzim founded on the Golan Heights. As to the moshavim, some were founded in the spirit of the Labor movement, others under Beitar or Agudat Israel, and in still others Shas has more of a stronghold. Without resorting to comprehensive ecological analysis of the overall ballots versus individual and general census data, the investigation into trends in ticket splitting does lead to initial and partial conclusions. For purposes of this chapter the data was grouped at the ballot level but were not verified against individual data. Hence, one should be somewhat circumspect in ascribing broader validity to the conclusions derived—primarily due to the problematic issue of applying inferences based on ecological data to individual data.

This reservation is all the more relevant in light of the complexity of Israeli voting behavior. It is relatively easy to examine a classic majoritarian election system, like the one in the United States where voters essentially have two options—to split or not to split their vote. In Israel's case, gauging the split is infinitely more complex and, due to the plethora of parties, means including many more types of split-ticket voters.

To bypass some of the difficulties inherent in analyzing ticket splitting, this chapter proposes to distinguish straight voting from split-ticket voting within party blocs and split-ticket voting that transcends the boundaries of political blocs. The term straight voting refers to voters who supported the same-party representatives for the various Knesset and government posts. There is a high probability that those who supported the Likud (Mahal) will support Netanyahu and that those who supported the Ma'arach/Israel Ehat (Emet) in the 1996 and 1999 elections, respectively, will support the candidacy of Peres/Barak for the premiership. Here, too, there is no absolute certainty since presumably some Likud voters supported Ehud Barak in the 1999 elections and vice versa—however, the likelihood of such crossover support is not strong. It can be assumed that the behavior of those who supported one of the two major parties reflected loyalty to the party and to its candidate for prime minister. Nonetheless it should be emphasized that, based solely on general ecological data, there is no way to infer how many of the major-party voters remained loyal to their party compared to the previous election campaign. This is because some voters are first- time voters, because of the nature of the voting pattern of those who "abandoned" the major parties, and so forth.

Table 3.1 presents data pertaining to "major-party" voters and to voters for the prime minister. The difference between the two sets of figures was translated into percentages representing the straight voting levels. A macrolevel discussion of ticket splitting in Israel, based on the two major parties only, leads to the conclusion that straight voting in Israel is in steady decline, whereas the tendency for split-ticket voting among major-party voters increased significantly during the 1999 elections in comparison with the 1996 elections. In other words, the number of voters who supported the same party for both the Knesset and prime minister grew significantly smaller.

The difference between those who voted for Labor and those who voted for Shimon Peres for prime minister in 1996 stood at 44.4%, whereas the gap between those voting for One Israel and those voting for Barak for prime minister in 1999 stood at 62.7%. Similarly, the gap between those who voted for Likud and those who voted for Benjamin Netanyahu in the 1996 elections stood at 48.9% whereas the gap between those who voted for Likud and those who voted for Netanyahu in 1999 stood at 66.8%. Comparing the two election campaigns, there is a rise of nearly 20% in the level of split-ticket voting in relation to the two candidates. These figures point to a sharp decline in the rate of straight voting.

The explanation for the increased levels of ticket splitting between 1996 and 1999 may perhaps be a consequence of the gradual internalization of the new election system, which, during the elections for the Fourteenth Knesset,

Table 3.1 Percentages of Support for the Two Major Parties and the Two Prime Ministerial Candidates, 1996 and 1999

Number of municipalities	1996 Valid votes	Peres	Labor	Difference	% Difference	Netanyahu	Likud	Difference	% Difference
1,268	2,972,589	1,471,566	818,741	−652,825	−44.4	1,501,023	767,401	−733,622	−48.9
272	84,324	72,703	45,155	−27,548	−37.9	11,621	3,528	−8,093	−69.6
334	85,820	41,632	30,754	−10,878	−26.1	44,188	23,779	−20,409	−46.2
24	297,653	107,571	60,142	−47,429	−44.1	190,082	92,631	−97,451	−51.3
44	555,454	204,299	113,353	−90,946	−44.5	351,155	174,092	−177,063	−50.4
20	1,668,566	736,263	471,080	−265,183	−36.0	932,303	474,325	−457,978	−49.1
87	57,922	6,202	3767	−2,435	−39.9	51,720	20,740	−30,980	−59.9

Number of municipalities	1999 Valid votes	Barak	One Israel	Difference	% Difference	% Netanyahu	Likud	Difference	% Difference
1,268	3,048,924	1,711,160	638,241	−1,072,919	−62.7	1,337,764	443,697	−894,067	−66.8
272	80,417	72,108	39,828	−32,280	−44.8	8,309	2,076	−6,233	−75.0
334	87,387	48,789	27,866	−20,923	−42.9	38,598	14,937	−23,661	−61.3
24	303,096	126,015	41,308	−84,707	−67.2	177,081	49,977	−127,104	−71.8
44	576,742	246,468	78,353	−168,115	−68.2	330,274	89,934	−240,340	−72.8
20	1,650,510	847,255	358,537	−488,718	−57.7	803,255	265,713	−537,542	−66.9
87	63,926	10,740	3,669	−7,071	−65.8	53,186	14,189	−38,997	−73.3

prevented voters from maximizing their ticket-splitting potential. On this subject, it is interesting to note that internalization of the new system did not affect voting behavior alone. It also impacted on how prime ministerial candidates presented themselves to the electorate in 1999 as compared to 1996. During the 1999 elections both candidates severed their ties to the mother party to a large extent, thus enhancing trends of direct, personal democracy.

The data on the decline in straight voting corroborate the arguments regarding weakened party loyalty. Kibbutzim, a sector in Israeli society that is perceived as stable from an ideological point of view, showed a decline in their support for the Labor Party along with continued support for the party's candidate for prime minister. Similarly, moshavim identified with the Labor Party revealed a similar trend. In other words, even in "safe" party sectors, there has been a certain increase, albeit more moderate, in the split-ticket voting trend.

The term split-ticket voting refers to voters who support one party for the Knesset and another party for prime minister. In the case of Israel, due to the combination of direct election of the prime minister and an extreme form of proportional representation system to the Knesset, a distinction must be made between instances of split-ticket voting within the boundaries of the political bloc and split-ticket voting outside political blocs. For example, a split between Peres/Barak and Meretz would be perceived as split-ticket voting within the political bloc, but a split between Peres/Barak and the National Religious Party (NRP) would be considered split-ticket voting outside the political bloc.

The degree of politicization in Israeli society minimizes split-ticket voting outside political blocs, but the increase in direct elections in Israel has given rise to a number of cases where a similar split occurred during the 1999 elections. Furthermore, it was precisely this increase in direct elections that led to the blurring of the distinctions between right and left in the 1999 elections and rendered the discussion on ticket splitting even more complex.

When contemplating the results of the last two Knesset elections, one can identify four conceptual types of split-ticket voters which, to a large extent, are unique to Israeli society: The ideological split-ticket voter, the split-ticket voter motivated by personal interest, the split-ticket voter in the interest of balance and restraint, and the protest split-ticket voter.

1. The ideological split-ticket voter: This refers to ticket splitting within ideological blocs and it stems from the absence of prime ministerial candidates from small parties. If these had any candidates to offer, the voter most probably would support and identify with them. In their absence, he supports the premiership candidate closest to him from the point of view of his outlook. An analysis of the 1996 and 1999 election results reveals that Meretz, Shas, the NRP and Menachim Begin's party supporters were elected as poten-

tial representatives of the ideological split—in the absence of any prime ministerial candidate on their behalf.

2. The split-ticket voter motivated by personal or sectoral interests: This type of ticket splitting is characteristic of divided societies such as Israel's and it expresses a combination of support for a party that promotes personal or sectorial interests—such as immigrants' parties, women's parties, the handicapped, and pensioners—and support for a "default" prime ministerial candidate with whom the voter does not necessarily identify. Such split-ticket voters are not actually driven by ideological zeal, but rather by their desire to promote a specific interest. As such, for them the choice of a candidate for the prime minister is a case of facing a necessary evil.

3. The split-ticket voter in the interest of balance and restraint: For ticket splitting based on balance and restraint, the basic assumption is that the Israeli voter is politically aware of her actions and even sees her decisions as having immediate repercussions on her life. Thus, when the voter employs balance and restraint tactics, she does so out of an intent to restrain a candidate from an opposing bloc or to balance her political stance.

   Ticket splitting based on balance and restraint often stems from disappointment in a candidate or party; the basic assumption in this instance is that the voter exercises rational considerations and even acts out of a sense of accountability. The balancing split-ticket voter supported the centrist parties in the previous election campaigns and is disappointed in the "major parties." She understands, however, that she must choose one of the two candidates for prime minister since she believes this to be a fateful decision and she is not prepared to forego its impact. The centrist parties create a theoretical problem in the discussion of ticket splitting. On the one hand, these are parties that called for ticket splitting and granted voters freedom of choice, as did Yosef (Tommy) Lapid and Pnina Rosenblum in the 1999 elections. On the other hand, the act of selecting the centrist electoral list is a form of balancing between left and right.

4. The protest split-ticket voter: Ticket splitting based on protest or indifference tends to be rare in Israeli society. In this case, a given party is selected but an empty ballot is purposely cast for prime minister due to dissatisfaction with the level of candidates or ideological conflict with a candidates, or in order to voice protest. This phenomenon involves critical citizens expressing their disappointment in politics, a sense of channels being blocked, and sometimes even their desire to protest the shallowness of the messages conveyed by Israel's political platform.

Ticket Splitting Within and
Outside Political Blocs in Israel:
Some Case Studies

Focusing on a few cases studies and comparing the results of the 1999 and 1996 elections enables one to test the validity of the four explanatory types of ticket splitting in Israel and, through them, to propose a more detailed, involved explanation.

Ideological Ticket Splitting. When examining ideological ticket splitting, one can distinguish several types of voters. For the most part, the ideological split-ticket voter is stable and tends not to change her vote even when the system enables her to do so. For example, in Shomer Hatzair kibbutzim, Meretz has remained largely dominant, and a comparison of the 1996 and 1999 elections reveals that there is no significant change in the levels of ticket splitting in the last two election campaigns. In the 1996 elections, out of 323 valid votes at Kibbutz Baram, 321 voted for Peres and 229 for Meretz, thus the percentage of split-ticket Peres-Meretz voters equaled 71.3%. In the 1999 elections, out of 334 valid votes, 329 supported Barak and 224, Meretz; accordingly, the percentage of split-ticket Barak-Meretz voters equaled 68.4%. Thus, the difference in the levels of ticket splitting between the 1996 and 1999 elections amounts to an average of 3.1%.

A look at municipalities where Shas is prominent reveals that in some development towns (see table 3.2) Shas electoral power doubled, yet the degree of support for Netanyahu lessened or remained at par. For example, Shas electoral power doubled in Netivot, with 4,136 votes in the 1999 elections as compared to 2,136 votes in the 1996 elections. Support for Netanyahu, however, remained more or less identical: 7,461 votes in 1999 versus 7,175 votes in 1996. A similar trend was evident in Ofakim, Shlomi, Shderot, Migdal Haemek, and Kiryat Malachi. Similarly, in some moshavim, Shas electoral power doubled, whereas the support percentages for Netanyahu remained more or less identical. For example, in Moshav Zanuah support for Shas rose from 28 votes in 1996 to 117 votes in the 1999 elections. Support for Netanyahu, on the other hand, remained virtually identical: In 1996, 200 people voted for Netanyahu, compared to 196 in 1999.

Another selected category is the kibbutzim founded by Hapoel Hamizrachi, which have remained ideologically faithful over the years to the NRP. A comparison of the data for the 1996 and 1999 elections shows a decline in commitment to NRP alongside, in some cases, a shift in support from Netanyahu to Barak. For example, in Tirat Zvi, out of 405 valid votes in the 1996 elections, NRP won 285 votes, but only 175 votes in 1999.

Table 3.2 Development Towns

Left

Name	% of immigrants	1996 Valid votes	Peres	Labor	Difference	% Difference	1999 Valid votes	Barak	One Israel	Difference	% Difference
Ofakim	27.2	10,221	2,436	1,265	−1,171	−48.1	10,380	2,869	739	−2,130	−74.2
Netivot	21.3	8,082	907	342	−565	−62.3	9,353	1,892	278	−1,614	−85.3
Shlomi	23.3	2,026	598	320	−278	−46.5	2,176	811	207	−604	−74.5
Sderot	41.1	9,409	2,999	1,749	−1,250	−41.7	9,337	2,735	680	−2,055	−75.1
Migdal Ha'emek	33.3	12,317	4,506	2,714	−1,792	−39.8	11,985	5,119	1,872	−3,247	−63.4
Kiryat Malachi	15.6	9,701	2,313	1,395	−918	−39.7	9,465	2,248	859	−1,389	−61.8
Kiryat Gat	26.4	24,003	7,890	4,313	−3,577	−45.3	23,481	9,515	2,627	−6,888	−72.4
Hatzor Haglilit	11.9	4,455	922	581	−341	−37.0	4,539	1,156	436	−720	−62.3
Kiryat Shmona	17.6	10,910	3,372	1,852	−1,520	−45.1	11,128	4,281	1,566	−2,715	−63.4

Right

Name	1996 Valid votes	Netanyahu	Likud	Difference	% Difference	Shas	1999 Valid votes	Netanyahu	Likud	Difference	% Difference	Shas
Ofakim	10,221	7,785	2,473	−5,312	−68.2	2,509	10,380	7,511	1,180	−6,331	−84.3	3,341
Netivot	8,082	7,175	2,530	−4,645	−64.7	2,136	9,353	7,461	1,151	−6,310	−84.6	4,136
Shlomi	2,026	1,428	646	−782	−54.8	363	2,176	1,365	353	−1,012	−74.1	663
Sderot	9,409	6,410	3,068	−3,342	−52.1	1,842	9,337	6,602	1,349	−5,253	−79.6	2,179
Migdal Ha'emek	12,317	7,811	4,105	−3,706	−47.4	1,443	11,985	6,866	1,982	−4,884	−71.1	2,800
Kiryat Malachi	9,701	7,388	3,096	−4,292	−58.1	1,871	9,465	7,217	1,584	−5,633	−78.1	3,401
Kiryat Gat	24,003	16,113	7,760	−8,353	−51.8	3,415	23,481	13,966	3,501	−10,465	−74.9	6,362
Hatzor Haglilit	4,455	3,533	1,527	−2,006	−56.8	646	4,539	3,383	1,002	−2,381	−70.4	1,206
Kiryat Shmona	10,910	7,538	4,008	−3,530	−46.8	1,625	11,128	6,847	2,507	−4,340	−63.4	2,549

Similarly, support for Netanyahu decreased from 311 votes in 1996 to 223 votes in 1999. Support for Barak, on the other hand, rose to 141 votes versus 94 for Peres, despite the absolute decrease in the number of valid votes.

We can also learn about the increase in ticket splitting outside of political blocs by considering the data on settlements established outside of Israel's 1967 borders. In this instance as well, the ideological split-ticket voter must choose a prime ministerial candidate who does not belong to her mother party or necessarily reflect her worldview.

Table 3.3 illustrates that in Kiryat Arba, for example, the right-wing parties gained electoral power. In the 1996 elections, Moledet won the support of 211 voters in Efrata whereas in 1999 Benny Begin's party gained 911 votes. The interesting data concerns the ticket-splitting trends outside political blocs. In Efrata, for example, the support for Barak rises (to a total of 289 votes) compared with Peres (a total of 102 votes).

The argument that split-ticket voting across ideological borders has gained prominence is even more relevant when one looks at the election results in Ma'aleh Adumim. Whereas Peres won 1,577 votes in the 1996 elections, Barak garnered 2,424 supporters in 1999. Support for the Labor candidate almost doubled, with no absolute rise in the number of valid votes. Table 3.3 thus corroborates the impression that split-ticket voters who crossed ideological borders to shift their support to the left-wing candidate characterized the 1999 elections.

The Split-ticket Voter on the Basis of Sectoral or Personal Interest. To examine ticket splitting stemming from personal interests, one can focus on the immigrants from the former Soviet Union, some of whom have not yet forged a clear ideological identity (with regard to the electoral behavior of former Soviet Union immigrants, see Horowitz 1999, 151–155). Needless to say, the intent is not to reach sweeping conclusions regarding the entire immigrant public, but rather to test the hypothesis that the vote for prime minister reflects selection of a candidate due to lack of choice.

Table 3.4 illustrates municipalities in Israel with high concentrations (over 25%) of immigrants from the former Soviet Union. In all of these municipalities, without exception, there is a decline in the rate of support for Netanyahu versus a significant rise in support for Barak. Furthermore, there is a significant increase in support for the sectoral immigrant parties compared with 1996 election results.

Out of an overall Beersheva electorate of 80,152 in the 1996 elections, 49,696 supported Netanyahu whereas Natan Sharansky's party won the support of 10,932 voters. In 1999, however, out of an electorate totaling 81,544, 44,903 supported Netanyahu while the parties of Sharansky and Avigdor Lieberman, respectively, gained the support of 15,217 voters. In 1999, Barak

Table 3.3 Settlements Beyond Israel's 1967 Borders

Right	1996						
Name	Valid votes	Netanyahu	Likud	Difference	% Difference	Shas	Nationalist List
Alfei Menashe	2,293	1,636	1,297	−339	−20.7	45	96
Ariel	7,410	6,610	4,597	−2,013	−30.5	393	265
Kiryat Arba	2,393	2,305	594	−1,711	−74.2	38	518
Ofra	672	652	66	−586	−89.9	4	77
Alon Moreh	466	455	50	−405	−89.0	7	63
Elkana	1,521	1,502	184	−1,318	−87.7	15	89
Efrata	2,373	2,271	398	−1,873	−82.5	23	211
Bet El	738	733	79	−654	−89.2	1	136
Kdumim	990	987	188	−799	−81.0	9	175
Ma'ale Adumim	9,165	7,588	4,212	−3,376	−44.5	762	408
Kfar Etzion	231	190	19	−171	−90.0	4	5

Right	1999						
Name	Valid votes	Netanyahu	Likud	Difference	% Difference	Shas	Nationalist List
Alfei Menashe	2,322	1,216	774	−442	−36.3	87	163
Ariel	7,612	6,421	3,064	−3,357	−52.3	583	497
Kiryat Arba	2,545	2,429	314	−2,115	−87.1	268	959
Ofra	863	823	98	−725	−88.1	26	420
Alon Moreh	450	443	34	−409	−92.3	40	273
Elkana	1,665	1,578	164	−1,414	−89.6	54	437
Efrata	2,518	2,229	319	−1,910	−85.7	90	911
Bet El	1,627	1,611	68	−1,534	−95.8	69	1,026
Kdumim	1,206	1,185	119	−1,066	−90.0	87	572
Ma'ale Adumim	9,160	6,736	2,682	−4,054	−60.2	1,361	885
Kfar Etzion	211	155	23	−132	−85.2	7	65

was supported to the tune of 36,641 votes, versus 30,456 votes for Peres in 1996. These figures apply to the entire city of Beersheva and it is difficult to assess which percentage of immigrants split their votes right and which split left. However, it is safe to assume that a significant percentage shifted their loyalty toward Barak while intensifying their support for sectoral parties.

The Split-ticket Voter in the Interest of Balance and Restraint. The discussion of split-ticket voters motivated by balance and restraint considerations is the most complex because it is based on parties situated in the center

Table 3.4   Immigrants from the Former Soviet Union

Left

Name	% of immigrants	1996 Valid votes	Peres	Labor	Difference	% Difference	1999 Valid votes	Barak	One Israel	Difference
Ashdod	29.0	70,702	24,463	12,148	−12,315	−50.3	77,665	31,471	8,049	23,422
Ashkelon	25.9	45,545	15,298	8,213	−7,085	−46.3	47,630	18,739	5,831	12,908
Beersheva	25.3	80,152	30,456	18,651	−11,805	−38.8	81,544	36,641	12,781	23,860
Or Akiva	50.1	7,821	1,917	757	−1,160	−60.5	7,801	2,427	557	1,870
Afula	25.9	18,951	6,772	3,999	−2,773	−40.9	19,460	7,973	2,825	5,148
Katzrin	32.4	2,855	1,290	735	−555	−43.0	2,964	1,583	536	1,047
Kiriat Gat	26.4	24,003	7,890	4,313	−3,577	−45.3	23,481	9,515	2,627	6,888

Right

Name	1996 Valid votes	Netanyahu	Likud	Difference	% Difference	1999 Shas	NRP	Third Way	Israel b'Aliya
Ashdod	70,702	46,239	19,048	−27,191	−58.8	12,199	3,642	1,279	13,046
Ashkelon	45,545	30,247	14,203	−16,044	−53.0	4,967	4,768	905	7,686
Beersheva	80,152	49,696	25,217	−24,479	−49.3	10,635	5,369	1,724	10,932
Or Akiva	7,821	5,904	2,701	−3,203	−54.3	1,678	732	83	1,463
Afula	18,951	12,179	7,033	−5,146	−42.3	1,563	1,613	605	2,543
Katzrin	2,855	1,565	711	−858	−54.6	200	189	311	407
Kiriat Gat	24,003	16,113	7,760	−8,353	−51.8	3,415	1,791	345	3,713

Right

Name	1999 Valid votes	Netanyahu	Likud	Difference	% Difference	1999 Shas	NRP	Center Shinui +	Immigrant Parties
Ashdod	77,665	46,194	8,522	−37,672	−81.6	19,606	4,786	6,231	18,506
Ashkelon	47,630	28,891	7,950	−20,941	−72.5	10,562	1,177	3,222	10,617
Beersheva	81,544	44,903	11,486	−33,417	−74.4	19,287	1,377	6,978	15,217
Or Akiva	7,801	5,374	1,285	−4,089	−76.1	1,722	56	353	2,022
Afula	19,460	11,487	4,024	−7,463	−65.0	3,464	244	1,556	3,834
Katzrin	2,964	1,381	365	−1,016	−73.6	250	20	264	594
Kiriat Gat	23,481	13,966	3,501	−10,465	−74.9	6,362	536	1,642	4,994

Table 3.5 Large Cities—Supporting Right-wing, Immigrant, and Centrist Parties

Right	1996							
Name	Valid votes	Netanyahu	Likud	Difference	% Difference	Shas	Israel b'Aliya	Third Way
Jerusalem	217,534	151,492	58,190	−93,302	−61.6	22,642	9,430	7,102
Tel Aviv-Jaffa	231,966	103,960	63,990	−39,970	−38.4	20,057	6,290	8,121
Haifa	154,224	63,704	38,339	−25,365	−39.8	5,328	12,770	6,245
Ashdod	70,702	46,239	19,048	−27,191	−58.8	12,199	13,046	1,279
Bnei Brak	58,104	51,616	6,924	−44,692	−86.6	9,388	1,609	464
Bat Yam	83,758	47,635	28,103	−19,532	−41.0	9,388	7,354	2,417
Holon	100,403	52,681	33,366	−19,315	−36.7	11,140	4,852	3,923
Netanya	81,766	50,281	24,520	−25,761	−51.2	9,850	7,550	2,952
Petach-Tikva	92,675	54,361	26,446	−27,915	−51.4	9,469	6,983	3,599
Rishon-Le-Zion	97,639	49,045	31,194	−17,851	−36.4	6,852	6,502	4,341
Ramat-Gan	82,162	39,194	25,723	−13,660	−34.7	4,181	2,649	3,534
Beersheva	80,152	49,696	25,217	−24,479	−49.3	10,635	10,932	1,724
Herzlia	51,687	22,168	14,055	−8,113	−36.6	3,356	2,095	2,257
Hadera	35,689	21,411	12,117	−9,294	−43.4	3,460	3,433	1,253
Kfar Saba	41,422	18,682	10,772	−7,910	−42.3	2,962	2,372	1,812
Lod	27,106	17,263	9,113	−8,150	−47.2	3,628	2,066	469
Ashkelon	45,545	30,247	14,203	−16,044	−53.0	4,967	7,686	905
Rehovot	52,084	27,980	14,115	−13,865	−49.6	3,139	4,480	2,336
Ramle	30,521	20,329	11,234	−9,095	−44.7	6,124	1,613	467
Ra'anana	33,427	14,130	7,656	−6,474	−45.8	1,741	840	1,638

62

Table 3.5 Continued

Right	1999							
Name	Valid votes	Netanyahu	Likud	Difference	% Difference	Shas	Immigrant Parties	Center + Shinui
Jerusalem	206,231	132,653	32,765	−99,888	−75.3	36,844	9,040	19,175
Tel Aviv-Jaffa	224,516	80,567	36,117	−44,450	−55.2	25,522	4,302	28,802
Haifa	150,396	48,423	20,050	−28,373	−58.6	8,663	8,956	19,885
Ashdod	58,442	46,194	3,959	−42,235	−91.4	13,634	930	6,231
Bnei Brak	77,665	51,857	8,522	−43,335	−83.6	19,606	17,402	1,624
Bat Yam	77,916	39,148	15,274	−23,874	−61.0	5,899	1,490	9,479
Holon	79,398	43,796	15,555	−28,241	−64.5	11,511	6,594	14,257
Netanya	81,544	45,490	11,486	−34,004	−74.8	19,287	8,182	8,724
Petach-Tikva	82,935	47,830	14,579	−33,21	−69.5	14,915	5,702	11,449
Rishon-Le-Zion	92,529	40,392	15,332	−25,060	−62.0	13,370	6,454	15,024
Ramat-Gan	95,815	29,560	20,296	−9,264	−31.3	13,672	3,636	12,974
Beersheva	98,829	44,903	18,532	−26,371	−58.7	9,989	5,308	6,978
Herzlia	30,177	16,101	5,953	−10,148	−63.0	8,938	1,412	8,003
Hadera	30,203	19,532	5,287	−14,245	−72.9	6,627	2,914	4,008
Kfar Saba	35,393	14,774	4,553	−10,221	−69.2	2,423	552	5,784
Lod	36,719	17,809	7,113	−10,696	−60.1	4,811	3,578	1,985
Ashkelon	42,012	28,891	6,264	−22,627	−78.3	4,177	1,470	3,222
Rehovot	47,630	25,299	7,950	−17,349	−68.6	10,562	7,330	5,956
Ramle	49,631	18,981	7,742	−11,239	−59.2	4,405	1,194	1,800
Ra'anana	52,529	11,055	8,384	−2,671	−24.2	6,302	3,110	5,499

of the political map. These parties do not necessarily guide their supporters concerning which candidate for prime minister is desirable. The main difficulty, however, lies in the fact that it is difficult to sketch a profile of the typical centrist voter. When attempting to pinpoint demographic areas or socioeconomic distributions featuring a prominence of centrist parties, we found that the tendency to vote for centrist parties in the 1999 elections was actually typical of large cities. Table 3.5 presents the data pertaining to support for the Third Way Party in the 1996 elections as compared to support for the Center Party and Shinui in the 1999 elections.

The data reveal that in a number of cities more than 10% of the voters supported centrist parties: Rishon-Le-Zion (16.2%), Ramat Gan (13.5%), Haifa (13.2%), Tel Aviv (12.8%), and Bat Yam (12.1%). In most cases, the increased support of centrist parties is very noticeable compared with the 1996 elections, but there is no way to infer from the general data the extent of the ticket-splitting trends within or outside political blocs. To bypass these difficulties, detailed demographic analysis of all ballots is required.

The Split-ticket Protest. Judging by the number of disqualified votes in both elections and comparing the percentage of disqualified votes in the Knesset elections and the percentage in the prime minister vote, this type of ticket splitting is significant in scope. In the 1996 elections, 67,601 votes, making up 2.16% of the actual overall voters for the Knesset, were disqualified. By contrast, 148,681 votes, or 4.76% of the overall electorate, were disqualified in the prime minister vote. For the sake of comparison, the percentage of disqualified votes in elections for the Thirteenth Knesset was 0.8%, and for the Twelfth Knesset 0.97%. One could claim, of course, that at least part of the increase in the percentage of disqualified votes in the 1996 elections can be explained by the transition to the new election system. However, if in 1996 it was possible to explain this phenomenon as being a consequence of the lack of familiarity with the new system, the rise in this trend in 1999 calls for an alternative explanation. In that election there were major gaps between the percentage of disqualified votes in electing the Knesset—1.9% of the overall voting electorate, or 64,332—versus the percentage of disqualified votes for prime minister—5.3% of the overall voting electorate, or 179,458 votes.[4] Hence the explanation that beyond the percentage of Israel's Arab citizens who cast empty ballots, other voters also chose to voice their protest by casting an empty ballot.[5]

Conclusion

Ticket splitting in Israel was more pronounced in the 1999 election campaign in comparison with the 1996 campaign. The number of straight voters, that is, those who supported same-party candidates for the Knesset and the government, declined. Instead, the number of split-ticket voters, those who supported a prime ministerial candidate from one party and cast a different ballot when selecting a Knesset candidate, has increased. The data in this chapter support the argument that there has been a decline in party loyalty in Israel.

Given the complexity of the ticket-splitting phenomenon in Israel, this chapter sketches a conceptual profile of the various types of split-ticket voters and presents only initial conclusions. Among the four types selected, it is the ideological split-ticket voter who tends to remain within the boundaries of the political bloc she is affiliated with, whereas the other three types of split-ticket voters—the sectoral, the seeker of balance and restraint, and the protester—tend to transcend the boundaries of political blocs and shift their support to the opposing bloc's candidate.

Notes

1. Kimmerling claims that the new election system has led to a powerful centrifugal movement in Israeli society from the inside outward and a reorganization of six main subcultures, all of which existed before the 1996 elections.

2. Doron and Kook claim that changing the election system led to split-ticket voting and to the consolidation of two new types of vote-casting, specifically to authentic voting, which is limited to electing Knesset representatives, and to strategic voting for the prime minister. Kaufman raises a similar argument with regard to Israeli-Arabs whose voting combines both ethnic-national and instrumental strategies.

3. Since 1979, Ingelhart has conducted a series of research studies on the link between declining party loyalty and the postmaterial value system. See, for example; Ingelhart, *Cultural Shift in Advanced Industrial Society* (Princeton: Princeton University Press, 1990).

4. It should be noted that the Central Election Committee does not distinguish votes disqualified due to shortcomings in the election process and a percentage of votes that are disqualified because the ballots are left blank.

5. With regard to the abstention by Israeli-Arabs from voting in the 1996 elections, and their casting empty ballots for prime minister, see Kaufman and Israeli (1999, 124–136).

References

Arian, Asher, and Michal Shamir. "Introduction." 1999. *The 1996 Elections in Israel.* In Asher Arian and Michal Shamir (eds.). Jerusalem: Israel Democracy Institute, 9–34.

Arian, Asher, and Shevach Weiss. 1968. "Split-ticket Voting in Israel." *Megamot* 16, no. 1 (October): 75–84.

Barzilai, Gad. 1997. "Internal Elections in Tel Aviv-Jaffa (1993) and Split-ticket Voting." In D. Nachmias and G. Menachem (eds.). *Tel Aviv Research Studies: Social Processes and Public Policy.* Tel Aviv University: Ramot, 2: 141–163.

Bealey, Frank. "Ticket-Splitting." In *The Blackwell Dictionary of Political Science* 322.

Born, Richard. 1994. "Split-Ticket Voters, Divided Government, and Fiorina's Policy-Balancing Model." *Legislative Studies Quarterly* 19: 95–115.

Burden, Barry C., and David C. Kimball. 1998. "A New Approach to the Study of Ticket Splitting." *American Political Science Review* 92, no. 3 (September): 533–544.

Diskin, Avraham. 1999. *The 1998 Jerusalem Municipal Elections.* Jerusalem: Israel Research Institute.

Doron, Gideon, and Rivka Kook. 1999. "Religion and Inclusion Politics: The Success of the Orthodox Parties." In Asher Arian, and Michal Shamir (eds.). *The 1996 Elections in Israel,* 85–106.

Fiorina, Morris P. 1992. "An Era of Divided Government." *Political Science Quarterly* 107, no. 3: 387–410.

Frymer, Paul, Thomas P. Kim, and Terri L. Bimes. 1997. "Party Elites Ideological Voters and Divided Party Government." *Legislative Studies Quarterly* 22 (May): 195–215.

Goldberg, Giora. 1987. "Municipal Elections." In Daniel Elazar and Haim Kalcheheim (eds.). *Israel's Local Government.* Jerusalem: Jerusalem Center for Public and State Issues, 89–110.

Horkin, Amir, Yitzhak Katz, and Baruch Mevurach. 1998. *Local Hero: Municipal Elections in the Era of Direct Elections.* Tel Aviv: Ramot.

Horowitz, Tamar. 1999. "Ideologies, Identity and Frustration as Factors Impacting on the Voting Patterns of Immigrants from the Former Soviet Union." In Asher Arian and Michal Shamir (eds.). *The 1996 Elections in Israel.* Jerusalem: Israel Democracy Institute, 149–170.

Ingelhart, Ronald. 1990. Cultural Shift in Advanced Industrial Society (Princeton: Princeton University Press).

Kaufman, Ilana, and Rachel Israeli. 1999. "'Out of Many One Is Born': The Arab Vote in Israel's 1996 Elections." In Asher Arian and Michal Shamir (eds.). *The 1996 Elections in Israel.* Jerusalem: Israel Democracy Institute, 107–148.

Kimmerling, Baruch. 1999. "Elections as a Battle Arena for Group Identity." In Asher Arian and Michal Shamir (eds.). *The 1996 Elections in Israel.* Jerusalem: Israel Democracy Institute, 35–56.

Molcho, Sara, and Rafael Gil. 1974. "Knesset Voting Patterns and Ticket Splitting in the 'Beit Adam' Knesset and City Council Elections." *Trends* 11, no. 4 (September): 410–422.

Niemi, G. R., and H. F. Weisberg. 1984. *Controversies in Voting Behavior.* 2d ed. Washington, DC: Congressional Quarterly.

Plano, Jack C. 1989. "Split-Ticket." *The American Political Science Dictionary.* Holt, 97.

4

Social Cleavages among non-Arab Voters
A New Analysis

MICHAEL SHALEV WITH SIGAL KIS

This chapter takes issue with the authoritative literature on the politics of social cleavages in Israel. It presents the results of three different types of empirical analysis of partisan choice among non-Arab voters in Israel.[1] Using methods and data that have rarely or never been exploited in Israel, as well as modified versions of the standard multivariate analysis of survey data, we offer an empirical reassessment of voter behavior that departs substantially from previous research by attributing a major role to class along with other social cleavages.

Based on a systematic comparison of election surveys carried out over the last three decades the editors of this volume, Michal Shamir and Asher Arian, recently concluded that the distinction between secular and religious Jews is the predominant social division, followed by the ethnic split between Ashkenazim and Mizrahim. They described "the economic cleavage" as "weak to begin with" (1999, 270), and reported multiple regressions predicting the division of votes between the right and left bloc that yield insignificant results for socioeconomic indicators in most periods. While this particular article by Arian and Shamir is their latest and most comprehensive review of the evidence, it is representative in this respect of their decades of earlier

Yoav Peled and Oren Yiftachel provided much of the inspiration for this study. Valuable advice or assistance was received from Aaron Benavot, Abraham Diskin, Nadav Gabay, Ahmad Hleihel, Charles Kadushin, Michal Peleg, Zeev Rosenhek, Michal Shamir, Sigalit Shmueli, Natasha Volchkina, Gad Yair, and an anonymous reviewer. We thank the Sapir Center at Tel Aviv University and the Silbert Center at the Hebrew University for their financial support.

This chapter is a condensed version of a longer paper with the same title, containing additional results and more extensive methodological details. This paper is available from the first author's website at http://student.mscc.huji.ac.il/~method/voting.htm, or in hard copy as Discussion Paper No. 2-2000 from the Pinhas Sapir Center for Development at Tel Aviv University.

work (beginning with Arian 1972) and with other research on electoral behavior in Israel (e.g., Diskin 1991).

The apparent irrelevance of class to voting flies in the face of both evidence
of the persistence of class voting in other societies (Manza, Hout, and Brooks
1995) and everyday knowledge about Israel. Political commentators and rank-
and-file citizens alike are well aware of the sharp polarization of voting between
North and South Tel Aviv, between exclusive neighborhoods like Saviyyon,
and peripheral localities like Ofaqim—in short, between the well-to-do and
the poor. True, this polarization encapsulates ethnic as well as class differences,
but it is hard to believe that class voting per se is merely epiphenomenal.

It cannot be denied that most political parties in Israel fail to explicitly
articulate class cleavages and that there is a marked absence of subjective class
consciousness among voters. Still, as C. Brooks and J. Manza (1997) have
pointed out, class voting and class politics are theoretically distinct and they
need not (and in the American context do not) covary empirically. One obvious possibility is that in Israel class interests and cleavages have been sub-
merged in—but not eliminated by—the politics of ethnicity, nationalism,
and collective identity. Historically Zionism and the national conflict, and
related peculiarities of the Israeli Labor movement, left a vacuum of political
agents willing and able to speak for the disadvantaged in the language of class
conflict. Despite this, the political alienation of the Mizrahim from the "labor
establishment" and their gravitation toward the hawkish right have sometimes been interpreted as reflecting a hidden agenda of class conflict (e.g.,
Farjoun 1983; Peled 1989; Swirski 1984).

This view has been challenged by scholars who interpret the ethnic vote as
a reflection of status or identity politics more than class politics (Herzog
1985; Shapiro 1991). The Mizrahim are seen from this perspective as strug-
gling for recognition as social and political equals to the Ashkenazi founders
and to their descendants. For instance, Shas proposes a vision of Israeli society
and its collective identity that is more congenial to Mizrahi interests and values than the Ashkenazi model of a democratic secular state at peace with its
neighbors and closely integrated into Western culture and the liberalized
world economy (Peled 1998). This chapter will not take up this controversy
at length, although we will come back to it in the conclusion. Our central
preoccupation is not interpretive but foundational: we seek to document the
role of class in voting behavior relative to, and in conjunction with, other
social cleavages.

Three different methodologies have been employed. First, in the conventional fashion we use survey data to connect the social characteristics of
individual voters with their voting intentions. Next we offer an ecological

analysis of aggregate data on the vote distributions and socioeconomic features of many hundreds of small geographic units. As an alternative to the survey approach, ecological analysis has a number of strengths and weaknesses. But we recommend it for an additional reason: since the variables of interest (including class) are actually situated at the local as well as the individual levels, local context can be expected to exert an independent influence on voter behavior. The third and final empirical section presents the first attempt that we are aware of to apply multilevel analysis—a tool for distinguishing between individual and contextual effects—to the study of voting in Israel. Because of data limitations the results of the multilevel analysis are empirically tenuous, despite their analytical power. Yet some of these results converge so strongly with the findings of the ecological and survey analyses that they provide an irresistible challenge to the neglect of class by students of political behavior in Israel.

Evidence from Individual-Level Data

What can we learn from surveys of individual voters about the impact of ethnic, religious, and class cleavages on voting? The most economical approach to the problem is the one adopted by Shamir and Arian (1999). They used multiple regression to estimate the "net" contribution of each variable of interest, with other known influences on voting also controlled. To evaluate this approach we took the principal model used by Shamir and Arian (1999, table 2) to analyze the vote for prime minister in 1996 and applied it to their 1999 data. In addition to ethnicity, religion, and SES (measured by housing density, education, and family expenditure) this model taps demography (age and gender) and issue positions (on territorial compromise, capitalism versus socialism, and religion and state). We echoed Shamir and Arian's preferred statistical technique (logistic regression) and most of their choices and definitions of variables.[2]

The most striking result of this replication (table 4.1) is the strength of the ethnic effect. (To aid interpretation for dichotomous variables we show not only logistic coefficients but also their exponents, which yield "odds ratios.") Mizrahim were roughly three times more likely than Ashkenazim to choose Benjamin Netanyahu over Ehud Barak, with or without taking into account their other personal characteristics. In relation to class, two of the three SES variables have marginally significant effects in Model 2 but all three "wash out" when issue variables are added to the regression. The replication thus seems to confirm Arian and Shamir's skepticism regarding the relevance of class to voting in Israel.

Table 4.1 Determinants of the Vote for Barak vs. Netanyahu (Logistic regressions, 1999 preelection survey)

	1			2			3		
	b	Exp(b)	t	b	Exp(b)	t	b	Exp(b)	t
Constant	0.42		3.8	4.75		6.8	8.14		7.2
Ethnicity									
Ashkenazi	−1.18	0.31	−7.0	−1.08	0.34	−5.4	−1.00	0.37	−3.7
Sabra	−0.58	0.56	−3.2	−0.19	0.83	−0.9	0.01	1.01	0.0
SES									
Education				−0.23		−1.9	−0.20		−1.3
Income				0.06		0.8	0.18		1.7
Density				−0.39		−2.3	−0.25		−1.0
Religion									
Secular-religious				−1.08		−9.8	−0.35		−2.1
Demography									
Age							0.00		−0.4
Female							−0.26	0.77	−1.2
Issues									
Territories for peace							−0.78		−11.6
Capitalism vs. socialism							−0.46		−3.3
State & religion							−0.50		−3.5
N	831			757			713		
Percent classified correctly	61%			70%			85%		

70

We find these results unconvincing. The models assume that all of the independent variables are validly and accurately measured, and that they have linear (or more accurately, loglinear) effects none of which is conditional on other variables. An alternative approach is the use of less precise but more subtle exploratory methods resting on descriptive rather than inferential analysis. This approach is also much better equipped to handle peculiarities of the data. Inspection of the distributions of the SES indicators reveals that housing density and education both "bunch" at certain values.[3] In addition the most direct indicator of living standards, household expenditure, has questionable validity and reliability since it appears that many people do not know, or do not honestly report, how much their family spends in a month. The specific content of the question also gave rise to a worrying distortion in the results.[4]

These drawbacks of the available indicators of voters' class situation make it very problematic to treat them as continuous variables, and they virtually guarantee weak correlations with voting. However, reconstructing the indicators in categorical form with breakpoints specifically tailored to their idiosyncrasies yields a quite different picture of their association with political choice. As table 4.2 reveals, crowded households, less than college education, and low family expenditure were all powerfully associated in 1999 with strong support for Netanyahu, while the opposite conditions of economic advantage were linked to exceptional support for Barak. For both density and expenditure the gap between the polar categories in support for Netanyahu was very large, on the order of 30 percentage points.

In principle these gross effects of class might turn out to be ephemeral once we take account of ethnicity and religiosity, the other noteworthy social bases of voting in Israel. To evaluate this possibility, and also to test for interactions between the effects of different cleavages, we analyzed the association between combinations of the three social cleavages and the vote for Netanyahu versus Barak. The major results are as follows:

Table 4.2   Class Effects on the Vote for Netanyahu
(1999 preelection survey)

Housing density *(persons per room)*	Up to 1 = 40%	1 to 1.33 = 64%	More than 1.33 = 74%
Formal education	College degree = 37%	12 years = 50%	Less than 12 = 47%
Your monthly spending compared with the average	Above average = 36%	Average = 52%	A little below average = 63%

1. Irrespective of their ethnic or class background, members of the *dati* and *haredi* groups almost uniformly voted for Netanyahu.

2. The ethnic hierarchy in voting is clear (except for the heterogeneous "Sabra" category), with new immigrants from the former Soviet Union most strongly supporting Netanyahu and Ashkenazim most favorable to Barak. This broad hierarchy holds whatever further divisions are considered. However, Barak's Ashkenazi advantage was substantial only among secular voters.

3. With the exception of very religious voters, the impact of SES is pervasive. *Whether its effect is assessed in relation to religious practice, ethnicity, or the two in combination, there is a clear and consistent decline in support for Netanyahu as SES increases.*

Thus, all three social cleavages independently affect voter choice. Ethnic voting cannot be reduced to the class (or religious) composition of different ethnic groups. But class also seems to matter in its own right. Still, perhaps its effect is spurious, actually just proxying for the impact of issue effects on voting? We do not think so. It is more plausible to think of voters' issue positions as an intervening variable in the casual chain between the social milieu of the voter and his or her ballot. Moreover, the supposition that political attitudes play an independent causal role in electoral behavior is problematic to begin with, insofar as attitudes are consequences as well as causes of partisanship.

The impact of economic interests on the choice between Netanyahu and Barak in 1999 provides a striking illustration of the reciprocal relationship between political opinions and partisan preference. Given widening income inequality and rising unemployment in Israel in recent years (Shalev 1999), one might have expected economically disadvantaged voters to see themselves as the victims of poor economic performance and misguided economic policy, and to therefore vote against the incumbent. In practice of course the disadvantaged tended to prefer Netanyahu to Barak. They also had a rosier, not more critical view of recent economic performance and of Netanyahu's ability to deal with the country's economic problems. This seems to confirm our view that to the extent that political attitudes are actually symptoms of partisan identification, it would be mistaken to use them as "controls" when trying to predict voter preferences.

Aggregate Data Analysis

Revisiting the survey data and setting aside some of the assumptions on which analysis of these data customarily rests, we have just seen that there are good reasons to challenge the view that class is immaterial to voter behavior in Israel. We move now to a higher level of analysis, the locality. At this level it would hardly be surprising to find strong class effects on voting in the 1999 (and previous) elections.[5] It is after all on the basis of comparisons of aggregate results from differentially located polling stations that Election-Night pundits and analysts writing in the immediate postelection period routinely note the striking tendency in Israel for the advantaged to favor the left and the disadvantaged to support the right.

In contrast, scholarly interpretations reflect the hegemony of the survey method. For instance, except for the first edition, rarely has an ecological analysis appeared in the eight volumes published in the *Elections in Israel* series by Arian and Shamir.[5] The Israeli literature as a whole does include several ecological studies (especially Diskin 1991; Gonen 1984; Matras 1965), although they generally failed to look for class voting. A notable exception is a major but little-known study of the 1988 elections by Sergio DellaPergola, which concluded from a statistical analysis of 810 urban Jewish localities that "social class is significantly stronger than ethnic background as a correlate of party preferences" (1991, 101). On reflection, it should not be surprising to find that the impact of class on voting is stronger in ecological than in survey correlations. This is because (a) the higher quality of aggregate data allows more sophisticated conceptualization and measurement of class; (b) class (and other social variables) are in fact grounded in communities as well as in individuals; and (c) unlike surveys, comparisons across communities capture local biases as well as the effects of individual differences.

To investigate the association between politics and places in the 1999 elections, we begin in table 4.3 by presenting voting results for thousands of small localities known as "Statistical Areas," classified by either types of locality or their social composition. Two outcomes are shown: the prime ministerial ballot and support for Shas in the Knesset vote. It is evident that in the contest between Netanyahu and Barak, certain types of communities voted with extreme homogeneity: 90% of kibbutz voters supported the candidate of the left, while at least 80% of Jews living in the Occupied Territories and Haredi neighborhoods[7] supported the candidate of the right. Class and ethnic voting were both pronounced, especially for the Shas Party. Support for Shas in predominantly Mizrahi communities outnumbered its support in Ashkenazi localities by roughly six to one. A similarly wide gap separated the most and least affluent quintiles of Statistical Areas.

We proceed now to a more systematic analysis of geographic linkages between social background and the vote in the 1999 elections (for a discussion of methodological issues in ecological analysis, see Discussion Paper

Table 4.3   Vote by Type of Location

	Netanyahu	Shas
National total (Jewish)*	49	14
Type of settlement		
Kibbutzim	10	1
Moshavim: Ashkenazi-dominant	22	2
Development Towns	60	22
Moshavim: Mizrahi-dominant	68	29
Settlements (occupied territories)	83	12
Locally "dominant" social groups		
Ashkenazim	33	5
"Russians"	51	11
Mizrahim-North Africa	67	31
Mizrahim-Asia	68	29
Haredim	78	20
Class composition		
Affluence: highest 20%	25	4
Affluence: lowest 20%	68	28

*Aggregate results for 1,968 predominantly Jewish Statistical Areas (except for class composition, which excludes kibbutz and Haredi localities, $N = 1,491$). Definitions of the variables appear later in the text.

No. 2-2000 from the Pinhas Sapir Center for Development at Tel Aviv University). Three specific challenges must be met for ecological analysis of voting:

1. Creation of a merged dataset comprising both voting and social cleavage variables averaged across geographic units. Smaller units should increase our confidence in the results.

2. Construction of valid measures of social cleavages—in our case, the ethnic, class, and religious composition of geographic units.

3. Verification that there is enough spatial segregation between social groups to make ecological analysis worthwhile.

Merged Dataset

Political and demographic data for Statistical Areas (hereafter SAs) were obtained by merging geographic summaries of data from the 1995 census with the detailed results (by polling stations) of the 1999 elections. SAs are as close as Israeli government statistics get to "neighborhoods" although their size varies. Some of them are entire small communities while others are fine subdivisions of towns or cities. The average number of eligible voters in the SAs that we analyzed was just over 1,500. Most of them (some 80%) comprised between 200 and 3,000 adults.

Our working dataset contained 1,968 SAs after the following exclusions: (a) Arab localities or localities with significant Arab minorities, (b) SAs that were very small or suspected of being nonresidential, and (c) SAs that could not be matched in the census and election files. In addition, except for the kibbutz averages shown in table 3 all of our analyses exclude kibbutzim (272 SAs) because of difficulties in measuring and interpreting their class composition.

Valid Cleavage Measures

Ethnicity. In the Israeli discourse on *edot* (ethnic communities) Ashkenazi and Mizrahi (or Sephardi) are taken-for-granted categories. This discourse was constructed in part by the dichotomous treatment of the *edot* in official statistics, in which they are defined in biological and geographic terms (typically, the continent of origin of immigrants or their fathers). Our research also necessarily focuses mainly on the conventional, broad categories of Ashkenazim (Jews born in Europe or the Americas or whose fathers were born there) versus Mizrahim (Jews born in North Africa or the Middle East or whose fathers were born there). We did make a few modifications however. Because of the distinctiveness (including political behavior) of the recent wave of "Russian" immigration to Israel, we created a separate category for immigrants from the former Soviet Union who arrived from 1989 onward. In addition, where feasible we checked for the presence of internal differentiation between Mizrahim from North Africa and from Asia.

In some of our analyses (including table 3) we have classified SAs according to the *dominant* ethnic group, if there was one. Operationally a group was defined as dominant if it enjoys a plurality of at least 40% of the adult population. Using this criterion, 41% of our SAs were dominated by Ashkenazim and 34% by Mizrahim. Dividing Mizrahim between "African" and "Asian" yielded dominance rates of 10% and 7% respectively. Only 3% of SAs were dominated by "Russians."

Religion. We inferred the religious complexion of SAs from three types of indicators. First, census data on the proportion of men whose highest education was Yeshiva studies at the postsecondary level and second, the proportion of households that failed to turn in a census questionnaire. (The rationale for this indicator is that Central Bureau of Statistics (CBS) officials are convinced that among Jews, most of the substantial phenomenon of noncooperation with the 1995 census occurred among the ultra-Orthodox.) Third, we obtained data from the Ministry of Education on the distribution of male elementary school students between the three officially recognized streams of the state education system: secular, national-religious *(mamlachti-dati)*, and Orthodox-religious *(azmai)*.

Unfortunately, information on school trends was available only for whole towns or cities *(yishuvim)* and did not cover kibbutzim or moshavim. In view of this problem of missing data, two different analyses of the effect of religion are employed in our subsequent multivariate analysis of the social correlates of voting. The preferred measures (unavailable for nearly 500 SAs) are based on a factor analysis of all three indicators, which revealed one factor tapping the presence of Haredim and the other loading high on the proportion of *dati* students in the school system. As an alternative, we sacrificed the schooling data and aggregated the other two indicators (nonresponse and yeshiva education) into a single Haredi scale.

Class. With few exceptions (Yatziv 1974; Zloczower 1972), Israeli researchers have failed to problematize either their concepts or measures of class. Theoretically it is well-known that there are a variety of competing conceptualizations of economic stratification. Most of them revolve around three potentially independent dimensions: production (e.g., occupation); consumption (e.g., income); and "sectors." Examples of vertical or sectoral cleavages are the public/private employment division (e.g., Burstein 1978) or distinctions between different "housing classes" (Dunleavy 1979, 1980; cf. Svallfors 1999, 206–208).

While studies of class voting in the Western nations have typically focused on occupational class (see most recently Evans 1999), Israeli researchers have ignored sectoral divisions and relied heavily on "socioeconomic status." But SES blurs the difference between class and status, erases qualitative distinctions between different types and conditions of work, and ignores the possibility of sectoral cleavages. The ecological analysis that follows is based on a factor analysis of indicators culled from the 1995 census that make it possible to find at least tentative empirical referents for the production, consumption, and sectoral dimensions of class structure. In addition to income, housing density, and education, our indicators included (1) four direct indicators of consumption standards (ownership of cars and other consumer goods), (2) two measures of the occupational and sectoral composition of jobs,[8] and (3) one indicator of state intervention in housing.[9] A principal component factor analysis yielded three factors, collectively accounting for 70% of total variance, which passed the conventional standard of having eigenvalues greater than 1.

As anticipated, there is a clear distinction between the consumption and production spheres. The first and strongest factor, which we have labeled *affluence*, represents living standards. The second factor, labeled *work*, is dominated by indicators of the two employment contexts included in the analysis. The third and final factor is more difficult to interpret. It loads heavily on two consumer goods (telephones and washing machines) that are basic to contemporary lifestyles. Areas in which the possession of these goods falls significantly short of being universal suffer from a form of poverty that is apparently distinct from the extent to which a locality participates in consumer affluence (captured by the first factor). The association of the *poverty* factor with the prevalence of public rental housing may hint at the existence of housing classes whose effect would be more clearly seen outside of the factor analysis. In fact, public housing alone is more strongly correlated than the poverty factor with ethnic and political variables. Therefore in later analyses we rely on the former.

Ecological Segregation

For ecological analysis to yield plausible generalizations, whether about individual or contextual effects, it is desirable that the geographic units of analysis be internally homogeneous and externally differentiated. It is common knowledge that Arabs and Haredim are spatially segregated in Israel. In relation to ethnic differences among Jews (Ashkenazim vs. Mizrahim) two competing overall views have long characterized the stratification literature. Some scholars have emphasized the crystallization across different spheres, and the reproduction over time, of the subordinate class position of Mizrahim (e.g., Cohen and Haberfeld 1998; Nahon 1984), while others have pointed to the scope and growth of class differentiation among Mizrahim (Ben-Rafael and Sharot 1991; Benski 1994). Our data on the extent of ecological segregation between the two major ethnic groups and its class correlates indicate that both perspectives are relevant. There are hardly any Ashkenazi-dominated areas in the poorest quintile of SAs and almost no Mizrahi-dominated areas in the richest quintile. At the same time, dominance does not mean exclusivity. More than a fifth of all adult Jews live in areas where neither Ashkenazim nor Mizrahim "dominate."

To summarize, ethnic "domination" is sufficiently pervasive that there are reasonable grounds for using ecological analysis to analyze the effect of ethnic composition on local voting preferences. At the same time not all areas are dominated by one ethnic group, and even in areas where one group is numerically dominant the other constitutes a significant minority. This poses a problem for making ecological inferences about the behavior of individuals,

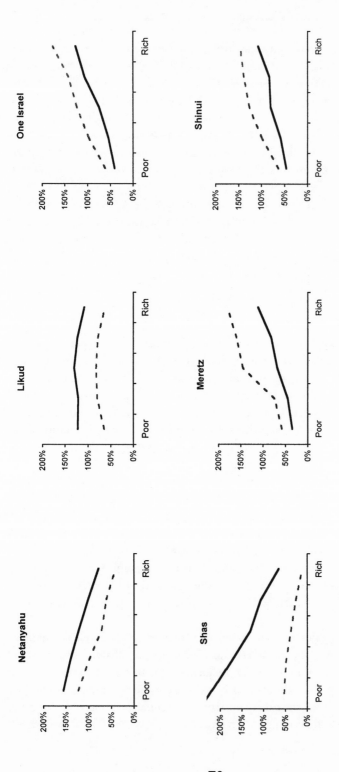

Figure. 4.1   Class, ethnicity and voting in 1999 (ecological data)

because we do not know whether or how the political preferences of members of the minority group are affected by those of the majority. At the same time, despite a striking degree of spatial overlap between ethnicity and class they remain incompletely crystallized (and religion is even less so).[10] Overall, the evidence justifies using ecological correlations to test for contextual influences, but it clearly poses dangers for making inferences to the individual level.

Class and Ethnic Effects

Figure 4.1 provides a graphic representation of the joint effects of ethnic and class composition on voting propensities across Statistical Areas. This analysis will be followed by multivariate regressions that estimate net effects controlling for other probable influences. However we have also endeavored to eliminate some possible confounding effects from the graphs, simply by excluding certain population groups. Specifically, we left out three groups that are characterized by both extreme partisan tendencies and distinctive ethnic or class composition—Haredim, kibbutzim, and Israeli settlements in the occupied territories.[11]

Three of the graphs relate to the two key political contests: Netanyahu versus Barak, and Likud versus One Israel (the expanded Labor Alignment). The other three cover the parties that most directly challenged the two leaders: Shas on the right and Shinui and Meretz on the left.[12] To maximize their comparability all six graphs have been constructed identically. The y-axis measures the mean vote for a party in SAs with a given class-ethnic combination, relative to the party's average in all the districts included in the analysis. The x-axis represents five equal divisions (quintiles) of the affluence factor. The relationship between class composition and the vote is shown separately for areas dominated by Mizrahim (continuous lines) and Ashkenazim (broken lines). Four findings are especially remarkable:

1. Ethnic voting is universal—in every case there is a sizable gap between the continuous and broken lines.

2. There is also very clear evidence of class voting. As we move from poorer to richer areas support for the left rises, whereas it declines for Netanyahu and Shas. The sole exception is the Likud. The disappearance in 1999 of the Likud's long-standing advantage among the poor—especially the Mizrahi poor—undoubtedly reflects its losses to Shas.

3. Voting for the two largest parties and for their prime ministerial candidates provides no indication of interaction between class and ethnic effects. Each variable appears to make an independent contribution to political preferences, unconditional on the other.

Table 4.4 Ecological Regressions

	Netanyahu			Shas		
	1	2	3	4	5	6
Constant	36.8***	31.5***	−3.64*	.42	.64***	.01
Ethnicity						
% Africa	.30**	.45***	.07*	.41***	.43***	.21***
% Asia	.36***	.45***	.06*	.37***	.32***	.14**
Russian dominant	2.35	5.80*	−1.23	.33	.38	.42
Class						
Affluence factor	−9.44***	−10.52***	−3.18***	−3.51**	−4.13***	−1.85**
Work factor	−4.96**	−2.43*	−.59	−2.18*	−1.54*	−.44
Public housing	.15*	.15	.04	.12*	.07	.05
Religion						
Haredi scale		10.77***	2.84**		2.43*	1.19*
Haredi factor	8.55***			2.75**		
Dati factor	4.06***			.72		
Type						
Settlements	20.69**	20.72***	−.23	−2.96	−6.77*	−1.12
Development towns	−1.63	−1.55	.67	−1.74	−1.43	−1.20
Mizrahi Moshavim		−4.90	2.58		−4.82*	−0.54
Vote in 1996						
Netanyahu 1996 (%)			.91***			
Shas 1996 (%)						.84***
Adjusted *R*-squared	.87	.81	.96	.77	.73	.86
N	1,204	1,689	1,678	1,204	1,689	1,678

*t > = 5   **t > = 10   ***t > = 15

N is the number of (predominantly Jewish) Statistical Areas, excluding kibbutzim.

4. On the other hand, interesting conditional effects are evident for the most important rivals of the two major parties. Ashkenazim of all classes seem to refrain from voting Shas, but not all Mizrahim support it—that depends (inversely) on class. For Meretz and Shinui, we observe relatively low support in poor localities almost irrespective of whether Ashkenazim or Mizrahim dominate ethnic composition. But a wider ethnic gap emerges (for Meretz it is especially wide) as we move up the class ladder.

Striking as the charts are, we would have more confidence in the results if they took into account influences on voting other than class and ethnicity. The ecological regressions in table 4.4 add several new features to the analysis of voting in the prime ministerial contest and for Shas. First, rather than relying on an arbitrarily chosen criterion of "dominance," we now measure ethnicity on a continuous scale. Second, finer ethnic categories are utilized: African and Asian Mizrahim are treated separately and the effect of the "Russian" presence is measured directly. Third, all three of the empirical dimensions of class are included. Fourth, we add indicators of the religious cleavage to the analysis of class and ethnic effects. Fifth, we test the effects of certain types of locality (e.g., "development towns") that are commonly believed to have effects on voting above and beyond their ethnic, class, and religious composition. Sixth, in some equations we estimate the determinants of the vote swing between 1996 and 1999.

The models perform well. The proportion of explained variance is high; nearly all coefficients are significant at conventional levels (hardly surprising given the large number of cases analyzed); and the effects of ethnicity, affluence, Haredi presence, and location in the occupied territories ("settlements") exhibit extremely high levels of significance. Multicollinearity—correlation between independent variables that hampers precise and reliable estimation of their individual effects—is not a serious problem.

Substantively the regression coefficients confirm the conclusions already reached by means of graphic analysis, but they add some interesting nuances.

Ethnicity. The effect of distinguishing between Mizrahim of Asian and African origin depends on which indicators are used for religion (and consequently, whether or not the dataset is truncated). It is clear that the Asia/Africa distinction makes little or no difference to the prime ministerial vote. But as might be expected, other things being equal the presence of North African immigrants and their children offers more of a boost to the Shas vote than residents of Asian origin. The "Russians" are more difficult to track because they are not a significant presence in most neighborhoods and only dominate a relatively small number of SAs. Netanyahu definitely did better in those neighborhoods, although his edge was smaller than in 1996.

Class. The regressions support our assumption that class is multidimensional: all three indicators had independent effects on voting. Given that factor scores are standardized the results imply that an increase of one standard deviation in the affluence factor added about 10 points to the Barak vote, whereas a similar increment to the work factor added a quarter to a half of that amount. The influence of the third class indicator, the proportion living in public rental housing, was more modest. In the results for Shas, the pattern is similar except that relatively speaking there is not such a big difference between the effect of affluence and the other two indicators of class composition.

Religion. Both indicators of Haredi presence had very strong and positive effects on the vote for Netanyahu. But Shas, whose origins in the mid-1980s were linked to internal disputes within the ultra-Orthodox political camp, did not benefit to the same extent from the overall presence of Haredim. Similarly, whereas Netanyahu profited substantially from strong "national-religious" as well as ultra-Orthodox streams, Shas did not.

Location. In table 4.3 we saw that Netanyahu's share of the vote among Israelis living in the occupied territories was 34 points higher than the national (Jewish) average. Table 4.4 shows that even after controlling for the three key social cleavages, a gap of more than 20 points remains. On the other hand, the above-average support for both Netanyahu and Shas in development towns appears to be fully explained by their class, ethnic, and religious composition. The same is true for the predominantly Mizrahi moshavim.

Three questions remain to be answered:

1. *How similar or different are the patterns encountered in 1999 from the preceding election?* Models 3 and 6 were included in table 4.4 to address this issue by using the 1996 vote as a control variable, in effect redefining the dependent variable as the rise or fall in the relevant share of the vote between the two elections. Broadly speaking the results suggest that the same factors that determined the overall outcome in 1999 also affected the swings. Still, there were differences. Netanyahu actually gained support in 1999 among Haredim (especially in Ashkenazi areas), while his already inferior position in affluent areas was further weakened.

2. *What is the relative importance of the different social bases of voting?* The unavoidable imprecision of most of our indicators and the presence of some multicollinearity between ethnicity, class, and religion in Israel make it difficult to reach clear-cut conclusions on this point. According to standardized coefficients of a regression analysis of the four leading factors defining aggregate vote for the premiership, all three cleavages had similar weight (not shown here).

3. *Can any significant interactions be detected?* Based on similar simple but powerful regression models run separately for Ashkenazi and Mizrahi-dominated areas, it is evident that the vote in Mizrahi areas was substantially more sensitive to class differences. Also in the voting for Shas, the effect of all three cleavages was much greater in Mizrahi-dominated areas than in Ashkenazi localities.

Cross-tabulations (also not shown here) reveal that in 1999 relatively affluent and Ashkenazi-dominated SAs led the swing to Barak, and they swam even more strongly than before against the currents pulling toward Shas. By contrast, in less affluent and Mizrahi-dominated areas it was more common to find deepened support for both Netanyahu and Shas.

The ecological findings thus show that alone or in combination with ethnicity and religion, class shaped both the distribution of votes in 1999 and vote shifts since the 1996 elections. This analysis was moreover based on data that are in many ways superior to those utilized by survey researchers: the dependent variable is *actual* voting, all parties and social groups are accurately represented, and it is possible to generate much more interesting indicators for the critical independent variable (class). Yet as we have cautioned, ecological relationships represent an uncertain combination of effects at the micro- (individual) and macro-(community-context) levels. The next section takes up this challenge.

Putting Voters in Context

While voting is ultimately an individual act, both the range of choices relevant to voters and the implications of individual differences between them are dependent on community context. To analyze these dependencies, as well as to overcome problems of inference from both micro- and macrodata, requires a methodology capable of recognizing and jointly evaluating both individual and contextual effects on voting. The ideal tool for this purpose is multilevel analysis (MLA), an innovative statistical technique that has become especially popular in research on individual differences in school achievement. Students of educational attainment employ MLA to disentangle the effect of individual differences between students from the effects of teachers, schools, and/or communities. The technique has obvious relevance to the study of voting behavior, in which individuals make decisions that are likely to be affected and conditioned by their spatial and social environment (e.g., Charnock 1997; Jones, Johnston, and Pattie 1992).

The essential requirement for MLA is a dataset integrating individual and aggregate-level information. The 1999 preelection survey conducted by Shamir and Arian was not designed for the purpose of multilevel analysis. However, because the sample was comprised of a diverse but limited selection of localities it was possible for us to identify in which of the 38 sampled areas each of the 1,075 non-Arab respondents resided.

Despite numerous limitations of the effective sample of 591 individuals living in 16 localities, the dataset opens an intriguing window onto the significance of local context for political behavior in Israel. For instance, the size and even the direction of the gap between Mizrahi and Ashkenazi voters differs enormously across localities. This finding throws into question the very notion of *the* ethnic vote. A particularly interesting finding is the comparison between "blue-white" Jerusalem and "red" Tel Aviv. There was no ethnic vote in 1999 in either of the two cities. In Jerusalem most survey respondents preferred Bibi and in Tel Aviv most preferred Barak *regardless of whether they were Ashkenazim or Mizrahim.*

Obviously, much more and better data would be required to validate and elaborate such local contrasts. But by combining microlevel data on individuals from the 16 available localities with macrolevel census data for these same localities, we can construct a dataset that is at least minimally adequate for the purposes of multilevel analysis. It should be remembered that our aim in using MLA is not to characterize local voting behavior and its causal origins in specific communities. We are interested in finding relationships between variables and levels that hold across a diverse selection of communities. Such relationships, if they exist, would enable us to make general inferences about whether location matters and why. These are the three specific questions that we would like to address:

1. To what extent are local differences in the vote merely the by-product of the type of people who live in different communities? The predominance of observant and traditional Jews in Jerusalem versus "secular" Jews in Tel Aviv is a good illustration of why the apparent impact of place on ethnic voting could be spurious, resulting merely from a *compositional effect.*

2. If voting does differ across localities irrespective of the types of people who live in them, what features of localities can explain these differences? Judging by the results of our ecological analysis we would expect all three social cleavages to have strong *contextual effects on how individuals vote.*

3. Localities may systematically bias the preferences of their residents toward one political bloc or another, but the magnitude of local bias may vary between types of voters. That is to say, community context may alter the impact of individual characteristics ("cross-level interaction"). We noted earlier that ethnicity had no apparent impact on voting in the two largest cities; but in Haifa and in several other localities there was a wide ethnic different in voting. Would this still be the case if we could set aside the impact of both individual and community-level determinants of voting?

MLA is designed to address precisely these three tasks: differentiating true contextual effects from compositional effects, explaining local bias insofar as it does exist, and identifying interactions between local and individual effects.[13]

In the spirit of an exploratory analysis that stretches the available data, our application of MLA to 1999 data rests on simple indicators and specifications. As explained in the next section a limited number of dichotomous explanatory variables are entered into the equations. For estimation, despite the advantages of logistic regression in analyzing dichotomous dependent variables, standard (OLS) regression is preferred. OLS is not only easier to interpret, but in the context of MLA it offers more tools for evaluating model performance and fewer estimation challenges. Nevertheless, to verify that the OLS results are not distorted all of the models were reestimated using logistic regression and one of these results is presented here.

The multilevel analysis reported in table 4.5 begins with the "empty" Model 1—so-called because it is devoid at this stage of explanatory variables (Snijders and Bosker 1999, 45–47). The purpose of this model is to decompose the overall variance in voting between each level: variation *within* localities (which can be thought of as representing individual differences) versus variation *between* localities (reflecting local bias). As is common in datasets where individuals are nested inside groups, only a modest share of the overall variance (12.5 percent) can be attributed to between-group differences. This ratio implies an "intraclass correlation coefficient" of .125, meaning that the clustering of voters in localities leads to some degree of similarity in their votes. Ignoring this clustering effect might cause an ordinary regression analysis to overstate the significance of pure individual differences, although in the present instance this exaggeration turned out to be quite mild.[14]

The empty model estimates the overall intercept for all the individuals sampled, which is similar (but not identical) to their mean probability of voting for Netanyahu. The multilevel analysis also provides a separate intercept for each locality. Comparing these intercepts it is possible to infer whether the "base level" of the dependent variable differs across localities. The statistic, that summarizes the extent of these differences is the average "reliability" of the differences between localities. This statistic is very high in Model 1 (just under .8).

Model 2 introduces four explanatory variables that we already know are powerful predictors of individual voting behavior: the most potent issue variable reported in table 4.1 (readiness to trade land for peace) as well as the usual three social cleavages. Ethnicity is represented in the equation by two dummy variables with Ashkenazim serving as the null category. We chose one indicator each for SES (housing density) and religious observance.[15] For ease of presentation all of the indicators are dichotomous and constructed so as to positively affect the vote for Netanyahu. The initial results (individual-level fixed effects) are as we would expect: all variables except housing density are statistically significant (t ratios of at least 2.0), with religiosity

Table 4.5   Multilevel Analysis of the Vote for Netanyahu vs. Barak

	Permit intercepts to vary by locality		Add predictors of individual differences		Add predictors of locality differences	
	1		2		3	
	b	t	b	t	b	t
Fixed effects						
Intercept	.546	*11.2*	.549	*11.3*	.633	*16.1*
Individual Level						
(N = 591)						
Mizrahi			.098	*2.6*	.098	*2.6*
Sabra			.105	*2.4*	.105	*2.4*
Crowded			.057	*1.3*	.057	*1.3*
Observant			.229	*5.6*	.229	*5.6*
Not dove			.515	*14.1*	.515	*14.1*
Aggregate Level						
(16 localities)						
Housing density					1.530	*4.2*
Contextual (random) effects						
Intercept (reliability)	.795		.863		.715	
Slope of Mizrahi (reliability)						
Slope of Mizrahi (variance)						
Model performance						
Unexplained variance						
Within localities	.219		.143		.143	
Between localities	.030		.033		.012	
Deviance	812.400		592.200		582.000	
Extra deviance/ Extra parameters			−44.000		−10.200	

Table 4.5 (continued)

	Permit slopes of individual predictors to vary by locality		Combine models 3&4		Reestimate Model 5 using logistic regression*	
	4		5		6	
	b	t	b	t	b	t
Fixed effects						
Intercept	.633	18.2	.633	18.2	0.25	1.8
Individual Level						
(N = 591)						
Mizrahi	.112	2.2	.112	2.2	.69 (2.0)	2.6
Sabra	.088	2.0	.088	2.0	.58 (1.8)	2.6
Crowded	.060	1.4	.060	1.4	.39 (1.5)	2.1
Observant	.216	5.3	.216	5.3	1.25 (3.5)	6.2
Not dove	.516	14.4	.516	14.4	2.73 (15.3)	12.9
Aggregate Level						
(16 localities)						
Housing density			1.470	4.7	8.20	4.0
Contextual (random) effects						
Intercept (reliability)	.868		.728		.649	
Slope of Mizrahi (reliability)	.383		.374		.385	
Slope of Mizrahi (variance)	.013 (p = .06)		.012 (p = .06)		.576 (p = .05)	
Model performance						
Unexplained variance						
Within localities	.140		.140			
Between localities	.033		.013		.359	
Deviance	588.000		579.600			
Extra deviance/ Extra parameters	−4.200		−2.400/−4.200			

Models were estimated using HLM for Windows 4.04 after deviating individual-level variables from their group means ("group centering"). Microdata were drawn from the Shamir-Arian (1999) preelection survey; macrodata are from the 1995 census. All data are for Jews only and microdata exclude recent immigrants from the former Soviet Union.

*Figures in parentheses next to dichotomous independent variables are odds ratios. Estimation method is the population-average model with robust standard errors.

and especially hawkishness having a pronounced impact on individual candidate choice.

The main purpose of Model 2 is to ascertain how much of the diversity of voting across localities disappears once we take account of key individual differences inside localities. This speaks to the crucial compositional question, whether differences in support for Netanyahu across localities disappear once we take account of their composition. The answer to this question is resoundingly negative. The reliability of local variation in intercepts is actually slightly higher than in Model 1. Naturally the extent of unexplained individual-level variance is considerably lower, but no reduction has occurred in the amount of unexplained aggregate-level variance. This is extremely important. It means that there are no grounds to suspect that local differences in aggregate voting patterns merely result from compositional effects.

The extent of each model's overall fit is addressed in the bottom rows of table 4.5 Multilevel models are estimated by likelihood methods that generate a "deviance" statistic. One of the reasons for estimating the empty model is to obtain a baseline measure of deviance against which subsequent models can be assessed. An accepted indication that one model is a significant improvement over another, is that it reduces deviance by at least twice the number of additional parameters that it estimates (Kreft and Leeuw 1999, 65). Not surprisingly, the addition of explanatory variables in Model 2 considerably improves the overall fit compared with Model 1.

Detecting variation in voting across localities that cannot be attributed to individual differences is only the first step in multilevel modeling. The next task is to uncover the sources of this variation by modeling the effects of differing local contexts. Using the rich dataset on localities collected for our ecological analysis we assessed the effect of variations in the ethnic, religious, and class composition of the sixteen localities included in the survey and analyzed here. Of these variables *only class composition* (measured by housing density) *was found to have a significant effect,* as judged by both its high t-statistic and the sizable reduction in unexplained variance between localities in Model 3 compared to Model 2. The coefficient showing the effect of local variations in housing density can be interpreted as follows. A unit increase on the measure is equivalent to the gap between Haifa and the Qrayot, or Herzliyya and Holon—and it was associated with 15 points more support for Bibi. This is a very large effect indeed.[16]

Note that between Models 2 and 3 the reliability of intercepts across contexts, an indicator of remaining contextual effects, declines; yet at .715 it is still very high. To further account for variation between localities we might need to incorporate other aggregate-level variables that are not in our dataset. It is also possible that different configurations of characteristics render localities qualitatively different one from the other. But one thing is clear: beyond the effects of individual differences, *place itself* and at least one characteristic (the standard of housing) of places matter a great deal for voting in Israel.

So far we have looked only at differences across contexts (localities) in "base" levels of support for Netanyahu versus Barak (intercepts). MLA can also tell us whether the impact of personal characteristics on individual votes is conditional upon features of the context in which the individual lives. To test for the existence of these cross-level interactions, we must permit not only the intercepts but also the *slopes* estimated in Model 2 to vary across localities. This is the purpose of Model 4, which reports the only individual-level variable (ethnicity) whose effect was found to differ significantly across localities. Reliability and variance, the two indicators of the extent of contextual differences in the ethnic vote, suggest that contextual variation is significant although modestly so. It seems that our earlier speculation that there may be no such thing as *the* ethnic vote may be well founded, although as with the other MLA findings reported here, more and better data will be needed to be sure. Data limitations may also account for the fact that nothing came of experiments (not shown in table 4.5) that proceeded to the ultimate stage of multilevel analysis, in which contextual variables are called upon to explain the varying impact of individual differences in different localities.

Our final two models, 5 and 6, integrate all three locality-level effects: differences in intercept ("base levels"), differences in slope (with respect to ethnicity), and the fixed effect of housing density at the community level. Combining the latter two effects, Model 5 lowers the overall deviance by a satisfactory margin with respect to both Models 3 and 4. Gratifyingly, when the same equation is reestimated using logistic regression (Model 6) none of the effects is found to lose significance. On the contrary, in this model the impact of housing density is statistically significant at the individual and locality levels alike. Voters are apparently influenced by both their own socioeconomic situation and, even more, the class composition of the communities they live in. We could hardly have hoped for more convincing evidence of the credibility of the class voting hypothesis.

Conclusion

We began this chapter with an analysis of survey data suggesting that the near-absence of class effects on individual voting in previous empirical research may have resulted more from methodological inadequacies than from the actual patterning of voter behavior. We then argued for the power of ecological analysis, largely untapped in previous works, to complement and in some respects even supersede the survey approach to electoral behavior.

By correlating aggregate election results with background characteristics across numerous geographic areas, we were able to verify the centrality of class voting in Israel. Ecological analysis thus elevated the class cleavage— a social basis of voter choice suggested by both theory and common knowledge—to its rightful place alongside other well-known social divisions in the Jewish electorate. Still, as we have taken pains to stress, micro- and macro-level data are not simply alternative sources of empirical information for modeling voter behavior. Multilevel analysis makes it possible to distinguish between the impact of individual differences and local biases. It appears that in Israel class influences voting at both the individual and local levels.

Beyond the recurring significance of class voting, our three methodologies did not always yield convergent results and indeed, given the differences and trade-offs between them, convergence could hardly have been expected. Which results are more credible? The ecological analysis is undoubtedly the most "solid" in terms of the size and quality of the database but, as we conceded, interpretation of ecological correlations is far from straightforward. MLA represents a vastly superior methodological strategy than either of the two conventional approaches on their own. However, the pooled dataset at our disposal does not fully meet its demanding requirements. What we hope to have achieved in this respect is a demonstration of the promise of multilevel analysis for addressing critical but unresolved issues in the study of electoral behavior in Israel. In order to realize this promise, we urge survey researchers to modify the size and composition of their samples in order to make them more suitable to the application of MLA.

Still, even by combining improved data with superior statistical techniques it will never be possible to eliminate tentative and inconsistent findings. These limitations are inherent to the ambition of making parsimonious generalizations about complex causal processes that operate at multiple levels of analysis. We regard the results of the present research as having accomplished our main purpose of questioning the paradigm and the techniques underlying the long-established view that class is located at the bottom of a well-defined hierarchy of social cleavages among Israeli voters. Our findings show that firstly, the effect of class is comparable to that of ethnicity and religion; and secondly, the impact of social cleavages is not purely additive but also interactive, although these interactions remain ambiguous. It might be possible to resolve this apparent contradiction using MLA, assuming appropriate survey data becomes available. Yet insofar as different *configurations* of class, ethnicity, and religious observance are accompanied by distinctive patterns of electoral behavior, the question of interpretation becomes no less challenging than the challenge of pinning down what is happening empirically. What is the glue that binds these configurations together and endows them with electoral significance? This question brings us back to the issue raised at the outset of this chapter, the problem of understanding class voting in a polity characterized by weak political articulation of class by parties and in political discourse.

C. Brooks and J. Manza (1997), who utilized the distinction between class voting and class politics to good effect in their study of political change in the United States, show that during the postwar period the members of an important class category (professional workers) have consistently tended to vote with their class (class voting). At the same time, the partisan preference of professionals has shifted from the Republicans (who presumably represent their economic interests) to the Democrats (who better embody their increasingly progressive positions on key social issues like racial and gender equality). Brooks and Manza do not explain this paradox. The "postmaterialist" thesis (Clark, Lipset, and Rempel 1993; Inglehart 1977) predicts the rising importance of social issue cleavages, but is unable to explain why the new politics has taken root only among certain classes. Clearly, the formation of professionals as a "voting class" rests upon different foundations than the factors that were responsible in the past for the political mobilization of blue-collar workers. Rather than union membership and class solidarity, professionals share a social outlook that helps sustain their distinctive collective identity and at the same time provides them with "cultural capital" that indirectly serves their material interests by maintaining social closure (cf. Bourdieu 1984; Parkin 1974). Thus, *noneconomic issue positions may reinforce rather than compete with class allegiance.*

Despite obvious differences in context, the Israeli case presents a puzzle that in principle is similar to the American one. Our research has shown that economically advantaged non-Arab citizens of Israel tend to vote together for the "left," while their less fortunate compatriots prefer the "right" and/or the ethnic-religious Shas Party. But as in the case just discussed, the most obvious correlates of these class-voting linkages are noneconomic: disputed issues of collective identity, the role of religion in personal and national life, and management of the peace process and future borders (Kimmerling 1999; Peres and Yaar 1998; Shamir and Arian 1999). In the spirit of Pierre Bourdieu it may be argued that in Israel, *struggles over identity and borders are by no means detached from class interests.* Peace, liberalization, and privatization are the indivisible components of a coherent formula for the success of the dominant group of middle and upper-class Ashkenazim in today's globalized, hi-tech, post Cold War world (Levy 1997; Peled and Shafir 1996; Ram 1999). It is in this context that Shas speaks to the material interests of its lower-class Mizrahi supporters, the losers from liberalization, by alternately directly providing them with subsidized social services or supporting a more generous welfare state. A second explanation derives from the high degree of overlap in Israeli society between ethno-class differentiation and the distribution of social status and political power. This approach suggests that *the main political cleavages between ethno-classes are reflections of status politics.* On this reading the success of Shas rests on its traditional religious conception of Israeli identity, which in the context of Israel's three-tiered status order (Palestinians, Mizrahim, and Ashkenazim) ensures the elevation of Mizrahim above the Arab citizens of the state and offers a platform for challenging Ashkenazi hegemony (Peled 1998).

These two perspectives need not be seen as mutually exclusive. Voting among lower-class Mizrahim and higher-class Ashkenazim is "overdetermined" by both class and status interests. Yet, despite a substantial overlap between ethnicity, rival subcultures, and class interests, we must also ask whether class or status politics triumph when these three planes are "misaligned." What may be gleaned from our data suggests that there is no clearcut answer. The individual-level evidence indicates that in the prime ministerial race ethnicity, religiosity, and class all contributed to predicting candidate preference. Survey data are too scanty to offer reliable explanations of why, where conflicts occurred, some individuals vote with their class and others with their identity. The ecological data confirm that where different cleavages fail to crystallize, each one plays a role in shaping voter preferences. Consider the eleven of the most affluent SAs in our dataset that are also located in the heartland of advantage, the Tel Aviv metropolitan area (they include Savyon, Kfar Shemarayhu, and Herzliyya Pituach). Netanyahu received an average of only 14% of the vote in these communities and Shas garnered a mere 1%—a testament to the potency of class voting. At the same time, the vote for both Shas and Netanyahu did vary across localities, and its variation was closely correlated ($r = .85$) with the representation of Mizrahim, which ranged from under a tenth to over a quarter. So even at this extreme on the class and voting spectra, there was far from a perfect overlap between class and ethnic composition and class voting did not suppress ethnic voting. In sum, while the interplay between class interests and cultural identities goes a long way to explaining voting behavior in Israel, where the two are in opposition the result is uncertain.

Notes

1. Given the significant number of non-Jewish Israeli citizens from the former Soviet Union in contemporary Israel, it would be inaccurate to describe our research population as "Jewish voters." See Lustick (1999).

2. Deviations from Arian and Shamir were as follows (1) Rather than treating "Sabras" (second-generation Israelis of unknown origin) as Ashkenazim we created a second dummy variable for them. (2) We did not include evaluations of candidates' competence in the model, on the grounds that these are so highly correlated with candidate choice that they should be regarded as a consequence no less than a cause of voting intention. In addition, note the following: (a) At Michal Shamir's suggestion we used a voting intention question that did not permit respondents to choose candidates other than Netanyahu and Barak. The ethnic bias of the Bibi/Barak vote would have been even larger if we had excluded voters who would have preferred Mordechai or another third-party candidate. (b) "Russians" (immigrants from the former Soviet Union since 1989) were excluded from the analysis. (c) We experimented with distinguishing between foreign and Israeli-born Mizrahim and Ashkenazim. The results for the two generations were almost identical for both ethnic groups.

3. Housing density for nearly one third of the respondents was precisely one person per room, and 60 percent reported twelve years of schooling.

4. Respondents were asked to evaluate their household expenditure relative to the mean for a family of four (NIS 9,000 at the time of the survey) *taking into account the size of their own family.* Apparently those with small families failed to make this adjustment and therefore understated their true standard of living.

5. Our speculation that other elections would reiterate the 1999 pattern is of course only a speculation. Generally speaking the empirics in this chapter are confined to the 1999 election.

6. This generalization does not hold for articles on the Arab vote, since until recently survey data was not available for this sector.

7. The criteria used to define the categories distinguished in table 4.3 are discussed in the next section. It should be stressed that identification of Haredi neighborhoods rests on a rough quantitative criterion that most probably causes understatement of the homogeneity of the Haredi vote.

8. In constructing indicators of the local job market we were limited to single-digit classifications of occupations and economic branches. Our first indicator, "proletarians," is the proportion of the employed who have manual occupations and who work in manufacturing, construction, or agriculture. The second indicator, "public professionals," is the proportion with technical, professional, or managerial occupations who work in social services (health, education, and welfare), public services, or community services. As well as honing in on different ends of the occupational scale, these indicators also have an obvious sectoral component.

9. The housing indicator is the proportion of households living in public rented dwellings, which are characterized by low construction standards and low market value (Werczberger 1995).

10. Complete "crystallization" would imply perfect correlation between the ethnic, class, and religious composition of SAs. However, excluding kibbutzim we find the following bivariate correlations with percent Mizrahim: affluence factor −.42, *dati* factor .36, *haredi* factor .22 (the parallel correlations for percent Ashkenazi were markedly lower).

11. We also took care that "Russians" would not confound our indicator of Ashkenazi domination, which is based on the proportion of Ashkenazim in each SA *excluding* immigrants since 1989 from the former Soviet Union.

12. The aggregate vote share for these candidates/parties in all 1,968 of the SAs in our basic dataset (including kibbutzim) was: Netanyahu/Barak 48.7/51.3%, One Israel 21.9%, Likud 15.7%, Shas 14.3%, Meretz 7.7%, and Shinui 5.6%.

13. For a clear textbook presentation of multilevel estimation, see Kreft and de Leeuw (1999).

14. Estimating Model 2 using standard OLS regression yielded almost identical coefficients but somewhat higher *t*-statistics.

15. Except for religious observance, all of the individual-level indicators are based on the same questions that were utilized in our replication of Shamir and Arian's logistic models.

16. Because this effect might have been inflated by "centering" the independent variables around their local means, we reestimated the effect of differences in density across localities by also including at the locality level the local means of the remaining individual-level variables (Kreft and de Leeuw 1999, 108), obtaining very close results to the models reported in table 4.5.

References

Arian, Alan, (ed.). 1972. *The Elections in Israel—1969*. Jerusalem: Jerusalem Academic Press.

Ben-Rafael, Eliezer, and Stephen Sharot. 1991. *Ethnicity, Religion and Class in Israel*. Cambridge: Cambridge University Press.

Benski, Tova. 1994. "Ethnic Convergence Processes under Conditions of Persisting Socioeconomic [and] Decreasing Cultural Differences—The Case of Israeli Society." *International Migration Review* 28, no. 2: 256–280.

Bourdieu, Pierre. 1984. *Distinction: A Social Critique of the Judgement of Taste*. Cambridge: Harvard University Press.

Brooks, C., and Manza J. 1997. "Class Politics and Political Change in the United States, 1952–1992." *Social Forces* 76, no. 2: 379–408.

Burstein, Paul. 1978. "Social Cleavages and Party Choice in Israel: A Log-Linear Analysis." *American Political Science Review* 72: 96–109.

Charnock, D. 1997. "Spatial Variations, Contextual and Social Structural Influences on Voting for the Alp at the 1996 Federal Election: Conclusions from Multilevel Analyses." *Australian Journal of Political Science* 32, no. 2: 237–254.

Clark, Terry N., Seymour Martin Lipset, and Michael Rempel. 1993. "The Declining Political Significance of Social Class." *International Sociology*, no. 8: 293–316.

Cohen, Y., and Y. Haberfeld. 1998. "Second-Generation Jewish Immigrants in Israel: Have the Ethnic Gaps in Schooling and Earnings Declined?" *Ethnic and Racial Studies* 21, no. 3: 507–528.

DellaPergola, Sergio. 1991. "Voting Behavior." In U. O. Schmelz, S. DellaPergola, and U. Avner (eds.). *Ethnic Differences among Israeli Jews: A New Look.* Jerusalem: Hebrew University Institute of Contemporary Jewry, 79–101, 98–204.

Diskin, Abraham. 1991. *Elections and Voters in Israel.* New York: Praeger.

Dunleavy, Patrick. 1979. "The Urban Basis of Political Alignment: Social Class, Domestic Property Ownership, and State Intervention in Consumption Processes." *British Journal of Political Science* 9, no. 4: 409–443.

———. 1980. "The Political Implications of Sectoral Cleavages and the Growth of State Employment: Part 1, the Analysis of Production Cleavages." *Political Studies* 28, no. 3: 364–383.

Evans, Geoffrey. 1999. *The End of Class Politics? Class Voting in Comparative Context.* Oxford: Oxford University Press.

Farjoun, Emmanuel. 1983. "Class Divisions in Israeli Society." *Khamsin (London),* no. 10: 29–39.

Gonen, Amiram. 1984. "A Geographical Analysis of the Elections in Jewish Urban Communities." In D. Caspi, A. Diskin, and E. Gutmann (eds.). *The Roots of Begin's Success: The 1981 Israeli Elections.* New York: St. Martin's, 59–87.

Herzog, Hanna. 1985. "Social Construction of Reality in Ethnic Terms: The Case of Political Ethnicity in Israel." *International Review of Modern Sociology* 15, nos. 1–2: 45–61.

Inglehart, Ronald. 1977. *The Silent Revolution.* Princeton: Princeton University Press.

Jones, K., R. J. Johnston, and C. J. Pattie. 1992. "People, Places and Regions: Exploring the Use of Multi-Level Modeling in the Analysis of Electoral Data." *British Journal of Political Science* 22: 343–380.

Kimmerling, Baruch. 1999. "Elections as a Battleground over Collective Identity." In A. Arian and M. Shamir (eds.). *The Elections in Israel, 1996.* Albany: State University of New York Press, 27–44.

Kreft, Ita, and Jan de Leeuw. 1999. *Introducing Multilevel Modeling.* London: Sage.

Levy, Yagil. 1997. *Trial and Error: Israel's Route from War to De-Escalation.* Albany: State University of New York Press.

Lustick, I. S. 1999. "Israel as a Non-Arab State: The Political Implications of Mass Immigration of Non-Jews." *Middle East Journal* 53, no. 3: 417–433.

Manza, J., M. Hout, and C. Brooks. 1995. "Class Voting in Capitalist Democracies since World War II—Dealignment, Realignment, or Trendless Fluctuation." *Annual Review of Sociology* 21: 137–162.

Matras, Judah. 1965. *Social Change in Israel.* Chicago: Aldine.

Nahon, Yaakov. 1984. "Ethnic Gaps—A Longitudinal Portrait." In N. Cohen and O. Ahimeir (eds.). *New Directions in the Study of the Ethnic Problem.* Jerusalem: Jerusalem Institute for Israel Studies, 23–43 (Hebrew).

Parkin, Frank. 1974. "Strategies of Social Closure in Class Formation." In F. Parkin (ed.). *The Social Analysis of Class Structure.* London: Tavistock, 1–18.

Peled, Yoav. 1989. "Labor Market Segmentation and Ethnic Conflict: The Social Bases of Right Wing Politics in Israel." Paper presented at the 1989 annual meeting of the American Political Science Association, Atlanta, August 31–September 3.

————. 1998. "Towards a Redefinition of Jewish Nationalism in Israel? The Enigma of Shas." *Ethnic and Racial Studies* 21, no. 4: 703–727.

Peled, Yoav, and G. Shafir. 1996. "The Roots of Peacemaking—The Dynamics of Citizenship in Israel, 1948–93." *International Journal of Middle East Studies* 28, no. 3: 391–413.

Peres, Yochanan, and Ephraim Yaar. 1998. *Between Consensus and Dissent: Democracy, Security and Peace in the Israeli Consciousness.* Jerusalem: Israel Democracy Institute (Hebrew).

Ram, Uri. 1999. "Between Colonialism and Consumerism: Liberal Post-Zionism in the 'Glocal' Age." In U. Ram and O. Yiftachel (eds.). *"Ethnocracy" and "Glocality": New Perspectives on Society and Space in Israel.* Beer Sheva: Negev Center for Regional Development, Ben-Gurion University, 41–100. (Hebrew).

Shalev, Michael. 1999. "Economics, Politics and Welfare" (Hebrew).

Shamir, Michal, and Asher Arian, 1999. "Collective Identity and Electoral Competition in Israel." *American Political Science Review* 93, no. 2: 265–277.

Shapiro, Yonathan. 1991. *The Road to Power: Herut Party in Israel.* Albany: State University of New York Press.

Snijders, Tom, and Roel Bosker. 1999. *Multilevel Analysis: An Introduction to Basic and Advanced Multilevel Modeling.* London: Sage.

Svallfors, Stefan. 1999. "The Class Politics of Swedish Welfare Policies." In G. Evans (ed.). *The End of Class Politics? Class Voting in Comparative Context.* Oxford: Oxford University Press, 203–228.

Swirski, Shlomo. 1984. "The Oriental Jews in Israel: Why Many Tilted Towards Begin." *Dissent* 31, no. 134: 77–91.

Werczberger, E. 1995. "The Role of Public Housing in Israel—Effects of Privatization." *Scandinavian Housing & Planning Research* 12, no. 2: 93–108.

Yatziv, Gadi. 1974. "The Class Basis of Party Affiliation." Ph.D. diss., Hebrew University of Jerusalem (Hebrew).

Zloczower, Avraham. 1972. "Occupation, Mobility and Social Class." *Social Science Information* 11, no. 5: 329–358.

Part II

Groups

5

The Continuing Electoral Success of Shas
A Cultural Division of Labor Analysis

YOAV PELED

Introduction

As far as Shas was concerned, the election campaign to the Fifteenth Knesset was conducted under the shadow of the conviction and then the sentencing of the party's political leader, Aryeh Deri, for bribery charges (Bilsky, 2001). In spite of these events, or perhaps because of them, Shas succeeded in raising its Knesset delegation from ten to seventeen members and became one of the three largest (albeit medium-size) factions in the house. Like in past election campaigns, this impressive achievement had not been predicted by the pollsters, who expected Shas to only retain its power (see, e.g., Plotzker 1999a, 1999b, 1999c; Shalev and Kis, in this volume).[1]

In this chapter I wish to explore the social origins of Shas's continuing electoral success, and consider its implications for our understanding of interclass and interethnic relations in Israel. The questions I will seek to answer are (1) What accounts for the sudden surge in Mizrahi political mobilization in the mid-1980s? and (2) Why has this mobilization taken place under the religious ideological banner of Shas, rather than under some other ideological formula?

My consideration of the second question, especially, will be informed by Anne Swidler's suggestion that the causal significance of culture for political action does not lie in "defining ends of action" by supplying it with values and norms. Its significance lies, rather, in "providing cultural components [or "tool kits"] that are used to construct strategies of action." Thus, "Explaining cultural outcomes . . . requires not only understanding the direct influence

I am especially grateful to Michael Shalev and Sigal Kis for providing me with statistical data, and to Yaron Tsur, Shlomo Deshen, Moshe Shokeid, Yehuda Shenhav, Oren Yiftachel, the two editors of the present volume, and Horit Herman-Peled.

of ideology on action. It also requires explaining why one ideology rather than another triumphs (or at least endures). And such explanation depends on analyzing the structural constraints and historical circumstances within which ideological movements struggle for dominance" (1986, 273, 280).

Analyzing the "structural constraints and historical circumstances" behind the political-cultural phenomenon of Shas requires a theory that can (1) explain the persistence and growth of ethnic identification in a modernizing society, where both the prevailing assimilationist theories of ethnicity and the prevailing nation-building ideology predicted its gradual demise; and (2) offer a conceptualization of the relationship between social structure and political culture. I believe that a modified version of Michael Hechter's "cultural division of labor" model would be most suitable for this purpose (1975, 1978).[2]

The cultural division of labor (CDL) model posits a stratification system in which groups marked by cultural differences are located differentially along both the horizontal and the vertical axes. Vertical differentiation, or "segmentation," occurs to the extent that particular groups are occupationally specialized; horizontal differentiation, or "hierarchy," occurs to the extent that particular groups are concentrated at the lower or upper echelons of the occupational ladder (Hechter 1978). The location of a particular group within the CDL is not *determined* by its culture, however, but by the timing and circumstances of its encounter with industrialization. Cultural markers are used only to *identify* particular groups as belonging to particular niches in the CDL. Thus, "the task of perpetuating the structure of inequality falls to ideas about cultural and racial differences" (Verdery 1979, 378).

The more pronounced the CDL, the greater will be the tendency for ethnic solidarity to prevail over other forms of solidarity, for two reasons:

1. The rigidity of the CDL determines the extent to which members of culturally defined groups would interact with one another, rather than with members of other groups in society. Endogamous interaction leads to in-group solidarity and to the maintenance, or development, of distinctive cultural patterns.

2. The CDL is usually legitimated by an ideology of the cultural superiority of the dominant group in society. Thus, for the groups at the bottom of the ladder, a reassertion of their own cultural identity may serve as a counterideology, a vehicle for "socialization, as well as political mobilization, contrary to state ends" (Hechter 1975, 37; 1978).

Hechter's theory was designed to account for the persistence of ethnic boundaries between the core English region of Great Britain and its Celtic periphery. While it has since been applied in a number of different case studies (ERS 1979), these have been mostly cases where ethnic marginalization resulted in separatist ethnic organizing. In the case of Mizrahim, as I will show in this chapter, their structural marginalization did not result in heightened ethnic, that is, separatist consciousness, nor in the development of class consciousness. It resulted, rather, in a resurgence of integrative, politicized religious consciousness, which expresses itself, electorally, in voting for Shas.

The reason for this divergence from the model, I will argue, is that the Mizrahim in Israel are not a peripheral, but a *semiperipheral* group, located between the Ashkenazi Jews on top, and the Palestinians, both citizens and noncitizens, at the bottom.[3] Being in this intermediary position, the Mizrahim have sought to ally themselves with the Jewish state and with the Ashkenazim who control it, rather than with the Palestinians. As a result, Mizrahi protest has rarely taken an unambiguously conflictual stand in relation to the dominant Zionist ideology (cf. Yiftachel, forthcoming). It has assumed, rather, the form of integral Jewish nationalism and, in the case of Shas, of politicized Jewish religiosity. In both cases, the Mizrahim's oppositional consciousness has espoused the integrative aspects of the dominant ideology, while negating its (inter-Jewish) discriminatory elements.

As formulated by Hechter, the CDL model does not include a notion of semiperipheriality, nor does it allow for cases where ethnic consciousness takes an integrative, rather than a separatist form. It also ignores the possibility of the formation of ethnic class fractions, that is, the evolution of different kinds of reaction to peripherialization in the different strata within the peripheral ethnic group (see Ayalon, Ben-Rafael, and Sharot 1988, pp. 307–308; Peled 1989, 7–9, 135–136). The latter possibility is also relevant for the case under study here, since it is primarily the Mizrahim of the lower socioeconomic strata that have been voting for Shas. These lacunae, however, do not make the model irrelevant for these types of cases, or diminish its general usefulness. What they call for, rather, is a refinement of the model in ways that would make it sensitive to a wider range of ethnic phenomena. This, as I will show, can be done without in any way harming the overall logical thrust of the model, or its internal coherence.

To explain the electoral success of Shas in terms of the CDL model, I will

1. Show that a CDL indeed exists among Jews in Israel, with Mizrahim overrepresented, as against Ashkenazim, in low-income, low-status occupations; and

2. Explain why, of all the ideological "tool kits" currently available to Israeli Jewish voters, Shas's definition of Jewish collective identity, which stresses Jewish unity and solidarity, is preferred by increasing numbers of poor, working-class Mizrahim.

My key argument will be that the roots of Mizrahi discontent do not lie primarily in cultural maladjustment but, rather, in their economic and social peripherialization within Israeli society. Their vote for *Shas*, as for *Likud*, does not signify, therefore, a yearning to recapture a lost, primordial past. It constitutes, rather, a rejection of Labor Zionist ideology that has been utilized to legitimate their deprivation in the present (cf. Deshen 1994).

Ashkenazim and Mizrahim in the Cultural Division of Labor

The Israeli control system (Kimmerling 1989), which until recently included Israel and the occupied territories, was characterized by a fourfold CDL. Each of the four segmentally and hierarchically placed groups—Ashkenazim, Mizrahim, citizen Palestinians, and noncitizen Palestinians—had its own socioeconomic, as well as political-cultural profile. Since my concern in this chapter is to explain the political behavior of Mizrahim, I will focus on their particular location within this system of stratification. However, the broader division of labor must be kept in mind as the general context that made, and continues to make, the location of Mizrahim meaningful (Semyonov and Lewin-Epstein 1987; Shavit 1990; Lewin-Epstein and Semyonov 1993).

In a study of social mobility in Israel conducted in 1974 it was found that

> Almost 70 percent of [Mizrahi males are] concentrated in the areas of skilled, semiskilled, and unskilled labor, as well as in service occupations and agriculture. By . . . comparison, only about 45 percent of [Ashkenazi] males are engaged in these occupational areas. Nearly one-third of the [Ashkenazim] are found in the upper nonmanual occupations . . . whereas only one-tenth of [Mizrahi] males hold positions of this kind. . . . These basic differences between the two ethnic groups are replicated in each of the age cohorts. The greatest dissimilarity in occupational distribution is found among the *youngest* cohort. (Kraus and Hodge 1990, 66; emphasis added)

During the following decade and a half (until the onset of massive immigration from the former Soviet Union in the late 1980s),[4] all ethnic groups within Israel's 1967 borders improved their socioeconomic status. This improvement, however, did not change significantly the relative standing of the two Jewish ethnic groups (Cohen and Haberfeld 1998; Kashti 1997[5] Nahon 1993a, 1993b; Shalev and Kis, in this volume; Smooha 1993). Most of the gains made by Mizrahim in this period have been either outstripped by the gains made by Ashkenazim, such as in the areas of education, occupational status, or income, or else have been in fields that have declined in their social significance. See table 5.1.

Table 5.1   Selected Socioeconomic Characteristics by Ethnic Origin, Different Years

	Ashkenazim	Mizrahim
Occupational status (3 top Categories), 1988		
Foreign Born	40%	20%
Israel Born	50	21
Income, 1988	100	80
Income per capita, 1988	100	64
Employee income (Israel born ages 25–54):		
1975	100	79
1982	100	70
1992	100	68
1995	100	69
College graduates:		
1975	100	100
1982	100	83
1992	100	88
1995	100	78
Housing (less than one person per room), 1988		
Foreign Born	60	32
Israel Born	40	23
Education (Israel-born employees ages 25–54):		
Years of schooling:		
1975	12.8	9.9
1982	13.8	10.5
1992	14.2	11.6
1995	14.4	12.0
% College graduates:		
1975	25.0	6.0
1982	25.5	8.7
1992	38.0	10.3
1995	36.6	10.3

SOURCES: Smooha (1993); Cohen and Haberfeld (1998); Cohen (1998).

Two examples of the latter kind are the earning of *teudat bagrut* (high-school matriculation certificate) and of officer ranks in the military. Matriculation certificates were held by 28% of Mizrahi 18-year-olds in 1995, compared to 17% in 1987 (the corresponding figures for Ashkenazim were 38.7% and 31.6%, respectively). During this period, however, these certificates had lost their status as guarantors of automatic university admission.

Thus, of the 1986–1987 cohort of *bagrut* earners, 45% of Ashkenazim but only 30% of Mizrahim had gone on to postsecondary education by 1995 (Adler and Balas 1997, 136–137, 153n11; Kashti 1997d).[6] Similarly, the inroads apparently made by Mizrahim into the higher military[7] ranks have paralleled the decline in the status of the military due to the liberalization of Israeli society (Erez, Shavit, and Tsur 1993; Kashti 1997b; Peled 1993, 259–291; Peri 1999; Smooha 1984b).

In only two social fields—self-employment/small business ownership and politics—can the Mizrahim be said to have improved their standing in relation to Ashkenazim. The rate of the self-employed (including employers of others) in the two groups was equalized by 1983, at about 17%. Ashkenazim, however, still predominated among large business owners, and the income gap between the two groups, while smaller than among wage earners, was still meaningful and was larger among members of the second than of the first generation (Nahon 1993c, 80–81; see also Shavit and Yuchtman-Yaar 2000; Yaar 1986). In politics, both local and national, Mizrahi representation has increased, in both absolute and relative terms. Still, Mizrahim have not captured yet the mayorship of any of Israel's three largest cities, and their enhanced presence in the Knesset and in the cabinet, since the 1970s, has been coterminous with a sustained decline in government social services and in economic equality (Ben-Rafael and Sharot 1991, 35; Grinberg 1993; Kashti 1997c).

Development Towns

The persistent gap between Ashkenazim and Mizrahim in general masks a growing socioeconomic disparity among the Mizrahim themselves. About one third of Mizrahim can now be classified as belonging to the middle class, and they have been more or less integrated into the Ashkenazi mainstream of society (Ben-Rafael and Sharot 1991; Benski 1993). This class differentiation corresponds, to some degree, to people's continent of origin, whether they hailed from Asia, primarily Iraq, or from North Africa, primarily Morocco. The key intervening variable connecting continent of origin with current socioeconomic status is time of arrival in Israel. Asians arrived mostly in the early 1950s and settled primarily in central areas of the country. North Africans arrived in the late 1950s and early 1960s and many of them were settled in "development towns" located in outlying areas (Benski 1993; Lewin-Epstein, Elmelech, and Semyonov 1997; Lewin-Epstein and Semyonov 2000). This partial correspondence between time of arrival and extent of integration in the society lends credence to Hechter's argument that the position of different groups in the CDL is determined largely by the timing of their encounter with modern industrial society.

Shas draws most of its electoral support from development towns (DTs) and from the sociodemographically similar poor city neighborhoods. Until the massive immigration of Soviet Jews in the early 1990s, between 15 and 20 percent of Israel's population lived in DTs (DTs have been defined differently for different official purposes), where the population was, on the average, 75 percent Mizrahi. This made DTs home to between one quarter and one third of the country's Mizrahi Jews (Ben-Zadok 1993). Since the early 1990s the demographic composition of DTs has changed. Their population has been augmented by 20 percent, on the average, due to the settling of about 200,000 immigrants from the former Soviet Union. This has brought the ratio of Mizrahim in DTs to 61 percent only (Carmon and Yiftachel 1994; CBS 1994, 1996b, 112; Yiftachel and Tzafdia 2000).

Socially, as well as geographically, DTs form a peripheral "spatial sector" within Jewish Israeli society (Ben-Zadok 1993; Don-Yehiya 1990, 25; Yiftachel and Meir 1998). In 1987 the Central Bureau of Statistics (CBS) computed the socioeconomic status (SES) of every urban locality in the country (not including the occupied territories), based on data from the 1983 national census. On a scale of standardized scores combining sixteen different socioeconomic variables and running from -2 (lowest SES) to $+2$ (highest SES), the average score for all development towns was -0.40. This score placed development towns between the fifth and sixth SES clusters, out of 20, or below 70 percent of the entire population (CBS 1987; CBS 1995; cf. Heimberg (Shitrit) and Dor, 1994; Yiftachel and Tzafadia 1999; 2000).[8]

While DTs constitute distinct social and administrative units, they share many of their social and economic characteristics with the other major concentration of working class Mizrahim—the poor neighborhoods of large and medium-size cities. Thus, the claims made in this chapter about Mizrahim in DTs can be seen as applying, in a general way, to the working-class Mizrahi population as a whole.

Characteristics of Mizrahi Politics

In Israel, "the task of perpetuating the structure of inequality" between Ashkenazim and Mizrahim has indeed fallen "to ideas about cultural . . . differences." These ideas, which prevailed in the dominant socialist-Zionist ideology, in mainstream Israeli sociology, and in the public discourse, labeled the Mizrahim as less modern and less committed to Zionism then the Ashkenazim and, therefore, as less capable and less deserving of integrating into the mainstream of society (Levy and Emmerich, 2001; Peled 1998).

Generally speaking, Mizrahim have not reacted to their marginalization by trying to engage in political mobilization on the basis of either class or ethnicity. This divergence from the expectations of both modernization theory and the CDL model can be explained by two factors:

1. As a semiperipheral group, Mizrahim have been inclined to emphasize their similarity to the dominant Ashkenazi group rather than to the subordinate Palestinians, with whom they share many socioeconomic and cultural attributes.

2. Zionist ideology has always stressed the value of unity among Jews, and has militated against autonomous ethnic political (as opposed to cultural) organizations.

Already in the Ottoman (pre-1917) period, (Jewish) Yemenite workers were complaining bitterly about being treated by Ashkenazi employers and workers as if they were Arabs. Their solution, however, was not to organize themselves separately (let alone together with the Arabs), but to demand equality and integration with the Ashkenazim (Shafir 1989, 118–122). During the British Mandate (1922–1948) several Mizrahi and Sephardi[9] parties participated in elections to the institutions of the Yishuv, and had some electoral success. This was tolerated, even encouraged, by the Zionist leadership, because under Mandatory law, membership in the Yishuv was voluntary, and disgruntled groups could simply opt out. The Zionist movement had an obvious interest in having the Yishuv encompass all Jews in Palestine, and they were willing to make concessions not only to Mizrahi groups but to anti-Zionist Haredi groups as well. Furthermore, since Mizrahim constituted a relatively small and *declining* portion of the Jews in Palestine (from 40 to 20% in 1918–1948), ethnically based political parties were not seen by the dominant Labor Zionist movement as a political threat (Herzog 1984; Horowitz and Lissak 1989).

Things changed dramatically, however, with the massive influx of Mizrahi immigrants in the 1950s. With the Mizrahi portion of the population reaching and then exceeding 50%, the specter of their coming to dominate the society, either politically or culturally, became a matter of serious concern. Major efforts at delegitimizing "ethnic" political organizations were undertaken by the dominant Ashkenazi institutions, and indeed, political parties catering to Mizrahim had almost disappeared from Israel's political scene (Herzog, 1985, 1986, 1990; Lewis 1985; Smooha 1978, 86–94).

The few "ethnic" political parties that did exist after 1948 failed to draw significant electoral support (Herzog 1986, 1990). Rather, until 1973, over 50 percent of Mizrahi voters had been voting for the Labor Party, in its various manifestations. This reflected both their desire to identify with the dominant political force in the society, and the virtual stranglehold the Labor movement had, through its various social and economic institutions, on employment opportunities and on the provision of social services to the immigrants (Shalev 1990; Shapiro 1989). Between 1973 and 1996, however, over 50% of Mizrahi voters had been voting Likud (Shapiro 1989, 178).

The mid-1980s witnessed the beginning of a profound restructuring process in the Israeli economy. When Likud came to power in 1977 it embarked on an ambitious program of economic liberalization that was designed to do away with the corporatist political-economic structures on which Labor had based its power for the previous half-century. The only tangible results of these efforts, by the mid-1980s, was an annual inflation rate that reached 445% in 1984 (Shalev 1992, 240). In 1985, the national unity government in which both Likud and Labor shared power, instituted a harsh anti-inflationary program known as the "Emergency Economic Stabilization Plan." The plan not only brought inflation to a halt, at the price of economic slowdown, lower wages, and increased unemployment, but prepared the ground for the liberalization process that has since reshaped the Israeli economy (Shafir and Peled 2000; Shalev 1992).

The primary goal of the 1985 economic plan, beyond stopping inflation, was to smooth the way for Israel's integration into the process of economic globalization (Shafir and Peled 2000; forthcoming). As Peter Beyer has argued, globalization can have adverse economic and cultural effects on the weaker sectors of society, who often react by reasserting their particularistic sociocultural identities through nationalist or subnationalist movements. Furthermore,

> In some circumstances, religion has been, and continues to be, an important resource for such movements, yielding religio-political movements in places as diverse as Ireland, Israel, Iran, India, and Japan. Because of their emphasis on socio-cultural particularisms, such religious movements often display the conservative option [of opposing globalization] with its typical stress on the relativizing forces of globalization as prime manifestations of evil in the world. (1994, 108)[10]

The earliest appearance of such religio-political movements in Israel, catering specifically to poor Mizrahim and enjoying meaningful support in DTs, was in 1984. In that year both Shas and Meir Kahane's Kach movement made their debut on the national political scene. Shas won four Knesset seats in the general elections of 1984, while Kahane's 1.2% of the national vote entitled him to one seat only. In DTs, however, Shas and Kahane had an almost equal share of the vote, around 3.5% each (Shafir and Peled 1986). In 1988, based on my own preelection survey, 8.5% of the voters in DTs were planning to vote for Kahane (making his party the third-largest party there, after Likud and Labor) while Shas was expected only to retain its 3% of the vote (Peled 1990).

Kahane's appeal for his voters, almost universally Mizrahim of low socio-economic status, was based on his calling for the "transfer" of all Palestinians, citizens and noncitizens alike, out of Eretz yisrael. The idea of total transfer was attractive to Kahane's potential voters for two reasons. First, if carried out, it would have removed Palestinian workers as competitors in the labor market (Peled 1990). Second, and more importantly perhaps, by calling for the transfer of all Palestinians, citizens and noncitizens alike, Kahane articulated a notion of Palestinian (or "Arab") identity that transcended the question of citizenship. By doing this he also articulated, as in a mirror image, a notion of *Jewish* identity that transcended the question of citizenship as well (cf. Roediger 1991).

As Erik Cohen has argued, the Mizrahim had always claimed, as against official Zionist ideology, that "mere Jewishness, rather than the internalization of any particular Zionist or 'Israeli' values, attitudes, and patterns of behavior, [should be] sufficient for participation [in the center of Israeli society]" (1983, 121). In Beyer's terms, this was a reassertion of particularistic, traditional Jewish identity, as against the modernizing, universalizing elements in the dominant, Labor Zionist definition of Israeli citizenship. It is precisely this reassertion that was echoed in Kahane's rhetoric.

In the actual elections of 1988, from which Kahane had been barred (Peled 1992), the Haredi parties, primarily Shas and Agudat Israel, had more than *tripled* their strength in DTs, from 5% in 1984 to 18% in 1988, as against a doubling of their strength nationally. Shas itself received 8.7% of the vote in DTs, while both Likud and Labor lost support there and the extreme right-wing parties, espousing the territorially expansionist ideology of Gush Emunim, retained their relatively low levels of support (Ben-Zadok, 1993; Don-Yehiya 1990; the figures, here and elsewhere, may vary slightly due to the different definitions of DTs used by different authors). The Haredi parties were not calling for "transfer," but the notion of Jewish identity that transcends the issue of citizenship is central to their worldview. It was thus they, rather than the extreme right-wing parties, who were able to benefit from Kahane's removal from the race.

By 1992, the demographic composition of development towns had undergone drastic change by the settlement of immigrants from the former USSR. Support for religious parties was virtually nonexistent among these new voters (Fein 1995), and indeed the religious parties' share of the vote declined in DTs by close to 30% (from 21% in 1988 to 15% in 1992) (CBS 1993). This would seem to indicate, however, that the level of support for religious parties among *veteran* voters in DTs remained more or less constant. Unlike 1988, however, of the Haredi parties only Shas had a significant showing in DTs and among Mizrahim in general in 1992.

Several reasons have been adduced for the virtual disappearance of support for Agudat yisrael among poor and working class Mizrahim in 1992. But no knowledgeable observer has suggested that one of these reason was Agudat Israel's neglect of its Mizrahi voters' ethnic concerns. (In this respect these voters should be distinguished from the Haredi-Mizrahi core of Shas activists who had seceded from Agudat yisrael precisely for this reason) (Deshen 1994; Don-Yehiya 1990; Heilman 1990, 149–50; Horkin 1993; Willis 1995, 130–131). Be that as it may, the significant point is that, at least once, voters who are usually identified as belonging to Shas's constituency were willing to support a strictly Ashkenazi Haredi political party. This would seem to indicate that the appeal Shas has had for this type of voters is based on something it shares with other Haredi parties, rather than on something that distinguishes it from them.

What Shas shares with other Haredi parties is a concern for the enhancement of the role of Jewish religion in the public and private lives of Jews in Israel. The concrete meaning of its slogan, *le-hahazir atara le-yoshna* (Restore the Crown to Its Old Glory) is "synagogues, ritual baths, keeping the Sabbath, yeshivot, torah schools, and the Wellspring" (*maayan ha-hinuch hatorani,* Shas's all-important elementary educational system) (Horkin 1993; Willis 1995, 123). The goals of El-ha-maayan, Shas's adult educational system, as stated in its incorporation by-laws, are "to promote the traditional and Jewish values of religious Jewry in Israel; . . . to promote religious Jewish education in the educational system in Israel; . . . to improve religious services; . . . to help improve the quality of religious life; . . . to supply the religious needs of haredi religious Jewry. . . ." (Horkin 1993, 82–83). It would be very difficult to find, in Shas's official pronouncements, political demands that refer specifically to Mizrahi culture. Students of Shas have even compared its political goals to those of the pre-1967 (mostly Ashkenazi) National Religious Party, before the latter had turned into an ultranationalist party (Heilman 1990, 146–147; Levy 1995, 129; Willis 1995, 134; Zohar, 2001).

In making this point I am not trying to suggest that Shas does not have its own unique characteristics or that it is not concerned with the plight of its Mizrahi constituency. My argument, rather, is that Shas was able to define the concerns of its constituency in terms of general Jewish religious concerns, and in this way organize its constituency around an integrative, rather than a separatist message (cf. Hen 1995; Herzog 1990, 108–111; 1995, 88; Levy and Emmerich, 2001; Zohar, 2001). Ezra Nissani, an important Shas operative, has described Shas as a movement that articulates the interests of the "popular strata." These strata have been excluded from the center of Israeli society and seek to transform that society, in order to take their

rightful place in it. They include "mizrahim, haredim and national minorities" (i.e., citizen Palestinians) and the values of the Jews among them are
"traditional-religious Jewish" values. Thus, restoration of these values, rather
than specifically Mizrahi values, however defined, is presented as a remedy for
both the cultural and the socioeconomic plight of mizrahim (1996).

In the 1999 elections Mizrahim of low socioeconomic status responded
to the Shas formula in unprecedented numbers. In DTs Shas became, in 1999,
the largest political party, with 22% of the vote. (In 1996 Shas came in second in DTs, after Likud.) In moshavim populated by Mizrahim (where the
population is ethnically more homogeneous than in DTs) Shas received 29%
of the vote. In the general electorate Likud lost to Shas the status it had enjoyed since 1977, that of the largest Mizrahi party (Shalev and Kis, in this
volume). As can be seen in figures 5.1 and 5.2, in both 1996 and 1999 the
vote for Shas in the different statistical areas (SAs), when these are divided
into quintiles by the affluence of their residents, was positively related to the
share of Mizrahim in the population and negatively related to their level of affluence.[11] These voting patterns were almost identical in 1996 and 1999,
with the vote for Shas in each quintile usually higher by about 50% in 1999
than it was in 1996. The rates of increase in the Shas vote in 1999 were also
positively related to the share of Mizrahim in the population of the different
SAs, and negatively related to their level of affluence. Among non-Haredi
Ashkenazim support for Shas is very low in the poorest SAs (reflecting, probably, the Ashkenazi Haredim who do live there) and nonexistent in the more
affluent ones. Shas has been, and remains, clearly the political party of poor
Mizrahim (and not of North-Africans, as is sometimes claimed). Whereas in
mizrahi SAs where economic conditions are reasonably decent the Shas vote
equals the national average (about 11% in 1996 and 14% in 1999), in the
poorest ones it is double that rate.

Conclusion

Shas's electoral success has been commonly interpreted as a separatist reaction
against the denigration of traditional Mizrahi culture by the Ashkenazi-
dominated institutions of Israeli society (Deshen 1994, 55–56; Don-Yehiya
1997). Thus, in concluding his anthropological study of Shas's performance
in the 1992 elections, Aaron P. Willis observed that "Shas has been innovative, forging a generic Sephardic identity, which even mixes Ashkenazi styles,
rather than arguing for a return to particularistic regional customs" (1995,
136). Willis is correct in pointing out that Shas is not a movement that looks
back to some primordial past. Indeed, Mizrahim (Sephardim in his terms)
as a group do not possess such a past; they crystallized into one collectivity
only in Israel, out of many disparate Jewish groups originating in a number of

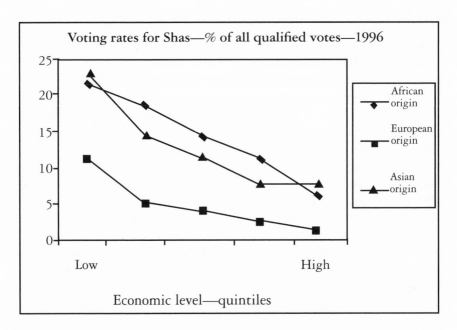

Figure 5.1

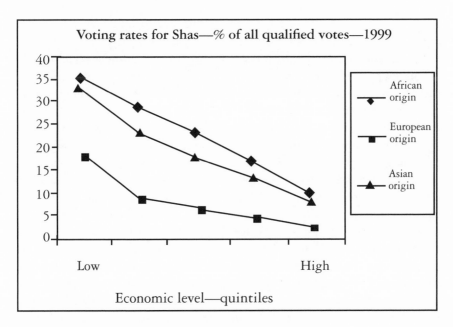

Figure 5.2

111

different countries. Willis, however, misses the fact that the identity that Shas is seeking to forge is an integrative Jewish identity, rather that a particularistic, Mizrahi identity.

Shas is indeed seeking to forge this identity against a dominant "other." That other, however, is not the Ashkenazim in general but the Zionist, especially Labor Zionist establishment that has marginalized Mizrahim since the beginning of Zionist settlement in Palestine. Being Ashkenazi is only one, though crucially important, characteristic of this establishment. Shas's political wisdom, and the secret of its success, lie precisely in its ability to direct the resentment of its constituency not against the Ashkenazi, but against the secular, modernizing component of the dominant culture. In counterposing Jewish, rather than Mizrahi identity to this dominant culture, Shas has provided its followers with an integrative, rather than a separatist principle of organizing "contrary to state aims." Rather than negating Israeli Jewish nationalism as defined by the Zionist establishment, Shas has sought to redefine it.

Since the message of Shas is not a particularistic, Mizrahi message, and since the majority of Shas voters have not been religiously orthodox, the appeal that Shas has had for so many Mizrahi voters cannot be explained at the level of culture alone. The explanation must be looked for at the level of the sociodemographic characteristics of Shas voters, hence at the level of the social structures that shape these characteristics.

While I find the CDL model I have employed very helpful for understanding Mizrahi political mobilization, there are two difficulties in applying it to the particular case of Shas: (1) The political-cultural formula espoused by Shas is not particularistic, but rather integrative with respect to the dominant "other"; and (2) the constituency mobilized by Shas does not encompass the entire relevant ethnic group, but only its lower socioeconomic strata. Both of these difficulties can be overcome by making the CDL model a little bit more flexible without harming the internal coherence of the model in any way.

As originally formulated, the CDL model posits a two-sided interaction, between a core and a peripheral group. In this situation, the greater the distance between the two groups, the more likely is the peripheral one to develop its own distinct culture. If another factor is added to this scheme, such that the group under discussion is faced not with one "other," but with two— a dominant and a subordinate "other"—the model should logically expect the group to develop a different kind of identity. Depending on the specific circumstances of the case, the group, which is now a semiperipheral group, can ally itself either with the group above it or with the group below it. In Israel, where Jewishness is the most important attribute defining membership in the society, it is not surprising that Mizrahim should opt to ally themselves with the dominant, Ashkenazi group, with whom they share their Jewishness, rather than with the Palestinians, with whom they share elements of the Arab culture commonly associated with the enemy.

As to the issue of ethnic class fractions, this can also be added to the model without too much difficulty. If, as claimed by the CDL model, the extent of hierarchy and segmentation shapes the collective consciousness of ethnic groups, it stands to reason that strata within ethnic groups that are affected differentially by hierarchy and segmentation would develop different forms of group consciousness. Thus, in Israel, Mizrahim who are relatively better off tend to join their Ashkenazi counterparts in voting Labor, those in an intermediate position tend to vote for Likud, while, as I have shown, the ones placed at the bottom of the socioeconomic ladder tend to vote for Shas (see Ben-Rafael and Sharot 1991, 189; Schmeltz, Dellapergola and Avner 1991, 100; Shalev and Kis, in this volume).

Notes

1. But the increase in Shas's Knesset representation fell short of the formula by which it had increased in all of the past national elections in which Shas had participated, except that of 1992—doubling, minus two, of the size of its delegation in the previous Knesset. By that formula Shas should have had eighteen members in the fifteenth Knesset, as was indeed predicted by Aryeh Deri.

2. For surveys of theories of ethnicity and their application to the Israeli context, see Zureik (1979, 8–30); Smooha (1984a); and Ben-Rafael and Sharot (1991, 36–53).

3. Noncitizen Palestinians were included in the Israeli control system until the establishment of the Palestinian Authority in the mid-1990s. Their current situation vis-à-vis Israeli society is both ambiguous and fluid. The most influential body of work utilizing the CDL model and treating Mizrahim as a peripheral group was done by Swirski and his associates. They predicted, indeed called for, separate Mizrahi organizing in all facets of social life, a prediction that has not materialized. See, for instance, Bernstein and Swirski (1982); Swirski (1984, 1989); and Swirski and Shoushan (1986).

4. These newly arriving immigrants, the vast majority of them Ashkenazim, have joined the society close to the bottom of the socioeconomic ladder. Since the early 1990s, therefore, the only comparison that is relevant for understanding the relative position of Mizrahim is that between second-generation members of the two groups.

5. Between April and October 1997, Ur Kashti published a series of reports in *Ha'aretz,* covering many aspects of the "ethnic gap" between Ashkenazim and Mizrahim. Three of the reports appeared in English as well (Kashti 1997f). Specific references will be made here only to articles actually cited.

6. Due to the military service required of Israeli Jews, two years for women and three years for men, there is normally a gap of a few years between graduating high school and starting postsecondary education.

7. The Israeli military does not release the ethnic composition of its personnel, so that all observations in this matter are educated guesses only.

8. The relative placing of development towns would have been much lower had the calculation been made for the Jewish population only; see Khalidi (1988, 133–138). A few Palestinian communities indeed scored below −2, the lowest end of the scale. Using the 1983 data is more appropriate for this study, because they were collected before the large-scale settling of formerly Soviet Jews in DTs.

9. For the distinction between the terms Sephardi and Mizrahi see Swirski (1984) and Ben-Rafael and Sharot (1991, 24–25).

10. I think Beyer's characterization of these movements is correct, and applicable to Israel. The movement he chose to focus on in Israel, however, *Gush Emunim,* is not a case in point. One indication of this is that *Gush Emunim,* and the political parties that express its agenda, do not enjoy much support among the poorer strata of Israeli society. The Israeli religio-political movement that fits Beyer's analysis is Shas.

11. For definitions of the variables and the method of calculation see Shalev and Kis, in this volume. I am grateful to Shalev and Kis for the calculations they made especially for this chapter and for allowing me to consult their findings before publication.

References

Adler, Hayim, and Nahum Balas 1997. "Inequality in Education in Israel." In *The Allocation of Resources for Social Services in Israel, 1996.* Jerusalem: Center for the Study of Social Policy in Israel, 121–155 (Hebrew).

Ayalon, Hanna, Eliezer, Ben-Rafael, and Stephen Sharot. 1988. "The Impact of Stratification: Assimilation or Ethnic Solidarity." *Research in Social Stratification and Mobility* 7: 305–326.

Ben-Rafael, Eliezer, and Stephen Sharot. 1991. *Ethnicity, Religion and Class in Israeli Society,* Cambridge: Cambridge University Press.

Ben-Zadok, Efraim, 1993. "Oriental Jews in Development Towns: Ethnicity, Economic Development, Budgets and Politics." In Efraim Ben-Zadok (ed.). *Local Communities and the Israeli Polity: Conflict of Values and Interests.* Albany: State University of New York Press, 91–122.

Benski, Tova. 1993. "Testing Melting-Pot Theories in the Jewish Israeli Context." *Sociological Papers* (Sociological Institute for Community Studies, Bar-Ilan University) 2, no. 2: 1–46.

Berstein, Deborah, and Shlomo Swirski. 1982. "The Rapid Economic Development of Israel and the Emergence of the Ethnic Division of Labor." *British Journal of Sociology* 33, no. 1: 64–85.

Beyer, Peter. 1994. *Religion and Globalization.* London: Sage.

Bilsky, Leora. 2001. "'J'Accuse'—The Deri Trial, Political Trial and Collective Memory." In Yoav Peled, ed., 2001 *Restore the Crown to Its Ancient Glory? Shas—The First Fifteen Years.* Tel Aviv: Yediot (Hebrew).

Carmon, Naomi, and Oren Yiftachel. 1994. *Israel's Population: Basic Data and Projections for Spatial Policy.* Haifa: Center for Urban and Regional Research, The Technion (Hebrew).

CBS. 1987. *Classification of Geographical Units according to the Socio-Economic Characteristics of the Population (1983 Census of Population and Housing Publications,* 15). Jerusalem: State of Israel, Central Bureau of Statistics (Hebrew).

―――. 1993. *Results of the Elections to the 13th Knesset.* Vol. 1. Jerusalem: State of Israel, Central Bureau of Statistics (Hebrew).

―――. 1994. *Special Supplement to Statistical Yearbook.* Jerusalem: State of Israel, Central Bureau of Statistics (Hebrew).

―――. 1995. *Characterization and Ranking of Local Authorities according to the Population's Socio-Economic Level in 1995.* Jerusalem: State of Israel, Central Bureau of Statistics (Hebrew).

―――. 1996a. *Statistical Abstract of Israel.* Jerusalem: State of Israel, Central Bureau of Statistics.

―――. 1996b. *Population in Localities: Demographic Characteristics by Geographical Divisions.* Jerusalem: State of Israel, Central Bureau of Statistics (Hebrew).

―――. 1997. *Income Survey 1996.* Jerusalem: State of Israel, Central Bureau of Statistics (Hebrew).

―――. 1999a. *Israel Statistical Yearbook, 1999.* Jerusalem: State of Israel, Central Bureau of Statistics (Hebrew).

―――. 1999b. "Percentage of College Graduates in Urban Localities." *Press Releases* www.cbs/gov.il/hodaot1999/99_20tb2.htm.

Cohen, Erik. 1983. "Ethnicity and Legitimation in Contemporary Israel." *Jerusalem Quarterly.* no. 28: 111–124.

Cohen, Yinon. 1998. "Socioeconomic Gaps Between Mizrachim and Ashkenazim, 1975–1995," *Israel Sociology* 1, no. 1, pp. 115–134.

―――, and Yitzak Haberfeld. 1998. "Second-Generation Immigrants in Israel: Have the Ethnic Gaps in Schooling and Earnings Declined?" *Ethnic and Racial Studies* 21, no. 3: 507–528.

Deshen, Shlomo. 1994. "The Religiosity of the *Mizrahim:* Public, Rabbis and Faith." *Alpayim.* no. 9: 44–58 (Hebrew).

Don-Yehiya, Eliezer. 1990. "Religiosity and Ethnicity in Israeli Politics: The Religious Parties and the Elections to the Twelfth Knesset." *Medina, Mimshal Vihasim Benleumiyim.* no. 32: 11–54 (Hebrew).

―――. 1997. "Religion, Ethnicity, and Electoral Reform: The Religious Parties in the 1996 Elections." *Israel Affairs* 4, no. 1: 73–102.

Erez, Yossi, Yossi Shavit, and Dorit Tsur. 1993. "Is There Ethnic Inequality in Promotion Opportunities in the IDF?" *Megamot* 35, no. 1: 23–37 (Hebrew).

ERS. 1979. *Ethnic and Racial Studies* (special issue: internal colonialism) 2, no. 3.

Fein, Aharon. 1995. "Voting Trends of Recent Immigrants from the Former Soviet Union." In Asher Arian and Michal Shamir (eds.). *The Elections in Israel, 1992.* Albany: State University of New York Press, 161–174.

Grinberg, Lev L. 1993. "Peripheral Ethnicity: Trends in Local Representation." In
    S. N. Eisenstadt, Moshe Lissak, and Yaacov Nahon (eds.). *Ethnic Communities
    in Israel—Socio-Economic Status,* Jerusalem: Jerusalem Institute for Israel
    Studies, 103–119 (Hebrew).
Hechter, Michael. 1975. *Internal Colonialism: The Celtic Fringe in British National De-
    velopment, 1536–1966.* London: Routledge and Kegan Paul.
———. 1978. "Group Formation and the Cultural Division of Labor." *American
    Journal of Sociology* 84, no. 2: 293–318.
Heilman, Samuel C. 1990. "The Orthodox, the Ultra-Orthodox, and the Elections
    for the Twelfth Knesset." In Asher Arian and Michal Shamir (eds.). *The Elec-
    tions in Israel, 1988.* Boulder, CO: Westview, 135–153.
Heimberg (Shitrit) Soli, and Isachar Dor. 1994. *Characterization and Ranking of Local
    Authorities by the Socio-Economic Level of Their Population in 1992.* Jerusalem:
    State of Israel, Ministry of Construction and Housing and Ministry of the
    Interior (Hebrew).
Hen, Ezra. 1995. "The Purposes and Goals of Shas's Educational System." Master's
    thesis, Tel Aviv University (Hebrew).
Herzog, Hanna. 1984. "Ethnicity as a Product of Political Negotiation: The Case of
    Israel." *Ethnic and Racial Studies* 7, no. 4: 517–533.
———. 1985. "Social Construction of Reality in Ethnic Terms: The Case of Political
    Ethnicity in Israel." *International Review of Modern Sociology* 15, no. 1: 45–61.
———. 1986. "Political Factionalism: The Case of Ethnic Lists in Israel." *Western
    Political Quarterly* 39, no. 2: 285–303.
———. 1990. "Midway between Political and Cultural Ethnicity: Analysis of the
    "Ethnic Lists" in the 1984 Elections." In Daniel J. Elazar and Shmuel San-
    dler (eds.). *Israel's Odd Couple: The 1984 Knesset Elections and the National
    Unity Government.* Detroit: Wayne State University Press, 87–118.
———. 1995. "Penetrating the System: The Politics of Collective Identities." In
    Asher Arian and Michal Shamir (eds.), *The Elections in Israel* 1992. Albany:
    State University of New York Press, 81–102.
Horkin, Amir. 1993. "Political Mobilization, Ethnicity, Religiosity and Voting for
    the *Shas* Movement." Master's thesis, Tel Aviv University (Hebrew).
Horowitz, Dan, and Moshe Lissak. 1989. *Trouble in Utopia: The Overburdened Polity of
    Israel.* Albany: State University of New York Press.
Kashti, Ur. 1997. "The Ethnic Gap," *Ha'aretz,* various dates, April–October (Hebrew).
———. 1997a. "A Clear Class Division." *Ha'aretz,* May 13 (Hebrew).
———. 1997b. "The Melting Pot Is Not Functioning." *Ha'aretz,* May 14 (Hebrew).
———. 1997c. "Still a Curiosity." *Ha'aretz,* June 1 (Hebrew).
———. 1997d. "More Units, More *Ashkenazim,*" *Ha'aretz,* June 17 (Hebrew).
———. 1997e. "First to Go Home," *Ha'aretz,* July 15 (Hebrew).
———. 1997f. "The Ethnic Gap," *News from Within* 12, no. 8, 23–27.
———. 1997g. "The Secure Center," *Ha'aretz,* July 8 (Hebrew).
Khalidi, Raja. 1988. *The Arab Economy in Israel: The Dynamics of a Region's Development.*
    London: Croom Helm.

Kimmerling, Baruch. 1989. "Boundaries and Frontiers of the Israeli Control System: Analytical Conclusions." In Baruch Kimmerling (ed.). *The Israeli State and Society: Boundaries and Frontiers.* Albany: State University of New York Press, 265–284.

Kraus, Vered, and Robert W. Hodge. 1990. *Promises in the Promised Land.* New York: Greenwood.

Levy, Gal. 1995. "'And Thanks to the Ashkenazim. . . .' The Politics of Mizrahi Ethnicity in Israel." Master's thesis, Tel Aviv University (Hebrew).

Levy, Gal, and Emmerich Zeev. Forthcoming. "From 'Natural Workers' to '*Sephardi-Haredim*': Ethnic Politics Between Labeling and Identity." In Yoav Peled, ed., 2001 *Restore the Crown to Its Ancient Glory? Shas—The First Fifteen Years.* Tel Aviv: Yediot (Hebrew).

Lewin-Epstein, Noah, and Moshe Semyonov. 1993. *The Arab Minority in Israel's Economy: Patterns of Ethnic Inequality.* Boulder, CO: Westview.

———. and ———. 2000. "Inequality in Home Ownership in Israel: Effects of Migration and Intergenerational Reproduction," a paper presented at the Second Taiwan-Israel Sociological Workshop, Taipei, Taiwan.

Lewin-Epstein, Noah, Yuval Elmelech, and Moshe Semyonov. 1997. "Ethnic Inequality in Home Ownership and the Value of Housing: The Case of Immigrants in Israel." *Social Forces* 75, no. 4: 1439–1462.

Lewis, Arnold. 1985. "Phantom Ethnicity: "Oriental Jews" in Israeli Society." In Alex Weingrod (ed.), *Studies in Israeli Ethnicity.* New York: Gordon and Breach, 58–133.

Nahon, Yaacov. 1993a. "Educational Expansion and the Structure of Occupational Opportunities." In S. N. Eisenstadt, Moshe Lissak, and Yaacov Nahon (eds.), *Ethnic Communities in Israel—Socio-Economic Status.* Jerusalem: Jerusalem Institute for Israel Studies, 33–49 (Hebrew).

———. 1993b. "Occupational status." In S. N. Eisenstadt, Moshe Lissak, and Yaacov Nahon (eds.), *Ethnic Communities in Israel—Socio-Economic Status.* Jerusalem: Jerusalem Institute for Israel Studies, 50–75 (Hebrew).

———. 1993c. "Self-Employed Workers." In S. N. Eisenstadt, Moshe Lissak. and Yaacov Nahon (eds.), *Ethnic Communities in Israel—Socio-Economic Status.* Jerusalem: Jerusalem Institute for Israel Studies, 76–89 (Hebrew).

National Insurance Institute. 1996. *Annual Survey 1995/96* Jerusalem: National Insurance Institute.

———. 2000. *Annual Survey 1998/99.* Jerusalem: National Insurance Institute.

Nissani, Ezra. 1996. "Teach the Children of the Poor to Fish." *Ha'aretz,* August 11, 1996 (Hebrew).

Peled, Alon. 1993. "Soldiers Apart: A Study of Ethnic-Military Manpower Policies in Singapore, Israel and South Africa." Ph.D. diss., Harvard University.

Peled, Yoav. 1989. *Class and Ethnicity in the Pale: The Political Economy of Jewish Workers' Nationalism in Late Imperial Russia.* Basingstoke, Engl.: Macmillan.

———. 1990. "Ethnic Exclusionism in the Periphery: The Case of Oriental Jews in Israel's Development Towns." *Ethnic and Racial Studies* 13, no. 3: 345–367.

————. 1992. "Ethnic Democracy and the Legal Construction of Citizenship: Arab Citizens of the Jewish State." *American Political Science Review* 86, no. 2: 432–443.

————. 1998. "Towards a Redefinition of Jewish Nationalism in Israel? The Enigma of *Shas.*" *Ethnic and Racial Studies* 21, no. 4: 703–727.

————. ed., 2001. *Restore the Crown to its Ancient Glory? Shas—The First Fifteen Years,* Tel Aviv: Yediot (Hebrew).

Peri, Yoram. 1999. "Society-Military Relations in Israel in Crisis." *Megamot* 39, no. 4: 375–399.

Plotzker, Sever. 1999a. "Only 4 Percent Really Swing." *Yediot Aharonot,* April 30.

————. 1999b. "Much Ado about Nothing." *Yediot Aharonot,* May 7.

————. 1999c. "The Polls: Where Were We Right, Where Were We Wrong." *Yediot Aharonot,* May 20.

Roediger, David R. 1991. *The Wages of Whiteness: Race and the Making of the American Working Class.* London: Verso.

Schmelz, Uziel O., Sergio Dellapergola, and Uri Avner. 1991. *Ethnic Differences among Israeli Jews: A New Look.* Jerusalem: Institute of Contemporary Jewry, Hebrew University.

Semyonov, Moshe and Noah Lewin-Epstein. 1987. *Hewers of Wood and Drawers of Water: Non-Citizen Arabs in the Israeli Labor Market.* Ithaca, NY: Cornell University, ILR Press.

Shafir, Gershon. 1989. *Land, Labor and the Origins of the Israeli-Palestinian Conflict, 1882–1914.* Cambridge: Cambridge University Press.

Shafir, Gershon, and Yoav Peled. 1986. "'Thorns in Your Eyes': The Socioeconomic Basis of the Kahane Vote." In Asher Arian and Michal Shamir (eds.). *The Elections in Israel—1984.* Tel Aviv: Ramot, 115–130.

————. eds. 2000. *The New Israel: Peacemaking and Liberalization.* Boulder: Westview.

————. Forthcoming. *Between Colonialism and Democracy: The Dynamics of Citizenship in Israel.* Cambridge: Cambridge University Press.

Shalev, Michael. 1990. "The Political Economy of Labor-Party Dominance and Decline in Israel." In T. J. Pempel (ed.). *Uncommon Democracies.* Ithaca, NY: Cornell University Press, 83–127.

————. 1992. *Labour and the Political Economy in Israel,* Oxford: Oxford University Press.

Shapiro, Yonathan. 1989. *Chosen to Command: The Road to Power of the Herut Party— A Socio-Political Interpretation.* Tel Aviv: Am Oved (Hebrew).

Shavit, Yossi. 1990. "Segregation, Tracking, and the Educational Attainment of Minorities: Arabs and Mizrahi Jews in Israel." *American Sociological Review* 55, no. 1: 115–126.

Shavit, Yossi, and Efraim Yuchtman-Yaar. 2000. "Self-Employment and Social Mobility in Israel," a paper presented at the Second Taiwan-Israel Sociological Workshop, Taipei, Taiwan.

Shokeid, Moshe. 1984. "Cultural Ethnicity in Israel: The Case of Middle Eastern Jews' religiosity." *AJS Review* 9, no. 2: 247–271.

Smooha, Sammy. 1978. *Israel: Pluralism and Conflict.* Berkeley: University of California Press.

———. 1984a. "Three Perspectives in the Sociology of Ethnic Relations in Israel." *Megamot* 28, no. 2–3: 169–206 (Hebrew).

———. 1984b. "Ethnicity and the Military in Israel: Theses for Discussion and Study." *Medina, mimshal vihasim benleumiyim,* no. 22: 5–32 (Hebrew).

———. 1993. "Class, Ethnic, and National Cleavages and Democracy in Israel." In Ehud Sprinzak and Larry Diamond (eds.). *Israeli Democracy Under Stress.* Boulder, CO: Lynne Rienner, 309–342.

Swidler, Anne. 1986. "Culture in Action: Symbols and Strategies." *American Sociological Review* 51: 273–286.

Swirski, Shlomo. 1984. "The *Mizrachi* Jews in Israel: Why Many Tilted Toward Begin?" *Dissent* 31 no. 134: 77–91.

———. 1989. *The Oriental Majority.* London: Zed.

Swirski, Shlomo, and M. Shoushan. 1986. *The Development Towns of Israel: Towards A Brighter Tomorrow,* Haifa: Breirot (Hebrew).

Verdery, Katherine. 1979. "Internal Colonialism in Austria-Hungary." *Ethnic and Racial Studies* 2, no. 3: 378–399.

Willis, Aaron P. 1995. "*Shas*—the Sephardic Torah Guardians: Religious 'Movement' and Political Power." In Asher Arian and Michal Shamir (eds.). *The Elections in Israel, 1992.* Albany: State University of New York Press, pp.

Yaar, Efraim. 1986. "Private Enterprise as an Avenue of Socioeconomic Mobility in Israel: Another Aspect of Ethnic Stratification in Israel." *Megamot* 29, no. 4: 393–412.

Yiftachel, Oren. Forthcoming. *The Making of an Ethno-Class: Policy, Protest and Identity in Israeli Development Towns.* Beer Sheva: Negev Center for Regional Development, Ben-Gurion University (Working Paper no. 10).

Yiftachel, Oren, and Avinoam Meir (eds.). 1998. *Ethnic Frontiers and Peripheries: Landscapes of Development and Inequality in Israel.* Boulder, CO: Westview.

Yiftachel, Oren, and Erez Tzfadia. 1999. *Policy and Identity in Development Towns: The Case of North-African Immigrants, 1952–1998.* Beer Sheva: Ben Gurion University, Negev Center for Regional Development.

———. 2000. "Political Mobilization in Development Towns: Struggle for Control of Place." Paper presented at the 2000 annual conference of the Israeli Political Science Association.

Zohar, Zvi. 2001. "Ovadia's Vision—'Restore the Crown to its Ancient Glory.'" In Yoav Peled, ed., *Restore the Crown to Its Ancient Glory? Shas—The First Fifteen Years.* Tel Aviv: Yediot (Hebrew).

Zureik, Elia T. 1979. *The Palestinians in Israel: A Study in Internal Colonialism.* London: Routledge & Kegan Paul.

6

Israel as an Ethnic State
The Arab Vote

AS'AD GHANEM AND SARAH OZACKY-LAZAR

Introduction

Arab citizens comprise about 11 percent of the Israeli electorate—a substantial bloc in terms of its latent potential, especially for the Israeli Left, which cannot gain power without Arab votes. Preparations for the elections among the Arabs began as soon as the motion was passed to bring forward the elections to the Fifteenth Knesset to May 1999, some eighteen months before they were due. As in the past, the election campaign was a stormy arena of political debates between parties as well as individuals and public activity in all Arab localities. These preparations were overshadowed by two fundamental facts:

1. The right-wing government and the increase in domestic ferment: The Likud government three-year rule marked a regression in official policy toward the Arabs; this was especially apparent after four years of the Rabin-Peres government, which worked to attain parity between Jews and Arabs in financial allocations, and in some cases even practiced affirmative action in favor of the Arabs (Sikkuy 1996). The change reflected in various categories in the socioeconomic and political fields (see more details in Sikkuy 1999), created a charged atmosphere among the Arab population and leadership, frustration, and hostility toward the government.

2. The suspension of the peace process: The right-wing government headed by Benjamin Netanyahu brought the peace process to an almost complete halt. The hardening of the Israeli position, with the stubborn refusal of Netanyahu and his government to implement Israeli commitments under the Oslo agreement, disappointed the Arab leadership and the public in Israel. A sense of frustration and distress prevailed as they followed the suspension of the process with grave concern. Like the other Palestinians they

laid the blame for the situation on the government and looked forward to the opportunity to vote netanyahu and his Likud government out of office.

These were the main parameters of the environment in which the elections to the Fifteenth Knesset took place. They constitute the key factors that explain the electoral behavior of the Arabs in the 1999 elections.

Two competing approaches to the electoral strength of the Arabs and their ability to influence decision and policy making can be found in the literature. The first is based on studies that claim that the Arabs' electoral strength is growing and that it gained a significant degree of influence over decision making, in both domestic and foreign matters that means a considerable advance in their civil status (Nueberger 1993; Ozacky-Lazar 1992; Smooha and Peretz 1993).

The second approach maintains that the Israeli Left has a strong commitment to the Jewish-Zionist state and to the preservation of exclusive Jewish control of major state institutions, lest Arab participation should alter the state's Jewish-Zionist character. For this reason the Israeli Left has seen fit to steer Arabs away from the main power centers, including the government. It is willing to use Arab votes as an electoral bulwark against the Right in order to win power, but unwilling to view them and their representatives as full partners. Both Left and Right in Israel hold that decision making should be solely in Jewish hands; therefore the vision of an emerging post-Zionist and civil society in Israel (Ram 1999) is not valid (Ghanem 1997).

A study of the 1999 election campaign and the Arabs' role in it provides another opportunity to verify or refute the two views. We shall present various aspects of the elections with regard to the Palestinian-Arab minority in Israel, and formulate some conclusions as to the validity of these approaches.

Preparations for the Elections: The Parties that Competed and the Discussion about the Race for Prime Minister

As in 1996, the May 1999 elections were contested on two tracks—for the Knesset and for prime minister. The Arabs, like the other voting groups, were not of one mind with regard to the two tracks. We shall briefly review the political forces that competed for Arab votes in 1999.

Parties Competing for the Arab Vote

As in the previous elections, Jewish-Zionist parties from all the political spectrum (right, left, center, religious, and secular) competed for Arab votes, along with nationalist or religious Arab parties and one Arab-Jewish party, the Democratic Front for Peace and Equality (DFPE), which for the purposes of our discussion can be classified as an Arab party.

Table 6.1   Distribution of the Arab Vote in Knesset Elections, 1949–1999

Knesset year	Valid votes	Participation %	ICP and DFPE	PLP	NDA	DAP and Islamic Movement	Arab lists	Labor Party	Other Zionist parties	Total
1949	26,332	79	22			28	10	40		100
1951	58,984	86	16			55	11	18		100
1955	77,979	90	15			48	14	23		100
1959	81,764	85	11			42	10	37		100
1961	86,843	83	22			40	10	28		100
1965	106,346	82	23			38	13	26		100
1969	117,190	80	28			40	17	15		100
1973	133,058	73	37			27	17	19		100
1977	145,925	74	50			16	11	23		100
1981	164,862	68	37			12	29	22		100
1984*	199,968	72	32	18			-	26	24	100
1988	241,601	74	33	14		11	-	16	25	100
1992	273,920	70	23	9		15	-	20	33	100
1996**	307,497	77	38			27	-	18	17	100
1999	321,201	75	22		17	31		8	22	100

SOURCE: *Ozacky-Lazar and Ghanem (1996) and researchers' calculations in 1999.*

*The Progressive List first appeared in 1984, when it won about 18 percent of the Arab vote; in the 1988 elections it won about 15 percent, and in the 1992 elections it won about 9 percent of the Arab vote.

**In 1996 the DFPE ran on a joint list with the NDA (National-Democratic Alignment), and on the DAP on a joint list with the Islamic movement.

123

All the Jewish parties targeted Arab voters and worked hard to persuade them to vote for them. One Israel called on Arabs to vote for its Knesset list and for its candidate for prime minister, Ehud Barak. It set up a special team to attract voters in the Arab sector, headed by MK Yossi Beilin, known for his dovish positions on the peace process and support for improving the government's attitude toward the Arabs. The Labor Party was also associated with efforts to increase the voter turnout among the Arabs, recommending to American Jewish funders to provide financial support to the al-Ahali Association, set up before the elections in order to encourage Arab citizens to vote and increase their participation. In addition, the party maintained a presence in the Arab press, through paid advertisements and long interviews with its central figures.[1] The Labor Party reserved two slots for Arabs among its first thirty candidates (considered safe in view of the polls): Nawaf Massalha, a Muslim from Kafr Qara in the Triangle, and Salah Tarif, a Druze from Julis in the Galilee.

The Likud tried to promote its political interests among the Arabs in various ways: through co-opting traditional and younger leaders, who viewed their personal standing as the main objective; through the extension of special benefits to some localities; through direct involvement in the local elections held in November 1998 and assistance to several candidates; and through interviews and advertisements in the electronic and printed media. The Likud reserved the nineteenth slot on its Knesset list for a Druze, Ayub Qara of Daliyyat al-Karmil.

Meretz, the left-wing Zionist Party, considered the Arabs to be a natural reservoir of votes, in view of its position in favor of peace based on the establishment of the Palestinian state alongside Israel as well as its consistent support for civil equality for the Arabs. Preliminary surveys predicted that Meretz would win only half the number of seats it held in the Fourteenth Knesset, so it needed every vote. Husnia Jibara of Taibe in the Triangle was elected by the party's general council to the tenth place on the list, which did not seem to be an assured seat at the time and it weakened Meretz's appeal to the Arabs. (Ultimately she did make it to the Knesset and became the first Arab woman in the House.)

Right-wing and religious parties, aside from the Likud, who were part of Netanyahu's coalition, also made significant efforts to win Arab votes. The religious parties went farther than the others: United Torah Judaism, representing ultra-Orthodox Jews of European origin, whose leader served as deputy minister of housing in the Netanyahu government; the National Religious Party (NRP), representative of the national-religious Jews and settlers, whose leader was minister of education and culture; and Shas, representative of the ultra-Orthodox and traditional Sepharadi Jews, which held the interior and labor and social affairs portfolios. All of them worked intensively among the Arabs, employing propaganda, visits, promises, and jobs, in the hope this would help them win Arab votes. Shas outdid the other two parties; its leaders visited Arab localities, made substantial promises, and named local teams to work at attracting Arab votes.

The secular parties in Netanyahu's coalition also attempted to win Arab votes. Israel b'Aliya, which represented the Russian immigrant community, and the Third Way, headed by the minister of public security, Avigdor Kahalani, should be noted. These parties used the same methods as the religious parties, exploiting the fact that they were in power and could order improvements in selected Arab localities, and co-opting influential Arabs.

The Arab parties (including the DFPE) worked among the Arab citizens on the assumption that this was the optimum if not indeed the only pool from which they could draw. These parties, old and new alike, tried hard to present attractive candidate lists. The DFPE expressed its desire to dissolve the bloc formed in 1996 with the National Democratic Alliance (NDA).[2] Soon it became clear that there was rampant dissatisfaction with its representatives in the Fourteenth Knesset, leading to a serious intention to bring about some changes that would refresh the list ahead of the elections—an historic and unprecedented step for the DFPE and its main component, the Israel Communist Party (ICP).

Intensive discussions about the composition of its Knesset list were conducted before the DFPE convention in late February. The party made an effort to put together a young alternative list, which represents the various religious and ethnic sectors. The party organ, *al-Ittihad,* functioned as its mouthpiece and disseminated its propaganda; the party also published advertisements in the Arab and Hebrew press in Israel and in Palestinian newspapers. The DFPE coordinated its efforts with leading figures in the Palestinian Authority (PA), to persuade Arab voters to support the candidate of One Israel, Barak, and also worked hard to frustrate the candidacy of MK Azmi Bishara for prime minister. The United Arab List (UAL), was formed in 1996 as an alliance of the moderate wing of the Islamic movement, headed by Sheikh 'Abdallah Nimr Darwish of Kafr Qasim in the Triangle, and the Democratic Arab Party headed by MK 'Abd al-Wahab Darawshe (Ozacky-Lazar and Ghanem 1996). It continued to function as a bloc and drafted an appeal to the other Arab parties to set up a single joint list, but the venture ultimately failed due to disagreement about the order of candidates. The UAL had to make do with adding MK Hashem Mahameed, who quit the DFPE toward the end of the term of the Fourteenth Knesset. Mahameed, who for years had expressed a secular and antireligious position and opposed the Islamic movement, joined the UAL and was given the third slot in its list, and thus kept his seat in the Knesset.

The list's propaganda consistently featured the line dictated by the Islamic movement, characterized by religious expressions and messages. It was disseminated by the list's leaders in meetings in Arab towns and villages, through the electronic and print media, and in the newspaper of the Islamic movement's southern wing, *al-Mithaq*.

The third-largest party was the National Democratic Alliance (NDA), which decided to sever its partnership with the DFPE and run on its own. The party gave the first slot, unchallenged, to its chairperson, Bishara, and the second to Jamal Zahalqa of Kafr Qara. At first, it looked for ways to restore its partnership with the DFPE, on better terms, or even to link up with the UAL, but all these attempts failed. One day before the deadline for submitting Knesset lists (on Land Day, March 30, 1999), the NDA reached an agreement with Dr. Ahmad Tibi and his party, the Arab Movement for Change, granting the second slot on the NDA list to Tibi.[3] Together they set up the United Democratic Alliance, a union that caused internal problems in the NDA. A number of prominent members suspended their activity in the party, arguing that Tibi, known for his ties with Yasser Arafat on the one hand and with the leadership of the Labor Party on the other, did not command their trust. They accused Bishara of taking steps without consulting the party institutions. An exceptional action taken by the NDA was running its chairperson Bishara, for prime minister—the first Arab party to do so.

Two other small Arab political groupings competed for Arab votes. The New Arab Party, led by Macram Mahoul of Yaffa, and the Democratic Action Organization, headed by Samia Nasser of Majd al-Kurum in the Galilee. Both groups were marginal throughout, in terms of propaganda, the attempts to set up a bloc, and in the results—each received only about two thousand votes and disappeared after the elections.

The Race for Prime Minister

Parallel to the parties' preparations for the Knesset campaign, they also made preparations and conducted discussions about the race for prime minister. In the early stages there were a number of meetings to discuss the basic positions of the parties, leadership, and the Arab public regarding the appropriateness of publicly supporting one candidate or another. Early on it became apparent that there were a number of Jewish candidates for the post: The idea of running an Arab candidate seemed strange in the political circumstances of the Jewish state of Israel.

Starting in February 1999, following prior declarations by MK Bishara, a number of Arab university lecturers, journalists, and political and social activists raised the possibility that he might run for prime minister. They discussed the idea in private meetings, public forums, and in the press. From the outset the DFPE expressed its opposition in principle to such a step proclaiming its commitment to support the candidate "with the best prospects of replacing Netanyahu," without explicitly naming Barak. The UAL was hesitant and declared its intention of examining the electoral advantages and disadvantages of such a step. The only party to sympathize publicly with Bishara was his own NDA, which sought to clarify the implications of having its chairperson run for prime minister—a post seen by many as the exclusive property of Jews.[4] The arguments for and against an Arab candidate for prime minister can be summarized as follows:

A. *In favor:* Most NDA supporters and activists, as well as a number of university lecturers, journalists, social activists, and influential personalities plus Palestinian political figures from the West Bank, Gaza Strip, and Palestinian Diaspora, among them the head of the political department of the PLO, Farouq Qadumi—all took a clear stand in favor. The main considerations that guided them, which were scrutinized by the electronic and print media and aired in dozens of meetings, were as follows:[5]

1. The separation of the Knesset elections from the race for prime minister increased the prominence of the latter and eroded the significance of the Knesset campaign. The press, decision makers, and officials hardly paid attention to the parties' statements, platforms, and ideologies (which in any case had been devalued in the age of privatization and retreat of ethical and ideological positions). Party platforms had become a marginal item and some parties did not even bother to update, rewrite, or print and distribute them. Public debate focused chiefly on the candidates' positions, personalities, and plans for the future. Every candidate won broad coverage, so an Arab candidate could place her community's needs and aspirations on the Israeli agenda.

2. The Jewish candidates presented their positions on a solution to the Palestinian problem without taking into account the positions of most Israeli-Arab citizens—which is identical to that of the PA and the official position of the PLO. They support the establishment of a Palestinian state in the entire territory of the West Bank and Gaza Strip, occupied by Israel in 1967, including East Jerusalem as the capital of this state. Only an Arab candidate could advance such a position, give prominence to its existence on the Israeli side, and influence Israeli public opinion in this direction.

3. In light of the expectation that more than two candidates would compete, and given the political stalemate between right and left in Israel, it seemed unlikely that the election would be decided in the first round. Accordingly, it was thought, an Arab candidate

could compete and express her opinions and platform as part of the general political discourse without endangering the candidate of the left and ultimate prospects of victory, since the decision would be made in a runoff.

4. An Arab candidate would heat up the public debate, in Israel in general and among the Arabs in particular; this would bring out more voters on Election Day thus increasing the number of Arab Knesset members.

5. An Arab candidate could reach an agreement with the candidate of the Labor Party before the runoff and thereby boost the number of Arab voters in the second round, which was expected to be rather low. Only an Arab candidate who won a significant percentage of the Arab vote could influence the public and political agenda between the two rounds in favor of the Arabs' interests, positions, and aspirations.

6. The main considerations behind the idea of putting up an Arab candidate for prime minister was the political distress of the Arabs in consequence of the competition between right and left in the Israeli political arena. The Arabs in Israel belong, ideologically and politically, to the left side of the political spectrum; in difficult moments of political crisis they are "forced" to support the Labor Party and Meretz, even though the latter frequently disagree with them and often hold positions that are hostile to the Arabs. This situation summarizes the essence of the political distress in which the Arabs found themselves in recent years (Ghanem 1997). To escape it would require a bold step, by which the Arabs could threaten the Zionist left forcing it to accept their positions, even if only in part (Ghanem 1996). In light of the aspiration of the candidate of the Zionist left, Barak, to attract support from the center and right, the Arabs had to take a step that would threaten him in practice and not merely utter meaningless words. The presence of an Arab candidate for prime minister, who could win a significant chunk of the Arab votes, ostensibly "guaranteed" to Barak, would imperil his chances of winning in the first round and compel him to relate to the issues that trouble the Arabs.

7. The presence of an Arab candidate would also serve to protect the Arabs against the specter of intervention in their domestic affairs by leaders of the PA, including propaganda and financial support for political parties that were willing to accept its dictates and public opposition to parties whose activists criticized the Oslo accords or protested human and civil rights violations by the PA and its denial of fundamental rights to its citizens. The NDA and

its activists believed that running a candidate would pose a threat to the PA, by endangering its preferred candidate, Barak. In fact, NDA people used this card both overtly and covertly and to warn the PA that if it intervened against the NDA or gave massive support to other Arab parties, the NDA would call for a boycott of the elections for prime minister. This threat served as a deterrent influence on PA personalities who had campaigned against the NDA arguing that it was liable not to cross the threshold and votes for it would be wasted.

8. NDA activists hoped that entering their chairperson in the race would give him broad exposure as well as the party's platform and positions, thereby increasing support for it. This expectation proved to be correct.

B. *Against:* Those who opposed an Arab candidacy for prime minister could be divided into a number of subgroups, of which the most important comprised activists of rival parties, a number of influential personalities, journalists, and PR people who marketed the various parties, as well as Arab and Jewish politicians and some leaders of the PA. The main explanations for their opposition were as follows:

1. An Arab candidate would imperil the possibility of changing the regime, not only in the first round but even in the runoff. It is a demonstrative but hopeless step that might leave Netanyahu in office.

2. Rival Arab and non-Arab parties were afraid that if the NDA ran a candidate for prime minister he would attract voters to the NDA at their expense.

3. Such a controversial step, which could not win a majority of Arab votes, would present a disunited front to the outside world and have a negative impact on the Arabs' bargaining power, showing that the candidate of the Jewish left represented the Arabs better than their own candidate did.

4. An Arab candidate, who would be seen and heard in local and international media, would contribute to the picture of Israel as an exemplary democracy that permits its Arab minority to compete for every public post, including the most important of all. This would weaken the Arab argument concerning the ethnic and nondemocratic character of the State of Israel.

As the deadline for the submission of candidacies for prime minister approached, following the failure of all attempts to find a consensual Arab candidate, the NDA decided, after a protracted debate, to have its chairperson,

Dr. Bishara, run for prime minister. Bishara accepted the nomination in the hope that it would help further these arguments; on many occasions he even declared that he was not really interested in the position but was using it as a means to advance the Arabs' interests. The NDA managed to collect about 56,000 signatures supporting his candidacy, more than the 50,000 required.

The Results of the Elections: Voter Participation and Distribution

The analysis of the results of the elections for the Fifteenth Knesset and prime minister in May 1999 relates to three main aspects: participation or abstention, the distribution of valid votes for the Knesset, and the distribution of votes for prime minister.

Voter Participation

According to official statistics that can be verified with some precision— namely, the results in all-Arab localities—some 75% of the 429,000 eligible Arab voters went to the polls. This is slightly lower than the 77% turnout in the 1996 elections. There are various explanations for the decline in the participation rate; some are historical and have characterized Arab voting since the birth of Israel (Ghanem 1997), while others are contemporary and apply only to these last elections. The historical explanations are as follows:

1. The hopes for the establishment of a unified Arab list that would fully exploit the Arabs' electoral potential was not realized; this caused disappointment and abstention.

2. There was a sense of marginality in the Israeli political system and an inability to be full partners in political activity.

3. There was also disappointment with the existing Arab parties— ideological, personal, and practical.

4. Some members of the small Sons of the Village movement and elements of the Islamic movement refrain from voting as a matter of ideology.

In addition to these arguments, a number of more localized developments influenced the decision to refrain from voting. This was particularly conspicuous in light of the fact that a survey we conducted about a month before the elections indicated clearly that Arabs intended to vote in large numbers.[6] The new factors that influenced the participation rate were as follows:

1. Both candidates—Barak and Netanyahu, ignored the Arabs and their needs. Barak, who had the best chance of winning and was acceptable to most Arabs, did not express positions sympathetic to their needs and wishes.

2. Bishara's withdrawal from the race two days before the elections braked the momentum and caused some Arabs who reject Zionism to reconsider their intentions.

3. The main group of those who did not vote this time but had voted in 1996 comprised, in our view, traditional voters for the Labor Party. The party made almost no attempts to encourage Arabs to vote for its list and focused on getting them to vote for its candidate for prime minister, generally through activists of the Arab parties and Meretz.

4. A significant factor that is difficult and perhaps impossible to verify is inherent in the Netanyahu government's general disposition toward the Arabs. Its frequently discriminatory and even hostile attitude was felt as an assault on the Arabs' civil status and reinforced their sense of marginality. This led to a decline in their evaluation of the importance of active citizenship and a general feeling that there was no point in participating in the elections, because in any case their situation would not improve afterward.

5. Local and technical problems contributed to a decline in the percentage of voters. Most prominent was the incident in the town of Baqa al-Gharbiyya in the Triangle, where the day before the elections inhabitants clashed with Palestinian collaborators. In the clashes, two local youths who had attempted to burn the collaborators' house were killed. Community leaders proclaimed a day of mourning on Election Day, including a commercial strike and a decision to stay away from the polls.

The Distribution of Votes for the Knesset

Continuing the trends that became more defined during the last two decades, the election results point to the crystallization of four political camps among the Arabs in Israel.

1. The "Israeli-Arab" stream over the years developed ideological positions close to those of the Jewish-Zionist parties. Its political behavior is manifested by voting for Jewish parties, from Meretz on the left to Shas and Likud and even the NRP on the right. In 1999, the distribution of Arab votes for Jewish parties—28% of the Arab vote—was as follows:

The Labor Party (and its successor, One Israel), has traditionally received the most significant chunk, because it held unbroken power during the first decades of the state and used state and Histadrut institutions as a tool to recruit Arab votes (Lustick 1980). This time, however, there was a 50% decline in the rate of support for Labor—to about 8% of the Arab votes, as against 16% in the 1996 elections.

Meretz is the second most popular Jewish party, because its positions are the closest to the Arab consensus.[7] Support for Meretz, too, was halved—from 10% in the last elections to 5% in 1999. The Likud, Israel b'Aliya, Shas, and other parties on the right also received some Arab votes because of the large investment they made and because they were in power from 1996 to 1999 and could distribute their largesse to Arab groups and individuals. Taken together they won about 5% of the Arab vote. The rest of the Arab vote were given to small Jewish parties, some of them new.

2. The Communist stream since 1948 has found its organizational expression in the Israel Communist Party and later in its front organization, the DFPE. The Communist Party has maintained its organizational and electoral primacy among the parties active in the Arab sector for many years (Ghanem 1994; Rekhess 1993). But it has recently undergone a process of gradual regression, since the collapse of the Communist bloc and as a result of internal changes in Arab society and in the party itself (Ghanem 1994). In the elections to the Fourteenth Knesset in 1996 the DFPE and its then-partner, the NDA, received about 38% of the valid Arab ballots, which translated into five seats in the Knesset.

In 1999 the DFPE ran alone and its support dropped to about 22% of the Arab votes, and three Knesset seats. This result constituted a severe defeat in the eyes of the party leadership and supporters, who started a thorough internal debate in an attempt to understand the causes for their party's decline. In our estimation, the vigorous competition among the various parties and the replacement of the traditional leadership by lesser-known faces were among the key factors.[8]

3. The "national camp" has had various organizational expressions since 1948. At one time it appeared as the al-Ard movement, in the 1970s it was represented by the Sons of the Village movement, and in the 1980s by the Progressive List for Peace (Reiter and Aharoni 1992). In 1996 the nationalist stream formed the NDA and ran for the Knesset on a joint list with the DFPE; its representative, Bishara, received the fourth place on the joint list. Profound differences emerged between Bishara and other members of the faction during the term of the Fourteenth Knesset, attempts at reconciliation before the elections failed and the NDA ran alone for the Fifteenth Knesset, reinforced by Tibi. It won about 17% of the valid Arab votes, a fine achievement that brought Bishara and Tibi to the Knesset. It seems, nevertheless, that the NDA did not realize its full potential because of conspicuous organizational weaknesses and the lack of collective leadership.

4. The Islamic stream is represented organizationally by the Islamic movement, which split in advance of the 1996 elections over the question of participation in Knesset elections. The "southern" wing formed an alliance

and joint list with the Democratic Arab Party of MK Darawshe;[9] together they received 25% of the valid Arab ballots in 1996, good for four Knesset seats. Before the elections to the Fifteenth Knesset it added MK Mahameed to its list, and won about 31% of the valid Arab ballots and five mandates—the largest Arab representation. This impressive achievement can be attributed mainly to its solid organizational efforts and to the ethnic tension among the Arabs in Israel.

To sum up, except for the UAL, all the other parties emerged with a sense of not having realized their potential. The results will force the secular Arab parties, the DFPE and NDA, to do some serious soul-searching and consider whether they should have contested the elections as a bloc.

Electing a Prime Minister

On Saturday, May 15, two days before the elections, Bishara announced in a press conference, broadcast live on Israeli television, that he was withdrawing from the race, and explained that the fundamental objectives of his candidacy had been fully attained. He asserted having reached an understanding (not an agreement) with the Labor Party as to the need for appropriate and thorough attention to the problems facing the Arabs. That included immediate attention, after the elections, to a number of acute problems like the legalization of unrecognized localities, resolution of the lands problem (including that in al-Ruha near Umm al-Fahm), employment of Arabs in senior positions in the civil service, and economic development of Arab communities. That evening the Labor Party endorsed Bishara's stand, as did the Arab rivals of the NDA, who claimed his withdrawal proved that their opposition to his candidacy had been right all along.[10]

A close study of Bishara's candidacy and its practical outcome leads to contradictory conclusions. It can be argued that he indeed achieved his goals and that his last minute withdrawal paved the way for other candidates, making it possible for the race to be won in the first round. It actually saved two expensive weeks of campaigning—as significant for Israel as a whole as for the Arab sector.

On the other hand, it can be argued that his candidacy was a total failure judging by the chief motive for an Arab's running for prime minister, namely, to bring about a serious change in the attitude of the Zionist center and left to the Arabs and their electoral potential. His candidacy, which was intended to call into question the Arabs' automatic support for the Labor Party candidate for prime minister (Ghanem 1996) in the absence of a discussion of their demands and commitments to them—did not achieve this objective. Bishara withdrew from the campaign without Barak's ever agreeing to speak, meet, or make any commitment to him, because of Barak's fear that this would reduce his support among Jewish groups in the center of the spectrum. This is the most prominent testimonial to the Arabs' political distress in the Israeli political system. Bishara's unconditional withdrawal was premature and caused him to miss his declared objective.

The failure to achieve a breakthrough in the attitude of the Zionist left and Labor Party toward the Arabs stemmed from the fact that the other Arab parties did not line up behind Bishara, owing to short-term electoral considerations as well as to immediate political and individual reasons.

Barak emerged victorious, with 56% of the vote, against 44% given to Netanyahu. Barak received some 95% of valid Arab ballots, an overwhelming majority that can be explained as a sweeping expression of Arab protest against Netanyahu and his government. This landslide was nourished by expectations among the Arabs for a revival of the peace process begun by the Rabin government in 1992–1996 and a continuation of its policies favoring equalizing the Arabs' socioeconomic level with that of the general population. The Arabs also expected that the government formed by Barak would be more attentive than its predecessors to Arab parliamentarians and even include them in the coalition.

The Status of the Arab Parties After the Elections

Historically, Arab parties in the Knesset were a permanent opposition in the Israeli system of government. They were treated as representing the "hostile" Palestinian-Arab minority, which must not be trusted and could not be accepted as part of a government coalition—except, of course, for Arab parliamentarians who were members of Jewish factions that belonged to the coalition. Despite the significant electoral weight of the Arabs, no Arab minister has ever been appointed and the handful of Arab deputy ministers were given responsibility for affairs relevant to "minorities" and not to the population in general. Israel was established and has always functioned as a Jewish-Zionist entity and as the state of the Jewish people. This was a key element in its Declaration of Independence, which received clear legal status in 1985 with the passage of Amendment 9 to the Basic Law: The Knesset. The amendment makes a party's participation in Knesset elections contingent on its own recognition of Israel as "the state of the Jewish people" (Rouhana 1997). Despite the improvement in the attitude toward Arabs over the years, Israel as a state sees Jewish affairs as its chief concern. By exclusion of the Arab from full partnership in the executive branch, the state keeps them from having an active and equal influence on the decision-making process that affects fateful issues relating to the Jewish people.

Over the years the "Arab" parties—the DFPE, the Progressive List for Peace, and the DAP—maintained an aggressive line and adopted an anti-Zionist stance. In their publications they rejected the definition of Israel as the state of the Jewish people; viewing it as unfair to the Arab citizens of the country, they wanted to designate it "the state of all its citizens" or, in the best case, "the state of the Jewish people and its Arab citizens" (see Ghanem 1990). This position in practice is compatible with the position of most Arabs in Israel, who reject the Jewish-Zionist character of the state (Smooha 1992).

The Arab parties and their Knesset representatives also disagree with, and are conspicuously opposed to, government policy on extremely important questions such as the allocation of resources within the state and the resolution of the Israeli-Arab conflict in general and of the Israeli-Palestinian conflict in particular (Ghanem 1990). This disagreement, which in practice coincides with the disagreement between most Arab citizens and the Jewish majority (Smooha 1992), intensifies Jewish suspicions of the Arabs and reinforces the perception that they are a "hostile minority" and potential fifth column. This mistrust deters the Jewish political leadership from accepting the Arabs as full coalition partners.

After the establishment of the Rabin government in July 1992, the Arab parties supported it from the outside and were not full members in the coalition, even though it depended on their votes. Withdrawing their support from the Rabin government would have been interpreted a vote of no confidence, causing the peace process to fail, while no Arab Knesset member could risk that.

Netanyahu's victory in 1996 returned the Arab factions to their previous status as marginal opposition having no influence on the shaping of events. The Arab parliamentarians became irrelevant in the contest between right and left, both inside and outside the Knesset; only in isolated cases were they able to work extremely minor changes in the policy of the Netanyahu government toward the Arabs and the conflict in general.[11]

When the results of the 1999 elections became known, the winners, Barak and the Labor Party, initiated contacts to form a new government. Throughout the process they ignored the Arab parties almost totally, even though they and their supporters had brought Barak his landslide victory (he received only 51% of the Jewish vote). Barak, who before the elections had shied away from any contact with representatives of the Arabs, so as not to endanger his support in the center, did not publicly recognize the Arabs' contribution to his victory. Barak's noncognizance led to turmoil among the Arabs and their representatives, who began to publicly air the idea that they were not "in Barak's pocket" and would vote against him when he presents his government, should his attitude persist.[12] Barak was not deterred, since his short experience with the Arab leadership had taught him that their declarations had no real backing and were not translated to practical steps. He assumed that in the end, the Arab MKs would support any government he put together, as long as it was committed to continuing the peace process and parity between Jews and Arabs.

The attitude toward the Arabs displayed by Barak and his aides during the coalition negotiations stemmed from two main factors: First of all, the Arabs' sweeping support before the elections for Barak's candidacy, including Bishara's withdrawal, were not accompanied by any demands. The Arab parties set the defeat of Netanyahu as their primary objective—a "negative" goal that was not balanced by any "positive" demands from Barak. This detracted from their bargaining power after the elections.

Secondly, Barak was guided by his Jewish-Zionist vision seeking to base his government on a Jewish majority and avoiding being perceived as dependent on Arab votes, as Yitzhak Rabin had been. He preferred to expand his government with religious and right-wing parties who supported Netanyahu before and in the elections, so the critical political moves he planned would be voted for by a large "Jewish majority." Barak relied on the Arab support from the outside assuming that the Arab parties could not team up with the extreme right to bring down his government.

Conclusions

For the Arabs, the 1999 elections were dominated by their desire to replace the right-wing government headed by Netanyahu with one that would revive the peace process and work more forcefully toward real civic equality between them and the Jewish citizens in Israel. For the first time in Israel's history an Arab citizen presented his candidacy for prime minister. As a result of Bishara's withdrawal two days before the elections, and the support of most of the Arab parties for Barak, about 95% of the valid Arab ballots were cast for the Labor candidate, contributing to his wide margin over Netanyahu in the first round. Barak received more than 56% of the total votes, but only 51% among the Jews—that is, Arab voters added 5 percentage points to his margin of victory.

The picture in the Knesset elections was more complicated. The voting patterns continued the trend begun in 1996, when the Knesset elections were first separated from those for prime minister. About 72% of the Arab voters cast their ballots for "Arab" parties and about 28% (a decline from 1996, 33% and 1992, 52%) for Jewish parties. The attempts to unite forces failed as in the past.

After the elections, during the period of the coalition negotiations conducted by the prime minister-elect Barak, all Arab parties and their supporters were relegated to the sidelines and were never included in coalition calculations or in the government's power base, not even consulted by Barak and his people.

The idea that the Israeli political system was gradually opening up to the needs of the Arabs and willing to include them as legitimate partners, seems to have been premature and overly optimistic. A comparison between Rabin's attitude toward the Arab parties in 1992 and Barak's in 1999 shows a clear marked regression by the latter. Rabin was willing to meet representatives of the Arab parties and have them participate in discussions and decisions, and even approved an agreement with them in which he promised to resolve a number of fundamental problems they presented to him (Ozacky-Lazar and Ghanem 1996). Although Rabin too did not include them in his coalition, he did give them legitimacy as partial partners.

The government established by Barak included religious and right-wing parties who supported Netanyahu almost without reservation. Barak preferred them to the Arab parties because he wanted to form a "Jewish coalition" not dependent on Arab support. This proves, in our opinion, the strength of the second approach presented in the introduction: the Israeli Left headed by the Labor Party is strongly committed to the Jewish-Zionist character of the state and to the preservation of exclusive Jewish control over its major institutions, the government being the leading one. The Zionist parties, including Meretz, who is a senior partner in Barak's coalition, are seeking the Arab votes without giving the Arabs full access to the decision-making centers. Even though the Arab electorate and political representation increases—their power remains marginal and they cannot tip the balance between the two political blocs. Labor prefers Shas, Likud, Israel b'Aliya, and even the National Religious Party, to the Arab parties who hold close political positions to it, on the major issues at stake. The 1999 elections point to Israel's character as an ethnic state.

The election results and their aftermath reinforced the argument that while Israel is moving toward peace agreements with the Palestinian Liberation Organization (PLO) and the PA; the standing of its own Arab-Palestinian citizens is deteriorating. This is due to two parallel but contradictory processes: On the one hand, the Arabs in Israel have developed high expectations for achieving full civil equality and they demand to be recognized as a national minority. They develop militant though legal ways of struggle and protest. On the other hand, the internal split among the Jews is expected to broaden as a result of territorial compromises with the Palestinians and the Syrians, and the Jewish majority is not willing to make additional "concessions" within the state. From the perspective of the Jewish majority, it will be imperative to create mechanisms of solidarity reinforcing the Jewish identity of the State of Israel—antithetical to acceptance of the Arab demands (Ozacky-Lazar 1999).

The election campaign also highlighted the weakness of the present Arab leadership and the political trap in which it finds itself. Arab politicians did not exploit the wooing of the Arab vote by Barak and his people to win substantial agreements and promises that would benefit their voters. The Arab representatives were not included in the negotiations toward the formation of the government and were not taken in consideration when the numerical calculations were made prior to the coalition agreement. They continue to sit in the opposition as in the past, unable to cooperate with the other opposition forces.

Notes

1. See especially *al-Sinara* in the weeks before the election.

2. On the cooperation in 1996, see Ozacky-Lazar and Ghanem (1996).

3. Two other small groups also joined this alliance: supporters of Hashem Mahameed who had not followed him into the UAL, and the remnants of the Progressive Movement for Peace, led by Ahmad Jarbuni from 'Arabe in the Galilee.

4. In the waning months of the Fourteenth Knesset the right-wing MK Michael Kleiner submitted a bill to ban non-Jews from running for prime minister; the bill was voted down in its preliminary reading, but expressed the wishes of many Jews.

5. See the discussion published in the NDA weekly, *Fasal al-Maqal,* for the entire period from the decision to advance the elections through Election Day (May 17, 1999).

6. In the survey conducted by the Institute for Peace Research at Giv'at Haviva about a month before the elections, some 87 percent of the respondents said they were willing to come out and vote.

7. On the consensus in Arab positions, see Al-Haj (1988).

8. The historical leadership of Tawfiq Toubi, who was a member of the Knesset from 1949, and Meir Wilner, the party secretary-general, and especially the loss of Tawfiq Ziad, the mayor of Nazareth, killed in a traffic accident in 1994. In the Fourteenth Knesset they were replaced by Hashem Mahameed of Umm al-Fahm, who bolted the party in 1999 because of a threat to his continued Knesset membership; Salah Salim of Ibillin in the Galilee; and Dr. Ahmad Sa'd of Abu Snan in the Galilee. At the beginning of the campaign for the Fifteenth Knesset, they were replaced by the DFPE secretary-general, Muhammad Baraka of Shefaram and by Isam Mahoul, the ICP spokesperson, from Haifa. MK Tamar Gozansky kept her number-three slot, reserved for a Jew, on the list. These persons were less-well-known outside the party and among Arabs in general.

9. Even after the establishment of this alliance this stream should be called "Islamic," because the members of the Islamic movement have clear control of the structure, operations, and messages of the joint list.

10. See, for example, the reaction of the DFPE in its daily, *al-Ittihad,* May 16, 1999.

Even had Barak won in the first round without Bishara's having withdrawn, the latter's persistence in the race would have meant that the Arabs are not a "sure thing" in any case, and that the Labor and Zionist Left must change their attitude toward them.

11. Thus, for example, during the deliberations on the 1999 state budget, the DAP faction was able to get the government to modify its stance on the issue of property tax in return for its abstention on the first reading of the budget bill.

12. See, for example, *al-Sinara,* June 1, 1999.

References

Al-Haj, Majid. 1988. "The Sociopolitical Structure of the Arabs in Israel: External vs. Internal Orientation." In John E. Hofman, (ed.). *Arab-Jewish Relations in Israel: A Quest in Human Understanding.* Bristol, IN: Wyndham Hall, 92–123.

Ghanem, As'ad. 1990. "Ideological Currents among the Arabs in Israel with Regard to Jewish-Arab Coexistence, 1967–1990." Master's thesis, University of Haifa.

———. 1994. "The Rise and Fall of the Israel Communist Party (Maki), A Discussion of the Causes." *Studies in the Rebirth of Israel* 4. Beer Sheva: Ben-Gurion Heritage Center, Ben-Gurion University of the Negev, 549–555.

———. 1996. "We Too Deserve Influence." Program to Study Arab Politics in Israel, Dayan Center, Tel-Aviv University.

———. 1997. "The Limits of Parliamentary Politics: The Arab Minority in Israel and the 1992 and 1996 Elections." *Israeli Affairs* 4, no. 2: 72–93.

Lustick, Ian. 1980. *Arabs in the Jewish State: Israeli's Control of a National Minority.* Austin: University of Texas Press.

Neuberger, Benjamin. 1993. "The Arab Minority in Israeli Politics 1984–1992: From Marginality to Influence." *Asian and African Studies* 27, nos. 1–2: 149–170.

Ozacky-Lazar, Sarah. 1992. "The Elections for the Thirteenth Knesset among the Arabs in Israel." *Surveys of the Arabs in Israel* 9. Giv'at Haviva: Institute for Peace Research (Hebrew).

———. 1999. "7 Roads: Theoretical Options to the Status of the Arabs in Israel." Giv'at Haviva, Institute for Peace Research, 26.

Ozacky-Lazar, Sarah, and As'ad Ghanem. 1996. "The Arab Vote for the 14th Knesset." *Surveys on the Arabs in Israel* 24. Giv'at Haviva, Institute for Peace Research.

Ram, Uri. 1999. "Guns and Butter: Liberal Post-Zionism in the Age of the Small World." In Uri Ram and Oren Yiftahel, *"Ethnocracy" and "Small-Worldli-*

ness": New Approaches to the Study of Society and Space in Israel. Beer Sheva, Negev Center for Regional Development, Ben-Gurion University of the Negev.

Reiter Yitzhak, and Reuven Aharoni. 1992. *The Political World of Israeli Arab.* Beit Berl: Institute for Israeli Arab Studies.

Rekhess, Elie. 1993. *The Arab Minority in Israel, between Communism and Arab Nationalism.* Tel Aviv: Hakibbutz Hame'uhad (Hebrew).

Rouhana, Nadim. 1997. *Palestinian Citizens in an Ethnic Jewish State: Identities in Conflict.* New Haven: Yale University Press.

Smooha, Sammy. 1992. *Arabs and Jews in Israel.* Vol. 2. Boulder and London: Westview Press.

Smooha, Sammy, and D. Peretz. 1993. "Israel's 1992 Elections: Are They Critical?" *Middle East Journal* 47, no. 3: 444–463.

Sikkuy. 1996. Association for the Advancement of Civic Equality. 1996 Annual Report. Jerusalem: Sikkuy.

———. 1999. Annual Report. Jerusalem: Sikkuy.

7

The "Russian" Revolution in Israeli Politics

Zvi Gitelman and Ken Goldstein

Introduction

Between 1989 and 1999, more than three quarters of a million people from lands that comprised the former Soviet Union (FSU) immigrated to Israel. This is the single largest aliyah in Israeli history. Ironically, it comes from a state that consistently opposed Zionism, armed and supported the Arab states and Palestinian military organizations, broke relations with Israel in 1967, and refused to allow Zionist and Hebrew education. Over the last three Israeli national elections, the introduction of such a large bloc of voters—with no previous political ties or partisan allegiances—into a highly competitive and evenly balanced political landscape has attracted the interest of both political strategists and scholarly observers.[1]

In all three elections (1992, 1996, and 1999), most of the immigrants from the FSU voted against the party in power and the incumbent prime minister. Their votes were probably decisive in the 1992 and 1996 elections, though not in 1999. Still, the behavior of the immigrants in the most recent contest is significant because it may portend a long-term trend of ethnic voting and the emergence of what may be an important swing party, and hence a key player in coalition politics. Furthermore, it is unlikely that future Israeli elections will be decided by such a large margin, and this large bloc of immigrant voters (16 percent of the electorate in 1999) is likely to remain a key constituency for those seeking to lead Israel.

We would like to thank Prof. Jack Kugelmass, chair of the Jewish Studies Department at Arizona State University, and the Frankel Center for Jewish Studies at the University of Michigan for providing the funds necessary to conduct the exit poll. We would also like to thank Prof. Zach Levy, of Haifa University, Maia Aksakalova, Tel Aviv University, and Rita Margolina, Yad Vashem Institute, for helping us deal with some of the logistic hurdles that were involved in fielding our study.

Accordingly, our goal in this chapter is to explain systematically why "Russians"[2] voted the way they did in the 1999 contest. Why did a majority of immigrant voters choose Ehud Barak for prime minister and one of their own ethnic parties in the Knesset? What attitudes and beliefs were most important in determining their vote for the two offices? What demographic characteristics are correlated with immigrants' votes? What happened in the campaign that enabled Barak to turn the "Russian" vote around? What, if anything, differentiates those who voted for the Israel b'Aliya Party, led by Natan Sharansky, from those who voted for the other "Russian" party, Israel Beiteinu, headed by Avigdor Lieberman?

We answer these questions by merging qualitative assessments from the campaign, taken from our observations and press accounts (in Hebrew, Russian, and English), with the results of an exit poll of close to 1,800 immigrant voters (see the appendix). We begin by providing an overview of the nature and influence of "Russian" immigrant voting over the past three Israeli electoral contests. We then use the exit poll to describe briefly the demographic characteristics and basic issue attitudes of the immigrants. After examining the course and content of the campaign in the immigrant community, we return to the exit poll data to explain voting patterns in the elections for prime minister and for the Knesset. In the final section, we summarize our principal findings and discuss longer-term consequences of the entry into the electorate of the massive wave of immigrants from the FSU.

The Consistent Oppositionists: Patterns of "Russian" Voting

In the 1992 election, the last one contested under the old system of a single vote cast for a party (rather than separate voting for the Knesset and prime minister), approximately 250,000 recent immigrants from the FSU were eligible to vote and they comprised 8% of the electorate. Most accounts of the 1992 contest identify immigrant dissatisfaction with the absorption process as their major concern and credit Labor's victory to the support it gained from these new immigrants (Fein 1995; Gitelman 1995; Reich, Dropkin, and Wurmser 1993). Although the Labor Party headed by Yitzhak Rabin won 12 more seats and 250,000 more votes than the Likud list headed by Yitzhak Shamir, the balance between the left and the right/religious bloc in the final Knesset results was only slightly in the left's favor (61 mandates to 59 mandates). Exit polls indicated that 58% of the Soviet immigrants supported Labor and parties to the left of it, and 24% supported Likud and parties to the right. The immigrant vote was clearly decisive in driving Shamir and the Likud out of power.

Evidence suggests that the vote was a protest vote against the Likud government more than it was a vote for Labor. In a study by Zvi Gitelman

(1995), satisfaction in Israel was the most powerful predictor of voting for Likud or Labor. While 69% of Likud supporters were satisfied, only 39% of Labor supporters were satisfied. Twice as many of the unemployed preferred Labor to Likud. The dissatisfaction of "Russian" immigrants provided the narrow margin that allowed Yitzhak Rabin to form a governing coalition and to return Avodah to power.

A Soviet immigrant party, "DA," also emerged in the 1992 elections. After much indecision and even a few changes of heart, Sharansky (the most famous Jewish "refusenik," formerly Anatoly Shcharansky) declined to head up the party's list. In the end, the party only got 11,697 votes, about 5% of the immigrant vote (0.4% of the total vote), not nearly enough to win representation in the Knesset.

In 1996, the first elections contested under the new dual system, approximately 400,000 immigrants voted and they comprised 13% of eligible voters. In the contest for both the Knesset and prime minister, most accounts indicated that they again voted against the party in power. Reports after the election estimated that Benjamin Netanyahu received from 65% to 70% of the "Russian" immigrant vote in his victory over Shimon Peres (Eldar 1999; Weiss 1997). With the new system of directly electing the prime minister, one does not have to add up Knesset seats or comprehend complicated coalition politics to see the decisive effect that the immigrant vote had. Netanyahu won by less than 15,000 votes, but enjoyed somewhere between a 120,000 to 160,000 vote margin of victory (depending on which estimates one believes) among immigrants from the FSU.

Some observers cited concerns about security as the primary explanation for the immigrant vote in 1996 (Horowitz 1999). An alternative explanation is that, as in 1992, dissatisfaction with their resettlement experience in Israel played the largest role in determining how immigrants from the FSU voted. A third explanation, perhaps the most convincing, is that while the immigrants were initially inclined to support Peres and Labor, the latter party neglected the immigrant voters, while Likud courted them, and the Russian-language media strongly supported Likud and especially Netanyahu. A typical Likud message was an ad, far bolder and cruder than anything in the Hebrew press, in the largest circulation Russian-language newspaper, *Vesti*. It was printed in the colors of the PLO and was headlined, "Hail to Comrade Peres, head of the Palestinian state! . . . The red Peres [means] a black future . . . Peres = Meretz, plus the Arafatization of the whole country!" A Soviet hammer and sickle was displayed as part of the PLO flag (*Vesti,* May 23, 1996, p.7). When Sharansky swung his support to Netanyahu, the "Russians" followed suit and drifted away from the party and leader who seem to have neglected them. In the simultaneously contested elections for the Knesset, more than four in ten (43%) immigrants voted for the Israel b'Aliyah list. This gave the party seven mandates, making it the sixth largest party in the Knesset and a key player in coalition politics.[3]

Despite the fact that the immigrants voted for a different party in 1996 than the one they voted for in 1992, their behavior was consistent: in both years they voted against the party in power, largely because they felt the government had not done enough for them. But in contrast to 1992, in 1996 immigrants not only voted against the incumbent party's candidate for prime minister, but also for a party of their own—an ethnic or parochial party led by Sharansky (Israel b'Aliya). "Russian" voting in 1996 thus foreshadowed some of the crucial elements in the 1999 election: they voted out the party and prime minister who were in power, they followed the lead of their own ethnic party, the campaign made a crucial difference, and they voted against those who associated themselves with the religious sector.

In January 1999, following Netanyahu's call for early elections, attention was once again focused on this huge bloc of immigrant voters. In this contest, one out of every six eligible voters (16%) would be an immigrant from the FSU who had come to Israel in the last ten years. Most observers, not to mention Likud Party and Netanyahu strategists, assumed that these immigrant voters would once again hold the key and that Netanyahu could count on their support. Early polls of immigrant voters seemed to confirm these assessments as Netanyahu consistently enjoyed a two- or even three-to-one advantage over his challenger, former army chief of staff, Barak.[4] Although Barak was not well-known in the immigrant community and there were still a sizable number of undecided voters, most immigrants were assumed to have views on the peace process closer to Netanyahu's. Moreover, some believed that to the extent that Barak's Labor Party was identified as "socialist," those who had lived under Soviet "socialism" would vote against it.[5] Furthermore, the Russian language press—there are four Russian-language dailies and at least forty weeklies and monthlies in Israel—was firmly in the right-wing camp. Therefore, most observers felt there was little opportunity for Barak to get his message out and little room for his support to grow. Finally, former Netanyahu advisor Avigdor Lieberman was starting his own immigrant party. The conventional wisdom was that this would increase turnout among immigrant voters—and especially among more right-wing immigrant voters—and thus increase Netanyahu's vote share (Shapira 1999).

Yet, when all was said and done, Barak beat Netanyahu by 13 percentage points among Russian-speaking immigrants (57% to 43%), a margin that was virtually identical to Barak's margin of victory among the electorate as a whole.[6] Unlike the 1992 and 1996 races, the immigrant vote did not determine the outcome. Overall, Barak beat Netanyahu by 388,546 votes, while

Barak beat Netanyahu by about 62,000 votes among Russian-speaking voters. Russian-speaking voters provided approximately 16% of Barak's margin of victory—which is about their proportion of the electorate. Even had Netanyahu beaten Barak among the "Russians" by the same 70 to 30 margin by which he had bested Peres in 1996, he still would have lost to Barak by over 100,000 votes. In fact, to beat Barak, Netanyahu would have had to win 83% of the votes of Russian-speaking immigrants.

Examining marginal results only, there is little that distinguished Russian-speaking immigrants from other Israelis in their votes for prime minister. In other words, like previous waves of Russian immigrants, these newer arrivals seem to have been socialized into a voting pattern nearly identical to that of the Israeli population as a whole. Still, although these more recent immigrant voters may look a lot like other Israelis at the aggregate level, these aggregate similarities may mask differences in attitudes and motivations at the individual level. Furthermore, while giving their votes for prime minister to one of the two major party candidates in the 1999 contest, more than half these voters cast their ballots for immigrant parties, giving Sharansky's Israel b'Aliya Party six seats and Lieberman's Israel Beitenu Party four seats.[7]

Thus, although not the deciding factor in the 1999 elections for prime minister, the "Russian" vote was crucial in the Knesset elections, putting one immigrant party into the coalition and another into the opposition in the Knesset. Moreover, the fact that Israel b'Aliya has now been well represented in two successive parliaments raised the possibility that it might be another Shas, an ethnic party with a stable constituency and a long-term player in Israeli politics. If it is able to maintain such high levels of support from the immigrant community, Israel b'Aliya is well suited to play a key role in many kinds of coalitions. This is due not only to the number of Knesset seats it controls, but because it could be more flexible than other possible coalition partners on the major issues—the disposition of the territories, religion's role in public life, and the economy.

A Profile of the Immigrants

Unlike the previous Soviet immigration in the 1970s, where over half the immigrants came from Georgia or the Baltic states, the aliyah of the 1990s was much more geographically and culturally representative of Soviet Jewry as a whole. Table 7.1 reports voters' places of origin before moving to Israel.

A large majority of immigrants were from Russia (32%) and Ukraine (31%), with sizable numbers from Central Asia, Belarus, and Moldova. Interestingly, according to our survey, one in four immigrant voters (25%) was not registered as a Jew in his or her Soviet identity papers and over two thirds

Table 7.1   Place of Origin of Immigrants, 1989–1999

Republic	Percentage of Immigrants
Russia	32%
Ukraine	31%
Central Asia	13%
Belarus	8%
Moldova	6%

SOURCE: *10 let alii, Novosti nedelii, March 31, 1999.*

described themselves as either not religious (52%) or atheists (17%). This is consistent with earlier surveys that show the proportion of those believing in God ranging from one in five to one in three, though only a small minority of these people practice any form of religion (Chervyakov, Gitelman, and Shapiro 1997; Gitelman 1977, 1985, 1989, 1991, 1992).

Overall, according to our exit poll, most immigrants were satisfied with their lives in Israel (53%). A little more than four in ten (41%) reported that their standard of living in Israel was better than their standard of living in the FSU and fewer than two in ten (18%) reported that it was worse. Eight in ten indicated that they would certainly (45%) or probably (35%) move to Israel again. We did find, however, that immigrants had fairly low levels of political efficacy with over half (56%) agreeing with the statement, "People like me don't have much say about what the government does."

The amount of time an immigrant had lived in Israel was slightly correlated with a more positive outlook on most of these measures. For example, 62% of immigrants who moved to Israel between 1989 and 1992 said that they were satisfied with their life in Israel, while less than half (48%) of immigrants who came after 1996 reported that they were satisfied. Not surprisingly, earlier immigrants were also more likely to report a higher standard of living and a stronger sense of political efficacy. There was virtually no variance between the immigrant cohorts on the question of whether they would make aliyah again.

More than three in four voters questioned in our exit poll reported family incomes of less than NIS 8,000 (about $2000) per month.[8] We also asked voters for a retrospective evaluation of how they were getting along compared to a year ago. A little over half (52%) reported that their financial condition was about the same, while 20% indicated they were doing better and 25% reported they were doing worse.

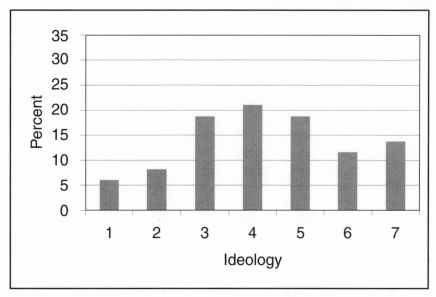

Figure 7.1   Left-Right Self-Identification

Politically, nearly 60% of the immigrants defined themselves in one of the three middle categories of a seven-point ideological scale (see figure 7.1). Still, on the extremes, more immigrants identified with the right (26%) than with the left (14%). Consistent with this rightward tilt, only small minorities were willing to give up all (3%) or part (16%) of the territories for peace. A majority was willing to give up only a small part (60%).[9]

The challenger, Barak, enjoyed some advantages. Most immigrants did not identify themselves on the ideological right and a majority felt that their financial situation had either gotten worse (25%) or stayed the same (52%) compared to the previous year. Furthermore, the great majority of immigrants reported incomes below the median in Israel. Still, on balance, the political environment appeared to benefit the incumbent prime minister, Netanyahu. Immigrants leaned to the right, were wary about giving up any amount of territory, and were generally satisfied with their situation in Israel. Barak's job in the campaign was to change the subject from territorial compromise to economic insecurity. His other task was to refocus the campaign from ideology to Netanyahu's personality. As we will see in the following section, he was able to achieve both goals as well as take advantage of Israel b'Aliya's focus on a completely different issue.

The Campaign

Whereas in 1992 and 1996, security and resettlement issues, and perhaps religious issues, influenced immigrants' votes significantly, in 1999 Israel b'Aliya primed the visibility of another issue, the administration of the Ministry of the Interior by the Shas Party. Broadly, this issue has to do with the Jewish character of the state and the extent to which religious conceptions define it. More narrowly, this issue concerns the non-Jewish relatives of Jewish immigrants and the Jewish status of many of the latter. The Ministry of the Interior decides these matters and thereby affects people's prospects for obtaining citizenship under the Law of Return, eligibility for officially recognized marriage and divorce, and, at least indirectly, social status. Since Shas is an ethno-religious party, with a strong following among those of North African descent, many "Russians" regard it as representing the "darker" elements (the *dubl' entendre* is deliberate) in Israeli society. In turn, Shas spokespersons have on occasion castigated the immigration from the FSU as composed of *goyim,* criminals, prostitutes, and other undesirables. When Israel b'Aliya began to focus on the issue of who controlled the Ministry of Interior, the nature of the campaign among the FSU immigrants changed, and so, ultimately, did their voting patterns. As in 1996, the campaign by the two major parties and Israel b'Aliya's position proved decisive in shaping the votes of immigrants from the FSU and its successor states.

In retrospect, Netanyahu made a crucial mistake when he made Lieberman, a former aide, his stalking horse among the FSU immigrants. As he did with many others, the prime minister seemed to distrust his coalition partner, Sharansky, and covertly supported the formation of a second "Russian" party headed by a closer confidante—against whom he turned eventually as well. As a result, the Likud campaign closed down its department for electioneering among FSU immigrants headed by the immigrant political activist and journalist, Ze'ev Geizler. Sharansky reacted angrily to what he saw as Netanyahu's attempt to undermine him by sponsoring a second "Russian" party and he adopted an official posture of neutrality in the prime ministerial contest. However, he spared no effort in attacking Lieberman, himself a very aggressive politician, and Israel Beiteinu. Since they were associated with Netanyahu, one could reasonably deduce that behind Sharansky's neutrality in the prime ministerial race lay a preference, if only *faute de mieux,* for Netanyahu's rival Barak. Moreover, acting on the suggestion of a non-"Russian" campaign adviser, Sharansky began to link the Likud and Netanyahu to Shas, a major partner in the Likud coalition government, and to make Shas' control of the Interior Ministry the focal point of Israel b'Aliya's campaign. Neither the territories, nor the future of Jerusalem, nor security—the issues on which Netanyahu concentrated—were featured or even mentioned in most of Israel b'Aliya's campaign propaganda. Instead, the party became identified with the catchiest slogan of the campaign, "*MVD pod nash kontrol', a nie pod Shas kontrol'*." Though in Russian (and grammatically incorrect), the idea that the Ministry of the Interior (MVD) should be under our *(nash)* control rather than under Shas's control struck a responsive chord among the immigrants and even caught on with the general Israeli public.

Once Israel Beiteinu came into existence, Likud-oriented local activists of Israel b'Aliya had to work with the local Labor infrastructures because Likud was with Lieberman (*Vesti,* May 20, 1999). Later Netanyahu distanced himself from Lieberman and reopened the "Russian" department in Likud campaign headquarters, but by then, it was too late. Voters saw him as having betrayed Lieberman and this gave credence to the One Israel Party's claim that Netanyahu betrayed his allies and was untrustworthy. Moreover, Israel b'Aliya was not united behind Netanyahu or Likud. Immigrant Resettlement Minister Yuli Edelstein was identified with the Likud, Member of Knesset Roman Bronfman was identified with Labor, and Sharansky was seemingly neutral. In addition, a group of local officials and vice-mayors (e.g., Mikhail Reif, vice-mayor of Rishon le-Zion) from the FSU came out for Barak (*Novosti nedelii,* May 19, 1999).

In contrast to Labor's indolence and indifference in 1996, the One Israel campaign worked the immigrant neighborhoods. It managed to circumvent the hostile Russian-language press by inserting multipage pamphlets in the papers, publishing books in Russian about Barak, issuing pamphlets and other materials.[10] Barak had at least four such inserts, Netanyahu only two—and those came late in the campaign. One Israel was also undoubtedly behind the pro-Barak newspaper ads taken out by *Olim vatikim za smenu kursa* (Veteran immigrants for a change in course) or "*Grazhdanie protiv diskriminatsii/Ezrahim neged aflayah*" (Citizens against discrimination) or "*Hamoetsah leshalom uvitakhon*" (Council for peace and security).

A sensation was created in the latter part of the campaign, especially among immigrants, when Yaakov Kedmi (formerly Yasha Kazakov), head of the prime minister's Liaison Office (Nativ or Lishkat Hakesher) which had for decades dealt semisecretly with Soviet Jews, accused his nominal boss of indifference to the immigrants. Kedmi, known as an extreme hard-liner who could not be suspected of sympathy for Barak's and One Israel's platform, accused Netanyahu of cynically manipulating a trip to Russia in order to enhance his electoral prospects. Kedmi resigned as head of the Liaison Office in April following the leak of his letter of resignation, written five months previously, in which he charged that Netanyahu had done nothing for post-Soviet Jewry and had failed to fulfill any of his promises. Netanyahu had not met with Kedmi for eighteen months, demonstrating his lack of genuine interest in post-Soviet Jewry. (*Haaretz,* April 26, 1999). Kedmi's unrelenting attacks in the press and in television and radio interviews blackened Netanyahu's name more than any other political figure dared to do in the campaign. Thus, despite the support Netanyahu and his erstwhile ally Lieberman enjoyed in the Russian media, there were significant countervailing forces available to move the "Russian" voter. As one can infer from the following data, Netanyahu's lack of integrity, rather than his policies and platform, became very important in the campaign as he failed to retain the support among the "Russians" that he had enjoyed in 1996.

The Vote For Prime Minister

Political campaigns, no matter where they are contested, are about securing one's base vote and winning the support of undecided or persuadable voters. Although previous voting patterns and a right-leaning tilt to the Russian electorate seemed to give Netanyahu the advantage, Barak and his allies in Israel b'Aliya did a masterful job of priming issues other than military security. As already discussed, after achieving a basic level of credibility on security issues, they made Netanyahu's integrity, the role of Shas, and the immigrants' financial situations the primary focus of the campaign.

In the following two tables, we use information from the exit poll to show how Barak and Netanyahu did among voters with different sorts of personal and ideological predispositions. Table 2 portrays the relationship between reported vote in 1996 and reported vote in 1999. Table 3 shows the relationship between ideology and reported vote in 1999. The two tables together tell a relatively simple, but powerful story. Those voters with predispositions toward Barak (Peres voters in 1996 and those who described their ideology as

Table 7.2   Reported 1999 Vote for Prime Minister
by Reported 1996 Vote for Prime Minster

	Netanyahu (44%)	Peres (24%)	Did not Vote (23%)
Netanyahu (41%)	62%	12%	34%
Barak (54%)	33%	84%	63%
Other (4%)	5%	4%	3%

Table 7.3   Reported 1999 Vote for Prime Minister by Ideology

	Left (33%)	Center (21%)	Right (46%)
Netanyahu (41%)	15%	34%	68%
Barak (54%)	82%	62%	27%
Other (4%)	3%	4%	5%

leaning to the left) were much more loyal than voters with predispositions toward Netanyahu (Netanyahu voters in 1996 and those who described their ideology as leaning to the right).

As table 7.2 shows, 84% of voters who cast their ballots for Peres in 1996 cast their ballots for Barak in 1999. On the other hand, while he still won the majority of their votes, fewer than two in three (62%) of Netanyahu's previous supporters voted for him in 1999. Furthermore, among first-time voters—a subgroup of swing voters within this large block of swing voters—Barak beat Netanyahu by nearly a two-to-one margin (63% to 34%).[11]

When we look at ideology (table 7.3), we see a similar story. More than eight out of ten voters (82%) who considered themselves on the left (one, two, or three on the ideological scale) voted for Barak. A little more than two in three voters (68%) who considered themselves on the right (five, six, or seven on the ideological scale) voted for Netanyahu. Those voters in the middle chose Barak by almost a two-to-one margin (62% to 34%).

Given the nature of the campaign, an official endorsement by Lieberman of Netanyahu and a tacit endorsement of Barak by Sharansky, we would expect to see strong correlations between Barak votes and Israel b'Aliya voters and between Netanyahu voters and Israel Beitenu voters. This was in fact the case. Nearly two in three (65%) Israel b'Aliya voters chose Barak and a little more than two in three Israel Beitenu voters (71%) chose Netanyahu. The correlation between Barak voters and Israel b'Aliya votes is all the more impressive when compared to the 20-percentage point advantage that Netanyahu enjoyed among these same voters in 1996.

Why were Barak voters more loyal than likely Netanyahu voters, and why was Barak able to win the support of first-time voters and those with weaker predispositions? In earlier sections, we described some of the basic attitudes of immigrant voters as well as the types of issues discussed during the course of the campaign. If we look at how some of those attitudes and characteristics correlate with votes for prime minister, some clear patterns emerge.

Voters who were more satisfied in Israel and believed that their economic lot had improved over the last year were more likely to vote for the incumbent, Netanyahu. Voters who believed their financial status had stayed the same or gotten worse were more likely to cast their ballots for the challenger. Looking at the issues that most concerned the voters, we see that creating jobs (which the Barak campaign stressed) and changing the role of religion in public life (which the the Israel b'Aliya campaign stressed) were in the top tier of issues that immigrant voters wanted the new government to tackle. In that first tier were creating jobs (25%), military security (23%), and changing the role of religion in public life (20%). Far down the list in a second tier of responses was improving the absorption process (6%), improving relations with Palestinians (5%), improving relations with the United States (2%), and improving relations with Russia (1%).[12] Not surprisingly, voters who believed that military security should be the main concern of the new government were more likely to vote for Netanyahu. Voters who felt that jobs, the absorption process, and the role of religion in public life required government attention were more likely to vote for Barak.

Still, bivariate analysis can mask the true influence of causal factors. So in order to identify the independent influence of these basic attitudinal and demographic factors on individual voting behavior, we estimated the following multivariate vote-choice model using logit regression:[13]

$$\text{Probability (Barak Vote)} = \text{Constant} - (B2 * \text{ideology}) - (B3 * \text{land for peace}) + (B4 * \text{jobs}) - (B5 * \text{security}) + (B6 * \text{role of religion}) - (B7 * \text{retrospective economic evaluation}) - (B8 * \text{satisfaction in Israel}) - (B9 * \text{religiosity}) + (B10 * \text{age}) - (B11 * \text{sex}) + (B12 * \text{IAB Voter})$$

Ideology controls for basic predispositions. Attitudes toward the return of territories and assessments of what issue should be the first priority of the government control for issue positions. Questions on personal economic well-being and satisfaction controls for personal retrospective evaluations. We also include a dummy variable for whether or not a respondent voted for Israel b'Aliya. Finally, we control for a series of demographic characteristics, age, sex, and religiosity. We report the findings in table 7.4.

With other factors held constant, ideology, retrospective financial evaluations, attitudes toward security and the peace process, as well as attitudes toward the role of religion in public life all have statistically and substantively strong influences on immigrant votes for the prime minister. Holding other variables in the model constant at their means and translating the logit coefficients into more easily comprehensible probabilities shows that an immigrant who thought he or she was worse off than last year was 15 percentage

Table 7.4   Causes of Vote for Barak for Prime Minister

Variable	Coefficient	Standard Error
Ideology	−4.21	.38
Land for peace	1.09	.37
Jobs	.09	.20
Security	−.53	.21
Role of religion	.70	.21
Retrospective economic evaluation	−.77	.24
Satisfaction in Israel	−.19	.30
Religiosity	−.23	.34
Age	−.05	.05
Sex	.19	.14
Israel b'Aliya Voter	.49	.15
Constant	2.62	.44

N = 1,011
Percent Predicted Correctly = 73.79%
Null Model = 57%
Log Likelihood = 1085.19

points more likely to vote for Barak than an immigrant who thought that he or she was better off. A voter on the far left was 75 percentage points more likely to vote for Barak than a voter on the far right. An immigrant who believed that military security was the top issue for the new government was 10 percent points less likely to vote for Barak, whereas an immigrant who believed that the government should focus on the role of religion in public life was 13 percentage points more likely to vote for Barak.

Even with these other factors held constant, a vote for Israel b'Aliya also has a strong and significant effect on one's probability of voting for Barak. Specifically, a Israel b'Aliya voter was 9 percentage points more likely to vote for Barak. Some of the strength of this coefficient is clearly due to other causal factors omitted from this very rudimentary model. Nevertheless, the finding suggests that Israel b'Aliya's organization on the ground did help Barak's efforts.

Although military security and ideology had strong independent influences on the vote, not enough people felt that military security was a top problem and not enough voters had right-wing predispositions to counterbalance the fact that only one in five immigrants thought their financial situation was better. Immigrants do lean to the right and appear to be more hawkish on security issues than most Israelis. Still, in the 1999 elections, our analysis shows that it was a combination of classic economic retrospective voting, concern about Shas, and Israel b'Aliya's help on the ground that were the decisive factors.

The Knesset Vote

While the change in electoral laws encouraged most Israelis to split their votes, our exit poll data show that almost eight in ten "Russian" voters (79%) chose the One Israel or Likud nominee for prime minister and voted for one of the other parties to represent their interests in the Knesset. More importantly, as we already noted, more than half of the "Russian" Knesset vote (54%) went to their own "ethnic" or parochial parties. Only Arab voters chose their own parochial parties in such large numbers. It was this behavior that really distinguished immigrant voters in 1999.

Although it is theoretically possible that strong support for such parochial parties would have emerged even in the absence of any change in electoral rules, we do know that previous immigrants from the FSU did not support their own ethnic parties and generally voted like other Israeli Jews—though, admittedly, they arrived with different "cultural baggage" and were more disposed to "become Israeli" as quickly as possible. Still, in the early 1990s cohort, close to 250,000 voters had a chance to vote for an immigrant party in the 1992 elections (contested under the old rules) and did so in very small numbers (11,000). In the election of 1996, however, about 43% voted for Israel b'Aliya or for a very small immigrant party headed by Efraim Gur (which got only 0.56% of the total vote). Finally, our exit poll reveals that in 1999, even among respondents who arrived in time to vote in the 1992 elections—when they could have voted for DA but did so in very small numbers—51% voted for either Sharansky (34%), or Lieberman (17%).

Clearly, electoral rules matter and the emergence of ethnic voting habits among this large bloc of new voters may be one of the most dramatic and long-term effects of the change in Israeli electoral law. Therefore, we take a closer look at two questions. First, what factors explain voting for an immigrant or ethnic party? Second, what factors explain for which immigrant party they voted? We also use our exit poll data to speculate on the long-term success of these parochial parties.

As one might expect, immigrants less satisfied with their situation in Israel were more likely to vote for one of the immigrant parties. Less efficacious voters were also more likely to vote for one of the immigrant parties. Put another way, those immigrants more confident in their abilities to navigate the Israeli system were more likely to cast their ballots for a nonethnic alternative. The data also show that more conservative voters were more likely to vote for one of the Russian parties. All in all, our data suggest that as the absorption process continues and when (or if) immigrants become more satisfied with their lives and more confident of their abilities, voting for ethnic parties

Table 7.5   Russian Party Vote for Selected Subgroups

	Israel b'Aliyah	Israel Beitenu	Non-Russian Parties
Ideology			
Left	27%	7%	66%
Center	39%	18%	43%
Right	27%	24%	49
Satisfaction in Israel			
Least Satisfied	41%	17%	42%
Most Satisfied	32%	18%	50%
Most Important Problem			
Jobs	415	15%	44%
Military Security	28%	25%	47%
Role of Religion	33%	13%	54%
Efficacy			
Low Efficacy	43%	17%	40%

may decline. Nevertheless, over four in ten (43%) of the most satisfied and the most efficacious (44%) still voted for one of the two Russian parties. It remains to be seen whether these still relatively high numbers will further decline if Israeli electoral laws still provide the opportunity and even the incentive to vote for more parochial interests on the Knesset ballot.

Looking at the competition among the parochial immigrant parties, Israel b'Aliya beat Israel Beitenu in every demographic and attitudinal subgroup. As illustrated in table 5, while Lieberman's alternative party did better with right-wing voters and with those concerned about military security, Israel b'Aliya still managed to win a plurality of even the most conservative voters. Table 7.5 also shows that Israel b'Aliya did its best with those who were least satisfied with their situation in Israel and who were in the middle of the ideological spectrum. Israel b'Aliya also did well among those voters who wanted jobs to be the chief priority of the new government and who said that their financial situation had declined in the last year.

Interestingly, voters who identified changing the role of religion in public life as the most important issue were actually less likely to vote for a Russian party and 4 percentage points less likely to vote for Israel b'Aliya than those who identified other issues. Although it is hard to tell for sure, the anti-Shas campaign may have helped Barak's bid for prime minister and the Meretz and Shinui campaigns for Knesset more than the campaign of its sponsor, Israel b'Aliya. Meretz (19%) and Shinui (10%) did their best with those voters who wanted attention paid to the role of religion in public life.

Israel b'Aliya is the largest and most broad-based immigrant party and as just demonstrated, showed strength among all subgroups. Still, although the Downsian middle may be where a party wants to be under the old system, it may be a dangerous place in the new system. Such a party is susceptible to attacks from more narrowly focused groups. In this most recent contest, Israel b'Aliya appears to have lost votes to Meretz and Shinui on the left on the religious issue and to Israel Beitenu on its right on the security issue. Israel b'Aliya voters will continue to be a target for other Russian parties as well as other parties trying to get voters on single issues. Party competition for immigrant voters over the next few elections will likely be fierce. In fact, the very same electoral laws that created the incentive for Israel b'Aliya to form and attract so many voters may make this success difficult to sustain. Furthermore, as Russian Jews become more comfortable and economically secure, and if immigration from the FSU tails off, Israel b'Aliya's base of reliable voters will be reduced.[14]

Conclusion

Israel's new voting system has allowed "Russian" parties to establish a stable constituency. Under the old system "Russian" voters may have reasoned that "voting for Israel b'Aliya gets us six to seven seats but gives us no say over who is elected prime minister; to do that we have to vote for one of the two big parties." In 1996 and 1999 they could have their cake and eat it too— they could vote "ethnically" on one level and "as statespersons" on the other. Over time the "ethnic" or parochial vote may be gradually transformed into a vote for a party whose origins were in ethnic protest but that evolved into a more broad based party. If loyalty to Israel b'Aliya develops and if party identification becomes solidified, it might be able to shift its focus gradually from immigrant concerns but still retain their loyalty. It could transform itself in a longer run into a stable centrist party with a broader base than immigrants from the FSU. Nevertheless, as our data suggest, given the types of voters that it attracts, this will be a difficult task.

In the shorter run, "Russians" are a swing vote who can be crucial in a vote for prime minister (1992, 1996) and are probably going to be crucial for every coalition government. But while they may swing from one partner party to another, they have been consistent in voting against whichever party controls the Knesset and against the incumbent prime minister. If they develop an "oppositionist mentality," which might be especially pervasive among people who for much of their lives could only vote "yes" to what was presented to them, they may be the second place a nonincumbent looks to for support after her own party.

While these points are speculative, it can be safely asserted that the past three elections in Israel demonstrated that under certain conditions campaigns make a great deal of difference. Among people who have no strong party identification (unlike most Israelis), or where both prime ministerial candidates are not in one's preferred party, the campaign made a difference. Its importance is perhaps enhanced among "Russians" both because they are voracious readers and because, as people for whom free elections are still a novelty, they make their choices carefully.

Another conclusion one may safely draw is that the success of two "Russian" parties, and the emergence of a third "Russian" party based on the non-Ashkenazi immigration from the FSU, further solidifies the trend to identity politics, a trend begun by Shas. The irony is that in the 1999 election Shas was the main target of the "other" ethnic party. However, Israel's political history is one of a dominant culture (and, for twenty-nine years, a dominant party) submerging the cultures imported via immigration, albeit with some concessions and assimilation of some elements of the new cultures. Especially if the immigration from the FSU declines as the reservoir of Jews and their relations continues to dry up, the immigrant parties may fade as the FSU immigrants blend into the mainstream population. Still, the example of Shas is instructive. Thirty years after the largest wave of immigrants from North African countries arrived in Israel, and after most of them had been acculturated to predominantly Ashkenazi Israeli norms, an assertive party claiming to defend them against discrimination and to restore Jewish tradition to a place of pride consistently wins a very large proportion of their votes and those of their children and grandchildren. The *bete noire* of the "Russians" could be the model they will follow.

Appendix: Exit Poll Methodology

Sample precincts for the exit poll were chosen in two stages. First, using information from the Israeli Central Bureau of Statistics on the distribution of immigrants from the former Soviet Union, cities and locales were allocated exit poll precinct sites in proportion to the size of their immigrant populations. Undergraduate and graduate students (all native Russian language speakers) from Tel Aviv University, Haifa University, the Technion, and other institutions who lived in the chosen cities and locales were re-cruited to conduct the exit polls in precincts with high immigrant popula-tions. The proportion of immigrants in these precincts ranged from 30 to 90 percent.

Interviewers were trained in basic data collection techniques and were instructed to screen all voters for eligibility. Eligible voters were then asked to complete the self-administered exit poll questionnaire and to deposit the questionnaire in a secret ballot box. Although some older voters asked our in-terviewers to help them fill out the questionnaire, every effort was made to make the survey confidential and anonymous. All in all, 1,795 surveys were conducted in 40 precincts across the country. We estimate a miss and refusal rate of close to 50% that compares well with other exit polls—not to mention telephone surveys—conducted in Israel and in other countries.

Drawing and completing interviews with a large representative sample of immigrants to Israel from the FSU is logistically difficult. For example, not all have phones and many move frequently before they can purchase their own apartments. Nevertheless, since well over 80% of Israelis (includ-ing new immigrants) typically turn out to vote, an exit poll in precincts with high concentrations of immigrants is an excellent, efficient way to gather survey data on immigrant attitudes and political behavior. Another important advantage of an exit poll is that only voters are questioned and they are asked their opinions immediately after the act of voting. The main drawback to this exit poll was that we missed immigrants living in mixed or majority Israeli neighborhoods. We would expect that these immigrants would show less distinctive voting patterns. Also, experience in the United States (Goldstein 1993; Teixeira 1993) show that higher educated and younger voters are less likely to complete exit polls. Still, the proportion of seniors in the exit poll was virtually identical to estimates of their share of the population.

In general, the exit poll survey results match up extraordinarily well with actual election results. First, most media reports estimate that Barak received between 55 and 60% of the immigrant vote. Our survey gave Barak 57% of the two-party vote. Second, we estimate that 480,000 Russian-speaking im-migrants voted. In our exit poll, Israel b'Aliya received 35%, translating to 168,000 votes. Official vote totals show that it received 171,705 votes. Also, in our exit poll, Lieberman's Israel Beitenu received 17% of the vote, which translates to 81,600 votes. Official vote totals show that Lieberman's party received 86,153 votes. Third, the survey cited from the 1996 elections had Netanyahu beating Peres by 64% to 36%. Our question asking about previ-ous voting behavior puts it at 65% to 35%.

Notes

1. Previous to this immigration, approximately 170,000 immigrants from the Soviet Union came to Israel from 1968 until 1988. As far as one can tell, they voted in the last twenty-five years pretty much as the rest of the Jewish population of Israel, though probably not as much for religious parties and perhaps somewhat more for Likud and for parties on the right than Labor and parties on the left.

2. Immigrants from the FSU are commonly referred to in Israel as "Russians," though the great majority are Jews and many have come from republics of the FSU other than Russia. Similarly, immigrants from English-speaking countries are sometimes referred to as "Anglo-Saxons." Language rather than ethnicity seems to determine others' perception of one's identity.

3. According to the newspaper *Haaretz,* 43% of the *olim* voted for Israel b'Aliyah, 26% for Likud, 12% for Avodah and Meretz, 13% for religious parties (which seems high, though Mafdal, the National Religious Party probably got some of their votes), and 6% for other parties (May 18, 1999).

4. For example, a poll reported in a Russian newspaper, *Novosti nedelii* (January 1, 1999), had Netanyahu leading Barak by a 27% point margin (45% to 18%) among immigrants. A Gallup poll in March had Netanyahu at 54% and Barak at 14% (*Maariv,* March 26, 1999). Most other polls throughout the spring had Netanyahu in the mid-40s and Barak in the high teens or low twenties.

5. Barak actually ran as the candidate of a coalition of Labor and two small factions and renamed his party "One Israel," but Likud and others still tried to pin the "stigma" of socialism on his party.

6. Interestingly, in our survey the Jewish-Russian vote (53% to 47%) was also almost identical to the Jewish vote among the population as a whole (52% to 48%).

7. Israel b'Aliyah got 171,705 votes; Liberman's Israel Beiteinu got 86,153, and there were two other immigrant parties—Tikvah (7,366 votes) and Lev (6,311 votes)—which did not pass the threshold for entry into the Knesset.

8. Our income question gave respondents a very wide range within which to place themselves and we are aware that self-reporting, even with such wide ranges, is often inaccurate. Median monthly gross income per household was 8,320 NIS in 1997.

9. We mistakenly did not include an option of "give up no territories at all" and a few respondents wrote on their questionnaires comments such as "not one inch should be yielded!" Over one in five respondents refused to answer this question.

10. Examples are *Edinnyi Izrail—informatisionnoe prilozhenie* [One Israel—informational supplement], no. 3, May 13, 1999, a 6-page tabloid insert into several Russian-language weekend newspapers; *Kniga rekordov 'Ginessa'* 1999 [the 1999 Guiness Book of Records], a 16-page brochure that claimed to document Netanyahu's record-breaking number of lies; *Lozungi ili dela* [Slogans or deeds] a dense 20-page pamphlet outlining One Israel's platform, and *Politika lzhi Netanyagu; uchites' chitat'* [Netanyahu's policies of lies—read and learn] an 8-page brochure purporting to expose Netanyahu's falsifications.

11. First-time voters include immigrants who turned 18 between 1996 and 1999; immigrants who simply chose to vote in 1999 after not voting in 1996; and immigrants who arrived after the 1996 election. Among the most recent arrivals, Barak won 60% to Netanyahu's 37%.

12. We note that this last finding goes against much of the conventional wisdom that claimed that immigrants felt close to, and were concerned about, Israel's relationship with their old homeland.

13. For this simple model, we ignore the simultaneity that clearly exists in the equation.

14. Israel b'Aliyah's long-term future will also depend on its ability to consolidate power in the Ministry of Interior and to use the ministry as an effective partronage machine.

References

Chervyakov, Valery, Zvi Gitelman, and Vladimir Shapiro. 1997. "Religion and Ethnicity: Judaism in the Ethnic Consciousness of Contemporary Russian Jews." *Ethnic and Racial Studies* 20, no. 2 (April): 280–305.

Cohen, Aryeh Dean. 1999. "The Kedmi Conundrum." *Jerusalem Post,* April 30, B4.

Eizenshtadt, Yaacov. 1997. "Bekhirot 1996 b're'i haitonim Vesti veVremiia basafah harusit" [The 1996 elections in the Vesti and Vremiia Russian-language newspapers]. In David Prital (ed.). *Yehuday brit hamoetsot bema'avar* 3, no. 18 (Jerusalem).

Eldar, Akiva. 1999. "Hakoach hekhadash shel Natan Sharansky." [Natan Sharansky's new power] *Haaretz,* May 13.

Fein, Aharon. 1995. "Voting Trends of Recent Immigrants from the former Soviet Union." In Asher Arian and Michal Shamir, (eds.). *The Elections in Israel 1992.* Albany: State University of New York Press.

Gitelman, Zvi. 1977. "Soviet Political Culture: Insights from Recent Jewish Emigres." *Soviet Studies* 29, no. 4 (October): 543–564.

———. 1985. "Resettling and Integrating Soviet Immigrants in Israel and the United States: A Comparative Analysis." In Rita Simon and Julian Simon, (eds.). *New Lives: The Adjustment of Soviet Jewish Immigrants in the United States and Israel.* Boston: Lexington Books.

———. 1989. "Jewish Nationality and Religion in the USSR and Eastern Europe." In Pedro Ramet, (ed.). *Religion and Nationalism in Soviet and East European Politics.* Durham, NC: Duke University Press.

———. 1991. "Ethnic Identity and Ethnic Relations among the Jews of the Non-European USSR." *Ethnic and Racial Studies* 14, no. 1 (January): 24–54.

———. 1992. "Judaism and Jewishness: Religion and Nationality in the USSR." *Nationalities Papers* 20, no. 1. (Spring): 75–86.

———. 1995. *Immigration and Identity: The Resettlement and Impact of Soviet Immigrants on Israeli Politics and Society.* Los Angeles: Wilstein Institute.

Goldstein, Kenneth. 1995. "Who Votes . . . Early?" Paper presented at the Annual Meeting of the American Association of Public Opinion Research.

Horowitz, Tamar. 1999. "Determining Factors of the Vote among Immigrants from the Former Soviet Union." In Asher Arian and Michal Shamir (eds.). *The Elections in Israel 1996.* Albany: State University of New York Press.

Kontorer, Dov. 1999. "Ultima Thule—prichiny porazhenia." [Farthest Thule—reasons for the shock] *Vesti,* May 20, 4.

Makovsky, David. 1999 "Sharon's Own Spin on His Game of Russian Roulette." *Haaretz* (English edition), May 26, B2.

Novosti nedelii. 1999. "My priveli Baraka k pobede" [We gave Barak the victory], May 19.

Reich, Bernard, Noah Dropkin, and Meyrav Wurmser. 1993. "Soviet Jewish Immigration and the 1992 Israeli Knesset Elections." *Middle East Journal* 47, no. 3 (Summer): 464–478.

Shapira, Inna. 1999. "A Pawn Trying to Be a Rook." *Haaretz,* May 18.

Teixeira, Ruy. 1998 "The Real Electorate," *The American Prospect* 9, 37 (March-April).

Weiss, Shevach. 1997. "Nituach hahatzba'ah bekerev yotsai brit hamoetsot" [Analysis of the vote among Soviet immigrants]. In David Prital (ed.). *Yehuday brit hamoetsot bema'avar* 3, no. 18. Jerusalem.

Part III

Political Parties and
the Election Campaign

8

The Triumph of Polarization

Daphna Canetti, Howard L. Frant, and Ami Pedahzur

Introduction

At the beginning of 1999, the future looked bright for the new Israeli Center Party. According to opinion polls, party leader Yitzhak Mordechai was the only candidate who could defeat the Likud leader, Prime Minister Benjamin Netanyahu, in head-to-head elections. The party called on Labor voters to desert the Labor candidate, Ehud Barak, and to unite behind Mordechai. As for the party itself, this group of well-known political figures, who had left their political homes in Likud and Labor, promised a new dawn in Israel's political life: no more conflict, no more alienation, a new style of politics. Their slogans were extremely appealing at a time when Netanyahu was attacking the old elite, the ultra-Orthodox population was at war with the Supreme Court, and tensions were high between the Mizrahi Jews (with origins in the Arab countries) and new Russian immigrants. The polls indicated the party would win at least twenty seats in the legislature.

At the same time, Shinui, Israel's old Center Party, established in 1974, was preparing for defeat. A split in the party had left it with only one seat in the current Knesset, and the party faced extinction. Only three months before the elections, the party went through a major upheaval. Instead of sticking to vague center values, Shinui became a "single-issue party"—a secular party devoted to struggle against the ultra-Orthodox camp. Its hardworking but non-charismatic leader, MK Avraham Poraz, stepped aside and cleared the stage for a new leader, former TV personality Yosef "Tommy" Lapid, known for his straightforward, even aggressive, style.

As Election Day came closer, the popularity of Shinui rose while that of the Center Party declined. In the end, Shinui slightly outpolled the Center Party, and each party ended up with six seats in the new Knesset. Mordechai withdrew as a candidate for prime minister before the elections. How could this be? Why did the new hope of the Israeli political system end up as a small, even marginal party, while a party on the edge of extinction dramatically increased its representation?

In this chapter, we propose an explanation based on Giovanni Sartori's (1966, 1976) concept of "polarized pluralism." Briefly, our argument is as follows: the Israeli political system has always had intrinsic structural and social features predisposing it toward fragmentation. But structural changes made shortly before the 1996 election greatly increased those tendencies. The effects of those changes are perceptible in the results of the 1996 election, but were magnified in the 1999 elections, both because adjustment to the new environment took time and because of external political changes.

Moreover, both the external political changes and structural changes reduced the importance of what had previously been the main dimension of political conflict. The paradoxical result is that while the two largest parties moved toward greater consensus, smaller parties found new dimensions of conflict, along which they could gain electoral benefits by staking out extreme positions. Israel today is characterized by polarization along multiple dimensions.

In what follows, we first discuss the meaning and implications of polarized pluralism, and describe the new features in Israeli politics that characterize it. We then offer an explanatory model for the shift from a moderate party system to an extreme or polarized one. We conclude with a brief discussion of the implications for Israel's future.

What Is Polarized Pluralism?

The concept of polarized pluralism was first introduced by Sartori (1966). Party systems with many parties, but without a large ideological distance between them, he terms *moderate pluralism*. Those with many (at least five or six) parties and a large ideological distance between the extremes he terms *extreme pluralism* or *polarized pluralism*.

In a later book Sartori considers Israel explicitly, but he is puzzled by it; he says that Israel's party system from 1948 to 1973 "hardly belongs to any type" (1976, 154). Specifically, it "belongs to the class of extreme pluralism," yet "it is not polarized." However, Giora Goldberg (1992, 44–49) claims that by the late 1980s Israel was close to Sartori's model of polarized pluralism; the only thing keeping it from being the perfect archetype was the absence of a viable center.

We assert that the Israeli polity by the late 1990s had arrived at a system of polarized pluralism. The absence of a center is explained by the fact that the two previously large parties, Likud and Labor, now occupy the center. This is why the new Center Party failed in the 1999 elections: there was no vacuum to be filled.

Sartori says that party systems of polarized pluralism have eight distinctive features:

1. *The presence of relevant antisystem parties:* Though such parties may have various ideologies, they all share the property of questioning the legitimacy of a regime and of undermining its base of support.

2. *The existence of bilateral oppositions:* There are two incompatible oppositions that are ideologically on opposite sides of the governing coalition and so cannot join forces.

3. *The center of the system is occupied:* The presence of a center means that political conflict is no longer bipolar, but triangular (at least). Paradoxically, this encourages extremism: Since parties cannot compete electorally over the center, they adopt extreme positions.

4. *Polarization:* Because the center is occupied, polarization results—the parties at the extreme ends are very far apart ideologically. Sartori notes, "This is tantamount to saying that cleavages are likely to be very deep, that consensus is surely low, and that the legitimacy of the political system is widely questioned" (1976, 135).

5. *The prevalence of centrifugal drives over centripetal ones:* Although the center is occupied, Sartori sees polarized pluralism as characterized by "the enfeeblement of the center, a persistent loss of votes to one of the extreme ends (or even to both)" (1976, 136).

6. *Ideological patterning:* The system "contains parties that disagree not merely on policy but also, and more importantly, on principles and fundamentals" (1976, 137).

7. *The presence of irresponsible oppositions:* Because of the presence of extreme parties that are destined never to govern, an irresponsible opposition develops that knows it will never be held accountable for its promises.

8. *Politics of outbidding:* Because some parties do not need to be responsible, they can engage in wild promises that they know they will not be able to keep.

Goldberg (1992) asserts the Israeli polity already had most of these characteristics by 1992, lacking only a viable center. In particular, while Sartori asserted in 1976 that Israeli politics is "not polarized," Goldberg sees an increased ideological distance between extreme left and extreme right since 1981.

What do left and right mean in this context? Traditionally the Israeli political system has been dominated by security considerations. Since the 1960s, the main left-right axis as perceived by Israelis was a hawk-dove axis

(Diskin 1999). The period leading up to Yitzhak Rabins's assassination was marked by intense conflict along this axis, particularly on land issues.

In the 1996 elections, both major parties moved toward the center. Reuven Y. Hazan (1999) attributes this to the decision to give priority to the prime ministerial elections, in which both parties were competing for the center. By the 1999 elections, the parties were largely locked into moderate positions. The right-wing Likud-led government had already handed over some land on the West Bank, which suggested that territorial maximalism was no longer a viable alternative. The attempt of the National Union Party to challenge the Likud on the right was a failure; it ended up with fewer seats than its constituent parts had held in the previous Knesset. There was seemingly a broad social consensus around the peace process.

It might appear, therefore, that the Israeli party system is becoming less polarized. But this is not so. A trend that has been little remarked upon[1] is that polarization now is multidimensional in Israel. While the hawk-dove axis has collapsed, polarization has spread to other axes.

The Role of the Center

As we just saw Sartori challenges the commonsense assumption that center parties are always a moderating force in politics. In his theory, when the center is occupied the moderate parties cannot compete for center voters, and so become more extreme in order to attract voters. Hazan (1995, 1997) finds support for this prediction; in a study of Western European parties he finds that the growth of center parties is accompanied both by the growth of extreme parties and by the movement of moderate parties away from the center. Goldberg (1992, 45) notes that Israel lacks center parties and so does not perfectly fit the definition of polarized pluralism.

The presence of a significant center is thus one of the most important recent changes in Israeli politics. Circumstances have pushed Likud and Labor toward each other. The two parties traditionally viewed as the large parties of left and right are the real center parties of Israel today.

In recent years, both Likud and Labor have displayed great flexibility, and have ignored or abandoned previous ideologies. Since the 1978 Camp David accords, Likud has adopted pragmatic policies in issues of land and peace. It oversaw the withdrawal from Hebron and the signing of the Wye River accords, and began land transfers to the Palestinian Authority. The 1999 campaign platforms of Likud and One Israel are markedly similar on national security issues: both pledge to seek peace with Israel's Arab neighbors, and to keep Jerusalem united.

As Likud eschews extreme rhetoric on the hawk-dove axis, so One Israel has abandoned socialist rhetoric in the economic field. Its 1999 platform embraces the free market. Only in religious affairs are there significant differences, with One Israel calling for abolishing the ultra-Orthodox military exemption, and Likud pledging to "keep the status quo in matters of religion and state."

It is thus clear why the Center Party did not live up to expectations. The center was already occupied. There was no void for them to fill.

In Sartori's theory, the fact that the center was occupied should have led other parties to become more extreme in order to compete for voters. This is indeed what happened in Israel, but in a quite unexpected way. Essentially the same external conditions that pushed the two major parties toward the center also caused the disappearance of the hawk-dove axis as an arena of electoral conflict.

The External Factor

An obvious and salient fact about Israel is that it has not been at peace with its neighbors since its founding. Because of the continuous threat, domestic unity was highly valued (Horowitz and Lisak 1990). Sartori himself suggests this as one possible reason why Israeli politics escaped polarization: "Israel is a small, encircled country fighting for survival and exposed to overriding external threats. . . . On these grounds solidarity and coalescence become a must" (1976, 154).

By 1999, with progress in the peace process, the public's sense of external threat had diminished Asher Arian's threat perception index (1999, 197–198) is based upon beliefs about the possibility of peace with the Arabs in the near future, and on an evaluation of the Arabs' aspirations. The perceived threat decreased drastically between 1986 and 1998. Similarly, the Peace Index of Yaar and Hermann[2] demonstrates the optimism of the Israeli public in the 1990s regarding peace.

The result was the near-collapse of the hawk-dove axis. The change was dramatic even from 1996 to 1999, perhaps aided by the decision of the hawkish Likud-led government to hand over some territory in the West Bank. Abraham Diskin (1999) reports that in 1996, 52% of Jewish voters said that foreign and defense policies were the main reason why people supported a specific party; by 1999 that percentage had fallen to 32%. (The decline was roughly proportional among non-Jewish voters, from 22% to 15%.)

In Israel, the collapse of the hawk-dove axis made extremism on this dimension an untenable strategy, as shown by the dismal performance of the hawkish National Union Party in the 1999 elections. But as the importance of that issue faded, so did the value placed on unity in other matters. Differences in ethnicity, religiosity, and lifestyle, always present but overshadowed by the national-security issue, emerged into prominence. The same survey found that from 1996 to 1999, the proportion of voters saying that people support particular parties because those parties "represent people like themselves" rose from 18% to 26% of Jewish voters, and from 33% to 38% of non-Jewish voters.

Parties looking to attract voters were thus moved to polarize along the multiple axes suggested by the words *people like themselves.* To understand what happened requires a look at the social cleavages in today's Israel.

The Social Factor

Deep social cleavages have always characterized Israeli society (Horowitz and Lissak 1990), but in recent years, the cleavages have become deeper and society has become more fragmented (Yatziv 1999). Baruch Kimmerling (1999) identifies six distinct cultures and subcultures in contemporary Israeli society: Jewish secular, ultra-Orthodox, national religious, traditional oriental, Russian, and Arab. Each group has different needs and different demands from the political process.

The large *secular* (almost entirely Ashkenazi) group has traditionally been the dominant culture in Israeli society, shaping Israeli society since the beginning of the twentieth century. The "establishment" and the social elite of Israel was, and to a large extent still is, drawn from this group. It was also dominant politically from 1948 until the election of the first Likud government in 1977. In 1999, the anti-Orthodox Shinui Party drew its support from this group.

The *ultra-Orthodox* camp has traditionally kept a distance from many of the institutions of Israeli society. It is distinguished from the secular not only by attitudes about religion but also by poverty. Current, two thirds of ultra-Orthodox men do not work; many of these, of course, are engaged in religious study. Ultra-Orthodox families (with an average of 5.5 people) are larger than secular families (an average of 3.3 people), meaning that government child allowances are a significant source of income (Ilan 1998). Because of this, along with the traditional exemption of the ultra-Orthodox from military service, "parasite" has become a common epithet used by the secular in referring to the ultra-Orthodox.

The *national-religious* camp is made up of those who identify themselves as religious, but also as Zionists participating fully in Israeli life. This camp was originally seen as a bridge between the ultra-Orthodox and the secular camps, but now it has its own internal dissension. One group emphasizes the religious aspect and holds policy positions not too different from those of the ultra-Orthodox. The other group has identified itself with, and is strongly represented among, Jewish settlers in the occupied territories.

In the 1999 elections the first group tended to vote for the National Religious Party (NRP), the traditional political voice of the national-religious camp, while the second group tended to vote for the National Union, which had a territorial maximalist agenda. The NRP's seats declined from 9 to 5.

The *traditional Mizrahi* camp is mostly comprised of Jews who emigrated from Arab countries to Israel in the 1950s and 1960s. This group perceived the secular Ashkenazi elite as discriminating against them, and maintains a strong ethnic consciousness today (Zfati 1999). They also tend to be more religiously observant than the secular elite and to have lower socioeconomic status.

The former leader of the Likud, Menachem Begin, was the first to mobilize the Mizrahi potential vote as a coalition of the underprivileged. A major factor in the decline of Likud has been a gradual shift of Mizrahi support to Shas, an explicitly ethnic-based and religious party.

Since late 1980s, a wave of almost one million immigrants from the former Soviet Union has created a new "Russian" community in Israel. Many had problems arising from their ambiguous status in terms of religion and nationality (many were not Jewish under religious law, but were entitled to come to Israel under the less stringent criteria of the Law of Return), and had difficulty integrating into the Israeli labor market. They felt excluded by the secular elite, but, being largely secular themselves, faced hostility from the traditional-Mizrahi camp, exacerbated by the suspicion of new immigrants common in those of lower socioeconomic status, who perceive them as competitors.

As early as the 1996 elections, a Russian political party, Israel b'Aliya, had won representation in the Knesset. A second Russian-based party, Israel Our Home, appeared in the 1999 elections, and it and Israel Be'aliyah won four and six seats, respectively.

By any measure, the most peripheral subculture is the Arab one. The Arabs have faced discrimination and hostility from the Jewish majority, and are socioeconomically disadvantaged. In 1961, almost half of all Arabs had no education at all. Educational levels among Arabs have improved dramatically since then, but in 1996, 36% had eight years of education or less, compared to 15.5% of Jews; although Arabs make up about 20% of the population, they comprised only 7% of university undergraduates (Gavizon and Abu-Ria 1999).

The Arabs, too, have responded by forming their own political parties, which have won Knesset representation. Although these parties never participated in ruling coalitions, and were largely excluded from political dialogue on security issues, they did have some voting power and sometimes supported governments from outside. In recent years the divisions *within* Arab society, mainly religious ones (Christian vs. Muslim) have increased.

To sum up, Israeli society is characterized by deep cleavages, with groups that not only have widely different cultures and needs, but that are deeply suspicious of one another. Yet this has long been true. It is just these conditions that led Sartori (1976, 154) to expect Israel to be polarized, and to be surprised that "it is not polarized, even though the tensions and conditions of a polarized development are well in the picture." With the reduced perception of external threat, though, these latent tendencies became more apparent.

The Electoral Exploitation of Cleavages

The reinvention of Shinui is in some sense a prototype of how parties were able to reposition themselves. Shinui found a niche in firm opposition to the ultra-Orthodox parties, promoting itself as hostile to "religious coercion."[3]

While there are other parties, such as Meretz, with a reputation for anti-clericalism, none had anticlericalism as its chief distinguishing feature, until Shinui. Meretz holds traditionally "left" positions not only on the religion-state issue, but also on hawk-dove, economic, and constitutional issues. This is not true for Shinui, which was originally right-of-center on economic issues and now downplays all issues except religious-secular conflict. Unlike Meretz, Shinui refused to join a coalition containing ultra-Orthodox parties.

The other notable winner in the 1999 elections was Shas, which soared from ten to seventeen seats. Shas represents polarization on at least two dimensions at once. First, it is an ultra-Orthodox party, at the opposite extreme from Shinui on the religious-secular divide. Second, it is a preeminent example of a "people like us" party, representing Mizrahi voters on the Mizrahi-Ashkenazi axis

The second of these axes was probably more significant electorally. Shas portrayed the conviction for bribery of its leader, Aryeh Deri, as an attempt by the Ashkenazi elite to silence a successful Mizrahi. There was also a bitter fight between Shas and the largest Russian-immigrant party, Israel b'Aliya. While the larger issue was the character of the state, this crystallized into Israel b'Aliya's demand for the Interior portfolio, at that time in the hands of Shas. The Shas minister of the interior, Eliyahu Suissa, accused the Russian population of wanting control of the Interior Ministry because they feared that a Shas minister would crack down on shops selling pork and would stop "forgers, swindlers and call girls" from entering the country (Alush 1999).

The elections even saw polarization on a class axis, left-right in the traditional European sense, when a small union-workers' party, One Nation, split off from Labor. It later refused to join a One Israel-led coalition (including the two main parties of the left) that it considered insufficiently socialist.

All of these cases illustrate the process of transition. From a single-axis structure, hawk versus dove, the party system has moved to a structure of multiple, sometimes overlapping, axes: ultrasecular versus ultra-Orthodox, Ashkenazi versus Mizrahi, and economic left versus right, among others.

To recapitulate: changes in external conditions led to a convergence of the two largest parties, driving other parties toward extremism. But those same external changes led to a reduction in the perception of threat by the Israeli public, leading to a collapse of the hawk-dove axis. The existing cleavages in Israeli society provided the opportunity for other parties to find new dimensions to polarize along. None of this, however, would have been feasible without structural features of the Israeli electoral system that predispose it to fragmentation.

The Structural Factor

The Israeli party system has always been prone to fragmentation. The very first Knesset had twelve parties in it, and this has been about the average since. There are two structural elements supporting the emergence and representation of small and sectarian parties; one is long-standing and one is new.

First, the basic Israeli electoral system has always been nationwide proportional representation with a very low representation threshold. Currently, a party can be represented in the Knesset if it receives 1.5% of the total vote.[4] In Germany, by comparison, a party must receive 5% of the vote before it can be represented. Israel's electoral system makes it relatively easy for small, narrowly based parties to get seats, giving them little incentive to merge into larger parties, or to moderate their ideology to appeal to a wide audience.

This is an important factor in fragmentation and in the proliferation of small parties but, as noted, it is a long-standing feature of the Israeli political system. In important ways, the Israeli system is now becoming *more* fragmented. This can be seen most clearly not in the total number of parties in the Knesset, but in the reduction in strength of the largest parties in the last two elections. As shown in figure 8.1, while in 1992 Likud and Labor gained together 59.6% of the total vote (76 seats in the Knesset), in 1996 the two parties received only 51.9% (66 seats), and in 1999 only 34.3% (45 seats).

One might think that this trend is explained by the meteoric rise of Shas, which in the 1999 elections came close to displacing Likud as the second-largest party. But in fact, the share of the four largest parties (Labor/One Israel, Likud, Shas, Meretz) fell from 85 seats in the Fourteenth Knesset to 72 in the Fifteenth pointing to a general increase in fragmentation.

The long-standing structural characteristics discussed earlier cannot explain this change. There has, however, been one important change in the

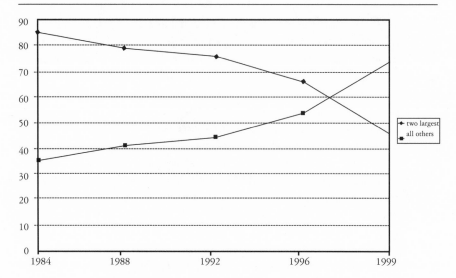

Figure 8.1.   Knesset Seats of Two Largest Parties

1990s: the new electoral law, passed in 1992, but first taking effect in the 1996 elections. The new law (Basic Law: The Government) provides for direct election of the prime minister. Voters cast two ballots, one for prime minister and the other for party in the Knesset.

The result is that voters have no incentive to consider whether the party they are voting for has stands they are comfortable with on a wide range of issues. They can affect the general direction of the government in their vote for prime minister, and then are free to indulge their special interest in voting for a party.

The "enfeeblement" of the two large parties has been largely a product of the two elections since the passage of the law on direct elections. But why the increase in fragmentation from 1996 to 1999? We attribute it to the increasing sophistication of both voters and parties as they adjust to the new system. It may have taken everyone time to grasp the implications of the new idea that ticket-splitting is possible.

Indeed, the new law may have contributed to the collapse of the hawk-dove axis in Knesset elections. First, Likud and Labor both moved toward the center in order to compete in the prime ministerial election (Hazan 1999). Second, to the extent that differences remain on hawk-dove issues, they are now fought out in the arena of prime ministerial competition, rather than in Knesset parties. Diskin's (1999, table 5) survey data show that there remained sharp differences between Netanyahu and Barak voters on such issues as evacuating settlements in the territories (the West Bank and Gaza). Similarly, Asher Arian and Michael Shamir (2000) find that the territories are the dominant issue in predicting voting in the 1999 prime ministerial race. But minor parties were able to appeal to voters by arguing that they could express their opinion on such issues in the prime ministerial vote, and on other issues in the Knesset vote. This opened the way for parties to carve out extreme positions on new dimensions.

Discussion

The increased polarization of the Israeli party system has been the result of three factors, each necessary but not by itself sufficient. First, there are long-standing deep cleavages in Israeli society. Second, the convergence of the two largest parties toward the center made it electorally profitable for smaller parties to stake out extreme positions, even while the collapse of the hawk-dove axis made it necessary for parties to seek out new dimensions of conflict. Finally, old and new characteristics of the voting system inherently tended toward fragmentation, making small "niche" parties viable.

The evolution of the Israeli party system has confounded forecasters. Goldberg predicted that the "probability of decline of polarized pluralism is greater than the probability of increase" (1992, 255). He foresaw a tendency for parties to become less ideological, with institutionalization of the anti-system parties, greater responsibility by previously irresponsible ones, and a decline in the politics of outbidding. Why were these forecasts not borne out?

Goldberg correctly foresaw that "the small parties may get further apart, but the large parties will come together" (1992, 257). What he could not foresee, because it did not really begin to happen until after passage of the direct-election law, was that the large parties would cease to be large. That is a worrisome development for the stability of the Israeli political system.

Similarly, Reuven Y. Hazan (1999, 183), looking at the 1996 elections, was "optimistic" about centripetal tendencies in the new system. No one foresaw—indeed, it is not generally recognized even today—the extent to which, as the hawk-dove dimension faded, new dimensions, with new forms of extremism, would spring up to take their place.

In the 1999 elections, the centripetal movement of the two largest parties was overshadowed by the centrifugal, center-fleeing, tendencies of the others. But extremism is no longer a simple matter of left and right, as was traditional in Israel. Rather, it is now multidimensional. Not only did the smaller parties flee the center—they fled, one might say, in all directions.

As Likud and Labor have moved toward the center, they have become "enfeebled." One should not conclude, however, that they have necessarily followed a bad electoral strategy. With three fifths of the Israeli voting public having centrist views (Arian 1999, 250) and a multiplicity of small parties, moving to the center may have been the best electoral strategy available to them.

The convergence of the large parties, however, has not led to the end of ideology in Israeli politics. Basic questions of economics, religion, ethnicity, and the future of Israeli democracy are very much on the agenda, but these questions are being raised by the small parties, not by the large ones. Two remarkable examples are the union-workers' party, previously affiliated with Labor, which refused to join a One Israel coalition it considered insufficiently socialist, and Shinui, which refused to sit in a coalition with ultra-Orthodox parties.

Conclusion

In the 1999 elections, the Center Party's attempt to create a centripetal force in Israeli politics collided with the powerful centrifugal tendencies of today's party system. In the end, its expected triumph melted away.

In contrast, Shinui was in tune with those centrifugal tendencies—it literally fled the center. But it did so in a new way, by being extremist on a new dimension. Shinui did not attract voters on a platform of territorial maximalism or pacifism. It is essentially a single-issue party of polarization, and at this point, its approach appears to be the wave of the future.

The potential consequences are not trivial. Sartori notes, "The only thing we know for sure is that if a polity is centrifugal at all levels—electoral, parliamentary and party leadership level—then it is doomed. . . ." (1976, 195). As examples of such polities, he cites Weimar Germany and Salvador Allende's Chile.

In Weimar Germany, of course, increasing polarization made the government incapable of dealing with economic crisis, and led to the coming to power of the Nazi Party with an minority of the popular vote. In Chile, increasing polarization following the election of a left-wing government led to political paralysis, followed by a bloody military coup and years of brutal repression.

Such outcomes seem highly improbable for Israel. But it would be a mistake to assume that political polarization is merely a neutral reflection of social polarization. Rather, it may exacerbate it. Roger B. Myerson argues that when voting systems favor minority representation there is an incentive for candidates "to create special interest groups and minority conflict even when it would not otherwise exist" (1993, 868). Under current electoral rules, it is clearly in the interest of parties to find ways to accentuate the already deep cleavages in Israeli society.

No one would wish for a return of the external threat as a way of increasing the stability of Israeli politics. But whether the Israeli polity will be able to counteract the centrifugal tendencies of the electoral level, or whether structural changes will be required (and politically possible) remains to be seen.

Notes

1. An exception is Hazan and Rahat (2000).
2. Peace Index data—http://www.tau.ac.il/peace/p_index.htm.
3. All platforms are taken from the following web sites:
One Israel - http://www1.knesset.gov.il/knesset15/oneisrael_m.htm;
Shinui - http://www1.knesset.gov.il/elections/knesset15/shinui_m.htm;
Likud - http://www.likud.org.il/b2a-1.html;
National Union - http://www.aquanet.co.il/vip/haichudhaleumi/matsa.htm;
Hadash - http://www.hadash.org.il/matza/platform.htm;
United Torah Judaism - http://www1.gov.il/yahaduthatora_m.htm.
4. Until the 1992 elections, the threshold was even lower, 1%. The threshold was raised to reduce fragmentation, but the change was evidently not large enough to have much impact—since 1948 the number of parties in the Knesset has fluctuated slightly, but shows no trend up or down.

References

Alush, Zvi. 1999. "Minister Suissa Against Israel Be'aliya: They Are Afraid that We Will Not Allow Criminals and Prostitutes to Enter Israel." *Yediot Ahronot,* May 5 (Hebrew).

Arian, Asher. 1998. *The Second Republic: Politics in Israel.* Chatman, NJ: Chatman House Publishers.

————. 1999. *Security Threatened: Surveying Israeli Opinion on Peace and War.* Tel-Aviv: Papirus.

Arian, Asher, and Michal Shamir. 2000. "Candidates, Parties and Blocs: Evidence from the 1999 Election." Discussion Paper 1-2000, Pinhas Sapir Center for Development, Tel-Aviv University.

Diskin, Abraham. 1999. "The New Political System of Israel." *Government and Opposition* 34 no. 4: 498–515.

Gavizon, Ruth, and Isam Abu-Ria. 1999. *The Jewish-Arab Cleavage in Israel: Characteristics and Challenges.* Jerusalem: Israel Democracy Institute (Hebrew).

Goldberg, Giora. 1992. *Political Parties in Israel: From Mass Parties to Electoral Parties.* Tel-Aviv: Ramot (Hebrew).

Hazan, Reuven Y. 1995. "Center Parties and Systemic Polarization: An Exploration of Recent Trends in Western Europe." *Journal of Theoretical Politics* 7, no. 4: 421–445.

————. 1997. *Centre Parties: Polarization and Competition in European Parliamentary Democracies.* London: Pinter.

————. 1999. "The Electoral Consequences of Political Reform: In Search of the Center of the Israeli Party System." In Asher Arian and Michal Shamir (eds.). *The Elections in Israel 1996.* Albany: State University of New York Press.

Hazan, Reuven Y., and Gideon Rahat. 2000. "Representation, Electoral Reform and Democracy: Theoretical and Empirical Lessons from the 1996 Elections in Israel and their Unintended Consequences." Forthcoming. In *Comparative Political Studies.*

Horowitz, Dan, and Lissak, Moshe. 1990. *Trouble in Utopia: The Overburdened Polity of Israel.* Tel-Aviv: Am Oved (Hebrew).

Ilan, Shachar. 1998. "One Works, Two Don't." *Ha'aretz,* March 17 (Hebrew).

Kimmerling, Baruch. 1983. *Zionism and Territory: The Socio-Territorial Dimensions of Zionist Politics.* Berkeley: Berkeley University Press.

————. 1999. "Elections as a Struggle Arena for Collective Identity." In Asher Arian and Michal Shamir (eds.). *The Elections in Israel—1996.* Jerusalem: Israel Democracy Institute, 35–56 (Hebrew).

Myerson, Roger B. 1993. "Incentives to Cultivate Favored Minorities under Alternative Electoral Systems." *American Political Science Review* 87, no. 4: 856–869.

Sartori, Giovanni. 1966. "European Political Parties: The Case of Polarized Pluralism." In Joseph LaPalombara and Myron Weiner (eds.). *Political Parties and Political Development.* Princeton: Princeton University Press.

————. 1976. *Parties and Party Systems: A Framework for Analysis.* New York: Cambridge University Press.

Yatziv, Gadi, 1999. *The Sectorial Society.* Jerusalem: Bialik Institute (Hebrew).

Zfati, Yariv. 1999. "The Ethnic Genie in Israel: Inside the Bottle on a Low Flame." *Megamot.* Forthcoming (Hebrew).

9

Barak, One—One Israel, Zero, Or, How Labor Won the Prime Ministerial Race and Lost the Knesset Elections

GIDEON DORON

Introduction

Ehud Barak's three-year political drive against the incumbent, Benjamin Netanyahu, was successfully translated into victory in the May 1999 election. Labor on the other hand, the party he chaired since 1997 (and that ran under the banner of One Israel), was not as successful. It lost close to 30 percent of its power, obtaining only 26 seats in the Fifteenth Knesset—the lowest number of representatives ever. Postelection, while still the largest party and the pivot in Barak's ruling coalition, Labor provided its leader with neither a firm parliamentary base for legislation nor the flexibility needed for governance.

Barak's electoral success may be attributed to three not mutually exclusive factors. The first is his long-term and highly effective campaign strategy. The second is the effects of the 1992 electoral reform that allows voters to differentiate between preferences for the prime minister and for the Knesset. The third is the subperformance of the incumbent both on the substantive policy level and the management of his campaign. Given the built-in theoretical and practical advantages of the incumbent (Doron and Harris 2000), Netanyahu's mismanagement helped Barak win the election.

Labor lost because, like Likud in 1996, its leaders adopted the thesis that executive ruling and parliamentary representation are two values that need not, because they can not, simultaneously be maximized. Hence, when forced to choose, they opt for the proposition that it is more important to maximize the winning-chances of its leader than to secure its traditional parliamentary base. To obtain this Likud paid, in 1996, 14 of its potential Knesset seats to both Gesher and Tzomet. Its poor performance in 1999, when it obtained only 19 Knesset seats, is partial result of that trade-off. Labor too, by altering its name to One Israel (Yisrael Achat), thus providing its leader with more spatial flexibility, allocated safe slots on its Knesset list to members of Gesher and Meimad. Its failure to sustain its size in the Knesset however can be attributed to other factors; most importantly, an almost complete emphasis—in terms of energy, attention, and resources—on Barak's personal campaign.

The main argument presented here is that given the specific design of the new electoral rules that do not permit a candidate to compete independently of his party, the opportunity costs of Barak's 1999 victory are directly related to Labor's electoral loses. Consequently, the intentions of the reformers—to strengthen the governance capabilities of the prime minister—backfired. Without a large and loyal party to back his policy programs, even routine decisions such as the approval of the annual national budget risk governance stability.

The first part of this chapter concentrates on the strategy used in Barak's campaign. Special attention is given to the "politics of amotot," ad hoc civil associations founded to bypass legal and other limitations imposed on the activities of candidates and parties. The second part analyzes the electoral outcomes of both Barak and Labor. The third provides an assessment of the governance capability and glomming prospects of Barak's coalition.

Barak vs. the Labor Party

Barak's quest for the post of prime minister began upon his 1995 retirement from the army. Many observers of his impressive military career anticipated this decision (Kaspit and Kfir 1998). Upon the request of Yitzhak Rabin, the five-time decorated retired Israel Defense Forces chief of staff assumed the post of minister of interior. Following Rabin's assassination in November 1995, he was appointed foreign minister under Shimon Peres. While learning the ropes of politics and the art of diplomacy, he projected the image of the most right-wing minister among his Labor colleagues. In the government, he refused to support steps to implement the Oslo Peace Agreement with the Palestinians, or to explicitly recognize their right to an independent state (Shitrit 1998). During the 1996 election Barak was in charge of the incumbent's personal headquarters. Following Peres's defeat, however, public blame for the loss was directed toward Haim Ramon who was responsible for the campaign, and toward the candidate himself (Kasbit, Kristal, and Kfir 1996). Barak succeeded in avoiding the public reputation of a "loser" that was associated with Peres and Ramon. This led senior members of Rabin's camp within Labor to select Barak as their leader. While considered by most observers as the most natural candidate to lead the Labor Party, he still however needed to formally capture the party's chairmanship.

The primaries elections within labor were held on June 3, 1997 and included four candidates. Barak's challengers included Efraim Sneh, former minister of health; Yossi Beilin—the architect of the Oslo Agreement; and Shlomo Ben-Ami—former Israeli ambassador to Spain. Barak needed only 40% of the votes to win in the first of the two designated rounds but he was aiming for more. Out of the 114,000 party members who took part in this election, he obtained 50.3%. Beilin, came second with 28.5%, Ben-Ami third with 14.2%, and Sneh lagged last with only 6.6% of the votes (Pedut 1997). Formally, Barak became the chairperson of the party. Practically, however, there was one final obstacle. To avoid a potential structural split in the party, he decided against appointing Peres to the newly invented title of party president, as suggested by his followers. Instead, he promised to treat the senior leader with great respect. Therefore, in 1999, some of Peres's loyalists left Labor to join the newly established Center Party.

Barak's first step was to understand the nature of the political battlefield. Under the new Israeli electoral system, as specified in Basic Law: Government 1992, the Knesset can dissolve itself and oust the prime minister when only 61 members support a nonconfidence vote. To approve a "special election" for the prime minister, a majority of 80 members is needed. Although the difference between these two sizes of majority is designed to provide some measure of stability to the rule of the prime minister, he is really not protected against the threat of impeachment. When 61 members know their term of office is about to end, they would presumably find it easy to recruit the extra members needed to secure their own posts. Since it is unclear when new elections might be called under this system, the opposition must continuously be on their guard.

Furthermore, the composition of Netanyahu's coalition, his policy zigzagging and personal conduct triggered intensive criticism. Moving forward on the peace process often raised opposition from some superhawks members of the National Religious Party and of his own party. A move back to the right was often confronted by the resistance of David Levy, or Yitzhak Mordechai, two of his senior ministers, or from the four members of the Third Way Party. Similar constraints existed in the economy sphere. The poor and the unemployed, including many Likud voters, did not favor the prime minister's support of a free market approach to the economy. To bridge contradictions, he manipulated the media by using his remarkable spinning skills, initiated frequent changes in the public agenda or, quite often, simply lied publicly. While these techniques enabled him to prolong his rule, gradually members of his party including some members of his cabinet started to defect. These included Benny Begin (the minister of science), Dan Meridor (the finance minister), Levy (the foreign minister), and finally, just months before the election, Mordechai (the minister of defense).

During these developments Barak and especially Ramon, intensified their criticism of the prime minister. Indeed, contradictions, defections, and criticism were among the factors that forced Netanyahu to call for an early election, more than a year before its designated legal time. But more importantly, faced with these political uncertainties, Barak began to implement his grand campaign strategy. Several components were involved in this strategic design.

Definition of the Strategic Goal. The election for the prime minister is designed as Two-Stage-Majority Rule, similar to that used in the French Fifth Republic (Rae 1967). While it is difficult enough to anticipate voters' patterns of behavior even when they are conducted in one round, predicting how they would vote in the second round is speculative. This is because except for municipal and intraparty elections (Horkin, Katz, and Mevorach 1998), second-round elections have never been tried in Israel. Hence there is no experience upon which to establish "habitual behavior" pattern (Shachar and Shamir 1995), so as to indicate how certain groups would vote when asked to cast a vote for only the prime minister. Hence, the net effect of the extra personal costs components added to second-round voters' participation calculus is thus not clear. The uncertainties that might be generated concern the patterns of electoral behavior of, in particular, two groups that are used as cornerstones for the strategic designs of both candidates: the right-oriented ultra-Orthodox community and the left-oriented Israeli-Arabs. The fluctuation in the rate of voting of these two groups may have significant affect on the outcomes. Thus, for example, the relatively low turnout rate among Arab voters in favor of Peres, and the complete mobilization of the ultra-Orthodox community against him, provided Netanyahu with the winning edge in the 1996 (Peretz and Doron, 1996).

Furthermore, the second round is assumed to take place after the results for the Knesset are known, and potential coalition profiles may be constructed. Given this information, it is unclear what would be the motivation of voters to support a candidate who would not be in a position, even if elected to the post of a prime minister, to serve the interests of these particular voters. Hence, there is a built-in incentive for at least one of the candidates to design a strategy that maximizes the probability of wining in one round. As just mentioned, Netanyahu in 1996 paid dearly to increase the probability of winning in one round. In 1999, Barak followed suit: in an agreement signed on March 2, 1999 he promised Levy the post of a senior minister (i.e., foreign minister) and to his party, three places within the first group of thirty Labor representatives. Likewise, one ministerial position was promised to a member of Meimad, a liberal religious party.

Except for Barak and Netanyahu three other candidates competed for the prime minister post. Begin representing the extreme right, Azmi Bishara the Arabs, and Mordechai the center. Of them, only the last one was capable of sending Barak to a second round. Therefore, to cause him to remove his candidacy he was apparently willing to pay as much as Netanyahu had three years before. But Mordechai's insistence gradually lowered his price once it became clear that Barak was capable of securing on his own the 50 percent threshold. Hence, the prime strategic goal of winning the election in one round could be obtained since only two competitors were left in the race.

Spatial Positioning. Only a median strategy can assure winning in a two-person race, regardless of the distribution of voters' preferences (Brams 1985). To obtain this position Barak held a similar position to that of Netanyahu on the security dimension. Indeed, because of this similarity he was often referred to as "Bibi [Netanyahu's nickname] Compatible." From this position, as theoretically expected (Shepsle and Bonchek 1997), he needed only to emphasize his personal attributes: that is, that because of his military experience and mature personality, he could become a better negotiator for Israel's security than the incumbent. Barak's spatial positioning was similar to the one held by Rabin in 1992, and to the right of the one held by Peres in 1996 (Peretz and Doron 1996). Indeed, all that Netanyahu had to do in 1996 was to "adopt" peace as a preferred solution to Israel's security problems. In 1999 however, Barak's, and later even Mordechai's positions, made it more difficult for Netanyahu to repeat a similar strategic move to the left and toward the median.

Also, as theoretically expected (Downs 1957) a median position of the principle candidates might lead to voters' abstention or indecisiveness due to alienation if they are located at the extreme sides of the overall preference distribution, or due to indifference if they are median voters. Consequently, the number of unidentified potential voters at the early stages of the two-year long campaign was large enough to lure the three other candidates to the race. None, however, had a winning chance; in particular Mordechai, who spatially too, located himself at the median, just like the two principle candidates. He positioned himself there, with no interesting differentiating message, no new dimension to cut the support of his two main opponents, no effective organization and resources to back his drive, and without an appealing personality. His main issue—"bring Netanyahu down," was shared by the other four challengers. His campaign message promoting him as the "only candidate who can win in the second round" aimed at the so-called strategic voter was logically defective. The support recorded in public polls was indicative of a preelection pivotal position that could be used for bargaining, just as Levy used it in 1996 with much lower statistical figures, not of a meaningful electoral strength. How can one win the second round when he is surely to lose in the first?

The prevalence of a left-right continuum as defining Israel's electoral politics and where most voters' relevant issues converge, dates back to the 1980s (Arian and Shamir 1983). Roughly speaking, security, economic, social, religious, and other issues converge to one dimension. Likud, whose traditional position is on the right side of the continuum, tends to have a competitive advantage over Labor when security issues become salient. To win, therefore, Labor should have developed an advantage over a different dimension, but it failed to do so until 1992. Then, in an artificially constructed two-person race between the security-minded Rabin representing Labor, and the incumbent Yitzhak Shamir of the Likud, the former spatially positioned himself to the right of the median of voters' preference distribution. Also, by promising to alter the "order of national priorities" and to finance these changes at the expense of the "political settlements" he was able to attract some votes from traditional Likud supporters (Doron 1996).

Here too Barak followed suit. He chose to develop the social dimension because many of Likud's voters were potentially susceptible to policy solutions that promised to improve their economic well-being. Unlike Rabin, however, who used an ambiguous language to promote his social messages, Barak used a specific one. He promised, among other things, free education from age three through university, 300,000 new jobs within four years, and $1 billion investment in new infrastructure. Unlike Netanyahu's sectarian government, "My government," he promised, "will be for all citizens." "Hospital beds will come before settlement spending and work place before money to yeshivot. Student loans will be more important than the West Bank bypass roads to nowhere" (Jerusalem Post [North American Edition] No. 1993, January 15, 1999, p. 7).

As just mentioned, candidates' median positioning often generates a motivation among some potential voters to abstain. Indeed, in 1999 the rate of voting was amongst the lowest in Israel's electoral history reaching 78.7%. Only the elections to the Second and to the Thirteenth Knessets with 75.1 and 77.4%, respectively, recorded lower rates. Also, the rate of abstention (i.e., disqualified paper ballots) was the highest ever. It reached 5.32% for the election for prime minister and 1.88% for the election to the Knesset. For comparison, in 1996, the rate was 4.76% and 2.16%, respectively (Central Bureau of Statistics, 1999 publication # 1054). This could mean, among others things, that since people had no sincere preference for a prime minister, they simply cast a "blank ballot."

Defining Target Populations. To win Barak needed to improve upon Peres's 1996 performance. The strategic task was to improve upon the turnout rate of Peres's loyalists and to attract new groups. These new targeted groups were the Sepharadi (especially of North African origin), the Russians, and the moderate religious voters. In a zero-sum fashion, a vote supporting Barak by members of these three groups who tend to support Likud, should be counted as two votes, since the one added to his side has to be subtracted from his rival. To penetrate these groups, a long-term strategy had to be designed (Tzemach 1998). Part of this strategy was asking North Africans for their "forgiveness" in the name of his party, for their mistreatment by Labor-led governments when they arrived at Israel during the early 1950s. This controversial act was effective in opening up this sector to Barak's social programs as well as motivating some of the traditional Likud (and Shas's) voters to switch their votes in favor of Barak. As argued in the next section, a comparison between Barak's performance with that of Peres in 1996, shows that while Netanyahu still dominates the North African voters, Barak was somewhat able to reduce the gap between them.

With the Russians he used a different strategy. He continuously, directly and by influential mediators (e.g., Peres) communicated with this diversified new group of voters, through their sophisticated network of printed and electronic media (Zeltzer 1999). He also translated his biography into Russian. Finally, he incorporated the moderate religious voters into his new political formation.

The Formation of One Israel. Like Rabin in 1992 who decided, for strategic reasons, to alter the name of his party from "Labor" to "Labor headed by Rabin," Barak presumably understood the difficulty for traditional right-wing voters to vote for someone representing Labor. Consequently, he changed the name of his party to "One Israel." This move was also compatible with Shlomo Ben-Ami's post-1996 election idea of restructuring Labor as a new alliance or federation consisting of new social groups in the spirit of the American Democratic Party, or more precisely, of the British New Labor (Ben-Ami 1998). To this new political construction he added, the Gesher and Meimad groups, along with some other small political factions and local organizations like Derch Hamerkaz and Lev, respectively. In April he promised to nominate their members to various public posts. He also promised various women's organizations to nominate at least three women to his government. Thus, his political appeal extended to groups and individuals driven by social, moderate religious, and gender agendas.

To support this formation and to finance his massive campaign he needed organization and resources. Labor, the largest party in the Knesset and therefore the one to enjoy the largest sum provided by the Party Financing Law could not, however, be of much help. By January 1998 the party was in financial debt of close to 90 million NIS, capable of extending it by only 30 million NIS (Cohen 1999). During that year Labor financed municipal campaigns that further drained its depleting budgets. Likewise,

Labor had no effective organization to speak of. The days the party relied on Histadrut's (the Federation of Workers' Unions) personnel; the Labor movement (i.e., Kibbuzim or Moshavim); and on public employees for political mobilization are long gone. To bypass these financial and personnel constraints a new system—Amotot—had to be developed, and Barak has been very effective in doing that.

The Politics of Amotot

The tension and contradiction that exist between the interests of the candidate for the prime minister post and those of his party are often ignored. These contradictions result from the particular construction of the 1992 electoral law permitting voters to differentiate between their preferences for the party and for the candidate. Prior to this law, the candidate for the post of prime minister was the head of the largest party (i.e., Labor) or of a party large enough (i.e., Likud) having the best chance of forming a winning coalition. Hence, the leaders of Labor and Likud had an incentive to expand their parties' ranks so as to increase their probability of forming a government. But since 1996 such an incentive does not exist. The new law does not provide the distinct means for conducting separate campaigns; hence the chairpersons of the big parties—that is, the candidates—must make an allocating choice: How much of the party resources should be spent on their campaign and how much on that of their party. Naturally, rational candidates will favor their own chances. Senior members of their parties who see a chance of becoming ministers do not, often, oppose. Airtime in the electronic media allocated by law to the party, and money awarded to it by the Party Financing Law will be directed toward the candidate's political bid at the expense of his party's exposure. Moreover, the substantive messages of the party's campaign must be coordinated with those of the candidate. Consequently, smaller parties are freer to transmit messages in a clearer manner, and de facto have even more airtime and money to do so.

This observation provides a partial explanation of the dramatic reduction in the size of the large parties. It nevertheless does not tell us what a candidate can do when her party has little or no resources at her disposal as was the case with the Labor Party in 1999. Anticipating such potential financial and personnel problems, Barak, like Netanyahu, began appealing to various private and corporate sources, for financial help. Because of questionable legality these moneys came under the investigation of the state comptroller and following his report on January 2000 (State Comptroller 2000), the police and the state attorney were asked to get involved in the matter. Therefore it is impossible to cite the exact amount generated in this way. However, judging from the massive expenditures on billboards that covered the entire country, it must have been very large sums—many millions of dollars.

Direct or indirect contributions from Israeli or foreign corporations or from noncitizens to parties and individual candidates are forbidden by paragraph 8 of the 1973 Party Financing Law. Also, paragraph 8 limits the sum of contribution a party may receive from private citizens or members of their household. In 1999 this sum was 1,700 NIS (or, a little over $420). For ambitious politicians, members of parties with depleted budgets, these sums are not enough. Therefore, some have bypassed the legal restrictions by founding amotot (citizens' associations). While the amota cannot support the candidate's efforts directly, because these are defined as political and hence must be accountable to the law, it can nevertheless invest in the development of conditions that might improve his or her electoral bidding chances. Moreover, it can operate relatively freely so long as its activities are not related to the election. In 1999 (and for that matter in 1996), because the election was scheduled before their designated legal time, Baraks's amotot were free to mobilize money and people until the beginning of that year. Because they were perceived as associated with the candidate, the police have been investigating whether they were in fact under his direct control.

An amota may promote any cause, even political ones. Yet, if it is constructed and activated before the election with a specific political goal, and mobilizes moneys from unidentified sources and directs them without official reporting into the candidate's campaign effort, it is in effect reproducing the activities of the political parties. And as such, it is in a possible violation of the law. Barak has several of such allegedly illegal amotot. The state comptroller cited some: "Israel of All of Us—Our One Israel" founded in January 1999 with the stated purpose of bridging social gaps and promotes education. It was activated for only one month and invested its $30,000 in billboards promoting Barak and attacking Netanyahu. "Our Hope Is Not Lost" (a line from the Israeli national anthem) was Founded in February 1999 with the purpose of increasing public awareness of social issues. It too, was activated for a short time during which it invested about 315,000 NIS in different phases of the campaign. "Students for Change" founded a month before the election spent about 160,000 NIS on a campaign against Netanyahu. And so did several other amotot that were found a year or two earlier: "The Association for the Advancement of Taxi Drivers in Israel," "Hope for Israel," "Alternative for the Advancement of Alyia (Immigration)," "Negev Now," "Citzens from Left and Right," "Students Want Change," and so on.

Two of the twenty-odd amotot that worked for Barak are of special interest. The first is AAA ("Citizens Supporting Ehud") that was founded in 1996 by Barak's brother-in-law. In addition to money, it was able to mobilize thousands of people. These people who were not necessarily party members, were gathered for long orientation weekends in hotels around the country, where they were exposed to Barak's visions and practical ideas. Consequently, "graduates" of this and other amotot were instrumental in mobilizing supporters for Barak's causes, as well as monitoring the polls on Election Day. The voting abuse that characterized earlier elections, especially in 1996, when thousands of Peres voters were disqualified resulting in rare 100 percent support for Netanyahu in some areas dominated by religious voters, was not repeated (Peretz and Doron 1996). The narrow margin of defeat (about 15,000 votes) in 1996 motivated Peres and Raanan Cohen, Labor general secretary, to condemn Likud's behavior and declare that the elections were "stolen" from them. Indeed, to make sure events would not be repeated, 446 "problematic" voting booths were carefully staffed and guarded by amotot members, under the organization of the so-called Vardi Headquarters. In these "Vardi's booths," located mainly in areas where religious and Russian voters concentrate, there were over 200,000 registered voters, most of whom were potential Netanyahu supporters. The general rate of voting in these places was reduced by 1.1%, from 77% in 1996 to 75.9% in 1999, while the support for Barak increased by 1.8% (Pedut 1999, 17). Applying the zero-sum logic, where a transfer of a vote from one side to the other should count as two votes, then the total affect of the reduction in voter turnout in these areas, and the extra support he obtained, provided Barak with many of votes that were missing in Peres's tally three years earlier. The supervising efforts paid off.

The other interesting amota is Dor Shalem. Rabin's people formed this Amota in 1993–1994 to provide, among other things, members of his camp, then a minority within Labor, with organizational capabilities. Over the years, following Rabin's assassination, however, the amota has transformed into a social movement with thousands of young activists, mainly students, who worked to help the poor and needy in their own neighborhoods. Rabin's son, Yoval, became the head of this amota and the main figure to mobilize contributions from both Israeli and foreign sources. During the campaign these volunteers worked for Barak, substituting for the missing party activists.

Netanyahu's decision to de facto retreat from his commitment to implement the 1998 Wye Agreement with the Palestinians positioned him on the right side of the Israeli political map. There, sandwiched between two new candidates, Begin on his right and later Mordechai on his left he had limited space to maneuver. His difficulties in gathering support for the 1999 Budget Law was a strong indication that the term of his government had come to an end. Indeed, when the decision was made to call for new elections in May, all he could rely upon was a two-stage election and an efficient transmission of political messages through the electronic media. As it turned out, his decision to rely on the regret minimizing (Nash 1951), "security before peace" messages, so potent in the context of repetitive terror incidents against Peres, were ineffective against Barak. When the challenger is perceived as a security hawk and no violent activities have been recorded for many months, such a campaign strategy, cannot work. Moreover, even in the area where Netanyahu clearly shines above other politicians with his media manipulation, he encountered difficulties. To the surprise of everyone, in an April televised debate between him and Mordechai, the latter, not known for his oratory skills (an event Barak cleverly avoided) seemed to win over the incumbent. Moreover, during the last days of his campaign when evidence was mounting that indeed, the race would be conducted only between him and Barak, he decided to stir emotions by attacking the "leftist" media, and the Ashkenazi "racists" of Labor, two items traditionally favored by Likud voters. But Barak who responded by promising to be "the prime minister of everyone" and who was flanked by prominent Sephardi politicians like Levy, Ben-Ami, and Ben Eliezer was not affected. When the candidacy of Mordechai was finally removed under mounting public pressures just two days before the elections, and he agreed to endorse Barak, it was clear that the incumbent lost his last chance of being reelected. Indeed, he did not wait much; about twenty minutes after both Israeli television channels announced the outcomes, based on partial data taken from exit polls, Netanyahu conceded defeat.

Analysis of the Outcomes: The Prime Minister Race

The outcomes of the Netanyahu-Barak race for the prime minister post are as follows: Barak obtainted 1,791,020 votes (56.08%) while Netanyahu received only 1,402,474 votes (42.25%) (*Haaretz,* May 20, section D). A decisive victory, indeed.

While Netanyahu was able to defeat Peres in 1996 by a margin of less than 1% in 1999 Barak's margin of victory over Netanyahu was close to 13%. Except for among the Israeli-Arab voters where Peres received .5% more votes than Barak, he fared better than Peres in all places, all sectors, and in all voting booths. In addition to preserving the support of all the groups that traditionally supported Labor, Barak was able to attract new voters. He was even able to penetrate into Netanyahu's power bases: the North Africans—many of whom are concentrated in development towns, and the new Russian immigrants. Compared to Peres in 1996, Barak increased his support among the first group by 5.3% and among the second group by 10% (Pedut 1999), indicating that his long-term strategy had been effective. Netanyahu did better than Barak in all concentrations of new immigrants who arrived in Israel after 1989 from the former Soviet Union except in the forty-eight booths located in areas with a predominant Russian majority (i.e., about 90%). Expectations, and hence disappointment, for more effective government resolution of collective and personal welfare were magnified in these areas. Only there, Barak was able to overcome Netanyahu by 6.8%. Almost as a rule, the greater the concentration of new immigrants, the greater Barak's marginal achievement (Pedut 1999, 13). This indicates that the hard fieldwork and utilization of the immigrant network of communication paid off (Zeltzer 1999).

One Israel Electoral Performance

In 1999, Labor, masquerading as One Israel, lost much of its power. In two rounds of elections since 1992 both Labor and Likud lost twenty-one seats each. Indeed, while both parties were able to present their leader as the only viable candidate for the prime minister post, this had not established any partisan advantage. On the contrary, as shown in the various analyses of the Israeli political system included in Dan Korn's (1998) volume, the two large parties were indeed in a disadvantage position vis-à-vis the other parties. Hence, the effects of the electoral reform are quite dramatic. The combined size of the two major parties has significantly and systematically been reduced over the last thirty years. Labor was able in 1969 during the peak of the dominant party period (Arian and Barnes 1974; Goldberg 1992) to almost solely control a parliamentary majority. Thirty years later, Labor together with the Likud, can control only about one third of the Knesset seats. Three years earlier while both of these two parties seemed to be able to hold a majority of 55% of the Knesset seats, in actuality Likud's parliamentary strength was even smaller, resting on the technical block that included also five members for each Gesher and Tzomet. Thus, the outcomes of 1996 and more dramatically those of 1999, demonstrate that the political system that had been dominated by the two major parties between 1974 and 1992 whereby their combined strength averaged about 70% of the electorate has been significantly altered.

There may be several explanations for this political realignment, but the 1992 electoral reform seems to be the simplest, boldest, and therefore the most likely one. The assumption or perhaps the naive expectation that voters would not choose to split their tickets in order to let the prime minister they elected have an unimpeded opportunity to more forcefully affect policy has been found untenable.

After satisfying themselves by a vote for the prime minister that could reflect either a preference over security issues and general public interests or a strategic position against the other candidate, voters could choose their representatives in accordance with their sincere and particular interests (Riker and Ordeshook 1973). Since 1996, more and more voters decided to go this particular route. Thus, those parties that could be broadly defined as "general," catering more to their conception of state and society than to the interests of a defined group of voters (i.e, One Israel, Likud, Meretz, Center, and perhaps the National Unity) together obtained 65 seats in the Knesset. The rest of the seats were awarded to particular interest or "sectarian" parties. In comparison, in 1988 there were 103 representatives of "general interests" parties, in 1992 their number was reduced to 84, and in 1996 it was further reduced to 78. This trend may continue, of course, and may impose governance difficulties as explained in the next section.

The immediate effect of this new election system on the reduction of the size of the Labor party can be found in the independent performance of several groups that attracted traditional Labor voters. Among them is the Center Party that included among its top-ranking politicians at least three "typical Labor" members (i.e., Amnon Shahak, Uri Savir, and Dalia Rabin). The other is One Nation (Am Echad), a party consisting of unionized workers, which was able to pass the 1.5% threshold and send two representatives to the Knesset. Others Labor defectors who were not so successful include the Pensioners (Gimlayim) and the Third Way. Their combined power could have awarded them two and perhaps even three seats, which should be, of course, deduced from the overall Labor tally.

In 1999 only 670, 484 voters supported One Israel, that is, 148,086 less voters than in 1996. If we consider the increase of about 9% of the number of voters, then the rate of reduction in the size of One Israel is about 27% (Pedut 1999). Indeed, when all attention is directed toward the Israel Wants a Change—Ehud Barak main campaign slogan, and very little time, resources, and energy are invested in the party, such negative consequences are expected.

During the campaign, Labor captured the public attention only during its February primaries when it selected its representatives and placed them on its Knesset list. The general assumption that guided the race was that the higher a person would rank on the party list, the most likely he or she would be awarded a ministerial portfolio in case of Barak's victory. Except for Barak, Peres, and Cohen, all senior Labor members ran in the primaries in the so-called national list. The only surprise was that Ben-Ami came first supported by everyone. The political future of winners in the party regions or districts races who were by design supposed to appear on the list only after the top "nationals" were placed there, was not assured. This is because places on the list were secured for the three dignitaries just mentioned, a woman in each group of ten members, and representatives of the Gesher party. Barak's attempt to include on the list a local "hero" representing right-wing voters was aggressively rejected by members of his party, who were motivated by an anticipated sense of scarcity of Knesset seats. The ranking of the regional representatives on the party list was somewhat manipulated by Barak's people to assure that loyalists would enter instead of others. Thus, for example, the second largest party region—Sharon and Shomron—has no representative in the Knesset while smaller-size regions like the Negev (i.e., MK Wizman Shiri) have. Furthermore, because Barak was using his apparatus to win the election, senior Labor members who had secured a safe place on the list were not motivated to work hard.

Consequently, Labor decreased its power almost everywhere, in almost all population sectors. It is therefore of little analytic value to try to assess the reasons for this subpar performance of the party, because at the time of the campaign it was hardly functioning as a vital political organization. Perhaps, however, the performance of Labor among the Arab voters is of some interest. In that sector, Labor experienced the greatest loss; only 9,777 out of 57,020 qualified Druze voters supported the party (i.e., a reduction from 40.8% in 1996 to 23.3%), and only 15,311 out of 392,502 Arab voters cast their votes in favor of Labor for a drop from 13.2% in 1996 to 5.3% in 1999. In fact, Israel One got more support among the settlers in the West Bank (i.e., 7%) than from the Arabs. The missing votes presumably went to the Arab parties.

Barak's Governance Capabilities

Elections are supposed to select both rulers and representatives. The large margin of victory has put Barak in a situation wherein he could have chosen several options to form a ruling coalition. Like Rabin (1993–1995) he could have formed a minority government in the European fashion (Laver and Shepsle 1994), consisting of his party (26), Meretz (10), Center (6), Shinui (6), Israel b'Aliya (6), Am Echad (2), and an outside support of the 10 members of the three Arab parties. This is a civil coalition consistent, more or less, with Abraham De Swan's formulation (1973) whereby the policy distance among its members over security issues (perhaps with the exception of Israel b'Aliya) is generally perceived to be not too far. Another option could have been to form a minimal winning coalition in William Riker's (1962) sense. For that, he needed to include only two parties, Likud (19) and Shas (17). While each one of these two parties could have turned out to be pivotal, of course, stability in governance could have been maintained. Policy direction, however, in this formation, would have to be sensitive to the desires of the partners.

Barak decided to construct a two-dimensional government (Sened 1996). The one dimension included his natural partners—the substantive "core" in Michael Laver and Kenneth Schofield's terms (1990)—to the future peace process with the Palestinians, and the Syrians. These parties are Meretz and Center and together with One Israel they count 42 members. The other dimension is the social-religious one, consisting of four parties that also served in Netanyahu coalition, Shas, Israel b'Aliya, the National Religious Party (5), and Yahadut Hatorah (5); together 33 members. These four are the so-called sectarian parties in a sense that their main ambition is to serve the interests of their defined community of voters more than to serve the general public interest broadly defined (Peretz and Doron 2000). The combined size of these two dimensions is 75 members. Like the other formations, this one is also problematic. In addition to containing internal contradictions (e.g., the hawkish attitude of the National Religious Party and Israel b'Aliya voters) it is a surplus coalition and hence defection should be expected. Indeed, the five members of Yahadut Hatorah could not stay in this formation for more than three months. However, these parties' concentration on the specific, perhaps myopic interests of their own communities permitted Barak to advance at least for a while with his peace initiatives.

The collusion between the members upon whom the two dimensions are constructed is based not upon love or short ideological distance, but upon interests, of course. The three sectarian parties that remained in the coalition need to service their communities and they can do that only with government resources and means. Therefore, their leaders would allow Barak much flexibility so long as the government continues to supply the agreed upon payoff and the choices their voters would have to make over his policies would not be "ideologically" critical. Socially and economically, Barak can do little without the approval of Shas, the second largest party and the pivot of his coalition. A defection of Shas would necessitate a new coalition, new policies, and perhaps new elections. Hence, to obtain the support of Shas he must continue to finance its independent educational system and the party's political organization. Armed with public money, Shas competes with other parties, and with the state, over education and over welfare transfers (Kook, Harris, and Doron 1999).

To expand his governance flexibility, reduce public pressures, and meet preelection commitments, Barak decided to expand the size of the government from 18 members as defined by Basic Law: Government 1992, to 24 members. This move, which drew much public criticism, allowed him to meet some preelection commitments, and include an additional woman and two more generals (Amnon Shahak and Matan Vilnai) in his cabinet. The internal and external pressures on his coalition, however, have not subsided by this expansion. Difficulties encountered in passing laws through the Knesset, especially over budget items, are indicative of the future governance problems and instability Barak may face when time comes to address the big issues: peace with Syria and the Palestinians.

Conclusion

Barak may somehow be able to "muddle through" politically. To expand his parliamentary base, he may use the loose framework of One Israel to include members of the Center Party, Shinui, Am Echad, and perhaps some Russians, thus providing him with a firm base of 42 members. The incentives of members of these parties to join are clear: in the context of Israel's new election laws and primaries, when the future of an incumbent MK is insecure, it is relatively safer to be included in a larger party list than in a smaller one. Instead of independently working hard to mobilize resources and people, MKs would presumably use their present bargaining powers (including their shares in the party financing allocation) to secure a place in the next Knesset. Most likely, however, because of internal contradictions, the present coalition will find difficulties to see the designated four years terms through.

To induce political stability, restore the ability to govern, and reduce the extent of illegal activities, the electoral reform must continue with another step: separate the campaign for the Knesset from the one for the prime minister as suggested in 1996 by Miriam Ben-Porat, the state comptroller (State Comptroller, 2000, 16–17). Indeed, not only should the financing law be reformed, but also the entire prime minister campaign should be disassociated from that of his or her party. The candidates for the prime minister post would then have to obtain the endorsement of several parties, potential members of his coalition. The parties on the other hand, would be free to conduct their own campaigns.

References

Arian, Asher, and Samuel H. Barnes. 1974. "The Dominant Party System: A Neglected Model of Democratic Stability." *Journal of Politics* 36, no. 3: 592–614.

Arian, Asher, and Michal Shamir. 1983. "The Primarily Political Function of the Left-Right Continuum." In Asher Arian (ed.). *The Elections in Israel, 1981.* Tel Aviv: Ramot.

Axelrod, Robert. 1970. *Conflict of Interest.* Chicago: Markham.

Ben-Ami, Shlomo. 1998. *A Place for All.* Tel Aviv: Hakibbutz Hameuchad.

Brams, Steven. 1985. *Rational Politics: Games and Strategy.* Washington DC: Congressional Quarterly Press.

Central Bureau of Statistics (Hebrew). 1999. 1996 Election Results, Publication 1054.

Cohen, Raanan. 1999. *The Main Consequences of the Elections Outcomes for the 15th Knesset and the Prime Minister* (June 9). General Secretary Bureau. Tel Aviv: Labor Party.

De Swan, Abraham. 1973. *Coalition Theories and Cabinet Formation.* Amsterdam: Elsevier.

Doron, Gideon. 1996. *Strategy of Election.* Rechuvot: Kivunim.

Doron, Gideon, and Michael Harris. 2000. *Electoral Reform and Public Policy: The Case of Israel.* Maryland: Lexington.

Downs, Anthony. 1957. *An Economic Theory of Democracy.* New York: Harper.

Goldberg, Giora. 1992. *Political Parties in Israel—From Mass Parties to Electoral Parties.* Tel Aviv: Ramot.

Horkin, Amir, Yitzhak Katz, and Baruch Mevorach. 1998. *Local Hero: The Election to Local Municipalities in Israel in the Era of Direct Elections.* Tel Aviv: Ramot.

Kaspit, Ben, Hannan Kristal, and Ilan Kfir. 1996. *The Suicide.* Tel Aviv: Maariv.

Kaspit, Ben, and Ilan Kfir. 1998. *Barak: Soldier Number One.* Tel Aviv: Alfa Tikshuret.

Kristal, Hannan, and Ilan Kfir. 1999. *The Sixth Commendation 1999 Elections.* Tel Aviv: Keter.

Kook, Rebecca, Michael Harris, and Gideon Doron. 1999. "Between G-D and our Rabbi: The Politics of the Ultra-Orthodox in Israel." *Israel's Affairs* (January).

Korn, Dan (ed.). 1999. *The Death of the Israeli Parties.* Tel Aviv: Hakibbutz Hameuchad.

Laver, Michael, and Norman Schofield. 1990. *Multiparty Politics: The Politics of Coalition in Europe.* Oxford: Oxford University Press.

Laver, Michael, and Kenneth Shepsle. 1994. *Cabinet Ministers and Parliamentary Government.* Oxford: Oxford University Press.

Nash, John. 1951. "Non Cooperative Games." *Annals of Mathematics* 54:286–295.

Pedut, David. 1997. *The Outcomes of the Elections to the Role of Labor's Chairman and its Candidates to the Post of Prime Minister* (June 3). Tel Aviv: Labor Party Publication.

———. 1999. *The Elections to the 15th Knesset and to the Prime Minister—Preliminary Analysis* (May). Tel Aviv: Labor, Planning and Research.

Peretz, Don, and Gideon Doron. 1996. "Elections in Israel 1996." *Middle East Journal* (December).

———. 2000. "Sectarian Politics and the Peace Process: The 1999 Israeli Elections." *Middle East Journal* (May).

Rae, Douglas. 1967. *The Political Consequences of Electoral Laws.* New Haven: Yale University Press.

Riker, William. 1962. *The Theory of Political Coalitions.* New Haven: Yale University Press.

Riker, William, and Peter Ordeshook. 1973. *An Introduction to Positive Political Theory.* Englewood Cliffs, NJ: Prentice-Hall.

Sened, Itai. 1996. "A Spatial Analysis of Coalition Formation: Theory and Application." In Doron, Gideon (ed.). *The Electoral Revolution.* Tel Aviv: Hakibbutz Hameuchad.

Shachar, Ron, and Michal Shamir. 1995. "Modeling Victory in the 1992 Election." In Asher Arian and Michal Shamir (eds.). *The Elections in Israel 1992.* Albany: State University of New York Press.

Shepsle, Kenneth, and Mark Bonchek. 1997. *Analyzing Politics: Rationality, Behavior and Institutions.* New York: Norton.

Shitrit, Shimon. 1998. *The Good Land Between Power and Religion.* Tel Aviv: Yediot Achronot.

State Comptroller. 2000. *Law of Parties Financing-1973.* (A report on the outcomes of auditing the accounts of the parties for the period of the elections to the Fifteenth Knesset). Jerusalem. (January).

Tzemach, Yaron. 1998. *A Plan of Action to Bring Labor Back to Competition in the Field Battle over the Mizrachi Public Opinion.* Tel Aviv: Segev Yaron Strategies.

Zeltzer, Marina. 1999. *Immigrant Press: The Case of Russian Language Press in Israel.* Tel Aviv University: Master's thesis.

10

The Likud's Campaign and the Headwaters of Defeat

JONATHAN MENDILOW

Introduction

The elections of 1999 dealt the Likud so stunning a blow that to describe it critics had recourse to natural calamities such as volcanic eruptions, or disasters like being run over by an express train. While Benjamin Netanyahu's bid for reelection ended in a landslide defeat, the party's share of the vote was reduced by almost 44%, thereby breaking the 1977 record held by Labor when its share was reduced by 37.88%. Several explanations were offered, one that the results constituted a repudiation of a style of leadership that had led to the desertion of top Likud leaders and to the waning of activist enthusiasm, another that the debacle resulted from the decline of the left-right cleavage over the destiny of the Territories and its replacement by an amorphous center or by a nascent ultra-Orthodox versus secular split. Still others pointed to penalties meted by voters for the economic decline and the stalling of the peace negotiations (e.g., Marcus 1999; Sontag 1999; Yovel 1998). While none of these explanations will suffice by itself, the problems they allude to in combination exacerbated underlying causes that serve as the board on which to fit together the jigsaw pieces and to present a coherent picture. Such a picture is necessary to determine whether it was merely the reaction of a temporarily irritated electorate, whether any lessons can be learned from the failure of the Likud's strategy, and what consequences may be foreseen for Israeli democracy as a whole.

My argument is that the headwaters of the defeat lie at the confluence of two sources. One was the difficulty faced by parties fielding credible candidates for the premiership to compete efficiently for the Knesset. The former race demanded a "presidential stance," transcending party interests and able to attract the widest possible electorate; the latter to differentiate between the party and its rivals and to unify the membership around common causes.

In effect, two different campaigns were run simultaneously by the same agents. As a result, the race between the candidates turned on images contrived by promotional teams, while their supporting parties faded into the background, shedding the vestiges of their distinctive positions and social referents, a form of electioneering that cost them dearly in the multiparty Knesset competition. Both in 1996 and 1999 the larger rivals lost heavily to communitarian parties (Lawson and Merkel 1998), aggregating the interests of ethnic, cultural, or narrowly defined social groups; a Balkanization that reached its apogee in 1999, when two Russian parties, a party of Histadrut affiliated manual workers, and an anti-ultra-Orthodox Party won representation, while Shas became the third largest party in the Knesset.

And yet, the losses incurred by the Likud in 1999 were disproportionately high. To explain this we must turn to the source unique to it: its failure to resolve a prolonged identity crisis that was carried over into government and intensified by the heterogeneity of the coalition and the need to take critical decisions. The Likud's 1996 feat was winning the premiership despite the fissure between those who argued that following Oslo the party must change its positions on the Land of Israel issue and that "anyone who refuses to acknowledge the reality had better stay at home" (Barnea 1996), and those who protested that the "credo remains as right and just as it ever was" (Honig 1996) and that without it the party "is unworthy to survive" (Tal 1993). Striding over the divisions, B. Netanyahu combined a readiness to negotiate within the context of the Oslo agreements with security demands that amounted to the traditional Likud stands rejecting both territorial compromise and the gradualism laid down at Oslo.[1] This enabled the party to attract the electorate to its right and to its left, as well as those hesitating between the options; yet its message designed to avoid coming to grips with the ideological dilemma, not to resolve it. The inexorable progress of the peace process consequently imposed on the Likud-led government double negotiations. Externally, it had to engage the Palestinians and the United States. Internally, the prime minister had to confront moderates and Rightists within the Likud and the coalition, and attempts to placate both led to inconsistent policies and loss of credibility. Deteriorating relations with the Palestinians and the Americans intensified the strains, forcing him to rely not on his own party but on coalitional communitarian parties with their separate and potentially conflicting agendas. It was this combination of pressures from within and without that brought about the lurching of the government from one crisis to another, until the final breakdown in December 1998.

In the campaign of 1999, the challenge of the Likud was to repeat its 1996 success, but it was now complicated by accusations of Netanyahu's lack of credibility and by claims of government ineptitude, rendered more acute because of an economic recession and growing unemployment. Furthermore, the credibility issue was also raised by Likud secessionists and an additional challenge was therefore to prevent the party's hemorrhage. In the earlier campaign Netanyahu could make ambivalent promises that could be interpreted as presenting the party ideology as well as its adaptation to the new realities. This subterfuge was now denied him. Consequently, the strategy was to concentrate on relations with Palestinians, where the government's wrestling between left and right and its overthrow by their united votes could be turned to advantage. This was possible through the presentation of Netanyahu as a hard-nosed pragmatist championing the center against both extremes. To do so however it was imperative not only to run against the ultra-Right but, more critically, to tear away One Israel's guise of being centrist, exposing the extremism lurking behind it. The resulting catchall style was therefore characterized by an emotional "challenger approach" focusing on the positions of the opponents, supplemented by a parallel appeal to the electorates of the communitarian parties, each in its own style and its own media, with the rejection of the "Left" as a common thread.

This strategy failed for several reasons. The presidential-like campaign with its focus on the candidate abandoned efforts to unite the party on other grounds, leaving its internal crisis unresolved. This left frustrated members open to the temptations of Shas, the National Union, and the Center Party, a problem magnified by the failure to defend the Likud's electoral territory by attacking predators whose electorates, it was hoped, would opt for Netanyahu in the first or the second round. Equally serious was the disappointment with the communitarian parties. Their squabbling put Netanyahu in midcampaign in the familiar position of having to win over opposing sides, with One Israel able to wedge away much of the Russian vote. What would have befallen the Likud had Netanyahu won is a matter of speculation. Certain it is that the results lost it the government, significantly reduced its numbers, and left it with its crisis of identity still unresolved. Beyond the fate of the Likud, the campaign it led can be considered as indicating a further step in the transformation of the Israeli party system. What seems to be emerging is a double system where on one level narrowly defined sectoral or ideological parties vie for Knesset seats, while on another the competition is between individuals who appeal to all and sundry on their personal merits, supported by compact cadres of professionals and loyalists. This in turn seriously questions the continued viability of Israeli democracy.

The Background: Netanyahu as the Overloaded Juggler

Netanyahu's victory in 1996 did not remedy the Likud's ideological predicament, but it did ensure a remission. The fact that the largest coalition partners were of the communitarian type furthered government stability, for they could be relied on to support the prime minister on national issues provided that it was made worth their while. What emerged recalls Lijphart's "consociational democracy": a partnership based on personal consultations and utilitarian interests between Netanyahu and the heads of the two strongest communitarian parties, Shas and Israel b'Aliya. Their ability to deliver the votes of at least most of their members of Knesset shielded the prime minister from frictions within his own party. During the first months these themselves had been reduced, with most of the party leaders moderating their tone, partly because those benefiting from government positions tended to be sensitive to the pragmatic aspect of governing on which their positions depended. But there was also a moderating factor relating to the peace process itself. The first problem was how to fulfill the previous government's commitment to a withdrawal in Hebron. This was a bitter pill to swallow, but firm international obligations were long overdue, and these could hardly be nullified. Most Likud leaders acceded to the inevitable, and even to the likelihood that further concessions would have to be made. The substitution of a relative "more or less" for the absolute "yes or no" in itself contributed to moderation. The resignation of Menachem Begin in protest did not signal a general revolt, while the resignation of Finance Minister Dan Meridor was unrelated to the peace issue. Nevertheless, from the very beginning storm clouds began to accumulate. They darkened throughout 1997 until, late in the year and more intensively in 1998, they broke out in periodic storms. The situation that developed lends itself to an apter metaphor: the prime minister as a juggler challenged by more and more balls that threaten his timing.

In the 1996 campaign the Likud succeeded to turn the debate between Israel and the Palestinians to one between itself and Labor. Whether the Palestinians would accept peace at the reduced price offered by the Likud to Israel was another matter. The insistence to renegotiate the terms of the Hebron withdrawal only deepened Palestinian suspicions and led to bitter bargaining till early 1997. But the acridity expressed itself also in clashes, the most serious of which occurred in late September 1996 when a tunnel along the outer wall of the Temple area was opened. The disturbances were the worst since the pre-Oslo era, while the urgent summit called by Clinton inaugurated a new phase in which the United States began to acquire the role of a direct participant, thereby limiting the maneuverability of the government. The ultra-Right too organized to pressure the government to adopt firm stands, prodded not only by frustration over Hebron, but because it signaled the continuation of the peace process.

Notwithstanding its campaign stands, once in power the Likud government found itself committed to three additional withdrawals. Unlike Hebron, the extent of these was left open, and the onus fell on the government to hammer it out with the Palestinians. In the atmosphere of mutual suspicion, the offer to fulfill the first phase by transferring to full Palestinian control 2 percent of "C territory," that already under joint control, was rejected out of hand. This meant haggling over the second phase, with the Americans in full involvement. Readiness to negotiate in such conditions was interpreted by settlers, who almost unanimously had supported Netanyahu in the elections, as reneging on his commitments. More ominously, the sense of betrayal was shared by member of Knesset of coalition parties, including several from the Likud itself. One expression of the malaise was the reawakening after a hibernation of several years of the veteran parliamentary Land of Israel Front. A nebulous forum chaired by an MK from Gesher faction of the Likud, it contained some seventeen members (the exact number varied) two of whom were from the opposition Moledet Party but the rest from the parties in the coalition: the National Religious Party (NRP), Israel b'Aliya, and the largest number from the Likud itself. Their demand for minimalizing the territories to be conceded was justified by Palestinian breaches of the Oslo agreement, and these should be countered by conditioning full compliance on further steps in the negotiations. Otherwise they would bring down the government, a warning reinforced by the fact that some of the hawkish Likud MKs were not associated with them. A day before the Wye memorandum was signed, Menachem Begin could claim that "it was the crystallization of forces in the Right questioning the political future of the prime minister that enabled us to delay the sale of the Land of Israel to the Palestinians" (*Yediot Aharonot,* October 23, 1998).

Attempts to placate right-wing supporters, took symbolic forms (e.g., Netanyahu's well-publicized tour by air over the West Bank on the eve of the Hebron deal) but also involved coupling moves forward with defiant moves back. The best-known examples were the post-Hebron authorization and the first steps of a building project in East Jerusalem, which led the Palestinians to cease negotiations and raised an international outcry. Netanyahu too froze negotiations several days later, accusing Yasser Arafat of giving a "green light" to Hamas attacks, followed by a major bombing incident in the heart of Tel Aviv. Some two years later, Thomas Friedman (1999) referred to this ongoing back-and-forth pattern in his description of Netanyahu as swimming laps across the Rubicon. However, despite the alternating efforts to accommodate both the United States and Likud and coalition moderates and the party and coalition nationalists the respites were short-lived and the prime minister was accused by all sides of inconsistency. In November 1997 the problem was compounded by an intraparty crisis when senior Likud leaders lined up against him in what was tantamount to a declaration of no confidence.

The implosion occurred when his supporters passed a resolution abolishing the primaries and transferring the selection of the party candidate slate to the Party Center. Netanyahu himself disclaimed any part in the scheme, but it was generally believed that he was behind it, further evidence of his lack of credibility. MKs and activists I interviewed agreed in their assessment of the motivation: primaries ensured the independence of the MKs, enabling them to adopt positions incompatible with the prime minister's line. The dependence of their political future on the Center, where Netanyahu wielded considerable influence, could therefore rein them back. Be that as it may, his promise of a referendum scotched an open rebellion, though at the cost of worsening his plight. The already cool relations turned into a deep chill, with Begin and others accusing him of dishonesty and Netanyahu characterizing those who had turned against him as "subscribers to a coalition of personal ambitions" and their supporters as "blind" (*Yediot Aharonot,* November 21, 1997). Signs increased of a double challenge from both wings. Contemplating leaving the Likud to oust Netanyahu from without were Begin and the Tel Aviv mayor, Roni Milo, who had moved during the 1990s from the right to the left of the party. The moderate Dan Meridor and the hawkish Olmert, the Jerusalem mayor, considered contesting Netanyahu from within for the party leadership. Except for Menachem Begin, what animated these nascent moves to depose Netanyahu was not directly ideological, yet it was clear that sooner or later bids would be made to woo disgruntled party members on ideological grounds as well.

Two additional burdens that weakened government against the escalating pressures were the competition between the communitarian partners and the deteriorating economic conditions. The ultra-Orthodox, the Russian immigrants, the Sephardim, and the West Bank settlers had little in common beyond the resentment of the highly educated, secular-minded Ashkenazi elite. Hence Netanyahu's constant use of Left, not in the sense of a point in an ordinal scale indicating the positions in a major cleavage but as a catchall term with negative associations for his coalition partners: those who "have forgotten what it means to be Jewish" (the words whispered by Netanyahu to the most senior of the Cabalists that were caught by the Israeli TV); the type of regime under which the new immigrants had suffered in the former Soviet Union; the fat-cat Westerners who had so discriminated against the fathers of the Eastern Jews, the economic and cultural underdogs; and those "delicate souls" who were prepared to deliver the Land of Israel to the enemy. But positive incentives were also necessary, and it was here that the parties competed for what resources were available. Worse still, their interests could clash, as in the case of the secular Russians and the ultra-Orthodox. Such strains were especially liable to surface whenever the national budget was being negotiated.

In 1996 the communitarian parties had just catapulted from opposition to government, or else were altogether new and as yet restrained in their demands. The year 1997 presented a different picture. In view of the trouble within the Likud, Netanyahu was in greater need of support, at a time when the United States was showing signs of impatience. This gave further power to the coalition partners' demands for practical incentives. In mid-December Netanyahu promised the American secretary of state to pass a resolution for a significant redeployment, but only after the budget had been approved. This was probably to prevent the opening gambits starting from a higher point, but it was also because of the inverse proportion between the demands and the ability to satisfy them at a time when symptoms of economic slowdown were growing increasingly acute.

In point of fact, indications of an impending recession preceded the Likud-led government. Restrictive fiscal policies aiming to curtail the deficit, coupled with the constraining monetary policies of the Bank of Israel may have been necessary countermeasures, but their effect was to stunt economic growth and infrastructure investment. What with the "Asian flu" and the decline in tourism they caused ever poorer economic figures to plague the government, with perhaps the most sensitive relating to the rise in unemployment from 6.6% in June 1996 to 8.7% at the start of the 1999 campaign (*Central Bureau of Statistics,* 1997, 1998; *Ma'ariv,* April 30, 1999). It was inevitable that the budget negotiations would be tortuous, yet that they would bring about the breakaway of Foreign Minister David Levy and his party was less foreseeable. The background was the prime minister's decision to give priority to Shas's demands, mostly for social welfare, over those of Gesher that had run as a faction of the Likud in the 1996 elections. But in the tacit competition between Shas and Gesher for the Sephardi electorate, the advantage was with the former. Seeing that the prime minister could not guarantee the Gesher MKs slots on the Likud candidate list for the next elections, Levi resigned, leaving the coalition in protest against a government "on its way to nowhere." The government majority was thereby reduced to sixty-one MKs, rebels included, so that each member had a veto power. Justice Minister Hanegbi summed up the situation as "the Last Supper" (*New York Times,* January 7, 1998). This turned out to be too gloomy, but the subtle timing of the juggler was disrupted at irregular intervals, threatening completely to overload his act.

Throughout 1998 the United States intervened to restart the Israeli-Palestinian dialogue and to hold Israel to its commitment to redeployment. At the beginning, the middle, and toward the end of the year, this peaked in meetings that were preceded by intensified pressures from both moderates and extremists in the coalition. The first occasion came immediately after the shrinking of the government majority, when the United States refused to postpone a planned summit in Washington. One day after Levi's resignation came into effect, Dennis Ross arrived to prepare the meeting. The equally impatient defense minister, Yitzhak Mordechai, threatened to follow Levy unless progress was made on the redeployment issue, while the Third Way Party indicated it would follow suit. The second occasion was an early May meeting in London with the secretary of state who two weeks later pressed Israel to accept an American compromise proposal of 13% redeployment. The departure of Netanyahu to the United States was accompanied by warnings that the NRP would abstain from Knesset no-confidence motions until the government published tenders for the Jerusalem construction that had stopped the negotiations in 1997; his arrival was greeted by accusations from Sharon that he and other ministers suspected him of readiness to sell out Israel's vital interests (*Yediot Aharonot,* May 13, 1998). The third occasion was the Clinton-Netanyahu-Arafat summit at the Wye plantation, where the second Israeli redeployment was finally agreed on. The pattern was repeated: the NRP declared it would overthrow the government should an unacceptable agreement be arrived at while hawkish ministers met to coordinate early elections should Wye fail to meet expectations. For his part, Avigdor Kahalani of the Third Way, announced that "should Netanyahu because of internal pressures come back without an agreement, I will not continue in government" (*Ma'ariv,* May 23, 1998).

The pattern also holds of the relative calm between these summits, when matters could be considered more peacefully. Following the first and second summits the government could discuss maps, and the fact that the sides were represented by the Likud's two military experts, the moderate Mordechai and the right-wing Sharon, also served to reduce the temperature. A body calling itself the "Secretariat of Yesha in the Likud" (1998) accused Mordecai of readiness to divide Jerusalem "to the delight of the Left and the Americans," and demanded "a [new] Defense Minister" for whom Hebron is not just a ruin and the Land of Israel is not just a map." But the party mainstream was unaffected by the hysteria. Moreover, from February, talks with Labor over the formation of a national unity government served as a warning to the party and to the coalition extremists that if they failed to toe the line Netanyahu could dispense with them and govern with the aid of Labor.[2] Yet the consistency of the pattern need not imply repetition. American browbeating steadily increased as did the dire warnings at home. Government positions likewise changed. At the beginning of 1998, there was only agreement on what territories could not be ceded. In the spring Netanyahu let it be known that he had reached "an inner decision" that a serious withdrawal was unavoidable" (*Jerusalem Post,* April 10, 1998). Later specific percentages were

debated, Sharon arguing for a maximum of 9 percent, but on the eve of the
Wye summit it became clear that it would be more. Netanyahu's tactics
changed too. If earlier Labor served as the dreaded enemy and later as a
potential ally, now he actually won from it a commitment for a "safety net":
it would vote with the government as long as it adhered to the Wye decisions.
At the same time he tried to shore up his position within the Likud by offering the Foreign Ministry to the moderate Meridor, and when this was rejected to the right-wing Sharon, whose appointment came into effect two
days before the summit.

But the critical divagation from the pattern was that in contrast to the relative calm between the previous summits, after Wye the temperature rose.
Settler leaders announced that "We have been tricked . . . a new leadership is
needed in Israel"; Land of Israel Front MKs vowed to bring down a prime
minister who "believes in certain ideas and acts exactly the opposite"; within
the Likud itself Shamir was not alone in condemning Netanyahu for "his
complete about-face" (*New York Times,* October 26, 1998, November 20;
Ma'ariv, October 23, 1998). Aware of what awaited him, Netanyahu decisively moved to the Right and again blamed the Left. Upon arrival at Tel
Aviv Airport he claimed that in Wye he had fought tooth and nail to whittle
down Labor's earlier commitment to a 90 percent withdrawal, and that only
he could foil Labor's conspiracies. "Who will see to it that the border will not
reach Tel Aviv? Who will protect Jerusalem?" (*New York Times,* October 26,
1998). Three days later, the Party Center, Netanyahu's stronghold, was convened to hear the same explanation (*Ma'ariv,* October 29, 1998). Its support
magnified however the intraparty division, for party MKs and most of its
ministers, not to mention other members of the coalition, remained un-
convinced. To win them over, a vigorous retreat from the Rubicon's further
shore was needed. Government ratification was delayed first by citing Palestinian failures to deliver plans for fighting terror, then by the demand that
the Palestinian Authority (PA) guarantee the arrest of thirty fugitive terror-
ists. The day the accord came into effect, the enlargement of Kiryat Arba was
announced. Ratification itself was shackled by the demand that the entire
Palestinian National Council meet to annul clauses from the Palestinian
covenant and to promise to limit the next phase of withdrawal to no more
than 1 percent. The government announced the beginning of the work in the
East Jerusalem project and threatened to annex parts of the West Bank should
the Palestinians unilaterally declare an independent state. The first phase of
the pullout mandated by the agreement was conditioned by the insistence
that the PA first gather the illegal arms of the Palestinian police, thereby
rousing the ire of the United States. All to no avail. Ratification was a shaky
victory for Netanyahu, for only eight of the seventeen ministers voted for it,

among them Sharon and Mordechai; the rest of the Likud ministers abstained. The situation even worsened, for the animus against Labor released it from its "safety net" obligation.

In this context the annual vote for the budget turned into a test of the government's survival. Failure to entice Levy to return led to desperate efforts to gain the cooperation of MKs of every shade. Pledges were made to Arab MKs and to moderates like Levy that in return for their votes Wye would be honored. Members of the Right wing were promised that Wye would be scuttled, and when this became known to both sides Netanyahu's credibility eroded.[3] Freezing compliance with the Wye agreement likewise failed to save the day. Netanyahu's last plea for a National Unity coalition met with laughter in the Knesset. Later Shimon Peres was to thank him for unifying the Left and the Right: against him (*Yediot Aharonot,* January 8, 1999).

Campaign Salesmanship, 1999

The political world, like the world of the senses that William Wordsworth described, is half perceived and half created. This is especially prominent at times of electoral campaigns, when citizens are called upon to evaluate different constructs of recent history offered by contestants in justification of future policies and of leadership teams to execute them. Consequently, the competition usually opens with a battle over the agenda, in which the rivals attempt to establish the grounds and the relevant facts on the basis of which the electorate will assess them. However, in so doing they cannot ignore generally accepted realities. They must also bear in mind the buffeting and counter-buffeting with opponents and craft their messages on the basis of a careful stocktaking of potential dangers and the available means to forestall them.

For the Likud the dangers were clear from the start. With the peace process at a standstill and a prolonged economic recession, the toppling of government rendered it inevitable that an issue overshadowing the campaign would be the functioning of the government. Simply to ignore it was impossible, but to address it head-on risked accepting the Labor agenda of attributing the miring of the peace process and the economy to failures in system management, and linking it to Netanyahu's dependence on extremists, thus refutating Likud's claim to represent the center. No less hazardous was the temptation of dispirited Likud supporters to transfer their votes to neighboring parties. The fall of the government unified the party, and the Americans and the Palestinians helped by relaxing their pressure in anticipation of the elections. Yet the secession of Begin to head a new party of the Right, and of Meridor and later Mordechai to join in forming the Center Party, meant that Likud members would be wooed from both directions. The appearance of new parties was no novelty, and few of them ever became viable. The danger of such arrivistes as the National Union and the Center Party hinged on their ability to siphon off a substantial following from the Likud. Ideological proximity and personal links between the leaders of the new parties and Likud members suggested that this was the case. On the eve of the Wye conference, Gallup polls predicted that should Sharon form a new party he could wean away a full half of the Likud vote (Crystal and Kfir 1999, 91, 98; Levi-Barzilai 1998). Begin was no Sharon, but he was the son of the founder of the Likud and one of the most respected of its leaders. He was also supported by such personalities as ex-prime minister Shamir, and polls conducted late in December 1998 pointed to some 10 percent of the voters supporting his bid for the premiership (Shalev 1999). Meridor was already in 1996 the candidate of a sizable group within the Likud for replacing Netanyahu, while the popular Mordechai was number two on the Likud 1996 candidate slate. A variant of the same hazard was that of Shas. Unlike the former parties, the issue here was neither ideological nor personal but socioeconomic and cultural, yet the lackluster spirit of the Likud[4] could extend the appeal of Shas to the Sephardi core-constituency, a phenomenon that in previous elections had already resulted in the loss of a significant number of Knesset seats.

Finally, the support of the communitarian partners could also be an albatross. This was demonstrated in the campaign waged by the ultra-Orthodox against the Supreme Court, climaxing in February, when a quarter of a million ultra-Orthodox demonstrated against what Rabbi Ovadia termed "the tyranny" of its "wicked . . . empty-headed evil-doers." Minister of Justice Hanegbi, the only Likud leader to attend a counterdemonstration in support of the Court, recounted after the elections how his fellow ministers responded to his query why they had absented themselves, "by stuttering about the approaching elections and their fear of quarreling with the ultra-Orthodox" (*Israeli Broadcasting Authority, Radio,* July 7, 1999). In the widening cleavage between the ultra-Orthodox and the secularists over the very nature of the state, the danger was that the Likud would be seen as caving in to the former. The conviction of Aryeh Deri, the Shas leader, on bribery charges complicated the problem. His friendship with Netanyahu threatened to compound the cost in the Sephardi vote by alienating secular elements in the electorate, especially the Russians, whose leaders were already at odds with Shas over the treatment of new immigrants by the Shas-controlled Ministry of the Interior.

The ongoing relationship between Netanyahu and his foreign consultant, Arthur Finkelstein, achieved even before the fall of the government a basic understanding on how to confront these challenges, and this was wrapped up during the latter's visit to Israel in the first days of January. From personal interviews and press releases of those connected with the campaign one can piece together its underlying premises, but hindsight provides perhaps the best guide. The first decisions concerned the voters to whom the message was to be directed and the antagonists against whom it was to be aimed. To be targeted were obviously the floating voters and last minute deciders. Whereas they were not demographically distinct, the Russians, the Sephardim, and the ultra-Orthodox were the fastest-growing sectors of the Jewish population and, being represented by communitarian parties, could be efficiently mobilized by their own leaders. This was especially true of the rabbi-led Shas supporters and the Ashkenazi ultra-Orthodox. The Russians were less predictable, but in 1996 they had voted strongly for Netanyahu, and the appearance of a new right-wing Russian party improved prospects from that quarter. A persuasive message had to be tailor-fitted to their particular interests, but in a way that would not alienate the ultra-Orthodox. Fortunately, the other way round was not necessary and the general effort to drive up Labor's unfavorables would suffice. All these were expected to vote for Netanyahu in the first round, whether or not they split their ticket with a communitarian party. The voters of the Center Party and the National Union were a different matter. Unlike the Russians and ultra-Orthodox these might vote for a candidate other than Netanyahu in the first round (the tendency to abandon preferred candidates who were certain to lose in favor of less desirable ones likely to win might persuade National Union voters to cast ballots for Netanyahu in the first round too). The effort should therefore be to ensure their support for him in the second. Voters for Begin had no option, but the danger following his defeat was one of apathy. Center Party voters might give their second round vote to Barak, and hence justified greater investment. Then there was the matter of the party membership. In the situation the party was in, heavy spending would be essential to deter members who were not keen Netanyahu supporters from voting for the National Union, the Center Party, or Shas. However, what caused the party to founder was the crisis of self-identity. Attempts to reach out to either side would not only alienate other members but would endanger the second round vote of those who had already rejected the party. The same considerations applied to the selection of the targets for attack. One Israel was obviously the main one. The decision was taken however to restrict the attack to it, and not to the Center Party, the National Unity, or Shas. In each case the same decision was made: to risk votes for the Knesset so as not to irritate voters supporting Netanyahu in the first or second round.

The need to forego attempts to energize activists whose enthusiasm had flagged, and to avoid feuding with the adjacent parties, together helped to solve the problem of operating on a shoestring. Reduced as it was from thirty-two to nineteen MKs, the Likud lost much of the campaign financing allocated according to numbers in the outgoing Knesset. This demanded focusing on the prime minister, with the lion's share of the resources devoted to the "Netanyahu for the Premiership" drive, the production of the TV campaign, and the emoluments for professionals. Little was left for printed information and even less for the expenses of activists. Contrary to previous practices, Likud-controlled municipalities such as Nataniya or Rosh Ha'ayin could not contribute to the party, being themselves in financial straits. Thus the budget for the Voting-Day Headquarters had been fixed at 3 million NIS (some $750,000) and only after a struggle this was raised by 1.9 million NIS, but it was for both the expected rounds. As against 1,200 NIS (roughly $300) per polling station in 1996 all that could be allocated was 400 NIS ($100) to cover all expenses, including telephone calls to voters who failed to show up. Similarly, the fleet of vehicles disseminating information all over the country was reduced from 40 in 1996 to 4 at the beginning of the campaign and then during the last month increased to 25 to form "a cavalcade of triumph." All this meant that participation in the common endeavor as an alternative to crating an esprit de corps by means of ideological distinctions received a lower priority than before (Yerushalmi 1999).

Similar calculations help to explain the message. The appeal had to fulfill two conditions. It had to be simple enough to come home to a large hetero-geneous public, and sufficiently ambiguous to allow nuanced appeals to dif-fering groups. Since the Likud itself consisted of such groups, it had also to provide a common sense of mission. The peace process provided a perfect answer to these needs, and so the primary objective was to base the campaign on it. As one senior Likud figure explained to the writer, "if on election day voters regard the ballot as a referendum on the negotiations with the Pales-tinians, Bibi has a chance." Seeing that the crises and fall of the government were connected with these negotiations there would seem to be a paradox here. However, the prime minister's record lent itself to favorable interpreta-tions. The defeat of a government by "those who wanted to scuttle the Oslo, Hebron and Wye agreements" proved his readiness to pursue peace unflinch-ingly, yet the repeated deferments and breakdowns in the process proved persistence, stamina, the ability to resist "the chimeral 'New Middle East'" and to stare down the Palestinians and the Americans (Netanyahu 1999b). Thus the apparent veering from side to side could be taken as testimony of a consistent maintenance of balance. The cardinal choice faced by the electorate would then one of trust: Who could they bank on to represent the state in the fateful negotiations about to be held with the Palestinians, Syrians, and Americans? In Netanyahu's words, "the real encounter will begin the day after the elections. This will be the struggle over the nature of peace, over the final borders, over Jerusalem" (Netanyahu 1998).

During the months preceding the TV campaign the most persistent theme of the Likud's message was therefore the hammering on Netanyahu's record on the Palestinian issue. Among the first battle cries were We Shall Not Compromise on Israel's Security and We Shall Never Compromise on Jerusalem. The self-description on both slogans was The Likud, A Strong Leadership. Positive reaction of focus groups led to Netanyahu's choice of the slogan A Strong Leader for a Strong Nation, (later A Strong Leader for the Future of Israel) as mainstay of the Likud propaganda after his nomination as the candidate for the premiership. It encompassed the image of a pillar of strength sustaining the nation and the claim of centrism attested by the balanced appeal to all nonextremists. As he had declared in his statement opening the campaign, "leadership means the ability to say 'Yes!' and 'No!' I said yes to progress towards a true peace; I said no to compromises that might endanger the state" (Netanyahu 1998). This middle-of-the-road consistency found its most concise form in the theme that was repeated throughout the campaign: "If they give they will receive; if they don't give they won't receive." This was a variant of the 1996 "Netanyahu! Making peace with security," professing a readiness both to go forward and to freeze the process. A related theme that was upgraded as the campaign proceeded was the allegation that the demand for reciprocity was responsible for the dramatic decline in terrorist activity. This in turn suggested that the acceptance by the Arabs of the reciprocity principle created an opening for a breakthrough toward a true, secure peace. The flip side of this coin was the persistent attack on "the Left" as extremists who would imperil the state by unilateral concessions and bring about the replacing of the principle of "territory for peace" by the paradox of "territory for terrorism" (Netanyahu 1999b). As a countertheme this received at least as much attention throughout the campaign, yet unlike the continuity marking the claims supporting the incumbent, it unfolded in a series of "drives" each replacing a predecessor that failed to achieve hoped-for results.

A brief comparison of Peres's 1996 campaign may throw light on that of Netanyahu in 1999. Largely turning on the peace process, each relied on memory-based vote, in effect appealing to the electorate to ignore temporary present concerns and base expectations on past performance. Each confronted challengers who campaigned on immediate, "on-line" issues (terrorism in 1996 and failures in system management particularly in the socioeconomic spheres in 1999) with memory playing a part only as an accumulating "on-line tally" (Lodge, Steenbergen, and Brau 1995, esp. 310–311). Similarly, both attempted to disparage their adversaries, Peres claiming that Netanyahu lacked qualifications and Netanyahu portraying Barak as an unprincipled front for Leftist extremists. Such efforts could also be bolstered by the tested "on-line" issue of the danger such extremists would pose to the unity of

Jerusalem. Nevertheless, both found it difficult to build a persuasive attack against challengers who had no prolonged political careers the negative recollections of which could serve as an organizational principle for the on-line tally. Furthermore, the challengers could deflect attacks, Netanyahu by his acceptance of the Oslo framework and Barak by his military career. Netanyahu's predicament in 1999 was however worse than that of Peres, seeing that the discrediting of the Left and of Barak were the linchpin of his entire campaign. Hence the continuous effort to change tactics to reach the same goals.

The first negative slogans presented Barak's statements I Don't Express Dovish Positions because I Want to Win the Elections and Had I Been a Palestinian I Would Have Joined a Terrorist Organization as evidence of his evasiveness as well as of his true opinions. The slogan Ehud Barak—Too Many Ambitions, Too Few Principles sought to support the first allegation, but the second was that there was a reason for the evasiveness. Here a parallel developed between the two main contestants. One Israel accused Netanyahu of being beholden to the extremists of the ultra-Orthodox and the settlers. The Likud, for its part, accused Barak of being a front for the extremists of the Left, whose true positions were totally unacceptable to the bulk of the population. Its slogans described Barak as "fleeing" from truth and from responsibility, echoing the accusation that as chief of staff he "fled" from the scene of a serious military training accident. It was implied also that "fleeing" was the basic philosophy of "the Left" according to which unconditional withdrawal would appease the Arabs. The argument against such weak-kneed naïveté served in turn as the basis for the readaptation of the successful venture of the 1996 campaign–the threat to Jerusalem. As just noted, this was an issue seized by Netanyahu on landing from Wye, and with the beginning of the campaign it became the main plank of a drive entitled "Barak will set up a Palestinian state with its capital in Jerusalem." But it was further maintained that the logic of those who would join a government headed by Barak would inevitably bring about the achievement of the Palestinian dream.

By the end of March it became clear that neither the Jerusalem nor the anti-Barak drives had swayed significant numbers of floating voters. The state comptroller's report on the training accident exonerated Barak, and the loss of credibility was deepened by Olmert's admission that no candidate would divide Jerusalem. The conclusion was that the manner though not the matter of both charges should be changed. The Jerusalem issue still played a leading role, but now mainly through a new assertive note that was sounded in late March. The trigger was highly publicized meetings in Orient House between the Jerusalem representative of the PLO and European Union consuls. The prominence given to this violation of Israeli sovereignty afforded the cabinet leaders (Netanyahu, Sharon, and the new defense minister Moshe Arens) an opportunity to convince the electorate that the battle over the city had actually begun. In early April a series of steps was taken, including the annulment of the privileges of PLO leaders, the closing of the Palestinian Authority News Agency and other offices, and finally the proclamation of the intention to close the PLO offices in Orient House itself. The activity of Minister of Internal Security Avigdor Kahalani, who for fear of bloodshed adopted a strategy of foot-dragging by conducting consultations with Palestinian figures ready to compromise, may have prevented a major conflagration, but it ensured the presence of the issue on the agenda up to, and including, most of the TV campaign.

An additional front opened at about the same time employed yet another 1996 strategy, to assert a hidden competition between Netanyahu and Arafat underlying the elections. Like the Jerusalem issue the allegation of a partnership between Arafat and the Left was part of the campaign from the start. In late December Netanyahu had already argued that "Arafat wants to conduct the final status negotiations with the Left" (*Yediot Aharonot,* December 28, 1998). At the end of March, the Israeli Arabs Supervisory Committee called upon MK Azmi Bishara to withdraw his straw candidature for the premiership so as to avoid splitting the Arab vote, thereby furthering Netanyahu's chances; media rumors were that this was at the request of senior members of the Palestinian Authority, thus confirming the Likud claim. A special meeting of the Knesset was convened to discuss Palestinian intervention and a new drive centered on such slogans as Arafat Votes for Barak and It Is Not for Arafat to Decide. Imputations made at the opening of the campaign (*Yediot Aharonot,* December 28, 1998) were revived: the Beilin-Abu Mazan plan included "a return to the Partition Plan and the ceding of parts of the Negev; what Yossi Beilin says today Barak will do tomorrow" (*Ha'aretz,* April 5, 1999). Toward the later part of April, however, indications were that this drive too had failed to influence the uncommitted voters. Considerable sums (about 30 million NIS or $7.5 million) had been wasted to little effect and, in addition, much of the material prepared ahead of the TV campaign had already been shown to be largely ineffectual.

The limited success of all these drives raised the premium of specially tailored appeals suited to narrowly defined sectors of the electorate. Among these most critical were the Russians, not only because of their numbers but also because a significant proportion of the undecided were Russians. Since the beginning of the campaign, the Immigrants Headquarters worked through the Russian media to translate the general propaganda and to evoke memories unique to the audience. The "Left," for example, was explicitly related to the socialist command-economies that the addressees knew all too well. But toward the end of March an implicit attempt was made to exploit more positive memories. This started with a brief but highly visible visit of Netanyahu to the Ukraine, Russia, and Georgia. His meetings with high dignitaries and Jews were beamed by the Russian TV watched by most immigrants. This was immediately followed by a series of visits made by Sharon, likewise featured on Russian TV. Such activities were supposedly independent of the campaign, but Sharon was quite frank. The key to the elections, he explained to William Safire, was the Russian-Israelis. Should these visits raise their support of Netanyahu from the two thirds they gave him in 1996 to 70 percent, that alone would be enough to clinch the matter (Safire 1999).

Further appeals to specific groups were made in mid-April, introducing a new tone at the ceremonial opening of the Likud campaign a month before voting day and almost four months after the campaign had actually started. These found their place within an expanded discussion of socioeconomic issues that conveyed greater Likud readiness to take on matters that One Israel emphasized. Hitherto, if mentioned at all, these took the form of sweeping generalizations, like the contention that what was at stake was "the conflict between free economy and the bankrupt socialist economy" (Netanyahu 1998), or that the Rabin-Peres government had favored their cronies and flooded the country with foreign workers.[5] A few days before the official opening of the Likud campaign, however, the government approved a number of economic palliatives for farmers, cabdrivers, Jerusalemites, and other groups. This served as a backdrop to Netanyahu's speech at the ceremony. The pride of place was still devoted to the "main issue," but concrete commitments were made for younger voters: subsidized loans for small-scale entrepreneurs, for people at the outset of their careers, and for students of all institutions of higher learning. Together with the continuation of privatization, it was argued, these measures would help the country to become "the world's Silicon Valley." Thereafter, the economic issue had a regular place in the agenda, chiefly on claims of performance that served to rebut the One Israel attacks: the reduction of deficit, lower inflation, longer school days for development towns and minorities, and a computer for every child.

The content analysis of the Likud's TV campaign in table 10.1 points to an amalgam of all these elements. As in the preceding months, the accent fell on Netanyahu's leadership and on peace and security. The relation between "positive" and "negative" appeals emphasizing the "challenger strategy" of the incumbent did not change materially. The overall picture, however, cannot bring out the most outstanding trait of the campaign—the increasing heat generated not merely by the rapid succession of broadcasts but as a deliberate strategy. Since quiet campaigns tend to work in favor of the status quo, it is usually the challengers who have an interest in stormy confrontations. But this depends also on the state of the party involved. Stormy campaigns arouse enthusiasm, encourage potential supporters not to abstain, and press hesitant voters who previously voted for the party to repeat their choice. This explains the Likud strategy for attracting the numerous wavering supporters and ex-Netanyahu voters who still had not made up their minds.

The opening broadcast employed a variation of the attack on the "Left" in an appeal to specific sectors. "We have turned Israel into a state of all of us," Netanyahu declared, "the religious and the secular, the Sephardis and Ashkenazis, the new immigrants and the veterans. We must never return to the reign of the Left, of a band of despotic elitists alienated from the people." This argument in its various forms appears in 6.5 percent of the net propaganda time taken as a whole, but at first in a much larger proportion following the denigration of the Likud partisans as "a rabble" by an actress at a Labor rally. The anger among lower-class Likud Sephardim, Netanyahu hoped, would "finally send the Likud engine on the right track" (*Yediot Aharonot,* May 7, 1999). "I am," he declared, "proud to be a member of the rabble." The TV schedule was altered to include the doctored screening of the lapse with a smirking Barak standing nearby, and Netanyahu made a whirlwind tour where he repeated his accusations. His words at the Tikva market were caught by TV: "[Barak's] elites hate the people. They hate the Sephardim, they hate the Russians, they hate all who are not like them, Ethiopians, Sephardim, Moroccans, the religious, they hate them all" (*Yediot Aharonot,* May 4, 1999). The new tone equally pervaded subjects already dealt with previously, such as Netanyahu's curbing of terror, illustrated by 1996 footage of blown up buses. The problem of Jerusalem, to take another example, was brought to a climax not only on the screen. A week before voting day the police served orders to close three Palestinian offices in Orient House, and Netanyahu was quoted on TV as calling Kahalani "chicken" for his warning of riots in the city and the West Bank (*Yediot Aharonot,* May 10, 1999). Concurrently the government came out with new spending plans that included grants for purchasing apartments in East Jerusalem and for infrastructure improvements in the new Jewish neighborhoods.

None of these turned the tide. The battle over Jerusalem subsided when a Supreme Court judge ordered the halting of the Orient House closures till after the elections; even the minister of treasury stigmatized the budgetary plans as an election ploy; the denunciations of the Left's elitism showed no effect on the undecided, while Netanyahu's words in the Tikva market generated a backlash within his own party. Worse was the clash between the Likud's communitarian allies. Israel b'Aliya's slogan was Shas Kontrol Nyet (Don't Let Shas Control the Interior Ministry). The Shas TV responded that

Table 10.1   Content Analysis of Likud Electoral Appeals Appearing on
Israeli Television April 26–May 15, 1999 (Excluding Party Jingles)
in Percentage of the Total Net Time

Content of appeal	A Entire campaign	B Apr. 26– May 7	C May 8– May 15
"Positive" Contents			
Building up the image of Netanyahu and other party leaders	43.00	35.50	57.50
Positive Likud traits and past achievements (credibility, strong negotiating team, etc.)	14.00	3.50	32.50
Achievements in the context of relations with Palestinians, including the curbing of terrorism	15.50	22.00	4.00
Domestic achievements (socioeconomic)	6.00	7.00	4.00
Confident assurance of electoral victory	1.00	0	2.00
Noncontroversial stands	2.50	3.00	1.00
Total "Positive"	82.00	71.00	101.00
"Negative" Contents			
The unreliability of Barak	4.50	4.00	5.00
Failures of the pre-1996 Labor government over relations with the Palestinians, including inability to curb terrorism	5.00	6.50	2.00
The socioeconomic failures of the Labor government	2.50	4.00	0
The elitism of the "Left"	6.50	10.00	0
Exposure of true Palestinian and Syrian aims vis-à-vis Israel	7.50	10.50	1.00
Warning of security dangers inherent in One Israel government	17.50	16.00	19.00
Jerusalem under threat	8.00	16.00	1.00
Criticism of rivals other than One Israel	1.50	0	4.00
Total "Negative"	53.00	67.00	32.00
Others	6.50	5.50	8.50
N (seconds)	3,008	1,944	1,064

Since each broadcasting second may contain more than one of the content items, the total percent of the content item to broadcasting time does not equal 100. Each broadcast was divided into seconds and each content idea was rounded to the nearest whole minute. Percentages were rounded to the nearest 0.5 percent.

the Ministry was the only defense against the prostitutes and criminals among the immigrants. Thereupon One Israel promised Natan Sharansky the post of minister of the interior in a Barak government. Polls showed a steep decline of Russian support of Netanyahu, and indicated that most Russians believed Netanyahu was giving in to the ultra-Orthodox whereas Barak would defend the rights of the secular (Cohen 1999). Though Netanyahu brought Shas's Suissa and Israel b'Aliya's Sharansky to a brief televised meeting of reconciliation, the latter stood by his aim to wrest the interior ministry from Shas, while a day later Rabbi Ovadia again tiraded against Russian criminals and prostitutes. In the mid-TV campaign Netanyahu had to start a new drive to plug the hole in the dike. Sharansky was offered a ministry that would be more important than the Interior; a series of benefits was announced for the Russian immigrants, and thousands of personal letters were sent arguing that only a reelected Netanyahu could continue cooperation between Israel b'Aliya and government, but all in vain. As a final straw, Mordechai's continued decline in the polls and his own comrades' questioning of the wisdom of his candidacy raised the fear that there would be no second round. Signs of growing hopelessness were media stories of quarrels within the Campaign Headquarters and of high-ranking Likud members blaming Netanyahu for the impending defeat (e.g., *Ha'aretz,* May 10, 12, 1999; *Yediot Aharonot,* May 12, 1999).

With little more than a week to go the campaign underwent a final shift. Table 1 shows that the overall tone had changed, with the emphasis shifting from the "negative" to the "positive." The party now featured in 32.5 percent of the time, and the appeal was explicitly directed to wavering Likud voters. The first intimation of change was when Sharon pleaded with them not to forsake the party. The following night Netanyahu apologized for disappointing party members who were now undecided, and requested them "to put aside other considerations" and "return home, to the Likud" for the sake of "our principles, our way." Other TV appeals depicted the party as "a beautiful rainbow, where all can find their own color" and pleaded, "stop wavering; let us remain in our home. We have no other." The logo changed too. Hitherto it was two voting slips, the one bearing the party acronym, the other Netanyahu's name. Now the full name of the Likud was added, with the caption "This is our home." An accompanying theme was the attempt to explain away the adverse polls: "The Likud loses all the polls except the final one." Netanyahu's image was also revamped. Hitherto he had been his own promoter, and the focus lay on his achievements in office. Now he was presented by others, and the focus shifted to his military past and to his personal qualities. But all this came too late. The dice had been cast.

Conclusion

Two elements were conspicuously missing in what became the longest campaign the Likud ever ran. One was its stand on controversial issues. No contestant really advocated the division of Jerusalem or the basing of relations with the Palestinians on anything but reciprocity. All that could perhaps be in dispute was whether Palestinian autonomy was better than statehood. Netanyahu did mention this at the beginning and the end of the campaign (Netanyahu 1999a, 1999b) but only in written statements, and no one else raised the matter. The party program likewise mentioned this, but it was buried in an anemic document that itself was largely ignored. This relative silence may be explained by polls indicating that most voters accepted Palestinian statehood as inevitable (e.g., Yaar and Hermann, 1999). Electoral considerations may also lie behind the virtual absence of the other element; the Likud itself. Distinguishing party supporters from other voters in a race concentrating on the prime minister would be counterproductive, and the last minute turnabout was an act of despair, born of the sense that the race for the top post was all but lost.

While this tallies with what is often referred to as the "Americanization" of the Israeli campaign, the Likud's fate illustrates the problematics of such a transplantation. In the United States presidential hopefuls commonly adopt in the primaries positions catering to the ideological supporters of their parties, after which they veer to the center where they converge in a general race. In 1996 Netanyahu adapted this strategy to the Israeli context by collapsing the two phases into a single campaign, so that by appealing to an electorate divided over issues at the heart of national identity he committed himself to both sides. Since the rift ran through the Likud itself, it found itself in office still facing an unresolved ideological crisis, and pressures deepened the schism. A little-noticed example was the call in the critical opening of the TV campaign for support of Netanyahu because of our "concern for the wholeness of the Land of Israel." Such a cognitive dissonance was a major agent in the overthrow of the government and in the secessions that had so reduced the Likud Knesset delegation. The only realistic option was a nonideological campaign focusing on Netanyahu, but it exposed the party to the predation of the Likud secessionists and of Shas.[6]

Over and above the Likud predicament there is the wider problem of Israeli democracy. The "American style" assumes a public largely uninterested in questions of political principle. It ranks salesmanship above rational discourse that lies at the root of democracy. That is why the Americanization of politics so disturbed Europe and scholars in the 1960s. A well-known warning is that of Otto Kirchheimer, that "voters may, by their shifting moods and their apathy, transform . . . the catch-all party into something too blunt to serve as a link with the functional powerholders of society" (1966, 200). This is doubly true of a country still in the process of defining itself. What happened to the Likud showed that the attempt to evade confrontation with issues of principle might not only erode the quality of democracy but be at the expense of parties adopting such a strategy. The reason lay in the unique combination of proportional representation and the premiership contest, and this was responsible for another democratic pitfall, namely, the rise of the communitarian parties. It was to them that the prime minister, turned to escape from the dilemmas of his own party. Each however pursued its own restricted interests, and mutual rivalry proved dependence on of them to be a broken straw. This highlights the mismatch of the principle of national representation by the prime minister and the communal representation of the parties whose support he hoped will win him the elections. Nevertheless there is something in common between the catchall race for the premiership and the narrow race for MKs in the Knesset. The latter, too, bypasses rational discourse on matters relevant to the main body of the nation. Between the desire to stretch the appeal to the utmost by avoiding general divisive issues and the desire to build on particular loyalties, democracy itself may become a victim.

Notes

1. For the balancing of these two positions in the Netanyahu message see Mendilow (1999, 199–206). The cardinal demands of the party ideologues were presented as essential for safeguarding personal security. These included ending the reliance on Arafat as a "subcontractor for Israel's security," permitting the security forces to operate at will within the areas controlled by the Palestinian Authority, establishing more Jewish settlements to cordone them and prevent their coalescence into a state, and substituting increased military presence in the territories for Labor's formula of separation from the Palestinians. Other matters related to the questions of the "final stage": the fate of Jewish settlements, the status and boundaries of the Palestinian entity, the rights of refugees to return, and the future of Jerusalem. With the exception of Jerusalem, the Likud propaganda was to present the predetermination of all these issues as vital for personal security and hence a sine qua non for peace. At the same time, the frustration brought about by the Likud's lack of positive solutions would be answered by a firm commitment to continue the peace effort. This was not to be satisfied by picturing white doves or by merely reciting that peace was the final goal of a Likud government, but by the firm assertion that "a Likud government would recognize the facts created by the Oslo accords" and insisting on the need for continued negotiations.

2. This was a new strategy. Hitherto such unity coalitions had been formed in times of national crisis (1967) or of electoral stalemate (1984, 1988). Now it was

used as a threat. When Levy resigned, Netanyahu even offered the Foreign Ministry to the "arch-Leftist," Peres himself.

3. For a short informative discussion of the attempts to secure a government majority see Crystal and Kfir, (1999, 33–56).

4. The Likud was now left with a mere nineteen MKs, among them members like Landau who openly criticized Netanyahu on ideological grounds and Livnat who seemed to be in two minds as to whether to leave the party altogether. Symptomatically, in the internal elections for the nomination of the party's premiership candidacy held on January 25, only 35 percent of the members bothered to participate, about half of the number in 1993. Netanyahu's argument that this was because everyone took it for granted that he would be elected is at best impersuasive. See Duweik (1999).

5. Fears that the government would engage in "election economics" were dispelled, and the only steps taken up to mid-April were the freezing of planned economic restrictive measures (e.g., raising past payments for clinic visits and medications or the reduction of tax cuts for development towns), increasing government 1999 expenditure by about 0.5 percent (Plotzker 1999).

6. The only defense against these came at the end of the TV campaign when a Likud member accused the Center Party of having no principles, and another confessed he had considered voting for it, only to find that this meant a vote for the "Left."

References

Barnea, Nachum. 1996. Interview with Dan Meridor. *Yediot Aharonot,* weekend supplement, February 16.

Central Bureau of Statistics (Hebrew). *Statistical Abstract,* 1997, 1998.

Cohen, Aryeh Dean. 1999. "Poll: Russian Immigrants Believe PM Caves in to Haredim, While Barak Will Support Secular Rights." *Jerusalem Post,* May 12.

Crystal, Chanan, and Ilan Kfir. 1999. *The Sixth Comendation: 1999 Elections—The Full Story.* Tel Aviv: Keter.

Duweik, Nechama. 1999. "The Members Voted With Their Feet." *Yediot Aharonot,* January 26.

Friedman, Thomas. 1999. "A Dangerous Peace." *New York Times,* January 12.

Honig, Sarah. 1996. "Packaging 'Bibi' for the Masses." *Jerusalem Post,* international edition, week ending February 10.

Kirchheimer, Otto. 1966. "The Transformation of the West European Party System." In Joseph LaPalombara and Myron Weiner, (eds.). *Political Parties and Political Development.* Princeton: Princeton University Press.

Lawson, Kay, and Peter H. Merkel. 1988. "Alternative Organizations: Supplementary, Communitarian and Antiauthoritarians." In Kay Lawson, and Peter H. Merkl, (eds.). *When Parties Fail: Emerging Alternative Organizations.* Princeton: Princeton University Press.

Levi-Barzilai, Vered. 1998. "In the Shadow of a Giant." *Yediot Aharonot,* weekend supplement, October 30.

Lodge, Milton, Marco R. Steenbergen, and Shawn Brau. 1995. "The Responsive Voter: Campaign Information and the Dynamics of Candidate Evaluation." *American Political Science Review* 89:309-326.

Marcus, Yoel. 1999. "He Sowed Hatred and Reaped Defeat." *Ha'aretz,* May 18.

Mendilow, Jonathan. 1999. "The Likud's Double Campaign: Between the Devil and the Deep Blue Sea." In Asher Arian, and Michal Shamir, *The Elections in Israel, 1996.* Albany: State University of New York Press.

Netanyahu, Binyamin. 1998. "The Real Struggle." *Yediot Aharonot,* weekend supplement, December 31.

————. 1999a. "Looking Forward." *Jerusalem Post.*

————. 1999b. "Vote for Me Because Only I Can Ensure that a Genuine Peace Prevails." *Jerusalem Report,* May 24.

Plotzker, Sever. 1999. "The Economic Balloon." *Yediot Aharonot,* weekend supplement, January 15.

Safire, William. 1999. "Meanwhile, in Israel." *New York Times,* April 4.

Secretariat of Yesha in the Likud. 1998. *A Call to the Members of the Likud Party Center.* Tel Aviv: private circulation.

Shalev, Hemi. 1999. "The Blossoming of the Cherry Tree." *Ma'ariv,* weekend supplement, January 1.

Sontag, Deborah. 1999. "Israel Is Weighing a Broad Coalition to Further Peace." *New York Times,* May 19.

Tal, Yevach. 1993. "Death Alone Can Release from the Platform." *Ha'aretz,* October 19.

Yaar, Efraim, and Tamar Hermann. 1999. "Majority Believe the Palestinian Demand for a State to Be Just." *Ha'aretz,* April 4.

Yerushalmi, Shalom. 1999. "One Man's Campaign: The Activists Stay at Home." *Ma'ariv,* weekend supplement, April 23.

Yovel, Yirmiyahu. 1998. "The Central Force." *Yediot Aharonot,* December 24.

11

The Appearance of the Center Party in the 1999 Elections

Nathan Yanai

The Center Party, established shortly before the 1999 elections, reflected changes in Israeli politics relating to both the political party and the party system and to the electoral competition in Israel. The formation of this party exemplified the perennial temptation to establish a party of the center and the special problems involved in that undertaking, as well as the difficulties in setting up a new party in Israel, despite the openness of the proportional system in the Knesset elections. The case of the Center Party will be discussed here within a comparative framework and in relation to the systemic factors that contributed to the nature of the elections in 1999.

The Center Party has been the subject of continual discussion in the research literature (see Daalder 1984; Downs 1957; Duverger 1959; Hazan 1995, 1996, 1997; Ieraci 1992; Kernan 1994; Sartori 1976; Scully 1992). Maurice Duverger (1964, 215), for one, negated the very existence of such a party, claiming that a "center" or centrist doctrine does not exist in politics. The center—according to his argument—is an artificial connection of the right wing of the Left with the left wing of the Right. Reuven Y. Hazan (1996, 226) argues that the use of the center label by a growing number of parties with differing ideologies in the various party systems of the expanding democratic world is an additional sign that the academic literature needs to reassess its perception of the center. The difficulty in identifying a center party, beyond its own declaration, stems from the difficulty in defining the center in any given party system and from the various possibilities for shaping the character of such a party—leaving aside the fact that the adoption of the center party name and a pretense of centrism may also manifest electoral manipulation.[1]

The definition of center party relates to two variables: (1) the party's location within the party system and its ideology, that is, its location between the principal political parties of the Right and the Left of the party system, or its intermediate ideological approach; and (2) its attempt to reach a consensus or compromise based on a rejection of the conflicting ideologies of the opposing wings within the party system.

Its intermediate ideological position brings the Center Party closer to an antiparty stand; one that rejects the very legitimacy of the political party because of its divisive impact. This negation is based on the claim that identifying with partisan ideology interferes with one's ability to relate to the system's main, objectives in regard to the community, nation, or state. This argument, found already in Jean-Jacques Rousseau's Concept of General Will, may be followed by an historical concept or legacy that has served, or may serve, as a guiding and unifying source for the general body. In other words, not only is the partisan ideology detrimental; it is also superfluous. The first claim is directed against the threat of divisive ideology, while the second claim suggests ignoring it because it has lost its vitality and meaning. At the outset of the World Zionist Federation, the General Zionists represented the antipartisan stand.[2] This movement argued against partisan division, since it threatened the unity of the federation and interfered with an ability to identify completely with the common Zionist objectives. It proposed the initial Herzlian vision as an enduring basis for unity. By comparison, it is possible to point to the French Radical Party, which, since its inception in 1901, has seen itself as representing the unique legacy of France, based on the rational "immortal principles," drafted in 1789, of the French Revolution (Larmour 1964, 60–77).[3]

The Splinter Syndrome

Occupying an intermediate position, the center actually harbors two contrasting orientations: one creates an opening to the right, and the other to the left. The clash between the two orientations generates the Center Party splinter syndrome. Indeed, when the General Zionists were forced (in 1929) to organize as a political party in order to stay in competition with the ideological Zionist parties, they immediately fell victim to this syndrome (in 1935). In their case, it involved a split between those who wanted to cooperate with the Labor movement (the Left) and those who wanted to cooperate with the political Right.

A later example of the splinter syndrome was the Liberal Party (1961), whose origins also lay in the historic General Zionist movement. The Liberal Party was formed by the merger of the General Zionist with the Progressive Party. Being disappointed by the outcome of the 1961 elections, and by Mapai's decision to favor the inclusion of Ahdut HaAvoda from the left rather than the centrist Liberal Party in its coalition government, the majority of the Liberal Party (the former General Zionists) decided to form an electoral and parliamentary bloc (Gahal) with the Herut Party, despite the objection of the former progressives. This decision resulted in a party split. The former General Zionists, now carrying the banner of the Liberal Party, moved toward full cooperation with the political right, while the former progressives reasserted their partisan independence as the Independent Liberal Party and resumed their traditional pattern of cooperation with Labor (Mapai). The case of Dash (1977) reveals the same syndrome in relation to participation in the Likud government. The antipartisan message is likely to provide a temporary advantage for a new center party in protesting the state of the existing party system or institutions. This same message, however, also erodes the ability to legitimize the formation of a new party. Moreover, a centrist position does not necessarily justify the formation of a center party; it is doubtful whether the establishment of such a party can be based solely on the rejection of past ideological cleavages. A recently published study (Kunsten 1998) points to the clear tendency of European parties, especially socialist parties, to move toward the center during the years 1982–1993. This general phenomenon was given institutional-partisan expression in the Israeli party system when Mapam (including its kibbutz element), the former Orthodox Socialist Party, was fully integrated into the Meretz Party, which was devoid of any socialist definition. Another example was the Labor Party's taking part in the 1999 elections within the framework of "One Israel," which intentionally blurred the party's historical identity. The phenomenon had also been seen earlier in the selection of a party standard bearer (Yitzhak Rabin in 1992) who was identified with consensual views.

The Formation of New Parties in Israel

The temptation to establish new parties in Israel is enhanced by the openness of its system of proportional elections and by a tradition of responsive politics in a system of coalition government. Nevertheless, the number of lists attaining Knesset representation has remained more or less stable (between ten and fifteen).[4] The overwhelming majority of the new parties that were established between 1949 and 1977 and that survived were created through the splitting or merging of veteran parties. The splits were carried out by organized factions with a tradition of collective action that professed at least a partially different ideological approach from that of the majority of the party. A decision to split the party was either forced by the majority, or it served the needs of a minority faction's leadership that found itself in a state of intensive intraparty conflict. Such a split either completed the institutionalization of a partisan organization, as in the case of Mapai's faction Bet in 1944, or renewed the institutionalization of a former party, as in the case of Ahdut HaAvoda, which had split from Mapam in 1954, and the Progressive Party, which had split from the Liberal Party in 1965. In the historic Israeli party system, mergers were made on the basis of programmatic negotiations and a calculation of the advantage of the merger versus the continued stalemate or an outright crisis in the electoral orientation of one or more of the merging parties. In a few cases, the unification was an attempt to reverse a historical split, such as the establishment of the Liberal Party in 1961 and of the Labor Party in 1968.

New Israeli parties can be assessed and classified on the basis of the principal rationale that led to their establishment. This assessment does not necessarily match the explanations offered by those involved in the formation of these parties. It has a significant but incomplete correlation with the identification of time periods. The classification, which relates only to those parties that gained Knesset representation, is based on three types of rationale for establishing new parties: partisan, communal, and electoral. These three types of rationale are not mutually exclusive; they can, and often do, coexist. The saliency of one rationale or the relationship among the three, however, reflects the changing character of political parties and politics in Israel.

Partisan Rationale—	Relates to traditional party features: viable ideology, cohesive leadership, and a tradition of collective political action.
Communal Rationale—	Relates to claims for group representation based on membership in a community. This claim may be generated by feelings of discrimination or even normative and social superiority. Issues relating to ethnicity, religion, or organizational (i.e., kibbutz) affiliation may be included in this category.
Electoral Rationale—	Relates to a sense of electoral opportunity shared by individual political figures and groups. In the absence of a partisan or communal rationale, the electoral rationale draws easily from the untapped claims of "new politics" and "deserving leadership."

Until 1977, one could identify the saliency of the partisan rationale in the establishment of new parties, which were built primarily on the basis of splits or mergers of veteran parties or party factions. The formation of Rafi in 1965 can be explained on this basis although some of the initial characteristics of the later model of the new Center Party can also be identified in the development of this party and the leadership group at its helm. The formation of the Democratic movement for Change, Dash, in 1977 signaled a retreat of the partisan-programmatic rationale and the advance of a new saliency, that of the electoral rationale. One can still trace, however, the connection between the two types of rationale in the efforts of the leaders of Dash to establish a party with a well-defined platform and elected institutions, and even to adopt a direct-democracy approach, through the use of primaries, in selecting party candidates to the Knesset. Nevertheless, the organization of Yigal Yadin's "Democratic Movement," which was formed to bring about a change in government by recruiting new leaders, its electorally oriented merger with Shinui, and in particular its attracting individuals and groups from existing parties highlighted the importance of the electoral rationale in the establishment of Dash. The primacy of this rationale, though, planted the seeds of this party's dissolution when Dash did not achieve its main objective in the elections. It may also be argued that the communal rationale was of some importance in the formation of Dash,[5] since it constituted an attempt to mobilize Israel's veteran elites to replace a faltering government, while trying to prevent its being taken over by the Likud Party, which drew support from constituencies, especially new immigrants and North African Jews, which threatened the social, economic, and political supremacy of these elites.

The weakening of the veteran political parties—first organizationally and later electorally—corresponded to the decline of traditional party ideology and the withering of the supportive political role of associate social organizations, primarily the Histadrut—the Israeli multiparty Federation of Labor—and the Kibbutz, the politicized collective-settlement movement. The process was certainly compatible with the saliency of new types of rationale for the formation of political parties: communal and electoral. This has been apparent in the formation of ethnic-communal parties: Tami (1981), *Shas* (1984), and Israel b'Aliya (1996); centrist parties carrying the claim of new politics: Dash (1977) and the Center Party (1999); and radical parties carrying a single message that was either neglected or rejected by the veteran parties: Ratz (1973), Kach (1984), Moledet (1988), and Shinui under the leadership of Yosef Lapid (1999).

Within this new reality, it is possible to identify two conditions for the success of a new party:

1. A unique public message answering the unmet expectations of a large group of voters—a message expressing both frustration and hope. The radical character of this message, in content and in form, is likely to contribute to the establishment of a new party although not necessarily to increase its chances of success. A wider legitimacy of the unique message of the new party among potential voters

contributes to its continued existence; this is notably the case of
Shas, with its dual religious/ethnic message, as opposed to the isolated ethnic message of Tami (Yanai and Aharonson 1986, 56–58).

2. A crisis in the functioning and legitimacy of the governing
party(ies) and the lack of a partisan-electoral alternative perceived as
legitimate by members of the elite groups and a significant number
of voters. This condition takes on stronger significance when central
parties collapse, thus creating the need for a legitimate political realignment. This extreme condition occurred in Italy as a result of
the left wing's being redefined after the dissolution of the Soviet
Union and, later, the collapse of the Christian Democrats following
the exposure of mafia connections in the government.[6]

Rafi—Forerunner of the Center Party?

In the case of Rafi—especially in the formation of Moshe Dayan's list, which
did not materalize prior to the 1969 elections—it is possible to identify the
forerunner of a center party carrying the flag of "new politics" and determined
to challenge the structure of the historical party system. Rafi, however, lacked
a clear, cohesive center-party philosophy, as it was still anchored in the organizational and programmatic tradition of Mapai and the Labor movement.
The formation of Rafi, not long before the Histadrut and Knesset elections
of 1965, was not a declaration of partisan independence by an opposition
faction within Mapai. It acquired, rather, the character of a new organization
that drew heavily from the circle of Ben-Gurion's supporters within Mapai,
but that frantically sought new recruits (Yanai 1969; 279–281). In this sense,
the formation of Rafi differed from the splitting of a cohesive programmatic
faction that continues as an independent party, the structure and tradition it
had maintained as an intraparty faction.

The development of Rafi's programmatic message was rooted in a number of sources: the reservations of Mapai's Young Circle over the party's class-
based ideological tradition, and its courting of Israel's new elites, especially
in finance, communication, academia, and the military. At the center of
Rafi's Knesset platform lay the concepts of "economic modernization" and the
rather vague concept of "national scientification." These concepts deviated
from Mapai's ideological legacy. Rafi's pretention at reforming the government was expressed in platform planks calling for a change in the proportional system of Knesset elections, for the direct election of mayors, and for
the "separation of powers" of government. Moreover, the platform included
the problematic plan, from the standpoint of Mapai, of creating a state
health-care insurance scheme. The change in Rafi's programmatic approach

and the emerging perception of its centrist position paved the way to its willingness to cooperate with right-wing parties in an attempt to set up an alternative coalition to the Mapai-led government. This willingness underlined Rafi's rigorous activity on behalf of establishing a National Unity government on the eve of the Six Day War.

The formation of Rafi through a broad membership-recruitment campaign corresponded with the Labor movement's historical model of a mass party. Moreover, its sectoral image on the eve of the 1965 elections was similar to that of Mapai, according to a study by Michael Lotan (Yanai 1969, 307–311). Nevertheless, Rafi's leaders showed particular interest, and were successful, in recruiting support among Israel's new social elites. Their success in this regard was apparent in 1969, when Shimon Peres and Dayan prepared the option for breaking away from the Labor Party and establishing a new party. The list of those involved in this aborted attempt, who were not members of the Labor Party, resembled the list of those who were later involved in establishing Dash. At first, Rafi appealed primarily to Mapai's historical constituency. Its new political orientation, however, made it possible to define a new constituency at the center of Israel's partisan map. If Dayan's List had been established in 1969, it would have served as the precursor to the new center-party model of Dash and the Center Party.

The Formation of the Center Party

The Center Party was established prior to the 1999 elections, not by a cohesive group of founders but at the initiative of three political personalities (Roni Milo, Dan Meridor, and Amnon Lipkin-Shahak), each of whom first offered his candidacy for prime minister[7] and established a separate support organization. These leaders found it difficult to cooperate with one another although it was clear to them that only one would have any chance of winning in the same partisan electoral space they had carved out for themselves. After a period of open competition and tense negotiations, the three finally collaborated in establishing a new party, an act made possible only by selecting a fourth candidate, Yitzhak Mordechai, for prime minister and to lead their new party. Mordechai had only recently left the Likud Party after being dismissed from Prime Minister Benjamin Netanyahu's government.[8] The search by these leaders for a political orientation turned the new Center Party first and foremost into an electoral arrangement. The formation of the Center Party requires, however, a broader explanation, relating to the circumstances that led to early elections in 1999 and to systemic changes and the changing character of Israeli politics—especially, the direct election of the prime minister and the shrinking power of the major parties.

The formation of a center party reflected the weakening of the partisan-programmatic rationale for creating a new party. The Center Party made use of the centrist partisan space left open after the Liberal Party merged with the Likud, and Shinui joined Meretz.[9] This space carried an historical tradition, which partially reduced the need for new legitimacy in creating the party; it was already a recognized political brand name, but one that had been neglected. The electoral success of the centrist appeal seemed an obvious certainty, particularly since the veteran parties had lost a firm grip on their historical constituencies; taking advantage of this electoral promise, however, was no mean feat. The possible advantages that accompany the centrist appeal are apt to narrow or even disappear precisely because of their problematic nature. Thus, the advantage of broadening the party's potential constituency may be negated by the loose definition of that constituency. An intermediate position reduces opposition, but also makes it difficult to create electoral identification and a strong partisan commitment. Carrying the banner of "new politics" invites an intense scrutiny of the nature and quality of the new partisan venture.

The Center Party (1999) presented itself to the voters as a political response to crises in government, society, and politics in Israel. Its platform contended that "Israel is in a state of deep crisis, with internal schisms between different sectors of society, an economic recession that has led to individual and societal suffering, and political stalemate." Furthermore, "Increasingly, Israel's international status is becoming undermined, and the peace process is not making progress. As a result, we can no longer fully use our strength in the ways that best serve the interests of citizen and society, and it is going to waste." According to the founders of the Center Party, "The eternal battle between the older parties does not reflect the public's opinions." In other words, the "older parties" had lost their relevance, and their contribution to society had become destructive. What was needed, therefore, was "a leading central force that will succeed in uniting the central forces in society . . . Israel currently needs experienced, reliable leadership to represent the vast majority of the nation."

The rest of the platform preamble has the flavor of an intellectual exercise, entailing all the commitments ever made in Israeli politics that might possibly suit the definition of a center party: uniting the right and left, the religious and the secular, veteran citizens and new immigrants; concluding the legislation for an Israeli constitution; decentralizing government and increasing citizen's participation in its work; depoliticizating services to citizens; presenting a balanced economic policy and avoiding sectoral preferences; "and security and peace policies with a long-range perspective, which will have the broad backing of the public." And lastly, "creating the basis for wide public support in favor of the correct policy for Israel."

The radical aspect of the party founders' message lay only in its critical appraisal of Netanyahu's personality. All of them sharpened their initial criticism,[10] which created a sense of urgency while producing the initial basis for merging their individual initiatives. This message reflected the feelings of alienation that had grown stronger between Netanyahu and most of Israel's elites. Four principal factors had led to its creation:

1. The assassination of Prime Minister Yitzhak Rabin contributed to the legitimate politicization of the country's economic, cultural, and social elites. The assassin's affiliation with the national religious camp made it difficult for people to come to terms with Netanyahu's election victory in 1996, because of the claim that the political and ideological circles backing him had created a public atmosphere enabling this political assassination.

2. The Netanyahu government changed in its orientation toward the peace process. The majority in this government, led by the Likud, regarded the Oslo Accord, signed by the Rabin-Peres government, as a political blunder. There was no way to nullify the agreement, but it was possible to limit its implications and to reduce the degree of dependence upon it. Netanyahu sought to minimize the advantages ostensibly gained by the Palestinian side in the Oslo agreement. The previous government, in contrast, considered the Oslo agreement a cornerstone in a process of reconciliation designed to put an early end to the Arab-Israeli conflict. Labor's argument concerning the opportune historical moment was followed up by the claim, supported by the economic elite, that only progress in the peace process could rescue Israel's economy from recession and pave the way for economic growth.

3. The change in political orientation brought about the need to sign the Wye Plantation Agreement. The suspension of the implementation of this agreement because of the claim of a lack of reciprocity created a crisis in the government's relationship with the American administration, which drew closer to the Palestinian Authority. An earlier crisis between Itzhak Shamir's Likud government and the Bush administration had remained unresolved through the 1993 elections, and led to the suspension of U.S. guarantees for a $10 billion loan targeted for Israel's absorption of Soviet immigrants. The Likud's defeat in both 1993 and 1999 reinforces the notion that U.S.-Israel relations are central to the position taken by the Israeli voter.

4. Netanyahu's leadership style was defined by his many rivals and critics as condescending and manipulative. Netanyahu's quick rise to the top leadership role in the Likud, despite the lack of extensive political background and/or a source of consensual legitimacy (e.g.,

the position of chief of staff as in the case of Rabin), made his acceptance uneasy, especially as it involved skipping over the previous
generation of those in the Likud who had sought this position (including Meridor and Ronnie Milo). Likud rank-and-file members
had actually imposed Netanyahu (who had served as deputy foreign
minister in the Shamir government) on the top echelon of the party
through the nominating primaries. It was no wonder that attempts
to oust him from his leadership position continued even after his
election as prime minister.

The sense of urgency and opportunity that initially led to the formation
of the Center Party derived not only from feelings of disenchantment with
Netanyahu but also from the lack of confidence in the ability of the Labor
candidate, Ehud Barak, to win the election. Skepticism at Barak's chances,
voiced within the Labor Party itself, was supported by media reports and
public opinion surveys.[11] In response, Barak initiated and successfully concluded a move to establish a new electoral alliance, "One Israel," based on
Labor's agreement with Gesher and Meimad.[12] This strategy was designed to
overcome the historical inhibitions of former right-wing voters and to create
a broader basis of possible identification with Labor's candidate, even at the
expense of his own party's representation in the Knesset. In the previous
elections, Netanyahu had initiated a similar move, albeit more limited in
public significance. He had reached an agreement with Gesher, which previously had broken with the Likud, and with Tzomet, which had identified itself as a member of the "national camp," concerning their appearance in a
joint electoral ticket.

The saliency of the Center Party's personal campaign was balanced by the
claim of "new politics." Five factors, however, lessened its ability to become
identified with this claim:

First, with the exception of former chief of staff, Lipkin-Shahak, the
Center Party was established by veteran Likud politicians who had been
pushed aside or who had broken with their party of their own free will. Having left the party of the right, they gravitated to the political center (Meridor
and Mordechai). Only Milo, while still a member of the Likud, began to
espouse a different political message. Each of the first ten candidates on the
Center Party's list had previously been identified with some other party; most
of them, in fact, joined the new party only after being promised a place on
its list.

Second, Lipkin-Shahak's entry into active politics only a short time after
his retirement from the IDF was hardly compatible with the claim of a new
type of politics. His sharp personal attack on the prime minister ("Netanyahu
is dangerous to Israel"), his superior in office during his service as chief of

staff, also did not support this claim. Neither did Mordechai's abrupt exit from the Likud following his dismissal from Netanyahu's government, which had come in the midst of Mordechai's simultaneous negotiations with both the three founders of the Center Party and the leader of the Likud.

Third, the oligarchic process used to appoint the Center Party's Knesset list clashed with the concept of party democracy that had become an important component of Israel's political reform philosophy. The composition of the list of candidates was left entirely in the hands of the four founding leaders, who basically acted as sole shareholders with total control of the new party.

Fourth, the leaders' control over the party's establishment and its nominating process, as well as the continuing rivalry among them, could have been at least partially balanced by the party's rapid institutionalization. This process was halted, however, at the level of recruiting member-supporters within the framework of the party's election campaign. The Center Party entered the Knesset without any sovereign institutions, even temporary ones, with the exception of its Knesset faction, which consisted of the four founders and two other members they had appointed to the list.

Fifth, the possible identification with the concept and image of "new politics" was diminished even further by the lack of a unique programmatic message that could have compensated for the saliency of the personal message during the party's divisive formative period. The platform commitment to complete legislation for drawing up a constitution for Israel within six months was perceived neither as the party's principal message nor as something unique or even radical.

Changes in Israeli Politics and Their Implications

The initiative to establish the Center Party was compatible with the processes of change in Israel's society, politics, and political culture. These changes contributed to the initiative to establish the Center Party and to its initial electoral promise. Most of them, however, also contributed to its early demise.

1. The Declining Power of the Major Parties

The decline of the two major parties in the Knesset began with the elections of 1984, when both parties significantly lost representation (Likud from 48 to 41 Knesset members; Labor from 47 to 44 Knesset members). The joint representation of these parties had reached its peak in 1981 (95 of the 120 members of Knesset). This electoral outcome, however, which may be defined as two-party dominance, could not become a permanent feature of the Israeli party system because of the openness of the proportional system of elections and the multicleavages characterizing Israeli society. The absence of a legal, systemic constraint paved the way to a gradual decline in the representation of the two major parties in response to the changing pressures of Israel's political society. This phenomenon took place in conjunction with the decline of the traditional ideological message of both parties and with their changing relationship, particularly in the case of the Labor Party, with auxiliary and supportive social organizations. It should be noted that the decline of both the Labor Party and the Likud occurred following the passing of the old guard (Golda Meir retired in 1974, and Menachem Begin in 1981) and the instituting of nominating primaries in the selection of their respective leaderships. The reduced organizational power of the major parties was not reflected in their membership rolls, which had remained relatively large, though not stable, primarily because of recruitment drives organized by the candidates themselves during the primaries.[13] Rather, the parties' organizational weakness manifested itself in the reduced functions of party headquarters and in the closing of party branches, in budgetary shortages, and in the decreasing significance attributed to party membership. This situation presented a temptation to challenge the dominance of the two major parties; at the same time, it damaged the public image of the party institution and made it more difficult to gain legitimacy for the formation of a new party.

2. Direct Election of the Prime Minister

The direct election of the prime minister has been the most important change in the Israeli system of government since the inception of the State. On the one hand, this legislation created an integrative constraint because it based this election on a unitary constituency. On the other hand, it created the possibility of ticket-splitting between the selection of a prime minister and the choosing of a Knesset list. In so doing, the new system of elections enhanced the fragmentation of the Knesset and accelerated the decline in the representation of the two historic major parties. The Likud's Knesset representation, which had numbered 32 in 1992, remained the same in 1996, but now it incorporated two smaller parties, Tzomet and Gesher; it then dropped precipitously to only 19 in 1999. Labor's Knesset representation fell steadily from 44 in 1992 to 34 in 1996 and to 26 (including the Gesher and Meimad parties) in 1999.

The direct election of the prime minister enabled a candidate to enter politics by competing directly for the highest governmental position. Although the candidate for prime minister must also submit a list of candidates to the Knesset, the new system put a premium on the role of the candidate's personality and on his capacity to attract the broadest possible constituency in order to be able to gain the majority support required to be elected prime minister. This change creates the possibility of a dramatic turnover in government, provided that the Knesset factions accept the decision of the electorate in this regard or that a similar change take place in the elections to the Knesset. The founders of the Center Party tried to take advantage of this new avenue to power in response to the political crisis and the sense of electoral opportunity that manifested themselves prior to the 1999 elections.

The dual competition, for prime minister and for the Knesset, created the need to combine an appeal to a partisan constituency with an appeal to the general electorate. This linkage at first seemed to be advantageous to the Center Party because of its consensual ideological orientation; it even created an initial promising forecast for its likely success (or lack of failure) in the race for the Knesset. It gradually lowered, however, the level of support for the Center Party's Knesset list because of the evaporating support for its candidate for prime minister. The rapid decline in the standing of the Center Party's candidate for prime minister, Mordechai, can be explained partially by the "third-candidate" syndrome. Remaining viable in a three-way race requires each candidate to possess a promising standing in the race in relation to at least one of the two other candidates. When, however, one candidate lacks this standing, the media begins to focus on the race between the two other candidates, thereby helping to produce the likely decline in the standing of the third candidate. This was certainly the case with the Center Party's candidate in the 1999 elections. A concerted effort by members of the Israeli elite and a significant number of Israeli journalists to stop Netanyahu in that race accelerated this process. Mordechai's early electoral claim that only he could beat Netanyahu lost meaning when polls showed that Barak could win even in the regular election and certainly in any second round.

3. Involvement of the News Media in Politics

The political involvement of the news media in a democratic society has been keenly observed (e.g., Cook 1998; Swanson 1991) although the full implications of such involvement, especially in relation to elections, are not entirely clear. The Israeli media's hostile attitude toward Netanyahu[14] did not prevent him from winning the 1996 elections, yet it is possible that the continuation of this attitude contributed to his defeat in 1999. This phenomenon strengthens the hypothesis concerning the importance of other variables in determining electoral behavior; it also raises an intriguing question concerning the implications of a consistently hostile attitude by the media or by the outcome of the backlash response it arouses.

The news media's involvement in politics did not annul the main systemic function of the political party in the organization of representative democracy

(Yanai, 1999, 5–17). Nevertheless, it modified and limited the party's role in organizing and shaping public debate on political issues and softened partisan identity and identification. It also tended to weaken internal party solidarity. The news media has become a legitimate partner, albeit an informal one, in the identification, recruitment, and promotion of political candidates. It, thus, opened the door for the appearance of a new candidacy for national leadership, based on public exposure and media legitimacy, not merely or chiefly on ongoing activity in the party. Indeed, the Israeli media contributed to a heightened sense of opportunity that accompanied the candidacies of Milo, Meridor, and especially Shahak, preceding the establishment of the Center Party. The media also documented the mishaps and failures in the establishment of this party. Center Party leaders, who were given a great deal of exposure in the media at the start of the election campaign, later complained that the media had prevented them from competing effectively with the two major parties.[15]

4. Political Mobilization of the Israeli Elite

Three related phenomena contributed to the enhanced political mobilization of Israeli elites prior to the 1999 elections:

    a. The participation of prominent members of the economic, cultural, and social elites in the campaign to enlist support for the peace process under the Labor government, including the direct involvement of some of these figures in deliberations on the economic aspects of peace.

    b. The traumatic impact of the assassination of Rabin, which has remained a significant and formative topic in Israel's ongoing public debate (Peri 1997).

    c. The changed orientation of Netanyahu government's toward the peace process and the subsequent crisis in relations with the United States; the stalemated peace process was frequently identified as the central factor halting the growth of the Israeli economy.[16]

All three phenomena, but especially the first two, gave legitimacy to the increasing political involvement of Israel's elite groups. The changing character of Israeli politics expanded the need and opportunities for such involvement. Successful businesspeople were even repeatedly mentioned as legitimate candidates for senior government positions. This phenomenon can be seen as an expansion and legitimization of the tradition of close and useful connections established during the Mapai era between members of the economic elite and party leaders.

The organizational weakness of Israeli political parties, prominently manifested in their financial distress despite a generous state subsidy, increased the need for campaign fund-raising among members of the economic elite. The system of nominating primaries created an even greater need for the personal funding of candidates. Moreover, the availability of campaign funding from sources outside the political parties made it possible to enter a political race without a party's organizational support (a notable case being Haim Ramon's successful campaign in the election to the Histadrut convention in 1994). In the absence of any appreciable membership base, the formation of the Center Party was entirely dependent on the financial support of a select group of donors.

The decline of the Center Party in the public opinion surveys limited its financial sources, and the party ended the campaign with a large deficit. The shared responsibility for covering this deficit became an important, although insufficient, reason for maintaining the Center Party's faction in the Knesset.

5. Changes in the Political Agenda and the Personalization of Politics

The political agenda of the democratic world has changed as a result of the end of the cold war and the dissolution of the Soviet Union, as well as owing to economic, social, and cultural changes in modern democratic society. Issues relating to citizens' rights, cultural identity, lifestyle, and the environment have become more prominent in the public debate at the expense of past issues, some of which had been anchored in traditional social ideologies. This saliency, which has been apparent in Israeli society despite the incomplete resolution of its external conflict with the Arab world, has placed controversial cultural issues at the center of public concern and political debate (Bennett 1998; Davison 1991; Gitlin 1995). The new agenda both reflected and fed cleavages between the secular and the religious and between Ashkenazim and Sephardim. Moreover, the historical ideological debate over Israel's borders, which was highlighted once again following the 1967 war, lost some of its relevance after the Oslo Accord with the Palestinians.

The process of detachment from the old political-ideological debate gave rise to the belief or illusion that it was possible to establish a political constituency through a new party, based on a changed agenda in Israeli politics. Milo, who was the first to initiate the establishment of the Center Party at the onset of the 1999 elections, wanted to base the party on assertive secularism in response to the perceived threat of religious coercion; he also expressed a readiness to search for a peace free of the ideological commitments of the past. Milo's partners in establishing the Center Party rejected this militantly secular message. Meridor emphasized the rule of law and the need to conclude the legislation of Israel's constitution in order to protect the integrity of public life. Shahak mainly emphasized the need for a leadership alternative. Mordechai, who had bolted the Likud, developed an entirely different political posture, one that was designed to win votes from traditional and religious Sephardic constituencies. In the end, the Center Party adopted a platform of reconciliation and rapprochement, not the radical, secular message of Milo.

Dash and the Center Party

The case of the Center Party in the 1999 elections calls for a comparison with the Dash Party (DMC) in the 1977 elections. Both parties appealed chiefly to the veteran Israeli society and positioned themselves in the middle of the party map. In both cases, the forming of the new party was based on an electoral rationale. With Dash, however, it is also possible to identify a certain partisan rationale in terms of the organizational processes that preceded the party's formation—the forming of the Democratic Movement Party and the institutionalization of the Shinui Party, the efforts to build a party based on a broad membership, the establishment of sovereign, active party institutions, and the adoption of a democratic nominating system of elections.[17] By comparison, the Center Party was actually founded by four candidates for prime minister; it was not fully institutionalized prior to the elections; and its list of candidates to the Knesset was formed by informal agreement among its principal founders.

In the case of Dash, a programmatic agreement was sought with groups that joined the party. The personal rivalries among the founders of the Center Party, as well as their joint sense of opportunity, repressed and delayed programmatic discussion beyond the initial subscription to the concept of a centrist party and the presentation of an alternative strategy to that of the Labor Party to defeat Netanyahu and the Likud Party. The primacy of the electoral rationale in the formation of the Center Party was manifested not only in the decision of the four candidates to join forces, but also in their agreement to appoint the party candidate for prime minister on the basis of public opinion surveys. Exhausted by their inability to accept each other's candidacy, the initiators of the Center Party finally recruited Mordechai for the task on the very day of his dismissal from the government and exit from the Likud. Up to that moment, Mordechai still insisted that he was "a Likudnik."[18] Settling on a candidate marked the beginning of the Center Party as a joint political venture of its four leaders. It was only later that these leaders articulated a common political program.

Despite their differences, Dash and the Center Party each adopted a similar political message, and their founders shared the same sense of urgency and opportunity. The latter derived from a crisis in government and a dissatisfaction with the available alternatives. In the case of Dash (in 1977)—the rifts and corruption in Rabin's Labor government, set against the background of the damaging memory of the failures of Meir's government at the outset of the Yom Kippur War (1973), and the apprehension among members of the veteran social elites at the alternative offered by the main opposition party, the Likud. In the case of the Center Party (1999)—the expanding opposition to Netanyahu, both within his own political party and outside it and the doubts concerning the ability of Labor's candidate, Barak, to defeat him. Both parties articulated a general promise to overcome the political crises by offering new leadership, reforming the process and rules of governing, and recovering integrity in public life. In the case of Dash, the message of reform overshadowed the subscription to a centrist ideology. In contrast, the founders of the Center Party claimed such an ideology even before the formation of their party. Like all centrist parties, these two parties found it difficult to define a clear interparty orientation. They did not answer the questions of which new structure they proposed for the future Israeli party system and which of the two principal parties, if at all, they wanted to replace. These questions arose from the assumption, shared by the leaders of all parties, that Israel would continue to maintain a competitive multiparty system despite the philosophy of unity and reconciliation presented by a center party. Keeping the answers to these questions vague or ambiguous might have helped to broaden a center party's electoral potential, but it also undermined its capacity to establish a clear, enduring partisan identity.

Neither party achieved its electoral objective. Both failed to generate partisan solidarity and, therefore, could not ensure their continuity. Of the two, Dash gained a significant number of seats in the Knesset (15). It did not succeed, however, in replacing the Labor Alignment as the principal party in government or in assuming a corrective role in Labor's government. Labor was crushed in the 1977 Knesset election (dropping from 51 to 32 seats) and replaced in power by the Likud, and Dash became an unessential partner in a government it did not favor.[19] After the elections, Dash played only a marginal role, one that differed significantly from the role it had originally set for itself.

The Center Party gained only a meager number of Knesset seats in 1999, especially when one considers the promise that had preceded its formation and the similar representation (6 Knesset seats) gained by a much less pretentious party (Shinui, under the leadership of Lapid), which had been put together hurriedly prior to the closing of party registration for the 1999

Knesset elections. Nonetheless, the leaders of the Center Party found some comfort in Netanyahu's defeat and indeed claimed significant credit for this outcome. Until the very last moment, however, the independent run of the Center Party had been directed not only against Netanyahu but also against Barak in an effort to gain entry into a second-round, two-man race with Netanyahu.

Both Dash and the Center Party failed to create leadership solidarity and the capacity for enduring collective action. The difficulty in creating such a leadership is common to all new parties in an open, competitive society. It is more difficult, however, in a party that lacks a unique, compelling programmatic message and a well-defined constituency; either element is likely to increase the demand for stronger personal identification with the collective body and to limit independent personal assertion. Other factors that made it difficult to establish leadership solidarity and efficiency were the divided origin of the new party, the penetration of a personal-leadership competition into it, and the lack of an institutionalized decision-making process. Dash was created by the merger of two major groups (Shinui and the Democratic Movement Party); however, it opened its gates to groups and personalities from diverse parties (Labor and the Likud) and from other civic organizations. With the agreement of its founders, Dash succeeded in forming party institutions before the elections. It also adopted the system of nominating primaries, which actually turned this new party into an opportune, competitive springboard for political leadership for those who sought such an opportunity and were ready to identify with the general principles of the new party. The outcome of the primaries validated the existence of a principal group of leaders and established the order of their appearance in the party's list of candidates without the need for either their approval or a decision by the party's central bodies. This democratic system contributed to the legitimacy of the new party and shaped its identity as a reform party. The primaries, however, also heightened personal competition during the party's formative period. Dash managed to cope with the divisive crisis of the primaries, and it effectively operated party institutions through a majority decision-making process during the election campaign. After the elections, a prolonged debate developed within the party about its entry into Begin's government. Over time, this disagreement created an unwillingness to accept the majority's decision on this issue.

The weakness of the principal leader (Yadin) among the founders of Dash, as well as the persistence of leadership rivalry, exposed this new party to the splinter syndrome of a center party: openness to the Likud government (on the right) versus openness to the Labor opposition (on the left), pressures that led eventually to its dissolution. During its single term in the Knesset—in the absence of a loyal party constituency before the 1981 elections—Dash broke into a large number of elements; several leaders dropped out of politics (Yadin and Meir Zorea), and some joined other parties. Only the Shinui Party, which had preceded Dash, remained, and it returned to what it had been, a small party with a cohesive group of leaders positioned at the center of the political map.

The Center Party, for its part, did not complete its institutionalization before the elections. The management of the party thus turned into a series of negotiations in search of agreement among its founder-leaders. During the campaign, for example, they had difficulty taking a uniform position on the issue of Shas and the sentencing of Aryeh Deri. This inability was sharply expressed in relation to the question of whether the party candidate, Mordechai, should remain in the race after it had become clear that he had no chance of winning even a second round, which he previously had been predicted to win. Mordechai was determined to continue the race despite his partners' increasing pressure on him to step down. He finally gave in two days before the elections, after being notified that two of the party's leaders (Milo and Meridor) were planning to announce their support for Barak.[20] Following the elections, the leadership rift resumed, primarily within its Knesset faction.

The respective experiences of Dash and the Center Party corroborate two general observations. First, forming a party list of candidates in a proportional system of elections—which permits an appeal to a small group of voters within a single, unified constituency requires only an electoral-based rationale to appeal to the public through the use of a marketing strategy. In order to survive, however, the new party must (a) develop a unique programmatic, cultural, and/or communal message that meets the important needs of a large group of voters and is perceived to be legitimate over time; (b) institutionalize the party organization; and (c) achieve leadership cooperation and solidarity. Second, both Dash and the Center Party can be seen as attempts to change the existing party system and as an instrument for unconventional political recruitment. Both parties' success in this endeavor was minor and only temporary. Defining a centrist position held greater advantage than being a center party. The sustained power of traditional politics (political institutions and culture) manifested itself in the fact that veteran politicians effectively took control of the attempts to establish the new centrist parties.

Notes

1. For example, the Third Way Party in the 1996 elections. Its election slogan was Let's Meet in the Center, but its central political message opposed a withdrawal from the Golan Heights.

2. Moshe Kleinman, the editor of *Ha'olam* (the journal of the World Organization of the General Zionists), writes, "General Zionism cannot be a party, because it is the essence of Zionism and its primary backbone is the Zionist Federation, first and foremost." See Kleinman (1945, 63). Yigal Drori notes that "the General Zionists became organized despite themselves. Their organization stemmed in the main from the fact that the other branches of the Zionist movement, from the left and the right, had reached a high level of organization, which strengthened their power and influence in the Zionist movement above and beyond their relative size" (1985, 129). See also, Sheari (1994).

3. See also De Tarr (1961, 233–245).

4. Source (up to the 1999 elections): Neuberger (1977, 239).

5. According to surveys by the Jerusalem Institute for Applied Social Research, 50% of Dash voters had 13 or more years of education (compared to 33.3% of Alignment voters and 26% of Likud voters); 46% of them earned more than NIS 5,000 per month or $1250 (compared to 33.4% of Alignment voters and 29.8% of Likud voters); and 68% of Dash voters were of a European/American origin. These data appear in Torgornik (1980, 83–84).

6. On the nature of the Democratic Christian Party in Italy and the factors leading to its decline, see Allen (1997).

7. On May 4, 1998, Ronnie Milo announced his departure from the Likud and presented his candidacy for prime minister on behalf of a new center party he intended to establish (*Ha'aretz,* May 5 1998). On December 22 1998 Dan Meridor announced his decision to leave the Likud and run for prime minister (*Ha'aretz,* December 23 1998). On January 6, 1999, Amnon Lipkin-Shahak announced his candidacy for prime minister and his intention to cooperate with Meridor and Milo in establishing a new center party.

8. Prime Minister Binyamin Netanyahu announced the dismissal of Yitzhak Mordechai from the government on January 23, 1999. Later that day, Mordechai announced he would head the Center Party and be its candidate for prime minister (*Ha'aretz,* January 24 1999). This event was preceded by a month-long series of negotiations to ensure Mordechai's position in the next Likud government as well as contacts between Mordechai and the founders of the Center Party, who wanted him to join them.

9. MK Avraham Poraz quit Meretz and announced the renewal of the Shinui Party for the 1999s election. He was involved in the initiative to form the Center Party but was deterred from joining it once Mordechai was named the leader and there was no chance that the party would adopt Milo's radical approach toward religion (*Ha'aretz,* March 1 1999). Later, Yosef Lapid was named leader of the Shinui Knesset list (*Ha'aretz,* March 21 1999).

10. In announcing his candidacy for prime minister, Meridor issued a call to "save the country from Netanyahu's false and dangerous charms." He added, "Someone who came to Israel from abroad only ten years ago has taken control of the [Likud], although through democratic means, and now is preventing his replacement. . . . We must consider what is more important, the form or the substance. There is no chance that the Likud will replace Netanyahu, but the State of Israeli must replace

him." Meridor said he would wait to announce his resignation until he had lost any hope that someone would come forward to compete against Netanyahu (*Ha'aretz,* December 23, 1998).

In announcing his candidacy for prime minister, Lipkin-Shahak was no less forthright than Meridor: "Netanyahu is dangerous to Israel, he must go. In his methods and under his leadership, he is leading Israel toward internal and external dangers. The responsibility for what has happened in Israel over the past two and a half years rests on his shoulders. He sees the schism, but uses it to his own ends" (*Ha'aretz,* January 7, 1999).

Following Mordechai's dismissal from the government, Milo attacked Netanyahu even more strongly: "Menahem Begin is turning over in his grave when he sees you [Netanyahu]. You, who profess to be his successor, bring shame to his path, the path of the Herut Movement and the Likud, the path of the students of Jabotinsky" (*Ha'aretz,* January 26, 1999).

11. Mina Zemach's survey, published in *Yediot Aharonot* (January 15, 1999), indicated that Netanyahu and Barak would tie for first place in the first round (Netanyahu—33%; Barak—32%; Shahak—15%) and the second round (Netanyahu—43%; Barak—43%), but Shahak was predicted to beat Netanyahu in the second round (45% vs. 40%).

12. On November 12, 1998, Barak announced his intention to establish a new movement, "One Israel"; on February 25, 1999, he reached an agreement with Meimad and Gesher on joining this movement; on March 4, 1999 the Labor Party's Central Committee authorized, with a 90% majority, the establishment of One Israel.

13. The number of Likud members during its primaries amounted to 160,000 (*Ha'aretz,* January 26, 1999); the number of Labor members during its primaries came to 163,000 (*Ha'aretz,* February 15, 1999).

14. See articles by Nahum Barnea and Carmit Guy, *Eye on the Week,* July 1999.

15. See *Ha'aretz,* May 3, 7, 9, 1999.

16. Announcing his candidacy for prime minister, Lipkin-Shahak exclaimed, "Economics is related to peace and *aliyah*" (*Ha'aretz,* January 7, 1999).

17. Before it decided upon the primaries method, Dash had only about 6,000 members; the number eligible to vote in its primary elections eventually totaled 33,176. More than 10,000 requests for membership were authorized in the days before the deadline. See Urieli and Barzilai (1982).

18. See *Ha'aretz,* December 30, 1998.

19. A survey that Dash commissioned in April, before the elections, revealed that 58% of Dash supported wanted the Alignment to remain in power and 55% believed Dash would form a coalition with the Alignment; only 3% wanted the Likud to win, and only 12% believed Dash would form the next coalition with the Likud. See Rubinstein (1982).

20. In an interview published in *Yediot Aharonot*'s weekend supplement, Milo said that the decision for Mordechai to drop out of the race for prime minister was based on the knowledge that the three other party leaders intended to announce their support of Barak (November 12, 1999).

References

Allen, Percy. 1997. "From Two Into One: The Faces of the Italian Christian Democratic Party." *Party Politics* 3, no. 1: 23–52.

Arian, Asher (ed.). (1980). *The Elections in Israel 1977.* Jerusalem: Jerusalem Academic Press.

———. 1997. *The Second Israeli Republic.* Haifa: University of Haifa and Zemora-Beitan.

Bennett, W. Lance. 1998. "The Uncivic Culture: Communication, Identity and the Rise of Lifestyle Politics." *P.S. Political Science and Politics* 4 (December). 741–761.

Cook, C. 1986. *A Short History of the Liberal Party 1900–1988.* Oxford: Macmillan.

Cook, Timothy. 1998. *Governing with the News: The News Media as a Political Institution.* Chicago: University of Chicago Press.

Daalder, Hans. 1984. "In Search of the Center of European Party Systems." *American Political Science Review* 78: 92–109.

De Tarr, Francis. 1961. *The French Radical Party—From Herriot to Mendes-France.* London: Oxford University Press.

Davison, James. 1991. *Culture Wars: The Struggle to Define America.* New York: Basic Books.

Downs, Anthony. 1957. *An Economic Theory of Democracy.* New York: Harper & Row.

Drori, Yigal. 1985. "The General Zionists in the Land of Israel in the Twenties." *Zionism,* Collection 10. Tel Aviv: Tel Aviv University and United Kibbutz Publications, 129 (Hebrew).

Duverger, Maurice. 1959. *Political Parties: Their Organization and Activity in the Modern State.* New York: Wiley.

Gitlin, Todd. 1995. *The Twilight of Common Dreams: Why America Is Wracked by Culture Wars.* New York: Henry Holt.

Hazan, Reuven, Y. 1995. "Center Parties and Systemic Polarization: An Exploration of Recent Trends in Western Europe." *Journal of Theoretical Politics* 7: 421–445.

———. 1996. "Does Center Equal Middle? Towards a Conceptual Delineation with Application to West European Party Systems." *Party Politics* 2, no. 2: 209–228.

———. 1997. *Center Parties: Polarization and Competition in European Parliamentary Democracies.* London: Pinter.

Hunter, James Davison. 1991. *Culture Wars: The Struggle to Define America.* New York: Basic Books.

Ieraci, Giuseppe. 1992. "Center Parties and Anti-System Oppositions in Polarized Systems." *West European Politics,* no. 15: 17–34.

Kernan, Hans. 1994. "The Search for the Center: Pivot Parties in West European Party Systems." *West European Politics,* no. 17: 124–148.

Kleinman, Moshe. 1945. *The General Zionists.* Jerusalem: Little Zionist Library, 63.

Kunsten, Oddbjor. 1998. "Expert Judgment of the Left-Right Location of Political Parties: A Comparative Longitudinal Study." *West European Politics* 21, no. 2: 63–94.

Larmour, Peter, J. 1964. *The French Radical Party in the 1930s.* Stanford: Stanford University Press.

Lynn, G., Benmnie, John Curtice, and Wolfgang Rudig. 1994. "Liberal, Social Democrat or Liberal Democrat? Political Identity and British Centre Party Politics." *British Elections and Parties Yearbook.*

Neuberger, Benyamin. 1977. *The Parties in Israel.* Tel Aviv: Open University, 239 (Hebrew).

Peri, Yoram. 1997. "The Rabin Myth and the Press." *European Journal of Communication* 12: 435–458.

Rubinstein, Amnon. 1982. *A Certain Political Attempt,* Jerusalem: Idanim, 175 (Hebrew).

Satori, Giovanni. 1976. *Parties and Party Systems: A Framework for Analysis.* Cambridge: Cambridge University Press.

Scully, Timothy, R. 1992. *Rethinking the Center: Party Politics in Nineteenth and Twentieth Century Chile.* Stanford: Stanford University Press.

Sheari, David. 1994. *From Just Zionists to General Zionists.* Jerusalem: Reuven Mass, 94–132.

Stevenson, John. 1993. *Third Party Politics Since 1945.* Oxford: Blackwell.

Swanson, David, L. 1991. "The Political Media Complex." *Communication Monographs.* 59, no. 4.

Torgornik, Ephraim. 1980. "A Movement for Change in a Stable System." In Asher Arian (ed.). *The Elections in Israel 1977.* Jerusalem: Jerusalem Academic Press.

Urieli, Nachman, and Amnon Barzilai. 1982. *The Rise and Fall of Dash,* Tel Aviv: Reshafim, 148–167 (Hebrew).

Yanai, Nathan. 1999. "Why Do Political Parties Survive?" *Party Politics.* 5–17.

———. 1969. *Division at the Top.* Tel Aviv: Lewin Epstein, 307–311.

Yanai, Nathan, and Shlomo Aharonson. 1986. "Elections 1984: A Test of the Political System in Israel." *State, Government and International Relations* 25: 47–90.

12

Candidate Selection in a Sea of Changes
Unsuccesfully Trying to Adapt?

GIDEON RAHAT

The methods political parties use to select their candidates may be analyzed from two perspectives. The first considers these methods as a dependent variable that reflects a party's response to changes in the political environment within which it operates. Manifested in changes to their candidate selection methods, this response implies an attempt to adapt to a changing political, social, and institutional environment. The political parties' adoption of primary systems in Israel to select candidates in the 1990s may be explained, for example, as an attempt to overcome the citizenry's increasing alienation from the parties. The second perspective analyzes the candidate selection method as an independent variable that influences the political environment. In the context of general elections, for example, a selection method may be presented as one that assisted in securing electoral success, or contributed to failure. This chapter will examine from both perspectives the changes that occurred in the Israeli parties' candidate selection methods in the run-up to the 1999 elections.

Methods for Selecting Party Candidates for the Knesset: A Comparative Framework

In order to analyze developments in candidate selection methods in Israel, we shall examine three principal dimensions for distinguishing between the different methods.[1] These relate to the level of inclusiveness of the selectorate; the level of decentralization in candidate selection; and the method of nomination, by appointment or a voting system.

245

The first dimension relates to the level of inclusiveness and deals with the composition of the selectorate: Who takes part in selecting the candidates? The body responsible for selecting Knesset candidates may include all citizens who are eligible to vote, which means a high level of inclusiveness; the members of a selected party institution—an intermediate level of inclusiveness, or a single party leader—a low level of inclusiveness. In the Israeli case, the party primaries method, in which the selectorate includes all members of the party, is the most inclusive method used. Candidate selection by party institutions (central committees, councils, conventions, etc.) is a less inclusive method, although it is more inclusive than the selection pattern current in mainly the ultra-Orthodox religious parties—appointment by nonselected committees of spiritual leaders.

The second dimension is the level of centralization in candidate selection. A high level of centralization is found when all candidates are selected by a single, central electorate, whether this be an individual leader or the entire electorate. A low level of centralization, or decentralization, in candidate selection is when candidates are selected separately for each distinct territorial or sectoral district. In territorial districts, candidates who live in a particular region are selected by the residents of that region; in sectoral districts, candidates are defined as members of a particular sector (e.g., Kibbutzim and Moshavim) or as members of a defined social group (e.g., ethnic minorities), and are selected by the members of that sector or social group. Since Israel employs an electoral system with a single nation-wide constituency, the decision to provide some territorial representation depends on the desire and capacity of each political party, as distinct from the majority of countries where the electoral system contains territorial districts that bind the parties to take this parameter into account.

In Israel, only the Labor Party primaries (in 1992, 1996, and 1999) and the Likud primaries (1996) have adopted systems that include guaranteed places on the candidate list representing territorial districts. In addition to districts, many Israeli political parties use the "reserved place" mechanism to ensure territorial, sectoral, and social representation. Under this system, candidates from groups with reserved slots on the electoral list compete alongside the other candidates for the votes of all members of the selectorate; if no such candidate secures the place reserved (or a higher place) in the vote count, the candidate from the same group who received the highest number of votes advances to the reserved slot. This mechanism embodies an intermediate level of centralization that may be more appropriate given Israel's single nationwide constituency electoral system. While selection by the entire electorate reflects centralization, candidacy itself is decentralized, in that places within the list are designated for candidates identified as representatives of a particular geographical region, sector, or social group.

The third dimension relates to the nomination system: Appointment or voting system. Under the appointment procedure, a small body or bodies determines the candidates' list without any formal voting procedure. Subsequent approval of the list by a party institution may or may not be required. The voting procedure, by contrast, determines the composition and ranking of the list according to the aggregation of votes cast by the members of the selectorate. For logistic reasons, in most cases the appointment method is implemented by an individual leader or small group, while voting takes place in larger selectorates. The distinction between the two methods is important to the level of control of the party leadership over the composition of the list: appointment allows a higher level of control than a voting procedure. A further distinction can be drawn between the different voting systems. In the candidate selection methods used in the 1999 elections, the main distinction was between majoritarian methods—which allow an organized majority within the selectorate to gain full control of the composition and rank of the candidates in the safe positions on the list—and semiproportional methods, which allow minority representation. The most widespread type of semiproportional voting method is the limited vote method, in which the number of candidates for whom each member of the selectorate may vote is smaller than the number of safe places on the list.[2]

In discussing the development of candidate selection methods, the emphasis is generally on changes in the level of inclusiveness of the selectorate. A transition from appointment of the list by a small "nominating committee" to selection by a selected party institution, or from the use of a selected party institution to a primary method involving all party members, is perceived as a substantive change reflecting democratization of the candidate selection method. A transition from selection by a smaller body to selection by a larger body also inevitably entails changes in the dimension of the nomination procedure, namely, determination of the list by voting rather by than by appointment. In most cases, candidate selection in Israel is a centralized process, reflecting the general electoral system in which the entire country functions as a single constituency. Despite this, in the 1990s there was a clear trend toward decentralization. This was seen in the decentralization of the selection process for part of the list—through adopting candidate selection through districts in the Labor Party (1992, 1996, and 1999) and in the Likud (1996)—as well as partial decentralization through adoption of the reserve place mechanism. Decentralization seems to be perceived as a means of democratizing candidate selection, particularly in regard to the representativeness of the candidate list.

Changes in Candidate Selection Methods
in the 1999 Elections

The Likud was the first party to introduce significant changes in its candidate selection method for the Knesset list. Before the party convention in November 1997, associates of the prime minister launched an initiative to amend the party's constitution, so that candidates on the Knesset list would be selected by the party's central committee rather than by all party members, as was the case in 1996. A fierce struggle erupted between the Likud government ministers and members of Knesset—who in 1996 had been selected to the list by the entire party membership and who wanted to preserve this selection method—and the majority of the members of the party's central committee, who tended to favor reinstituting committee selection of the candidates list (which the committee had relinquished in 1993), in order to regain the power they had lost. The prime minister took pains to distance himself from this struggle, but the fact that those initiating the change were his associates, and that the proposed change would give him more power in controlling the behavior of Likud Party ministers and MKs, meant that he was, nevertheless, identified with the change. Various attempts were made to prevent the proposed amendment being tabled before the party conference, or at least to postpone the decision. These efforts were in vain, however, and majority decision determined that the party's candidates for the Knesset list would in the future be selected by the members of the central committee.

These developments had a dramatic effect on the Likud. Once tempers had settled, a clear change could be discerned in most of the party's MKs and ministers, whose behavior became more disciplined and less independent; in particular, their comments in the media were much more restrained. The change also appeared to influence the decision of various key figures—such as Dan Meridor, Roni Milo, Benny Begin, and Yitzhak Mordechai—to leave the Likud, because of the fear they would be unsuccessful in the central committee, which was dominated by the prime minister and his associates, and the likelihood that it would prove difficult to maintain any internal opposition within the party.

The remaining components of the method for selecting Likud candidates were finalized after early general elections were called. These components concentrated all aspects of the selection process in the hands of the central committee. It was determined that the reserve slot method would be used to ensure representation not only of social groups (women, immigrants, youth, and non-Jews) as had been the case in the 1996 primaries, but also for representatives of the various territorial districts whose presence on the list was protected in the Likud constitution. It was determined that district representatives who, under the primary system, were selected solely by the party members in the relevant district, would now be selected by all of the central committee members (not just those members from their particular district). Moreover, the definition of "district representative" was broadened to include any candidate who was a resident of the district, other than those serving as ministers at the time of candidate selection.

Another significant change in the method for selecting candidates, one that passed almost unnoticed, related to the voting system. The Likud abandoned a majoritarian system in favor of a semiproportional one: A limited vote method in which the number of votes cast by each member of the selectorate was smaller than the number of safe positions on the party list. In Herut (the dominant faction within the Likud) since 1977, and in the Likud itself since 1992, majoritarian methods had been used, with each voter casting the same number of votes as the number of safe positions on the list. This method enabled "majoritization"—that is, an organized majority was able to control the composition of the Knesset list.[3] In 1999, a limited vote method was introduced whereby each member of the central committee was allocated just thirteen votes. Likud leader Benjamin Netanyahu was displeased with this change, preferring a majority system that would allow him to control the composition of the list. Under pressure from ministers and MKs, however, he refrained from attempting to alter the voting method (*Ha'aretz,* January 20, 1999). It seems the degree of his motivation in favor of changing the system was lessened because the vast majority of party figures who might have challenged him had already left the Likud.

An initiative was also launched in the Labor Party to abolish the primaries system and to transfer candidates selection to a selected party institution. This initiative was raised by associates of the party's candidate for prime minister, Ehud Barak, together with some heads of the party's district branches, who argued that the change would ensure internal harmony in the party. Senior Labor MKs were successful in blocking the initiative, when they threatened to quit the party if the primaries method was abolished. Still, various changes were made to other elements of the selection method that reflected the preferences of the party chairperson. These included granting to the party chairperson the authority to reserve places on the candidate list for candidates outside the party, with the approval of the central committee. Reserve slots that the central committee approved included one for the outgoing party chairperson and former prime minister Shimon Peres (1984–1986, 1995–1996), and for representatives of the Gesher and Meimad political parties—"virtual" parties that had never proven they enjoyed significant electoral support (Doron 1998). Meimad had participated in Knesset elections once, in 1988, and failed to exceed the minimum vote threshold, which at that time was 1 percent of the total votes cast. Gesher had never stood as an independent list, and opinion polls suggested it would fail to pass the minimum threshold. Although the reservation of places for the Gesher and Meimad representatives as part of the joint "One Israel" list was reminiscent of the Likud's reservation of places for Gesher and Tzomet representatives in 1996, the motives for these decisions differed. In 1996, the reservation of Likud slots for Gesher and Tzomet was intended primarily to prevent a situation in which the right wing would present more than one candidate for prime minister. The reservations on the One Israel list, by contrast, was intended to improve the image of Barak and the Labor Party among sections of the electorate who were problematic from the standpoint of the party—the Sepharadim (for whose sake Gesher was given reserved slots), and traditional and religious Jews (explaining the reserved places for Meimad).

As in 1992, the Labor Party continued to select some of its candidates in a central list, and others on territorial and sectoral districts. While the modifications to this method in 1996 were minor, before the 1999 elections significant changes were introduced in how district representatives were ranked within the overall list, as well as how districts were defined. In 1992 and 1996, district ranking was based on a weighted scale reflecting the number of party voters and members in the district. In 1999, the different districts were ranked arbitrarily, suggesting that some slots were tailor-made to suit the party chair's desire to ensure safe places for his associates and, in some cases, to respond to demands from groups that lacked representation. The voting system was also changed, although not at the behest of the party chairperson. The limited-vote principle—introduced by the Labor Party in 1988 for the central committee members, and in 1992 and 1996 for all party members—was maintained, but with an added preferential element. It was decided that in addition to marking nine to eleven candidates for the national list, party members could also mark their five preferred candidates. These five, it was determined, would enjoy special credits when the votes were counted. This change was introduced at the insistence of Haim Ramon, who saw it as a mechanism for protecting controversial candidates (e.g., himself) who enjoyed strong popularity among a relatively small group of party members but provoked strong opposition in other circles. The strength of this support was supposed to be reflected in the special markings, which would balance the opposition to such candidates as reflected in their not being included on the lists of other party members.

Thus, the underlying motivation of these changes in the Labor Party candidate selection method can be seen as increasing the representative character of the list. This was reflected both through coopting new forces (Gesher and

Meimad) and through the party's willingness to accommodate prominent members such as Shimon Peres (who received a reserved place) and Haim Ramon (whose proposed amendment was adopted) in order to ensure that these leaders would be ranked high on the party list. In the Likud, the party leader cooperated with the central committee, out-maneuvering the MKs and ministers in order to secure control; in the Labor Party, the leader reached a compromise with the leading figures in the party in order to ensure they would remain within the party, and to secure a majority in the central committee for his proposed changes to the selection method. Opposition to these changes was confined to backbenchers whose position was weakened by the reservation of slots for Gesher and Meimad, which relegated their districts position on the candidate list.

During this same period leading up to the 1999 elections, the Meretz political alliance included the Ratz and Mapam parties and part of Shinui with its former leader, MK Amnon Rubinstein. Another Shinui faction remained independent; the method it used to select its candidates is discussed separately at a later point in this chapter. In comparison with 1996, Meretz introduced numerous changes in its candidate selection method. First, the selectorates were replaced. In 1996, the first stage included a screening process in which the institutions of each party in the alliance selected a short list of candidates, and at the second stage all members of the Meretz alliance determined the ranking of these candidates in the Knesset list. Before the 1999 elections, the screening stage was transferred to the Meretz Council, a joint interparty institution with some 900 members. This process also included a separate screening of the seven serving Knesset members, who were required to secure the support of a special majority (60 percent) of the council in order to be eligible for candidacy for the next Knesset list.[4] The final decision on the list's composition and ranking was transferred from all the members of the alliance of parties to the alliance convention, with over 2,000 members. Second, changes were introduced in the mechanisms used to ensure representation. The position of women was improved, and the dimension of party affiliation (which in 1996 had determined in advance the position of the candidates from each constituent party within the list) was reduced to a provision that each party would have a representative among the top five places. Third, the ranking system used in the decisive second round, which in 1996 had used a semimajoritarian system, was replaced in 1999 with a new and more proportional system. Under this system the ranking of any candidate who did not receive enough support to ensure a given place, was determined according to a points system combining the fact of their selection with their ranking.[5] In 1999 the limited vote principle was adopted when each voter was allocated four votes in selecting each of the three groups of five candidates

(*Meretz*, February 11, 1999). Above all, these changes reflected the process of consolidating Meretz's joint framework.[6] The reduction in the size of the se-lectorate and the other new rules allowed the joint leadership to exert greater control over the list of candidates. An inclination to introduce new faces onto the list and to ensure their representation was combined with protection of the power already enjoyed by the alliance's senior leaders.

Shinui, which had participated in the 1996 elections as part of Meretz, stood independently in 1999. Advocates of right-wing economic policies in Shinui, led by MK Avraham Poraz, were unhappy about the affiliation with Meretz, which included social democratic and radical elements (Mapam and Ratz, respectively). In 1999, Shinui's list was determined in two ways. The first was selection by the party's central committee, which selected candidates for the second, third, and seventh places. Shinui once again opted for exhaus-tive ballot, whereby the candidate for each place on the list was elected sepa-rately and by an absolute majority.[7] Shinui also decided to reserve places for various individuals: The first place was reserved for the journalist Yosef Lapid; the fourth for Yosef Paritzky, the chairperson of the anticlerical associ-ation Am Hofshi; the fifth for MK Mudi Zandberg, who had quit Tzomet; and the sixth for a new immigrant. This was presented as an electoral move intended to strengthen Shinui's position as leading the struggle against reli-gious coercion—a struggle that was identified in particular with Lapid and with Paritzky (Shinui, March 25, 1999).

In the National Religious Party (NRP), the central committee continued to function as the selectorate. The method for ranking candidates was also maintained—a moderate points system, weighted for position and rank.[8] This method, which provides incentives for individuals and groups to cooper-ate, had in the past enabled the party to overcome factionalism (Rahat and Sher-Hadar 1999b). In 1999, however, a problem arose regarding representa-tion. Hanan Porat—who, along with his supporters, viewed himself as repre-senting the Jewish settlements in Judea, Samaria, and the Gaza Strip—was relegated to an unsafe position on the candidate list. The party leadership was highly alarmed by the protests from the national-religious public, which viewed the list as excessively moderate on political and security matters— a charge reinforced by the success of relatively moderate candidates to secure higher spots. The leadership feared its "moderate" image would cause votes to be lost to the new right-wing religious party, Tekuma. Accordingly, it was decided to include in the list a representative identified with the settle-ments and with right-wing elements in the party. Efforts to convince Porat to remain in the NRP in return for improving his position in the list proved unsuccessful. Porat quit the party and, together with another MK from the NRP, joined Tekuma. The second place in the NRP list was eventually reserved for Rabbi Druckman, who was perceived as one of the leaders of the Jewish settlements in Judea, Samaria, and the Gaza Strip.[9]

The immigrant's party Israel b'Aliya continued to use its central committee as the body responsible for selecting and ranking the party's list, but a significant change was introduced in its voting system. In 1996 the candidates for the leading positions (with the exception of Chairperson Natan Sharansky) were selected in several rounds. In each round, a group of three candidates was selected using the limited vote method (each voter having just two votes). The use of the limited vote method was a disincentive to "majoritization" and ensured minority representation. In 1999, by contrast, a majority method was introduced, with candidates selected separately to each position under a plurality vote. This enabled an organized majority bloc in the central committee to control all of the safe positions on the party's list. Before candidate selection took place, two MKs, who constituted an internal opposition to the party leaders, Sharansky and Yuli Edelstein, quit the party to join Israel Beiteinu, a new immigrant party established by Avigdor Lieberman, who was a veteran Russian immigrant and former executive director of the Likud.

When one compares the efforts of successful new parties in 1996 to adopt candidate selection methods with a democratic flavor, with the methods used to determine the lists of new parties in 1999, a tendency to restrict the selectorate can also be seen. In 1996, all three of the major new parties selected their candidates through a party institution: The central committee, in the case of Israel b'Aliya; a group including selected representatives and members of the founding council in the Third Way; and in Gesher, selection by the founding council.[10] In 1999, the most prominent new party, the Center Party, appointed its candidates through a restricted, nonselected body. As early as 1977, the Democratic Movement for Change—heretofore the principal example of a centrist party attempting to achieve a breakthrough in Israeli politics—had adopted the primaries method, which it championed as a model of democratic reform. Yet in 1999, after the selection of candidates by party institutions had become routine and the major parties, in 1996, had already introduced party primaries, the Center Party chose the well-worn path of an appointment committee. Another new party, Am Echad, led by the chairperson of the Histadrut (Labor Federation) Amir Peretz, also determined its list through appointment rather than selection by vote.

The use of the appointment method in the Center Party was justified on the grounds that the rapid establishment of this party made it impossible to establish a selectorate or to register members in a manner that would ensure balanced influence of the various forces that combined to form the party. The ranking of the top four candidates in the Center Party's list for the Knesset was determined according to an agreement among the leaders, which was influenced by opinion polls that tested the public support for their candidacy for prime minister. Accordingly, Roni Milo, who had founded the party, vacated the first place in favor of Dan Meridor, who had quit the Likud. Meridor in turn stepped down in favor of former chief of staff Amnon Lipkin-Shahak, after he had finished his period of service. Lastly, Shahak eventually stepped down in favor of Yitzhak Mordechai, the minister of defense in Netanyahu's government, who quit the Likud after he was dismissed by the prime minister.

Through a process of convoluted negotiations, this quartet also determined the ranking of the remaining candidates on the list. As a new party devoid of past accounts, the four politicians managed to put together a diverse list of candidates that was representative insofar as it addressed a broad range of political, social, and symbolic foci of identification that were relevant for a centrist party. The opening quartet in itself embodied an important blend in representative terms. Mordechai was a former defense minister and Likud member of Sepharadi origin; Lipkin-Shahak was a popular chief of staff who was identified as holding dovish positions; Meridor had served as a minister for the Likud and enjoyed a strong reputation for honesty and clean government; Milo, former Likud MK and minister, who also served as Tel Aviv mayor, was identified mainly with the struggle against religious coercion. This quarter concocted a list of candidates bringing together former members of the Likud, the Labor Party, Tzomet, and Meretz, or individuals who had identified with the political positions of these parties, in addition to representatives of diverse sectors such as women, immigrants, religious Jews, young people, and Sepharadim. This combination was considered significant at the time, since opinion polls predicted the new party would receive fifteen seats in the Knesset.

The ultra-Orthodox parties continued to employ their traditional method of selection, whereby lists of candidates were determined by councils of rabbis. As a subculture that may be typified as one that rests on traditional authority, it is hardly surprising that these parties were not affected by the general trend toward democratization of the candidate selection methods. Moreover, the maintenance of the party's electoral standing (in the case of United Torah Judaism) or the increase in it (in the case of Shas) provided no incentive for changing the candidate selection method. Despite this, there is some justification for claiming that the changes in the wider political, social, and media environment have also affected these parties, particularly given their attempts to appeal to a population that extends well beyond the ultra-Orthodox community itself. During the informal campaigns to influence the ranking of candidates in the parties' lists, the secular press provided a forum for illustrating the power and positions of the various candidates, and for demonstrating their capacity to break through to sections of the electorate outside the ultra-Orthodox community.[11]

In the Democratic Front for Peace and Equality (DFPE), as in 1996, the party's central committee served as the selectorate. Candidates were selected separately for each place on the list, using a two-round voting method. In the first round, a candidate receiving an absolute majority of votes was selected; if no such candidate emerged, a second round was held between the two candidates who had received the highest number of votes. Although the first two incumbents on the list were replaced, the DFPE maintained the traditional representative division among the different religions. This division, which is informal but strictly observed, dictates that the first three candidates will include a Muslim, a Christian, and a Jew. Unlike in previous elections, the Israel Communist Party (the dominant element within the DFPE) preferred to control the leading positions on the list, rather than allocate a secure place to a candidate who was not a member of the Communist Party.

The other Arab lists—the United Arab List and the Democratic National Alliance—were formed as aggregations of various parties and individuals. The leading places in these parties' lists were essentially determined by negotiations that continued until the last moment. Like the ultra-Orthodox subculture, the Israeli-Arabs also seem to be less influenced by, and interested in, developments in the candidate selection methods seen in the Zionist parties. As in the past, the Arab political scene continued to be dominated by personal rivalries and attempts to form and reform coalitions. Thus, for example, former DFPE MK Hashem Mahamid moved over to the United Arab List, while the leader of the Democratic National Alliance, Azmi Bishara, left the joint list with the DFPE. However, it seems some importance was attached to candidates being prominent and familiar in Israeli society as a whole, as reflected in the candidacy of two figures who had enjoyed considerable media abilities: Dr. Ahmad Tibi, who had served as consultant to the Palestinian Authority head Yasser Arafat, and Bishara.

The National Union was an alliance of three right-wing parties, including members of the "Land of Israel lobby" that had emerged in the Knesset. The alliance included Herut, the new party established by MK Benny Begin after he quit the Likud, along with MK Michael Kleiner, who quit Gesher; Tekuma, established by figures from the Jewish settlements and headed by the two MKs who had quit the NRP; and Moledet, an extreme right-wing party whose representatives in the joint list included its own two MKs as well as a third MK who had quit Tzomet. The allocation of places on this list was determined through protracted and tense negotiations between the three parties, with former prime minister Yitzhak Shamir acting as mediator.

The Dynamics of Change in
the Candidate Selection Methods

In considering the development of candidate selection methods from 1949 through the 1996 elections, two periods may be distinguished.[12] From the establishment of the state through the 1970s, the dominant pattern was maintenance of the status quo; in most cases, this meant the appointment of candidates by a nomination committee. A small group of party leaders, sometimes in cooperation with representatives of other elements (leading party bosses, representatives of social groups, and the heads of important party branches) determined the rank of the candidates on the party list (Brichta 1977). During the 1970s, the trend began toward expanding the selectorates. Candidate selection was transferred to selected party institutions, and appointment was replaced by voting system. By the end of the 1980s, most Israeli parties were already selecting their candidates through party institutions. Party primaries were introduced in 1992 by the Labor Party, and by 1996 were employed by the three largest parties in the Thirteenth Knesset: the Labor Party, the Likud, and Meretz.

The transition from appointment to voting systems during the 1970s and 1980s increased the need to ensure the representative character of the lists. In the 1992 and 1996 elections, the introduction of primaries was accompanied by a process of decentralization in the selection of candidates. This decentralization was reflected in two ways. The first method, confined to the major parties, was the creation of districts ensuring territorial and sectoral representation. The second method, the "reserve position," was used both by the major parties and by other political parties.

One of the main phenomena in the development of candidate selection methods in the 1990s, and particularly in 1996 and 1999, was the frequency of change. This frequency was in sharp contrast to the relative stability in the more distant past (until the 1970s), and the gradual evolution that had followed (during the 1970s and 1980s). Another prominent change related to the underlying trend in the development of candidate selection methods. The overall character of these changes will be discussed in the next section according to the three dimensions proposed for distinguishing candidate selection methods.

The most prominent development was the reduction in inclusiveness of the selectorates—a trend that was particularly evident in the abolition of the party primaries that had been adopted by the Likud and Meretz. The reservation of places for individuals and parties as implemented by both One Israel and the NRP may also be seen as part of the tendency for the leadership to usurp the role of the selection bodies. This tendency reverses the process of opening up the selection of candidates that had occurred from the 1970s through 1996, which had reached its peak in the adoption of party primaries.

In 1999, the trend to decentralize representation continued. In contrast to 1996, however, this process was characterized by the greater use of the reserve place mechanism rather than districts. This method constitutes decentralization in terms of representation, but not in terms of the identity of those selecting the representatives. The pattern of representation controlled by the central committee (as in the case of the Likud), and sometimes by the party leadership (as in the case of Labor/One Israel reservation of places), became a dominant feature.

Several changes also occurred in the methods of appointment and voting. As already noted, the number of personal appointments increased in 1999. This was particularly evident in the Center Party and in Shinui, but was also seen in those parties in which selection bodies continued to choose the majority of candidates. In terms of voting methods, however, no consistent trend can be identified. Developments in this dimension seem to have been influenced primarily by the situation within each of the parties, rather than by developments in other parties or in the political system as a whole.

The identified dynamic was toward restricting the selectorate, introducing the controlled decentralization of representation through the reserve position mechanism, and intervening in lists' composition through appointment. This trend reverses the trend observed from the establishment of the state through 1996 that included, first, the maintenance and, later, the expansion of the selectorates, as well as decentralization of the candidate selection process during the 1990s. This phenomenon may be understood in the context of two components: The dynamics of the process of change, and the motives underlying the changes.

The external pressure on the political parties to expand the selectorate (i.e., to introduce party primaries) was due mainly to the perception that this was "what the public wanted"—and that the public would reward parties that took this step. This perception was based on the juxtaposition of the Labor Party's introduction of primaries in 1992 with its victory in those elections. Toward the run-up to the 1996 elections, all parties—even the ultra-Orthodox—considered introducing primaries. Then the 1996 elections disproved the myth of a correlation between expanding the selectorate and electoral success. The three parties that employed primaries in 1996 saw their representation decline, while other parties in which the candidates were selected by a selected party institution or by appointment of nonselected committees managed to maintain or even increase their strength in the Knesset. The innovative character of the primaries faded, bringing growing awareness of the problems caused by this method. Free of pressure, the parties began to address the negative aspects of the primaries system: Temporary membership, vote trading, problems of representation, the advantage enjoyed by incumbent representatives and those with financial resources, and the tendency of MKs and ministers to ignore party discipline and policies (Begin 1996; Dror 1996; Hazan 1998; Peleg 1996; Rahat and Sar-Hadar 1999a). The various forces within the parties began to consider candidate selection methods in terms of their own interests, and no longer viewed primaries as an essential prerequisite.

Most of the changes that occurred in the candidate selection methods in the various parties may be explained by two principal motives: The desire to increase control over the behavior of the party MKs, and the desire to enhance the representative nature of the list. When lists of candidates are determined by a large selectorate and by voting, the leadership is less able to control the representative nature of the list, and selected MKs enjoy greater independence since their principal constituency is a broad body of voters. Once the myth that democratizing candidate selection method guaranteed electoral gains was destroyed, the parties were free to redress these two problems.

At the end of 1997, the Likud paved the way for the parties to abandon the primaries. The abolition of this method took place under conditions that differed from those that had obtained when the party adopted this method in 1993. In 1993, the Likud was under the influence of its electoral defeat; its adoption of primaries imitated the Labor Party, the victor in the 1992 elections. In 1997, by contrast, the Likud was in power. At this point, the elections seemed far off; the prime minister and the members of the party's central committee were interested in making the most of the advantages of power, and perceived the primaries as interfering with this goal. The Likud Central Committee, which Netanyahu had convinced to forego its role in selecting candidates in 1993, was now able, in coordination with elements close to Netanyahu, to reclaim this key function. As just noted, the pressure in the Labor Party to abolish the primaries proved unsuccessful, but the party chair was given leeway to introduce amendments and reserve places. In these conditions, Meretz also dared to abandon the use of primaries, while other parties adopted various procedures permitting greater control of the composition of their lists for the Knesset.

The reintroduction of candidates' selection by the central committee, as in the case of the Likud, was not the only development that enhanced the ability of party leaderships to control the behavior of ministers and MKs from their parties. On a more general level, the implementation of changes and introduction of new parameters in selecting candidates will always threaten MKs who were selected according to a given method. Other changes, such as voting systems that ensure majority control in candidate selection (as in the case of Israel b'Aliya) were also intended to secure this objective. The adoption of a screening process for Meretz candidates who were already serving in the Knesset, requiring them to secure the support of a special majority in the party's council, was another step to restore control over their behavior. The "tailor-made" method adopted by the Labor Party, including defined slots for candidates, also embodied a similar approach. In any case, and with the exception of the Likud and Israel b'Aliya, the principal motive for changing the system appears to have been an attempt to create more representative lists.

The districts and the reserve place mechanism were intended to ensure "representation as presence," that is, the perception that representation implies the presence in the party of persons with social characteristics similar to specific groups in the electorate (Philips 1995). In attempting to appeal to different segments of the electorate, places on the list were predetermined for competition among candidates sharing specific characteristics: Area of residence, sectoral affiliation, or social identification. By 1999 this mechanism seems to have been seen as inadequate, since presence in itself was not perceived as creating the desired image. This was due to the increasing importance attached to image which, it was felt, could be secured only through candidates and organizations perceived as labels that imply presence or represent a defined idea. Thus, in 1999 a tendency can be seen toward allocating places to individuals and parties with the objective of improving the public image of lists.

In the Labor Party, whose ranks include numerous individuals of Sepharadi origin and a senior figure from the religious Jewish population, places were reserved for parties symbolizing these foci of identification (Gesher and Meimad) in order to improve the party's image. Two of the candidates who secured safe positions in the NRP live in the settlements (Shaul Yahalom, in third place, and Yigal Bibi in fourth). However, the leaders of the NRP were so disturbed by Porat's failure to secure a safe position that they went so far as to redress the vote in the central committee, placing another "label" identified with the settlers, Rabbi Druckman, in second place on the list. In Shinui, which emphasized a strong position against religious coercion, the party chairperson relinquished first place on the list in favor of a journalist whom the public identified with this struggle on the basis of his media work, and who enjoyed much greater exposure and recognition than the chairperson himself. The reservation of places on the list for individuals and small parties also enabled parties to overcome the impossibility of reserving places for candidates through the definition of "presence." Thus, for example, within the context of Israeli political norms, the Labor Party could not have ensured representation of Sepharadi or religious candidates without actually reinforcing its image as an Ashkenazi, antireligious party. Reserving places for parties (such as Gesher and Meimad) which were defined as having such an identity was a way to overcome this problem. Similarly, the personal appointments in the Center Party enabled the new party to bring together a large pool of images within a relatively small number of candidates.

The tendency to adopt individual patterns of representation according to issues and identities should be appreciated in the broader context of the personification of Israeli politics. This framework creates a situation in which particular individuals are identified with groups and sectors; the mere fact of affiliation with a social group or sector according to set criteria is insufficient. In the past, senior figures in Israel politics symbolized ideological approaches and served as "flagships" for the entire party, as in the examples of David Ben-Gurion in Mapai, Menachem Begin in Herut and Likud, and Ya'akov Hazan and Meir Ya'ari in Mapam. In the 1990s, under the influence of telepolitics and growing sectorialism, personal identity has merged with representation as presence in the case of groups and social sectors.[13]

Changes in Candidate Selection Methods as Attempts to Adapt to a Changing Environment

One of the main characteristics of political parties is their ability to adapt to changes in their social environment. In most Western countries, current major political parties were established against the background of social cleavages that emerged in the 1920s (Lipset and Rokkan 1967; Mair 1991). Despite significant changes in the party political system in Israel, until the early 1990s it was possible to correlate the main political forces in Israel with their preindependence precursors. The parties proved able to adapt, and to recruit the support of the majority of immigrants who came to Israel after independence.

In the 1990s, this situation changed. Although the majority of votes are still given to parties that may be identified with their preindependence roots, parties based on ethnic grounds have enjoyed increasing success. Shas, which was established in 1984 and receives votes mainly from North African immigrants who came to Israel in the 1950s and 1960s, has achieved a dramatic increase in support; the number of seats it holds in the Knesset has increased from six in 1992 to ten in 1996 and seventeen in 1999. Contrary to past patterns, the parties representing immigrants who came to Israel at the end of the 1980s and at the beginning of the 1990s have managed to secure significant representation. Israel b'Aliya won seven seats in 1996—the first time it participated in the Knesset elections. Although the party's support fell to six seats in 1999, a new immigrant party, Israel Beiteinu, secured additional four seats.

Research on political parties includes two principal approaches to their development in democratic systems over recent decades. One approach argues that the role and functioning of parties has declined, while the other argues that parties have changed their form and function in a way that enables their adaptation to the changes that are taking place in their environment. In other words, the former approach emphasizes the increasing weakness of political parties relative to other political organizations, while the latter argues that, as in the past, parties have shown a considerable capacity to adapt to changes in their political environment.[14]

Against the backdrop of numerous developments in the 1990s, the electoral system for the Knesset constitutes a rock of stability in a stormy sea of change. In an era of personal politics fed by the increasing power of the electronic media, especially the visual media, and following the introduction of the system for direct election of the prime minister, the Knesset electoral system continues to be extremely impersonal. Not only are the lists of candidates completely closed, but election takes place in a single national constituency electing one hundred twenty representatives. This situation imposes on the political parties the main burden of adapting to personalized, image-based politics.

This is the context in which one should understand the changes, during the run-up to the 1999 elections, in the parties' candidate selection methods. The pace and direction of change in the patterns of selection methods in political parties in the 1990s reflect their attempts to adapt to the tremendous changes taking place around them. In preparing for the 1992 elections, and even more so in 1996 and 1999, the changes in selection methods were more numerous and profound than during the previous twelve election campaigns. The reversal of the trend in 1999, with a tendency to limit the selectorate and concentrate power in composing the lists, also reflects the tremendous pressure imposed by environmental changes.

The political parties are still searching for a formula that might enable them to adapt to the changes in their institutional, social, and media environment. In 1996, party members' involvement in candidate selection, through party primaries, was the main component in this attempt to adapt. The prevailing view was that expanding the body responsible for selection and increasing membership recruitment through offering an opportunity to participate and enjoy influence were the best ways for parties to cope with change. In 1999, the efforts to adapt centered on the field of representation. The 1996 emphasis on the elector as an active participant was replaced in 1999 by a perception of the elector as a consumer of individual labels reflecting identities and issues.

Did the methods for selecting candidates adopted in 1999 achieve the objective of enabling the political parties to adapt to their changing environment? We shall examine this question with regard to four parties: the Labor Party, the Likud, the Center Party, and Shinui.

The emphasis the Labor Party, within the One Israel framework, placed on the representative character of its list appears to have helped the party's candidate for prime minister, Ehud Barak, break free of the confines of the party's traditional electorate and increase his level of support among immigrants, Sepharadim, and traditional voters. The Knesset list declined in strength, however, receiving eight seats fewer than in 1996; the Labor Party itself lost eleven seats. In the Likud, emphasis on the party leader's ability to control the behavior of the Likud MKs encouraged senior figures who had lost any hope of achieving change from within to quit the party, contributing to Netanyahu's defeat in the elections. Neither did the Knesset list itself gain from this approach; it lost much of its appeal. The Center Party, which prepared a list that was consciously representative, eventually secured six seats in the Knesset. While this is a respectable performance for a new party, it is well below the results anticipated by opinion polls. Part of the reason for this was the emphasis on the contest for prime minister, which tended to eclipse the list itself. In the event, the party lost on both counts: Its candidate for prime minister, Yitzhak Mordechai, quit the race on the last day, leaving no time to shift the emphasis of the party's propaganda to its Knesset list. But the party's failure was also due to its tendency to blur its messages. While the polls predicted the Center Party would receive more than ten seats, Shinui was not even expected to pass the minimum threshold. In the end, both parties won six seats. In its messages and in the figures it recruited, Shinui emphasized its anticlerical stance. By contrast, the Center Party tried to blur its messages, since its function was to enable its candidate for prime minister to define the center ground and secure support from left and right alike. The Center Party even made a deliberate effort to obscure Milo's well-known opposition to ultra-Orthodox circles, in an effort to win support from religious and traditional Jews for its prime ministerial candidate.

These cases do not imply that parties failed because they adopted candidate selection procedures that antagonized the electorate; rather, they emphasize the secondary importance of changes in political parties relative to the incentives created by the system of direct elections for prime minister. This system leads to a situation where political parties are sacrificed to the cause of their candidate for prime minister.[15] However, even long-standing small parties, which did not face this issue, failed to gain from the direct elections. In 1996, the split vote promoted a phenomenon where the vote for prime minister was used to express an opinion on the principal policy line, while the vote for small parties was used to emphasize specific positions and identities. This led to the strengthening of existing small parties (Shas, the NRP, and the DFPE), and the success of an alliance between an old and a new party (the Arab Democratic Party and the United Arab List). In addition, two new parties entered the Knesset (Israel b'Aliya and the Third Way). In the 1999 elections, and with the exception of Shas, which did not face a close opponent, the long-standing small parties did not gain in strength; indeed, some declined. The opportunity that direct elections created for small parties was exploited mainly by new or revamped parties. These parties found their place in the multidimensional space that had opened up when alongside the centripetal tendency the system encouraged on questions of foreign affairs and security (Hazan 1999), centrifugal trends emerged on other issues (Hazan and Rahat 2000). Most parties had to content themselves with the establishment of new parties competing for the same sector of the electorate, and sharpening their own messages. Alongside Meretz, Shinui rose like a phoenix with its radical antireligious message; Israel b'Aliya faced the establishment of Israel Beiteinu, which attempted to channel the resentment of immigrants by presenting an anti-establishment approach; the NRP was challenged by Tekuma, which adopted a more emphatically nationalist position; while among the Arab parties, the National Democratic Alliance gained prominence vis-à-vis the DFPE for its strong nationalist message. Only among the ultra-Orthodox parties was there no such competition, after Shas managed to prevent the attempt to establish a rival list that will be supported by Rabbi Yitzhak Kaduri.

Most Israeli political parties, and particularly the major parties, had shown a high level of ability in the past to adapt to social developments; it is a different matter, however, to adapt to immediate institutional change. The adoption of the direct election for prime minister created new pressures and incentives, and offered new opportunities. In these conditions, a broad representative mosaic benefited the candidates for prime minister but not the political parties themselves, since the new system favored parties that emphasized their distinct positions and identity. This situation was also due to the continuation of the inflexible list system for Knesset elections. This absence of any individual component in the general elections is in stark contrast to the personalization of politics, and prevents different candidates within the same party from appealing to segments of the electorate who have differing identities and positions. It is possible that the adoption of electoral districts, where the size of the constituency would be much smaller than the present national system, and the adoption of a personal element (open-list system), might allow the major parties (Labor and Likud) to include prominent candidates and to attract a higher proportion of the votes. Given the existing system, however, direct election of the prime minister overshadows the voting for candidates lists, clearing the way for small parties with clear identities and messages. Primaries in the major parties did contain districts and were personal in essence. These, however, are no substitute for reform of the electoral system, particularly since they disconnect the issue of personal candidacy from the question of the parties' success in the general elections.[16]

Conclusion

The frequent changes in the candidate selection methods used by Israeli political parties during the 1990s, as well as the dramatic change in direction during the run-up to the 1999 elections, form part of a broader mosaic of changes occurring in Israeli politics in general, and in Israeli political parties in particular. Through evolutionary development, political parties in Israel and around the world have managed to adapt to enormous changes in their electorates, and in the electorates' attitudes toward politics and politicians. Institutional change, in the form of the Direct Elections Law, would seem to require a response on a level beyond the individual political party, due to the inherently nonevolutionary nature of this change. The parties cannot cope with this change on their own, since they face a paradoxical situation whereby the desire to secure power through presenting their own candidate for prime minister in the direct election is completely inconsonant with another of their interests: The desire to increase their representation in the legislature.

The solution to this dilemma may emerge in the not-too-distant future of Israeli politics. Disassociating the candidates for prime minister from the political parties would enable each to compete in a separate arena. This process may occur naturally if the current decline in support for the major parties (Labor and Likud) continues, leading to a situation where there will no longer be large parties that "automatically" present the candidates for prime minister. Such a development might require legislative attention, to separate the financing of political parties from the public financing of candidates for prime minister, for example, or to enable or require all political parties to support one of the candidates for prime minister or even to participate in funding this candidate. If and when such change occurs, the variable of which method is used to select candidates lists may once again become a source, and not merely an object, of influence, in terms of the functioning of the political system in general, and the success of political parties in particular.

Notes

1. For somewhat different frameworks for comparing candidate selection methods, see: Ranney (1981) and Gallagher and Marsh (1988). Another important dimension is the level of inclusiveness in the conditions for presenting one's candidacy for a party's Knesset list. These conditions may range from being a citizen of the state—reflecting a high level of inclusiveness—to conditions stipulating party membership for an extended period, or affiliation with, and activity in, its institutions and associated organizations—which is a low level of inclusiveness. In Israel, this dimension is negligible in importance: Experience shows that political parties tend to enable candidates to participate even if they do not meet the conditions of candidacy stipulated in the parties' constitutions. This takes place both by applying special clauses that permit exceptions to the rules in particular cases, and by simply ignoring the rules.

2. The number of safe places on a list is defined according to the number of seats the party won in the previous elections.

3. In 1992, the majority faction (led by Shamir and Arens) managed to control most of the safe positions in the Knesset list. David Levy's faction, which achieved very poor results under this system, demanded changes in the selection method and allocation of a lower number of votes than the number of safe positions in the Knesset list. After this demand was rejected, Levy quit the Likud and established Gesher, which later received five safe places on the joint list with Likud and Tzomet.

4. Each member of the Meretz Council was allocated five votes, so that in theory all seven candidates could have passed the screening stage. In practice, however, two incumbents were rejected at this stage; only five received 60% or more of the votes.

5. It was determined that a candidate in the first five places would receive a given place if 40% of the selectorate selected them for that place or a higher place. For the second five places, the required number of votes was 35%, and in the third 30%. In practice, however, none of the candidates secured these levels of support, and the ranking of all candidates was based on the points system.

6. At the time of writing, Meretz has not yet registered as a political party, and its constituent parties, Mapam and Ratz, continue to maintain their legal status as parties. This is because of the advantages that are gained under the laws governing political parties. For purposes of political funding, it is preferable to continue as separate parties, and for purposes of less intense state scrutiny, it is advantageous for Meretz to continue to be registered as an association.

7. In 1992 the exhaustive ballot method was used by Shinui to select its candidates. In 1996, it was used to determine which candidates would participate in the primaries held among all the members of Meretz. Under this method, candidates compete separately for each place in the list, in descending order. A candidate secures a place by winning an absolute majority. Until such a majority is obtained, repeated rounds of voting are held, with the candidate who receives the lowest number of votes in each round being eliminated.

8. Under the NRP's point system, each voter marked seven candidates in order of preference. Ten points were allocated for first place, nine for second and so on, down to the seventh candidate, who received four points. The candidate's ranking on the list was determined according to the number of points they received.

9. Both Porat and Druckman had quit the NRP during the 1980s in favor of parties further to the right, after Israel vacated its settlements in Sinai as part of the peace agreement with Egypt; both politicians later returned to the party.

10. In 1999, when Gesher was allocated slots as part of the joint list with the Labor Party, it continued to use its founding council for this purpose, although three years had passed since the establishment of the party. Gesher devoted no attention to establishing or developing selected institutions, and furthermore faced a severe crisis after its decision to "switch sides," leaving the right-wing camp in favor of cooperation with the Labor Party.

11. Shas is well-known as a party that appeals on ethnic grounds to a traditional, religious population that is not ultra-Orthodox. United Torah Judaism attempted to mimic this approach, appealing in its election propaganda to traditional-minded Jews to support the party as the guardian of true Judaism. United Torah Judaism also appealed to right-wing religious voters, emphasizing the involvement of Deputy Minister of Housing Meir Porush in expanding Jewish settlements (*Ha'aretz,* April 12, 1999).

12. For a discussion of the methods used in the past to select the parties' candidates for the Knesset, see Bar 1996; Brichta 1977; Doron and Goldberg 1990; Goldberg 1980, 1994; Goldberg and Hoffmann 1983; Hazan 1997; Rahat and Sar-Hadar 1999a, 1999b.

13. An additional phenomenon reflecting the personalization of Israeli politics is the movement of MKs between political parties. A large number of MKs (22) have left their parties, often because they anticipated that they would be unsuccessful in their efforts to be reselected in internal party elections, and in some cases after failing in such elections. In many other cases, party figures who had not served as MKs during the Fourteenth Knesset left their parties to join other parties, particularly new ones; these included former MKs and heads of local authorities.

14. Both approaches may be found in a collection of articles devoted to the subject of the development of political parties in Israel in the Nineties. See Korn (1998).

15. It might be argued that presenting a candidate for prime minister helps small or new parties, since it secures attention and prominence. Moreover, the fact of her candidacy gives the candidate's party a measure of power in bargaining with the major parties—in return for removing her candidacy, it might secure various promises, such as guaranteed positions in a future government. However, the smaller parties that presented candidates for prime minister—the Democratic National Alliance, the National Union, and the Center Party—did not secure particularly impressive electoral achievements. Neither does the representation that the Center Party secured in the government suggest that it gained any particular benefit from presenting a candidate for prime minister.

16. For a discussion of this issue and the problems inherent in primaries, as well as a recommendation for reform of the electoral system, see Rahat and Sher-Hadar (1999b).

References

Bar, Eliza. 1996. *Primaries and Other Methods of Candidate Selection.* Tel Aviv: Israel Democracy Institute and Hakibbutz Hameuchad (Hebrew).

Begin, Ze'ev B. 1996. "Primaries—The Price of Democracy." In Gideon Doron (ed.). *The Electoral Revolution.* Tel Aviv: Hakibbutz Hameuchad, 207–214 (Hebrew).

Brichta, Avraham. 1977. *Democracy and Elections.* Tel Aviv: Am Oved (Hebrew).

Doron, Gideon. 1998. "Real Parties and Virtual Parties." In Danny Korn (ed.). *The Demise of Parties in Israel.* Tel Aviv: Hakibbutz Hameuchad, 215–223 (Hebrew).

Doron, Gideon, and Giora Goldberg. 1990. "No Big Deal: Democratization of the Nominating Process." In Asher Arian and Michal Shamir (eds.). *The Elections in Israel—1988.* Boulder: Westview Press, 155–171.

Dror, Yechezkel. 1996. "The Ability to Govern as a Supreme Criterion for the Molding of a Regime." In Gideon Doron (ed.). *The Electoral Revolution.* Tel Aviv: Hakibbutz Hameuchad, 149–162 (Hebrew).

Gallagher, Michael, and Michael Marsh. 1988. *Candidate Selection in Comparative Perspective: The Secret Garden of Politics.* London: Sage.

Goldberg, Giora. 1980. "Democracy & Representation in Israeli Political Parties." In Asher Arian (ed.). *The Elections in Israel—1977.* Jerusalem: Academic Press, 101–117.

———. 1994. *The Israeli Voter 1992.* Jerusalem: Magnes Press (Hebrew).

Goldberg, Giora, and Steven Hoffman. 1983. "Nominations in Israel: The Politics of Institutionalization." In Asher Arian (ed.) *The Elections in Israel—1981.* Tel Aviv: Ramot, 61–87.

Ha'aretz (Hebrew).

Hazan, Reuven Y. 1997. "The Intra-Party Elections in Israel: Adopting Party Primaries." *Electoral Studies* 16, no. 1: 95–103.

Hazan, Reuven Y. 1998. "Your Destroyers and Ravagers Have Come From Within: The Ramifications of the Primaries for the Political Parties." In Danny Korn (ed.). *The Demise of Parties in Israel.* Tel Aviv: Hakibbutz Hameuchad, 78–90 (Hebrew).

———. 1999. "The Electoral Consequences of Political Reform: In Search for the Center of the Israeli Party System." In Asher Arian and Michal Shamir (eds.). *The Elections in Israel 1996.* New York: State University of New York Press, 163–185.

Hazan, Reuven Y., and Gideon Rahat. 2000. "Representation, Electoral Reform and Democracy: Theoretical and Empirical Lessons from the 1996 Elections in Israel." *Comparative Political Studies.* 33: 1310-1366.

Korn, Danny (ed.). 1998. The Demise of Parties in Israel. Tel Aviv: Hakibbutz Hameuchad (Hebrew).

Lipset, Seymour M., and Stein Rokkan. 1967. "Cleavage Structures, Party Systems and Voter Alignment." In Seymour M. Lipset and Stein Rokkan (eds.). *Party Systems and Voter Alignments: Cross-National Perspectives.* New York: Free Press, 1–54.

Mair, Peter. 1991. "Myths of Electoral Change and the Survival of Traditional Parties." *European Journal of Political Research* 24: 121–134.

Meretz. February 11, 1999. "An Analysis of the Results of the Election for the Ranking of Members of Knesset." (Hebrew).

Peleg, Molly. 1996: "Primaries and the Government: Two-Track Influence." In Gideon Doron (ed.). *The Electoral Revolution* Tel Aviv: Hakibbutz Hameuchad, 113–122 (Hebrew).

Phillips, Anne. 1995. The Politics of Presence. Oxford: Clarendon.

Rahat, Gideon, and Neta Sher-Hadar. 1999a. "The Party Primaries of 1996 and Their Political Consequences." In Asher Arian and Michal Shamir (eds.). *The Elections in Israel 1996.* Albany: State University of New York Press, 241–268.

———. 1999b. *Intraparty Selection of Candidates for the Knesset and for Prime-Ministerial Candidacy 1995–1997.* Jerusalem: Israel Democracy Institute (Hebrew).

Ranney, Austin. 1981. "Candidate Selection." In David Butler et al. (eds.). *Democracy at the Polls.* Washington, DC: American Enterprise Institute, 75–106.

Shinui. March 25, 1999. A summary of the meeting of Shinui's Committee (Hebrew).

13

Struggles Over the Electoral Agenda
The Elections of 1996 and 1999

GABRIEL WEIMANN AND GADI WOLFSFELD

One of the important aspects of modern politics is the struggle over the news media. The news media serve as the central arena for antagonists to promote their political positions and preferred images (Wolfsfeld 1997). This contest becomes especially intensive during election campaigns as each candidate and/or political party attempts to dominate the media agenda. Candidates want to pull their opponents onto the political battlefield where they have the greatest advantages.

Clinton's team in 1992, for example, was convinced that the secret to success was to keep the campaign focused on the economy (Arterton 1993). The now famous slogan written at campaign headquarters read, It's the Economy Stupid. Bush, on the other hand, would have preferred that the election be about foreign affairs and personal integrity. The content analyses of election news carried out by M. Just and her colleagues (1996) shows that Clinton was largely successful: the 1992 election was thought to be a referendum on the economy.

The news media however, often develop their own agenda that has little to do with the topics being promoted by the candidates. This phenomenon is especially well-known with regard to the media's tendency to take a cynical view of election campaigns by focusing on strategies, scandals, internal conflicts, and polls rather than on substantive issues (Blumler and Kavanagh 1999; Patterson 1993; Just et al. 1996). The news media can also exhibit an independent agenda with regard to substance. P. Norris and her colleagues found that in the 1997 campaign in Britain "the party and news agendas remained worlds apart (1999, 181)." While many of the political parties were talking about welfare, the economy, and education, little of this could be found in news about the election.

The authors thanks Asher Arian who worked with them on this project and the Israel Democracy Institute which provided the funds.

There is also increasing evidence that this struggle over the election agenda can have an important impact on voting choices. J. R. Zaller's work (1992) on priming is especially convincing in this area of research. Zaller argues that many citizens have conflicting "considerations" about public issues. The opinions they express vary in accordance with the ideas that are the most salient to them. Changes in the political environment serve to bring different considerations to the fore and this can have an important influence on how people relate to political issues and candidates.

This chapter attempts to examine the competition over the election news agenda using two election campaigns in Israel. The goal of the project was to better understand the factors that lead to success and failure in these contests. There are three major models that are often put forward in this area.

The most common factor cited by candidates and their advisors is *political bias.* The charge is that the news media prefer one candidate to another and this preference is reflected in the quantity and quality of news coverage given. In Israel, as in many countries, it is almost always the right-wing camp that accuses the news media of giving preference to left-wing candidates and issues. The conventional wisdom among political activists and journalists is that very few Israeli journalists vote for right-wing candidates and parties (Wolfsfeld 1997).

The same charges were also made in the '96 and '99 elections. The press was said to prefer Prime Minister Shimon Peres in 1996, and Ehud Barak in the 1999 campaign. The antagonism between Prime Minister Benjamin Netanyahu and the Israeli press was especially pronounced during the 1999 campaign. The peek of this tension took place in the final days of the campaign when Netanyahu appeared to be inciting his followers against the press. The candidate charged that the media were against him, that the press was "scared" that he was going to win. The scene of Netanyahu stirring up his crowd of followers with the chant "they are scared" was one of the most dramatic moments of the campaign. It is notable that no countercharges about media bias were made by the more leftist candidate in either election.

A second possible model would emphasize the advantages enjoyed by *incumbents.* The correlation between political power and power over the news media is one of the central axioms in the field of political communication (Bennett 1983; Entman 1989; Gans 1979; Molotch and Lester 1974; Peletz and Entman 1981; Reese, Grant, and Danielian 1994; Shoemaker and Reese 1991; Wolfsfeld 1997). Those in power are certainly given easier access to the media and are in a much better position to generate newsworthy events. If this proposition is true, incumbents should be in a much better position to dominate the media agenda than challengers.

The rules of access may change however during election campaigns. The news media become much more concerned with the issue of "balance," as do political activists and members of the public (Arian, Weimann, and Wolfsfeld 1999). Some countries also employ legal means to insure greater balance. In Britain, for example, editors use a "stopwatch policy" that strictly allocates news coverage in proportion to the number of seats parties have in the Parliament (Semetko 1996). In Israel concerns about the advantages of incumbents are linked to a (since repealed) law that prevents television and radio from presenting the images and voices of any candidates during the thirty days before election.

We believe that the competition over the electoral agenda is far more open than suggested by either of these approaches. While political bias and the advantages enjoyed by incumbents may influence the contest, the professional considerations of journalists are far more important. Editors and reporters are in the news business and their primary goal is to make the election interesting. This approach can be labeled the *drama first model.* It states that the best predictor of the media agenda in any election will be the dramatic appeal of the competing news stories.

The preference for drama is reflected in two journalistic routines. The first, noted earlier, is to focus on campaign stories that highlight the horse race and what is happening "behind-the-scenes." One of the reasons for this emphasis is that journalists assume (probably correctly) that stories about conflict and intrigue are more exciting than stories about policy proposals. The second routine is to give prominence to those substantive issues that provide the most exciting news stories. This helps explain why so much news about elections is negative (Patterson 1993). The most dramatic news concerning elections usually involves either scandals, disastrous mistakes by one of the candidates, or the emergence of an exceptionally distasteful conflict.

J. B. Manheim (1991) has argued that one of the primary reasons for the increase in negative advertising in Western countries is their newsworthiness. He labels this phenomenon the *multiplier effect* whereby candidates receive a great deal of free publicity when the attacks are publicized in the news media. T. Patterson (1993) also relates to this issue and demonstrates the dramatic increase in negative news about candidates in the United States. This may very well be part of a larger phenomenon that J. N. Cappella and K. H. Jamieson (1997) have called the "spiral of cynicism": politicians who want to survive are forced to provide the negativity the news media demand. Given this environment, modern politicians may find it much easier to convince the public of the opponents' shortcomings than of one's own strengths.

The key to success for any candidate and/or party is to find issues and events that meet two major criteria: (1) The prominence of the issue works to the exclusive advantage of one's own campaign. (2) The candidate's issue and/or event is considered more newsworthy by the press than the available alternatives. The first criterion is based on the previously discussed preference for candidates to compete on their home fields. While the prominence of some issues provides no real advantage to either candidate, others play to one side's strength and the other's weakness. The fact that crime became a major issue in the American election of 1988 campaign and that the economy was a major issue in 1992 provided important advantages to the first Bush campaign and to the first Clinton campaign, respectively. In 1996, on the other hand, Dole failed in his attempts to use the issues of crime and welfare to his advantage. Clinton preempted this strategy by promoting relatively conservative positions on both of these issues. The extent to which the prominence of certain issues will help one of the candidates and/or parties varies over political circumstance.

Meeting the second criterion of newsworthiness is more difficult. While a negative campaign is one way to insure newsworthiness, such a strategy can also backfire. The negativity itself can be come a major campaign issue. Those who fail to find anything newsworthy to promote, however, will have little control over the electoral agenda. The news media will either emphasize the issues that are raised by opponents or other issues that they themselves find newsworthy. Those who fail to feed a drama hungry news media will soon find the journalists eating somewhere else.

The struggle over the election agenda in the Israeli elections of 1996 and 1999 elections provide a useful demonstration of these principles.

The Setting

Israel has two major television stations that broadcast national news. Israel's Channel 1 operates as part of the Israel Broadcasting Authority (IBA), patterned on the British Broadcasting Corporation. The British model calls for nonpolitical appointments based on ability, professional expertise, and independence, but the Israeli system clearly deviates from that norm. The director general, for example, is appointed by the government and many of the members of the supervising council are representatives of political parties. The Broadcasting Authority lost its monopoly status in 1990 when the commercial Channel 2 was set up by law. The Broadcast Authority is funded by a user's fee; Channel 2 is funded commercially (Caspi and Limor 1995 122–133).

As one might expect, Israelis consume news at very high rates. In a survey of Jewish adults conducted before the 1996 elections, 8% of the respondents claimed they read more than one newspaper every day, 45% said that they read one paper every day, and an additional 20% said they read one, two, or three times a week. Only 6% stated that they never read a newspaper. Regarding television, surveys showed that between 50 and 60% watched one of the two news shows on any given evening.[1]

One of the more unusual aspects of election news on Israel television was a ban on showing or hearing political candidates during the thirty days before election. This law was initiated before the television era and was meant to apply to "newsreels" being shown in cinemas. The purpose was to prevent incumbents from having an unfair advantage in the production of news. This law was still in effect during the '96 campaign but was canceled for the '99 campaign.

Israeli television provides free airtime for political advertisements during the thirty days before the election. Time is given out in proportion to each party's number of seats in the outgoing Knesset (Israeli Parliament). In 1996, the same ads were broadcast during half hour slots at two times each evening: 8:30 and 10:30. Naturally, the previously noted ban on showing political leaders in the news does not apply to these ads.

The 1996 election campaign was marked by a number of important anomalies. First, the previously elected prime minister, Yitzhak Rabin, had been assassinated in November of 1995. His successor, Peres, had only been in office for a few months when he decided to call for new elections. In addition, the electoral system had been changed and the voters were asked to cast two votes: one for prime minister and one for the Knesset. Finally, in the beginning of April 1996, two months before the elections, the Israelis launched a military operation against the Muslim organization Hizbullah, based in southern Lebanon. During that month Israel carried out a massive attack: the "Grapes of Wrath" operation. Peres also held the position of minister of defense and this assured him a great deal of media attention (Arian, Weimann, and Wolfsfeld 1999). It is fair to say that the "real" campaign only began at the beginning of May, four weeks before the election.

The 1999 election campaign was more routine. Netanyahu had been forced to call early elections after he had lost his majority in the Knesset. The major challenger was Barak, a former chief of staff. Barak ran on the "One Israel" list that combined the Labor Party with some smaller ones. There were also a number of other candidates running who dropped out before Election Day. Netanyahu had trailed in the polls from the very beginning and the gap grew much larger as the campaign progressed.

Research Strategy

The goal of the study was to examine the struggle among candidates over the news agenda in two election campaigns. The focus on election news was quite intentional. It is here that voters are told what the election is about and where one is likely to find the clearest influence of campaign strategies. In any case, as the election gets closer, election items tend to dominate the news agenda.

The analyses were based on two major sources of data. The first was the election news appearing on television during the sixty days (April–May 1996 and March–May 1999) before each election. The news programs were taped and then analyzed by trained coders equipped with a prestructured code-book.[2] Any news item in which the word *election* was mentioned was included in the analysis. A total of 627 stories were coded in the 1996 campaign and 1,285 items were coded in 1999.

The second source of data came from a content analysis of the election ads that appeared every evening. The allocation of airtime was proportional to the size of the party in the Israeli parliament (ten minutes for every campaigning party plus three additional minutes for every member in the outgoing Knesset). Thus, in both elections Labor, as the leading party, was given more airtime, followed by Likud. A similar procedure was applied to the study of the television commercials: all the commercials aired by the two leading parties were content-analyzed by a group of coders trained together and using a simple and standard codebook containing the variables ISSUE (the same categories from the codebook used to analyze the news coverage), DATE, and PARTY.

We classified news items according to whether they were "substantive issues" (related to Israeli security, economy, welfare, relationships with the Palestinians, peace talks, etc.) or "campaign issues" (related to campaign strategies, surveys and polls, "sleaze campaigns," "deals," predictions of outcome, etc.). Intercoder reliability was tested by comparing the codes given by two additional coders with those of the original coders. Only those items for which the calculated reliability measures exceeded 85 percent were included in each database.

In keeping with the theoretical framework, we will focus most of our attention on the struggle over substantive issues. It is true that the news media devote a disproportionate amount of time and space to the "horse-race" aspects of the election. In addition, candidates often attack their opponents in areas that have little to do with policy. Nevertheless, studying the struggle over substantive issues has three major advantages for researchers: (1) Substantive issues are always an important part of election campaign while the centrality of campaign issues varies over time and circumstance. (2) Debates over substantive issues are likely to be more stable over the course of a campaign while strategy issues tend to be more erratic. (3) It is much easier to identify and code the rise and fall of substantive issues in both political advertising and the news media.

This study should be seen as two case studies rather than a rigorous testing of alternative hypotheses. The data tells us something about the topics being promoted by each side and the relative degree of success each enjoyed in controlling television news about the election. In order to untangle the reasons for this outcome we will rely on what we know about the political standing of the two candidates (incumbent and challenger), about their ideological differences (left and right), about the nature of the topics they were attempting to promote, and about how journalists construct news stories. The fact that we have evidence from two very different elections provides us with more confidence about the conclusions.

The first part of the discussion will look at the struggle over the agenda in the '96 campaign while the second will carry out the same analysis for 1999.

Round 1: The '96 Election Campaign

There was every reason to believe, in the spring of 1996, that Peres would win the election. Surveys showed that the majority of the population supported the Oslo peace process that had brought Israel both economic and diplomatic benefits. The Labor Party also expected to receive a good deal of support because of the Rabin assassination, especially as many considered Netanyahu tainted by that event. All the polls that were published showed Peres leading by at least 5%. In the end, Netanyahu pulled off a come-from-behind victory, winning the election by a mere 30,000 votes, nine tenths of a percentage point of the total vote.

The Peres campaign strategy inevitably focused on government achievements: the benefits and prospects coming from the peace process; the high level of growth in the economy; and the funds that had been allocated for education, welfare, transportation, and immigrant absorption. The major attack on Netanyahu was that he wasn't "fit" to be prime minister. The charges centered on his lack of experience and raised questions about his personal integrity.

The Netanyahu strategy also contained both positive and negative messages. The major slogan was Netanyahu: A Secure Peace, indicating that he would move the peace process forward, but at a slower, more cautious pace. For months before the election Netanyahu had been moving toward the center of the political spectrum. His major shifts from previous positions were his proclimations that he intended to honor the Oslo agreements that had been signed by the previous government and that he would be willing to meet with Yasser Arafat. His attacks on the government centered on three major issues: the "appeasement" of the Palestinians, the failure to prevent terrorism, and charges that the next Peres government would divide Jerusalem.

Table 13.1   Issues Promoted in the Netanyahu and Peres Commercials
(1996 Election Campaign)

Issue	In Netanyahu Commercials (%)	In Peres Commercials (%)	Difference
Terrorism, terrorist acts	23.31	6.60	+16.71
Palestinians, negotiations	24.51	36.93	−12.42
Jerusalem (split)	16.34	2.40	+13.94
Golan Heights + Syria	3.12	10.81	−7.69
Settlers, settlements	18.26	17.11	+1.15
Economy, finances	3.84	8.40	−4.56
Religion and state	2.64	2.10	+0.54
Education	4.08	8.70	−4.62
Israeli-Arabs	0.48	1.20	−0.72
Immigration and absorption	3.36	5.70	−2.34
Total	100% (N = 416)	100% (N = 333)	

The election commercials provide a convenient index of the major issues promoted by each side. The data in table 13.1 show the number of ads each candidate devoted to the ten major issues raised in the election campaign. We also calculated the difference in the proportion of ads that were devoted to each topic so that a positive number indicates that it was more a "Netanyahu issue" and a negative number means that it was more a "Peres" issue. The higher the level of difference the more the issue can be identified exclusively with one campaign.

The two major Netanyahu issues are terrorism and Jerusalem. The numbers provide a graphic illustration about the fact that the Likud was interested in emphasizing these topics while the Labor Party attempted to avoid them. While almost 40% of the Netanyahu ads dealt with these two topics, only 9% of the Peres commercials discussed them. As one might expect, many of the Peres ads on this topic were designed to defend the prime minister from Netanyahu's attacks.

The emphasis on terrorism was not surprising and certainly resonated with public concerns. In March 1996, a few months before the election, Israel suffered the worst wave of terrorism in its history. Dozens of Israelis had been killed in three bus bombings. The Peres camp's greatest fear was that there would be another bombing before the election. It never took place, but as discussed in the next section, terrorism became a major issue in the campaign.

Netanyahu's decision to focus on the future of Jerusalem was an attempt to raise a new issue onto the agenda. The charge was that if Peres remained prime minister he would hand over the eastern part of the city. While there is quite a bit of controversy concerning the future of the West Bank and Gaza, there is almost universal consensus within the country that Jerusalem will remain the undivided capital of Israel. The slogan, Peres Will Divide Jerusalem was everywhere and it constituted an important element in Netanyahu's campaign strategy. Peres attempted to ignore the issue, but in the end was forced to vehemently deny the charges.

One does not find a similarly important "Peres" issue. While Peres devoted proportionately more attention to the peace process with the Palestinians, Netanyahu was clearly not avoiding this issue. The dispute over the Oslo accords was the major point of contention between the right and the left during the three years leading up to the election. The left presented the Oslo accords as a major achievement, while the right attempted to portray the agreement as surrender to Israel's enemies. Neither side had any real reason to evade the topic, and it comes as no surprise that it became a major issue in the campaign.

The Peres campaign is also more interested in promoting the idea of peace with Syria in their election campaign. There had been an active peace process and significant progress had been made in the negotiations. Netanyahu was opposed to surrendering any land to Syria in exchange for peace, but it would seem that he was reluctant to emphasize this in his campaign. While the Peres campaign devoted almost 11% of their commercials to the Syrian issue, only 3% of the Netanyahu ads dealt with this topic.

The differences in the emphasis of other issues were relatively small. Both sides devoted a significant number of ads to the issue of the settlers living in the occupied territories. This too is a traditional point of contention between the two parties whereby the left opposes the settlements as obstacles to peace while the right sees them as an important means of guaranteeing Israel's security. The Peres campaign wanted to talk more about improvements in the economy and education, while these issues were rarely mentioned in the Netanyahu ads.

One topic was conspicuously absent from the Peres campaign: there was virtually no mention of the Rabin assassination. In the weeks following the assassination, Netanyahu had been accused by the left of indirect responsibility for the murder because of (what they called) his campaign of incitement against Rabin. Netanyahu's popularity dropped to an all-time low during that period (November–December 1995) and many thought he would never recover. This was the one negative issue Peres could have used against Netanyahu. While there are a number of theories about why the Labor Party refrained from using this weapon, a large number of political pundits expressed surprise.[3]

Looking at the top four issues of dispute—terrorism, Jerusalem, negotiations with the Palestinians, and the issue of what to do about Syria—it is clear that the major debate in this election was over the peace process. The Netanyahu campaign wanted to emphasize the dangers and threats associated with the process, while Peres wanted to talk about the opportunities it presented.

Media Coverage of the '96 Campaign

There were a total of 627 news items during the two-month period that was studied. Some readers may find these numbers surprisingly small given the high level of political interest in Israel. The reason for this anomaly has to do with the aforementioned Grapes of Wrath operation that dominated news coverage during the first month. The importance of this event in reducing the amount of election items will become especially apparent when we look at what happened in the next election.

The results presented in table 13.2 classify the items into different topic areas. The first thing to note is that, as in other countries, more attention is given to campaign issues than substantive subjects. Fifty-nine percent of the election news stories dealt with campaign issues. These campaign stories are the same as in other Western countries: stories about campaign strategies, sleaze campaigns, deals between the various political parties, polls, stories about television ads, and predictions about the outcome. By far the biggest category of issues are those that deal with the strategies of the two parties for winning the elections.

There are four major substantive topics for media coverage: the debate over the peace process with the Palestinians, the conflict over the settlements, the dispute over terrorism, and arguments about the economy. Less attention is given to the issues having to do with Syria and the Golan Heights, the Israeli Arabs, the issue of Jerusalem, religion and State, and education and immigration. At first glance, one can not detect any clear-cut winner in the battle over the agenda: there doesn't appear to be a clear preference for either Netanyahu issues or for those being promoted by Peres.

This picture changes when one separates the first month's coverage from the second. As discussed, due to the Grapes of Wrath operation, the campaign did not really begin until the second month. In any case, this is when the political ads began to air so this distinction provides a better indication of the impact of the advertising on the electoral agenda. Looking at table 13.3, one sees an important change over the two-month period that worked chiefly to Netanyahu's benefit.

The issues favored by the Peres administration were an important part of election news during the month before the ads began. This was the time

Table 13.2 "Substantive Issues" and "Campaign Issues":
TV Coverage of the 1996 Elections

Substantive Issues		Campaign Issues	
Issue	% of Items	Issue	% of Items
Terrorism, terrorist acts	15.3	Campaign strategies of the parties	55.8
Palestinians, negotiations	22.4	Divisions, conflicts within parties	6.8
Jerusalem (split)	5.3	Surveys, preelection polls	8.1
Golan Heights + Syria	8.7	Accusations, "bad-mouthing"	13.2
Settlers, settlements	19.7	Speculations (about "deals," nominations)	16.1
Economy, finances	11.2		
Religion and state	4.1		
Education	2.3		
Israeli-Arabs	7.4		
Immigration and absorption	2.3		
Total	100% (N = 268)	Total	100% (N = 385)

Table 13.3 The Salience of Issues in 1996 Election News:
First and Second Months

Issue	First month (%)	Second month (%)	Difference
Terrorism, terrorist acts	12.12	17.68	+5.56
Palestinians, negotiations	29.29	18.90	−10.39
Jerusalem (split)	3.03	6.78	+3.75
Golan Heights + Syria	18.18	3.04	−15.14
Settlers, settlements	7.07	27.43	+20.36
Economy, finances	14.14	9.75	−4.39
Religion and state	4.04	4.26	+0.22
Education	3.03	1.82	−1.21
Israeli-Arabs	7.07	7.92	+0.85
Immigration and absorption	2.02	2.43	+0.41
Total	100% (N = 99)	100% (N = 164)	

when people's attention was focused mostly on the war in Lebanon, although interestingly this never became a campaign issue. The two major issues discussed were the negotiations with the Palestinians and the Syrian issue, both of which were "Peres" issues. The issue of terrorism was further down the list and the subject of Jerusalem was barely mentioned.

There was a dramatic rise in the prominence of Netanyahu issues in the second month of the campaign. There was a significant increase in the number of election stories that dealt with terrorism and almost four times as many stories about the issue of Jerusalem. There was also an important drop in the number of stories about the Palestinians and the Syrian issue.

The most significant change was the increase in election stories about the settlements. Peres was supposed to pull out of part of Hebron before the election and most settlement stories centered on this issue. There was a great deal of tension and debate over this decision and many felt that such a controversial move would provide a considerable amount of ammunition to the opposition. Given the symbolic importance of Hebron, one can understand why the press devoted so much attention to this issue. In the end, Peres decided to avoid this controversial issue by not withdrawing.

The steep rise in the importance of the settlements story is an excellent example of how events can independently change the electoral agenda. The media follow the drama and in this case it led to Hebron. There is no reason to believe however that this provided any advantage to either candidate, because both referred to the settlement issue in their campaigns.

Rank-order correlations were calculated by comparing the order of the issues in each of the television campaigns with the order in which they appeared in the news. We were especially interested in the change between the first month and second month of the campaign because, as noted, the election ads only began during the last thirty days. The results show that during the first month, the correlation between the Peres campaign themes and election news was .80 while the corresponding figure for the Netanyahu campaign was .44. Some of this difference in the level of success can be attributed to the advantages enjoyed by incumbents. During the second month of the campaign, the correlation for the Netanyahu campaign rose to the .77 while the Peres coefficient dropped to .56. Thus, once the campaign got started, there was a genuine reversal of fortunes.

We would argue that the reason for Netanyahu's success in '96 was that his issues made for much better news stories than those being promoted by Peres. Terrorism was the most negative, divisive issue of the campaign. Although there hadn't been an attack for several months, the national wounds were still very fresh. There was also a good deal of discussion about how a terrorist attack could ruin Peres's chances. The accusation about Jerusalem was also an incendiary charge. The Peres issues were, by comparison, rather tame. If Peres had raised the specter of the Rabin assassination, the story might have come out differently.

In sum, the struggle over the '96 campaign was one in which the leftist incumbent Peres attempted to promote the government's accomplishments while the right-wing challenger Netanyahu talked about the government failures, especially with regard to terrorism. Netanyahu's issues were far more negative, divisive, and above all newsworthy. The fact that Peres was the incumbent may have helped him in the first month, but was of little use in the second. Once the political ads began, Netanyahu's issues rose in prominence while Peres's declined. There was also an extreme increase in media attention focused on the settlement issue, because of the political tension surrounding Hebron. The results, at least from this election, suggest that the "drama-first" model provides that best approach for explaining how the news media cover election campaigns.

Round 2: The '99 Campaign

The analysis of the '99 campaign allows us to look at these same issues within a very different context. This time the prime minister was from the right-wing camp and the challenger came from the left. If the incumbency model is correct, then Netanyahu should have been able to exploit his position in order to create newsworthy events that complemented his overall strategy. If the political bias model is correct, then Barak would have been given a clear advantage in promoting his own agenda. As shown in the next section, however, neither candidate was given any real advantage. Instead, the news media produced their own agenda for the 1999 campaign, based on the most dramatic stories available.

We again start by presenting the major issues being promoted by each candidate. As can be seen in table 13.4, Netanyahu employed almost an identical strategy as in '96. The majority of his ads focused on three major issues: terrorism, the peace process, and Jerusalem. It is also clear that Netanyahu was not interested in talking about domestic issues: only 8% of his ads dealt with the economy and there wasn't a single ad on either education or unemployment.

Barak, on the other hand, ran a very different campaign than Peres had in '96. The most striking difference is the amount of emphasis that Barak placed on security; it appeared more than any other topic. Barak's impressive military background was a clear advantage for this candidate and provided a critical counterweight to Netanyahu's warnings about terrorism. A good proportion of Barak's campaign was also devoted to social problems: unemployment,

Table 13.4   Issues Promoted in the Netanyahu and Barak Commercials (1999 Election Campaign)

Issue	In Netanyahu Commercials (%)	In Barak Commercials (%)	Difference
Terrorism, terrorist acts	18.7	1.7	+17.0
Palestinians, negotiations	25.3	6.1	+19.2
Jerusalem (split)	21.3	13.0	+8.3
Security	10.7	20.0	−9.3
Golan Heights + Syria + Lebanon	5.4	0.9	+4.5
Immigration and absorption	6.7	2.6	+4.1
Economy, finances	8.0	15.7	−7.7
Religion and state	0	1.7	−1.7
Education	0	16.5	−16.5
Unemployment	1.3	17.4	−16.1
Ethnic gap	2.7	0	+2.7
Welfare and health care	0	2.6	−2.6
Unity of Israeli society	0	1.7	−1.7
Total	100% ($N = 115$)	100% ($N = 75$)	

the poor state of the economy, and education problems. Barak also parted ways with Peres by virtually ignoring the peace process with the Palestinians. Only 6% of all his ads dealt with this topic.

As always, each candidate was attempting to play on his own field. Netanyahu believed that his major successes were on the Palestinian front: reducing the amount of terrorism and refusing to give in to their demands. An important element in this strategy was warning that a Barak victory would return Israel to the frightening period of violence that characterized the Peres regime. Barak wanted to have the electoral agenda focus on social issues where Netanyahu was the weakest. Many of his ads talked about the plight of the poor and unemployed. Whereas in '96 only Netanyahu had focused on negative issues, this time both candidates were using that tactic. The question is whether either had any impact on the television agenda.

Media Coverage of the '99 Campaign

One of the most important differences in the coverage of the two election campaigns was the dramatic rise in the amount of election news in '99. As noted, there were a total of 627 broadcasts in '96, but 1,285 in '99. There

Table 13.5 "Substantive Issues" and "Campaign Issues"
in TV Coverage of the 1999 Elections

Substantive Issues		Campaign Issues	
Issue	% of Items	Issue	% of Items
Terrorism, terrorist acts	3.9	Campaign strategies of the parties	52.1
Palestinians, negotiations	11.4	Divisions, conflicts within parties	9.8
Crime and corruption	25.1	Surveys, preelection polls	6.5
Jerusalem (split)	8.3	Accusations, "bad-mouthing"	13.5
Golan Heights + Syria + Lebanon	5.7	Speculations (about "deals" and nominations)	12.5
Settlers, settlements	2.5	Campaign tours and visits	5.5
Economy, finances	5.9		
Religion and state	5.5		
Education	0.7		
Israeli-Arabs	4.2		
Unity of Israeli society	4.6		
Social welfare	4.6		
Immigration and absorption	5.5		
Others	12.1		
Total	100% (N = 1107)	Total	100% (N = 1499)

were no major competing events in '99 and thus the election was a top news story for the entire two-month period. It is also possible that the change in the election law, which allowed the media to cover the candidates more directly, may have also played a part in this increase.

The massive increase in the number of election stories also allowed the media to deal with a wider range of topics (see table 13.5). Whereas we were able to use only ten categories of substantive issues in '96, the number jumped to fourteen in '99 (including an "other" category). The stories were also much longer than in '96, which explains the fact that so many more stories fell into multiple categories.

Interestingly, despite the significant increase in the number of news stories the proportion of stories dealing with campaign issues remained remarkably stable. Fifty-nine percent of the stories dealt with campaign issues in '96 and 58% fell into this category in the '99 election. One also finds a relatively consistent division *within* campaign stories. In both elections there were a little over 50% of the stories that dealt with campaign strategies, between 13 and 16% dealing with political deals and speculations concerning future governments, and around 13% that dealt with the accusations of the two sides. This is a surprising finding that is worthy of further study. These editors seem to have developed some type of professional norm by which they "know" how much space should be devoted to such topics.

The distribution of stories about substantive issues, on the other hand, is very different than in '96. In 1999, corruption and crime was by far the most important topic, a subject that did not even arise in the '96 campaign. Over 25% of all the news stories dealt with this topic. The major reason is that former minister Aryeh Deri was found guilty of bribery, fraud, and breaking his oath of office. Deri was the leader of the ultra-Orthodox party Shas, whose major constituency are Sephardic Jews. Although Deri had in the past served in a Labor government, he called on his followers to vote for Netanyahu in 1999. An additional scandal emerged when another Netanyahu associate, Minister Ariel Sharon, was indicted for corruption.[4]

As can be seen in table 13.6, the issue of crime and corruption continued to dominate election news in the second month of the campaign, even after the start of the television ads. While the salience of this issue declined somewhat, it remained the most important election issue throughout the campaign. Indeed, when compared to what happened in '96 (when there was a dramatic change in the second month) one finds very little variation in the news agenda. This would suggest that this time the televised political ads had very little impact in '99.

This conclusion receives further support when one looks at the specific issues raised by the two candidates. Neither candidate appears to have had significant influence on the campaign agenda. The most notable difference from the '96 campaign was the lack of media attention to the issue of terrorism. Although there was an increase in the amount of attention given to this issue in the second month, it remained a relatively minor issue throughout. The Netanyahu campaign could take some comfort in the fact that the negotiations with the Palestinians and Jerusalem were the second and third most important issues mentioned. Given the importance of the corruption story, however, this must have been very small comfort indeed.

The prominence of the Deri conviction was especially problematic for Netanyahu due to another development in the election campaign. A major conflict emerged between Deri's party Shas and the Russian immigrant's party, Israel b'Aliya. The confrontation centered on which party would take control over the Ministry of Interior after the election. Both parties were part of Netanyahu's coalition, and both sets of voters were critical to the prime min-

Table 13.6   The Salience of Issues in '99 Election News:
First and Second Month

Issue	First month (%)	Second month (%)	Difference
Terrorism, terrorist acts	1.3	5.6	+4.3
Palestinians, negotiations	9.8	12.4	+2.6
Crime and corruption	28.3	22.8	−5.5
Jerusalem (split)	7.1	9.1	+2.0
Golan Heights + Syria + Lebanon	9.2	3.5	−5.7
Settlers, settlements	2.5	2.6	+0.1
Immigration and absorption	3.8	6.7	+2.9
Economy, finances	6.0	5.8	−0.2
Religion and state	4.7	6.1	+1.4
Education	0.9	0.6	−0.3
Israeli-Arabs	3.3	4.7	+1.4
Unemployment	1.8	1.7	−0.1
Ethnic gap	2.7	3.0	+0.3
Welfare and health care	5.4	4.1	−1.3
Unity of Israeli society	3.6	5.3	+1.7
Others	9.6	6.1	−3.5
Total	100% (N = 448)	100% (N = 659)	

ister's hopes of being reelected. As the insults and accusations reached their peak, Barak implied that his minister of interior would come from Israel b'Aliya. This was an important turning point in the campaign as a growing number of Russian voters moved from supporting Netanyahu to supporting Barak.

Turning back to table 13.6, however, it is clear that the Barak issues also failed to catch on in the news. While the general emphasis on security may have been an effective response to Netanyahu's focus on terrorism, it was not a theme that could be easily converted into election news. The issues of unemployment and education were also not major topics in this campaign. The picture improves somewhat if one combines all economic problems into one category, but not by much. This is very similar to what was mentioned about the 1997 election campaign in Britain (Norris et al. 1999). There too it was difficult to get social issues on the electoral agenda.

It would appear that neither candidate was able to find a sufficiently newsworthy issue for journalists. The terrorism story was no longer considered relevant, perhaps because so much time had passed since Israel had been plagued by such violence. While the economic stories might have caught on in different circumstances, they could not compete with the dramatic impact of the Deri conviction. The rank-order correlations we performed confirm this conclusion: no significant correlation was found between either set of political ads and the news agenda.

Conclusion

The empirical evidence from both of these elections leads us to reject two of the three models that were presented in the beginning of this chapter. The incumbency model received the least support. Neither incumbent was able to dominate the electoral agenda. In 1996, Peres failed to ignite the press with his emphasis on the peace process, and in 1999 Netanyahu was no longer able to use the terrorism card. It would appear that once the election campaign begins, the incumbents lose many of their normal advantages as newsmakers.

There was also very little evidence pointing to the bias model. The conventional wisdom in both elections was that the Israeli press was united against Netanyahu. There is certainly no evidence to support such a belief, at least when it comes to the electoral agenda. In fact, the evidence suggests that the press may have played a part in Netanyahu's victory, especially by increasingly emphasizing the topic of terrorism. There is also little proof of bias in the electoral agenda of the '99 campaign. The news media barely mentioned any of the major issues promoted by Barak.

It is possible however that the media bias against Netanyahu came out in other forms. Some would argue that focusing on Deri's conviction during the '99 campaign was simply a more sophisticated method of ruining the prime minister's chances for reelection. The bias may also have come out in the newspapers, which were not analyzed in this study. The editorials that were written against Netanyahu would provide an especially promising venue for finding bias. A more comprehensive study would also include the many talk shows that are broadcast on both radio and television.

Nevertheless, the "drama-first" model provides the most compelling of the three explanations for how the news media construct their electoral agenda. The first priority of every journalist is to produce the most interesting news stories possible. This is why so much emphasis is placed on (what we have called) "campaign stories." Here we demonstrate that this same principle also has a major impact on the struggle over substantive issues. In '96, news attention was first focused on the Grapes of Wrath operation and then on the two most dramatic developments of the campaign: Netanyahu's scathing attacks about terrorism and the continuing tension about whether Peres would pull out of Hebron. In '99, it was the Deri's conviction that dominated election coverage, a story that would continue to reverberate long after the election was over. The electoral agenda worked in Netanyahu's favor in '96, and probably against him in '99. But the evidence suggests that in both cases the final lineups were based on legitimate editorial concerns about newsworthiness.

These findings contain both positive and negative implications concerning the role of the news media in elections. On the one hand, it would appear that the contest over the electoral agenda is a fairly open affair in which neither of the major candidates is given any inherent advantages. The playing field in other words, is fairly level. On the other hand, the fact that entertainment values have such a major impact on the construction of the electoral agenda is problematic. Such a process creates a situation in which decisions about the country's future depend on either the candidate's ability to produce dramatic stories or on unplanned events. This dynamic is likely to be especially important in close elections such as the Netanyahu-Peres contest in '96.

We clearly have a long way to go in this area of research. It will be especially important to look closer at the ways in which journalists construct campaign stories. Given the fact that such items make up such a large proportion of election coverage, it is critical to gain a better understanding of how political strategists attempt to influence such stories. As noted, it would also be helpful to look at how such contests take place in newspapers, radio, and other programs on television. The ultimate goal is to provide a model that better explains how candidates and parties compete for media attention and support.

Notes

1. The survey was conducted during May 1996 in face-to-face interviews among a representative sample of voters conducted by the Modi'in Ezrachi Research Institute, funded by the Israel Democracy Institute, and by the Sapir Center for Development of Tel Aviv University. The questionnaire was prepared by the editors of this volume, Asher Arian and Michal Shamir.

2. The coders were interns of Knesset committees in a program sponsored by the Israel Democracy Institute.

3. One theory put forth was that Peres advisors were reluctant to "heat up" the campaign due to their lead in the polls. The other was that focus groups with undecided voters had suggested that such an attack would prove to be counterproductive.

4. After the election, Sharon was exonerated of those charges and replaced Netanyahu as head of the Likud Party.

References

Arian, A., G. Weimann, and G. Wolfsfeld. 1999. "Balance in Election Coverage." In A. Arian, and M. Shamir (eds.). *The Elections in Israel, 1996.* Albany: State University of New York Press.

Arterton, C. 1993. "Campaign '92: Strategies and Tactics of the Candidates." In G. M. Pomper (ed.). *The Election of 1992.* Chatham, NJ: Chatham House.

Bennett, W. L. 1983. *News: The Politics of Illusion.* 2d ed., New York: Longman.

Blumler, J. G., and D. Kavanagh. 1999. "The Third Age of Political Communication: Influences and Features." *Political Communication* 16: 209–230.

Capella, J. N., and K. H. Jamieson. 1997. *Spiral of Cynicism: The Press and the Public Good.* New York: Oxford University Press.

Caspi, D., and H. Limor. 1995. *The Mass Media in Israel.* Tel Aviv: Am Oved (Hebrew).

Entman, R. 1989. *Democracy without Citizens.* New York: Oxford University Press.

Gans, H. J. 1979. *Deciding What's News: A Study of CBS Evening News, NBC Nightly News, Newsweek, and Time.* New York: Pantheon Books.

Just, M., A. Crigler, D. E. Alger, T. E. Cook, M. Kern, and D. M. West. 1996. *Crosstalk: Citizens, Candidates, and the Media in a Presidential Election.* Chicago: University of Chicago Press.

Manheim, J. B. 1991. *All of the People, All of the Time.* Armonk, NY: Sharp.

Molotch, H., and M. Lester. (1974). "News as Purposive Behavior: On the Strategic Use of Routine Events, Accidents, and Scandals." *American Political Science Review* 39: 101–112.

Norris, P., J. Curtice, D. Sanders, M. Scammell, and H. A. Semetko. 1999. *On Message: Communicating the Campaign.* London: Sage.

Paletz, D. L., and R. M. Entman. 1981. *Media, Power, Politics.* New York: Free Press.

Patterson, T. 1993. *Out of order.* New York: Alfred A. Knopf.

Reese, S., A. Grant, and L. Danielian. 1994. The Structure of News Sources on Television: A Network Analysis of "CBS News," "Nightline," "MacNeil/Lehrer," and "This Week with David Brinkley." *Journal of Communication* 44, 84–107.

Semetko, H. A. 1996. "Political Balance on Television: Campaigns in the United States, Britain, and Germany." *Harvard International Journal of Press/Politics* 1: 51–71.

Shoemaker, P. J., and S. D. Reese. 1991. *Mediating the Message: Theories of Influences on Mass Media Content.* New York: Longman.

Wolfsfeld, G. 1997. *Media and Political Conflict: News from the Middle East.* Cambridge, Great Britain: Cambridge University Press.

Zaller, J. R. 1992. *The Nature of Mass Opinion.* New York: Cambridge University Press.

Contributors

Paul R. Abramson is Professor of Political Science at Michigan State University. He is author of *Generational Change in American Politics, The Political Socialization of Black Americans, Political Attitudes in America,* co-author of *Value Change in Global Perspective,* and *Change and Continuity in the 2000 Elections.*

John H. Aldrich is Pfizer-Pratt University Professor of Political Science at Duke University. He is the author of *Before the Convention* and *Why Parties,* and the co-author of *Change and Continuity in the 2000 Elections,* among other books and articles.

Asher Arian is Distinguished Professor in the Ph.D. Program in Political Science at the Graduate School and University Center of the City University of New York, Professor of Political Science at the University of Haifa, Israel, and a senior fellow at the Israel Democracy Institute. His books include *The Second Republic: Politics in Israel; Security Threatened: Surveying Israeli Opinion on Peace and War,* and the co-authored *Executive Governance in Israel.* He has been editing the Elections in Israel series since 1969.

Dana Arieli-Horowitz is a lecturer at the Department of Political Science at Tel Aviv University. Her research focuses on the interrelations between art and politics in totalitarian regimes and on political behavior in Israel. She is the author of *Romanticism of Steel: Art and Politics in Nazi Germany.*

Daphna Canetti is a Ph.D. candidate and a lecturer of political science and political psychology in the Political Science Department, The University of Haifa, Israel. Her research interests are in political science, political psychology and Israeli politics and especially in mass beliefs and behavior in the socio-political arena.

Gideon Doron teaches political science at Tel Aviv University. Amongst his recent publications are *Political Bargaining* with Itai Sened (2001) and *Public Policy and Electoral Reform* with Michael Harris (2000).

Howard L. Frant is senior lecturer in political science at the University of Haifa. His work on the interaction between political institutions and public administration has appeared in the *American Journal of Political Science, the Journal of Public Administration Research and Theory,* and *the International Public Management Journal.*

As'ad Ghanem is a lecturer and researcher at the political science department at the University of Haifa. He is the author of *The Palestinian Regime: A Partial Democracy* (Sussex Academic Press, 2001) and *The Palestinian-Arab Minority in Israel: A Political Study* (SUNY Press, 2001).

Zvi Gitelman is Professor of Political Science, Preston Tisch Professor of Judaic Studies, and Director of the Frankel Center for Judaic Studies at the University of Michigan, Ann Arbor. He is the author, most recently, of *A Century of Ambivalence: The Jews of Russia and the Soviet Union* (Indiana University Press, 2001) and editor of *Modern Jewish Politics in Eastern Europe: Bundism and Zionism* (University of Pittsburgh Press, forthcoming 2001) and of *Jewish Life after the USSR: A Community in Transition* (Indiana University Press, forthcoming, 2002). Gitelman is currently engaged in a study of Jewish identities in post-Soviet Russia and Ukraine.

Ken Goldstein is assistant professor of political science at the University of Wisconsin-Madison. He is the author of *Interest Groups, Lobbying, and Participation in America*, published by Cambridge University Press. His research on political advertising, turnout, campaign finance, survey methodology, and presidential elections has also appeared in *The American Journal of Political Science, the Journal of Politics, Public Opinion Quarterly*, and*Political Communication* as well as in a series of book chapters.

Sigal Kis is a graduate student in Political Science at Tel Aviv University. Her research interests are in political behavior, political sophistication, and information.

Jonathan Mendilow is a professor of political science at Rider University, Lawrenceville, N.J. He has published extensively in the fields of political theory and comparative politics. His latest book, *Ideology, Party Change, and Electoral Campaigns in Israel, 1965-2001* will be published by the State University of New York press.

Sarah Ozacky-Lazar has a Ph.D. from Haifa University in Middle Eastern Studies. She is the co-directory of the Jewish-Arab Center for Peace and the director of "The Institute for Peace Research" at Givat Haviva, Israel. She writes extensively on the Palestinian-Arab community in Israel and its relations with the State. She co-edited the book *"7 Roads: Theoretical Options for the Status of the Arabs in Israel"* (Givat Haviva 1999) and edits and writes two series: *Surveys on the Arabs in Israel* (since 1990) and *Palestinian Studies* (since 1994).

Ami Pedahzur is a lecturer at the Department of Political Science, University of Haifa, Israel. He recently published a book entitled: *The Extreme Right-Wing Parties in Israel: Emergence and Decline?* (Tel-Aviv University: Ramot, 2000) (in Hebrew).

Yoav Peled is associate professor in the Department of Political Science, Tel Aviv University. His books include *Class and Ethnicity in the Pale: The Political Economy of Jewish Workers' Nationalism in Late Imperial Russia,* Macmillan, 1989; the co-authored *Being Israeli: The Dynamics of Multiple Citizenship,* Cambridge, 2002 (with Gershon Shafir). He has edited *Shas: The Challenge of Israeliness* (Hebrew), Yediot Ahronot, 2001, and co-edited *The New Israel: Peacemaking and Liberalization,* Westview, 2000 (with Gershon Shafir); *Ethnic Challenges to the Modern Nation-State,* Macmillan, 2000 (with Shlomo Ben-Ami and Alberto Spektorowski; and *Israel: From Mobilized to Civil Society?* (Hebrew), Van Leer and Hakibbutz Hameuchad, 2001 (with Adi Ophir).

Gideon Rahat recently received his PhD from the Department of Political Science at the Hebrew University in Jerusalem and was a Research Fellow at the Israel Democracy Institute between 1994-2000. His research interests include candidate selection methods, electoral systems and the politics of electoral reform. He has co-authored articles in *Electoral Studies, Comparative Political Studies* and *Party Politics*, published chapters in several books, and is the co-author of the *Intra-Party Selection of Candidates for the Knesset List and for prime Ministerial Candidacy 1995-1997* (1999).

Michael Shalev is Senior Lecturer in Sociology and Political Science, and Chair of the Department of Sociology and Anthropology, The Hebrew University of Jerusalem. He is the author of *Labour and the Political Economy in Israel* (Oxford University Press, 1992).

Michal Shamir is Professor of Political Science at Tel-Aviv University. Her research focuses on democratic politics, and in particular public opinion, elections, party systems, and democratic norms. She has been co-editing the Elections in Israel series with Asher Arian since 1984. Her most recent book is *The Anatomy of Public Opinion* (University of Michigan Press, 2000) co-authored with Jacob Shamir.

Gabriel Weimann is Professor of Communication and the Chair of the Department of Communication at the University of Haifa, Israel. He has published *Communicating Unreality* (Los Angeles: Sage Publications, 2000); *The Influentials: People Who Influence People* (State University of New York Press, 1995); *The Theater of Terror* (New York: Longman, 1994); *Hate on Trial* (Toronto: Mosaic, 1986); and *The Singaporean Enigma* (Jerusalem: Tzivonim, 2001). His papers and research reports have been published in scientific journals such as *Journal of Communication, Public Opinion Quarterly, Communication Research, Journal of Broadcasting and Electronic Media, American Sociological Review* and others.

Gadi Wolfsfeld is an Associate Professor of Political Science and Communication at the Hebrew University in Jerusalem. His most recent book was published by Cambridge University Press and is entitled: *Media and Political Conflict: News from the Middle East.*

Nathan Yanai is professor in the departments of Israeli Studies and Political Science at the University of Haifa. He is the author of several books on Israeli politics and also "Why Do Political Parties Survive?" *Party Politics* 5 (1999):5-17; the section on Israel in Frank Tachau, ed.(1994) *Political Parties of the Middle East and North Africa;* "The Political Affair: A Framework for a Comparative Discussion", *Comparative Politics* 2 (1990):185-98.

Index